THE SAVVY SHOPPER

Rose Prince is a freelance food journalist and writer, and the author of the highly acclaimed *The New English Kitchen: Changing the Way You Shop, Cook and Eat*, published by Fourth Estate. Her work appears regularly in the *Daily Telegraph*, the *Telegraph Magazine*, the *Independent on Sunday* and the *Tablet*. She has contributed to the *Food Programme*, *Women's Hour* and *You & Yours* on BBC Radio 4. In 1999 she co-produced *In the Footsteps of Elizabeth David*, a two-hour film for Channel 4 presented by Chris Patten. She lives in London with her husband, the journalist Dominic Prince, and their two children.

D0618862

Also by Rose Prince

The New English Kitchen:
Changing the Way You Shop, Cook and Eat

THE SAVVY SHOPPER

ALL YOU NEED TO KNOW ABOUT THE FOOD YOU BUY

ROSE PRINCE

FOURTH ESTATE · London

First published in Great Britain in 2006 by
Fourth Estate
An imprint of HarperCollins*Publishers*
77–85 Fulham Palace Road
London W6 8JB
www.4thestate.co.uk

1

A catalogue record for this book is
available from the British Library

ISBN-13 978-0-00-721993-3
ISBN-10 0-00-721993-8

Set in Granjon with Stencil Display by
Rowland Phototypesetting Ltd, Bury St Edmunds, Suffolk

Printed in Great Britain by Clays Ltd, St Ives plc

The author and publishers have made every endeavour to
ensure that all information was correct at the time of going
to press, but no responsibility can be taken for any changes
occurring after the book has been printed.

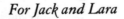

For Jack and Lara

CONTENTS

ACKNOWLEDGEMENTS

I am indebted to the hard work of Louise Haines, Jane Middleton, Robin Harvie, Julian Humphries and Silvia Crompton of Fourth Estate. A special thanks to Professor Tim Lang, who went out of his way to help with finding researchers, and Joanna Blythman and Nigel Slater for all their encouragement.

A huge thank you to my researcher, Bec Huxstep, for her hard work; Sophie Hart Walsh for her work on the directory, and Catherine Blyth for her work on earlier columns. Much gratitude is due to my editors at the *Telegraph*, who have nursed *The Savvy Shopper* since the beginning: Rachel Simhon, Michele Lavery, Casilda Grigg and Jon Stock.

I could not have completed *The Savvy Shopper* without the help of the following people, publications and organisations: Eve Alexander, Nishita Ashomull, Marlene and Rodney Belbin, Jon Bullock of the Meat and Livestock Commission, Fanny Charles, Helen Christofoli, Chantal Coady, Compassion in World Farming, Dr Alan Dangour, Philippa Davenport, DEFRA, Sheila Dillon, *The Ecologist*, Annabel Elliott, Ethical Tea Partnership, *Ethical Trader*, Ethical Trading Initiative, The Fairtrade Foundation, Hugh Fearnley-Whittingstall, The Food Commission, The Food Standards Agency, Peter Gott, Henrietta Green, Greenpeace, *The Grocer*, David Hammerson, Carolyn Hart, Michael Hart, Vivienne Jawett, Bob Kennard, Monika Lavery, Felicity Lawrence, LEAF, Jeremy Lee, Michael Lough, Marine Conservation Society, Marine Stewardship Council, Julie McGuckian, Clancy McMahon, Jennifer Middleton, Mark Newman, Summer Nocon, Oxfam, Pesticides Action Network UK, The Pesticides Residues Committee, David Pickering of the Trading Standards Office, Becky Price at Genewatch UK, *Resurgence*, Kay Robins, Paul Robinson, Karen Schenstrom, Slow Food, The Soil Association, Elaine Spencer White, Sustain, Carinthia West, Geoff Wheeler, Andrew Wilkinson, Natalie Winder.

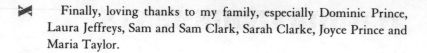

Finally, loving thanks to my family, especially Dominic Prince, Laura Jeffreys, Sam and Sam Clark, Sarah Clarke, Joyce Prince and Maria Taylor.

INTRODUCTION

The Savvy Shopper column first appeared in the *Daily Telegraph*'s Weekend section in October 2004. Its aim was to provide a guide not only to feeling good about the food we buy, but to also help find the food that gives the most sensory pleasure – that rare thing, a guiltfree shopping trip. The philosophy was rooted in ethical shopping, and the timing for the first column was perfect. Words and phrases like 'organic', 'Fairtrade', 'welfare-friendly' and 'food miles' were on our consciences, but there was no existing detailed guide tying food issues to a shopping directory.

The first Savvy Shopper article featured apples and must have touched a nerve. The letters began to pour in – concerned, intrigued, frustrated and curious. It was obvious that there is an army of discerning food shoppers in this country whose quest is to buy food with peace of mind and a clear conscience but also to enjoy great flavours, aromas and textures. A year and a half later, the column has developed a huge and enthusiastic following and, as so many correspondents admitted to cutting out and keeping the page, it seemed crazy not to collect it all into a book, expanding, updating and adding new suppliers and foods. Shoppers need an at-a-glance guidebook to chuck into the car, bag or pushchair when setting out to shop. And since many of the listed suppliers are also able to offer home delivery, it's one to keep by the telephone or laptop, too.

But savvy shopping doesn't just begin and end in your own kitchen – it has a wider influence, too. The food industry (the producers, manufacturers and retailers) has one objective: to please you. Over the eighteen months since the Savvy Shopper was born, the food industry's bigger businesses have made some remarkable policy changes. One supermarket chain has pledged to source fish more responsibly, another has promised to remove (most) artificial additives from its ready meal range and a potato crisp giant has promised to fry in 'healthier' oil. As I write, mission statements are popping up all over the place. Media exposure has a great impact on food issues, it's true, but the greatest impact on the food industry will come from us – the willing shoppers who want, and increasingly demand, to eat excellent, ethically produced food that tastes good.

FOOD'S BIG ISSUES

Food's big issues (what on earth do they mean?)

Food miles, genetic modification, pesticide residues, vCJD, GM terminator seeds, hydrogenated fats, interesterification, transfats, stalls and tethers, specified risk material, formed meats, cheese food, modified maize starch, hormone disruptors, irradiation, mechanically recovered meats, broiler houses, batteries, FADS, aquaculture, nature identical flavourings, stabilisers, emulsifiers and over 40 colourings, many of them artificial ...

A warm welcome to the food industry, and all the wiles and ways it employs to reap the most at the least cost. The words above have a connection to your kitchen. You probably bought something today that relates to at least one of them. We hear phrases like GM and food miles bandied about, but what do they really mean?

Food miles

Food miles relate to the total distance that each food travels from field or factory to our shops, and the impact they have on our environment depends on the method of transport: sea, road or air freight.

Transporting food is inefficient and depletes our supply of fossil fuels – we use more energy to transport an asparagus spear from Peru than it can give us in calories. Air freight is the least efficient, road is next; sea freight is the most economic in fuel terms.

The food that causes the greatest concern is that which travels the longest distance using the most fuel – so air-freighted Thai basil is more of a problem than sea-freighted frozen New Zealand lamb, especially as it has little nutritional importance in comparison to meat. The frustrating aspect of this for environmentalists is that both these foods can be produced in the UK; there is no real need to import them.

With year-round availability destroying seasonal eating, food miles ruin the pleasures of our gluts. Food miles, incidentally, negate the planet-saving intentions of organic farming; organic is best when it is local.

Food mile issues are not straightforward, however. While there is really no excuse for the midwinter airdrop of strawberries, a case can be made for importing nutritionally important, non-air-freighted foods that we cannot grow ourselves, such as bananas and citrus fruits. But then what about the poor African region whose economy boomed with the ability to fly green beans to the UK? If it is true that their water supply is protected, pesticide use controlled and their children are receiving an education, shouldn't they join in the global market fun? Surely their good fortune is worth the waft of kerosene. It's tricky stuff. Me? I eat the odd Kenyan bean, but it is not a dish for every day.

There is no question that long-distance transport has an impact on food's simple delights. Prospecting for the lucre that can be made by sending fruit to distinctly unsunny nations like ours has the plant breeders create strains of fruit that look good yet have no squelch.

And food miles can be cruel. Livestock are still transported long distances all over Europe. In spite of rules and guidelines regarding water supply, rough handling and resting time, their suffering remains shameful.

Local food

If organic has created the biggest buzz in food over the last five years, 'local food' will be seen as the latest remedy to treat the ills of the food supply chain. Local means traceable, which in turn means easy access for consumers to information about what they buy. Local means short journeys, so that's good for fuel consumption. Local means the freshest food. Local is welfare friendly – livestock are notoriously stressed by long road journeys.

Local means less dependence on a centralised food supply. So when the food chain is hit by a crisis, such as foot and mouth or another animal disease, the movement of food around the UK is minimal and easier to track.

A culture of local marketing boosts local economies. According to the New Economics Foundation (NEF), every £10 spent with a local food business, employing local people and buying ingredients locally, generates £25 for the local economy, compared with just £14 spent with a non-local food business. The NEF, among other environmental organisations, believes that if the major supermarket chains adopted local buying policies it would save the future of farming and fishing in the UK.

Local is good for regional identity, and for society. How much more distinctive for roadside cafés and motorway service stations to offer each region's favourite pie, gooey cake, curry or apple juice? Motorway meals would for once be worth some discussion, some analysis – you can't exactly discuss the excitement of finding yet another KFC meal deal while travelling, or yet another reheated sausage roll and can of Coke. Regional distinctiveness is also good for tourism – so that's more cash in the tin.

Local can fall flat on its face in big cities especially, where hectic lifestyles can distract from ethical shopping, and enormous rents prevent all but the richest food chains getting a look-in on high streets – or staying on them if they are already there. But the success of farmers' markets and food co-operatives speaks for itself, and the concept of local food is an earnest but not unusual subject for city shoppers frustrated by the dullness of food shopping.

Genetic modification (GM)

A war of technology against tradition, and public will. The majority of British consumers continue to reject the idea of genetically modified foods being sold in our shops. Supporters of genetic modification say it will remove the ills of pesticide use and create better-functioning foods that can feed greater populations. GM's detractors say the technology is not properly tested and its health impact not thoroughly monitored (some approved GM crops such as maize and soya are in use outside Europe). They also question the long-term benefits of GM as the answer to world food shortages, and whether it can bring the promised wealth so desperately needed by farmers in poorer countries or simply make a few seed-manufacturing biotech companies rich beyond their dreams. Opponents to GM suspect that the development of terminator seeds, plants modified so their seeds cannot be used after flowering, is also a ruse to make money and will never bring wealth to the farmers that grow them.

The functional aspects of GM foods remain uncertain. For example, one biotech company's early promises to bring vitamin-enriched 'golden' rice to India (for free) have yet to take off.

While the pro-GM sector fights anti-GM voices, GM 'contamination' is spreading anyway. It is now hard for UK farmers to avoid giving GM feed to animals unless they are in an organic system that polices the source of feed or a traditional system in which all food for livestock is produced only by the farm. (It is argued that because feed passes through an animal, only nutrients are absorbed and not genetic material, but opponents to GM say that there is some evidence of GM DNA material remaining and passing through the gut of animals. They add that testing the effects of GM feed is not adequate, and that labels should indicate when livestock have been given GM feed.) In the case of crops, GM trials can let seeds 'loose' on the environment and it is known that bees can carry pollen from a GM crop trial on to a conventional crop for some unofficial cross-breeding. It is also a fact that the organic sector would be damaged, if not destroyed, by the arrival of GM in the UK. After a time, it would be impossible for them to guarantee their food as GM free.

GM has an image problem. Few of us are at ease with the concept of enormous salmon, growing so fast you can almost watch them do it; moreover we fear the unconventional combinations of human with animal or animal with plant genes. But what consumers and environment groups are most fed up with is the arrogance of GM big business. The swagger of the biotech firms and their closeness to those in power is disturbing. Their apparent refusal to listen to the arguments against them, painting their detractors as muck-spreading hippies, provokes cries that they will eventually get their way and permission will be given for genetic modification to come into general use.

As it stands in the UK, seven plants that could be used in animal feed have Part C approvals from the EU, meaning that they are licensed to be sold. Two of these are herbicide-tolerant and insect-resistant maize varieties (made by the biotech firm Syngenta); two are herbicide-tolerant maizes (made by Bayer and Monsanto); there is an insect-resistant maize and a herbicide-tolerant soya bean (both made by Monsanto) and finally a herbicide-tolerant oilseed rape (made by Bayer). Three of the maize crops are licensed for cultivation in the EU, although none has yet been grown here. A larger number of GM crops are licensed to be grown outside the EU, in North and South America, South Africa, China, India and other parts of the Far East.

The US Department of Agriculture estimates that 46 per cent of the US maize crop and 93 per cent of the soya bean crop is genetically modified. More than 98 per cent of soya and 55 per cent of maize grown in Argentina is GM.

But can you tell if food is GM or has GM ingredients? In 2004 the EU established new rules for GM labelling: any food sold in the EU that is genetically modified or contains GMOs (genetically modified organisms) must carry this information on the label (or immediately next to non-packaged food). The presence of GM ingredients in ready-made foods (e.g. flour, oil, glucose syrup) must be shown on labels, but products made using GM technology (cheese produced with GM enzymes, for example) do not have to be labelled. Meat, milk and eggs from animals given GM feed also do not need to be labelled. Food that accidentally contains less than 0.9 per cent approved (by the EU) GM ingredients or 0.5 per cent non-approved GM ingredients need not be labelled. You can see why detractors of GM insist that gradual GM contamination of our food is taking place.

In January 2006 the organic sector reacted with horror when the EU announced plans to allow food to be labelled organic even when it contains 0.9 per cent of GM ingredients. The Soil Association says that any more than 0.1 per cent is unacceptable. They and the other environmental organisations are now campaigning against the EU plans.

The European Food Safety Authority (EFSA) tests GM foods on a case-by-case basis, deciding whether to permit them to be sold in

Europe after public consultation and referring to the various relevant food safety and agricultural authorities in member states. In the UK this means the Food Standards Agency (FSA) and the Department for the Environment, Food and Rural Affairs (DEFRA). Both the FSA and DEFRA have not exactly spoken out against GM, so it is no wonder its opponents are concerned. Shoppers are quite justified in opposing GM. To take part in public consultations regarding the licensing of GM crops, keep an eye on the EFSA website, **www.efsa.eu.int**.

Pesticides and other chemicals

For descriptive ease, I have used the word pesticide in this book as a cover-all term for agricultural chemicals, which include weed killers (herbicides) and fungicides.

In September 2004 the Royal Commission on Environmental Pollution (RCEP) issued a serious warning about the effects of pesticides and our government's failure to tackle the issue. The RCEP report covered health risks to bystanders and residents exposed to the use of pesticides on land near their homes. Its recommendations included a re-think of how risk itself is measured, making it clear that current risk assessment is inadequate. The lobby against pesticides is understandably elated at the report, but its concerns about pesticides are much wider. It alludes to the dangers farmers all over the world face when handling pesticides, the pollution of the environment, depletion of the ozone layer and the long-term effects of hormone- and endocrine-disrupting chemicals on human and animal reproductive systems.

In 2005 agricultural chemical watchdog, the Pesticides Action Network UK (PAN UK), published the List of Lists, detailing all the hundreds of dangerous pesticides in use around the world and how they can affect us. This list, which is too long to be included here, can be obtained from PAN UK, **www.pan-uk.org**. Thanks to the campaigns of environmental organisations including PAN UK, various worldwide conventions on pesticide use have ruled that many on the list (including the better-known poisons, DDT and lindane) can now be used only with prior consent between the importing/exporting countries. However, three on the list, namely aldicarb, DBCP and paraquat are not yet internationally regulated.

In the UK the government-backed Pesticide Residues Committee tests samples of food from various groups four times a year, and publishes the findings on the internet. For each pesticide it has established a Maximum Residue Level (MRL) to enable it to measure the safe use of pesticides. Council-funded local trading standards offices also test for pesticides. Anti-pesticide voices claim that MRLs are not low enough and pesticide residues are found on far too many everyday fruits and vegetables. They also say that the 'cocktail effect' of multiple residues poses the real danger.

The Soil Association, which operates the most stringent standards in the UK organic farming sector, permits its members in special cases to use six agricultural chemicals on crops: copper, sulphur, rotenone, soft soap, paraffin oil and potassium permanganate. They may use pyrethroids in insect traps. Those that defend the use of pesticides as a whole will always leap on this fact when attacking organic standards to weaken the position of the organic sector. It is a slim argument, taking into account the 450 or more chemicals available to conventional farmers and the fact that each individual organic farmer must go through hell and high water to get permission to use one of the six on a crop. The Soil Association argues that the pesticides they permit are either of natural origin or simple chemical compounds compared to the complex chemicals used in conventional farming.

As far as savvy shoppers should be concerned, the traceability of organic food and its comparative freedom from residues is a standard to chase. Farmers who strive to reduce pesticide use and reintroduce wildlife to farms, like those signing up for the environmentally concerned farming scheme, LEAF, should be encouraged – if not quite celebrated. But while no ideal system is in wide use, buying seasonally and locally boosts trust and is good value for money. Viewed another way, it is easier to check up on the tomato grower down the road than the one in Brazil.

Organic versus conventional

Organic is a great standard, especially when a producer has Soil Association accreditation, the most stringent in Europe. But conventional can mean high standards, too. It depends on the producer, and that is why buying food is a confusing business. A farmer might produce food responsibly but prefer not to go through organic conversion, which can be an expensive investment.

The organic movement (specifically the Soil Association in the UK) was founded on the principle of the holistic benefits of 'soil health'. It recognises a connection between human health and that of the soil. Organic crops grow in healthy soil fertilised with natural manures. Organically reared livestock are naturally fed on organically grown feed and standards of welfare are exceptionally high. But is this better than a responsible conventional farmer?

I have visited farms where enormous care is taken to prevent animal and plant disease through good husbandry, but which are not organic. They keep hedgerows, leave buffer zones between crops and hedges and, like organic farmers, will not spray unless absolutely necessary. I know farmers who care for their livestock, stock them loosely, give them proper shelter and plenty of water, and grow all their feed. Their animals are rarely ill or stressed and are totally traceable – but they are not organic. Some of the best cheeses, hams and even potato crisps in the UK are made by responsible, non-organic farmers.

Other conventional farmers blindly use every pesticide available to them, intensively rear animals in cruel systems and think only of the margins at the end of the day. The problem is that both types of conventional farmer dislike being put down as a bad farmer, even though only one has some justification in feeling this way. So organic standards get attacked – particularly, to my amazement, by the authorities. The Food Standards Agency, of all people, does not accept that the organic standard is one to strive for.

For shoppers, the problem is not how to choose organic food – if it has a Soil Association or other British organic logo, you can more or less rest assured – the real task is picking good conventional food out from the bad.

Organic always costs more. This is related to higher labour costs, slower growth rate of both livestock and plants, lower yields and the higher cost of ingredients in naturally processed foods. The only time I am wary of the pricing is when farm-gate prices of organic food match that of the same food in London shops. Sales at the farm gate should be cheaper than those that have gone through any middle man.

Animal welfare and disease

Animal welfare and disease should be grouped together because the latter is often a consequence of low standards in the former. Good animal welfare practice should include:

* Natural feed with a low protein content for slow growth, plus plenty of forage.
* Room to move – what is known in the business as low stocking density.
* Free access to outdoors in daylight.
* Good deep bedding, preferably straw.
* Access to plenty of water.
* Natural lighting.
* Freedom to behave naturally.
* No long road journeys.
* Low stress at slaughter, a rest beforehand and low noise levels.

The majority of farm animals never know a stress-free existence like this. As you will find out in this book, pig and poultry farms are especially intensive. With low stress, the incidence of disease is minimal. Viruses and bacteria spread in intensive rearing systems, and trucking livestock around the country does not help – as proven by the 2001 foot and mouth epidemic.

Eating meat is a big deal, and much respect is due to an animal that has been reared for food. With the emphasis on plentiful and cheap – a mantra followed in food supply for the last 50 years – the welfare of animals has somehow become unimportant to those who eat them. We have picked up some nasty habits: eating only the fillets and prime cuts as if the rest of the animal did not exist; eating a burger or chicken breast a day for just a few pennies; but, worst of all, a lack of curiosity. No one asks, so nothing changes.

Over the last decade, much time has been invested in debating how a fox should be killed, yet the majority of chickens we eat eke out their wretched existence in a broiler house, in conditions that should shame meat eaters. And animal welfare is a problem for vegetarians, too. Milk and egg production still see some of the cruellest practice in the food business. Dairy cows can spend their entire lives being unable to graze, going through lactation after lactation with all the inherent health problems that such a system can create.

Just a few questions when shopping for meat will make an enormous difference. There is much that shoppers can and should ask butchers and retailers before they buy. That is how free-range eggs found their way into supermarkets.

Finally it is worth bearing in mind that British animal welfare standards, while not good enough in the intensive farming sector, are still a vast improvement on welfare standards in Europe and elsewhere.

Country of origin

When shopping, keep one labelling legal loophole to the front of your mind: if a food has been grown or reared in, say, Holland but packed or processed in the UK, it can call itself British. So a side of pork that is cured in Holland and then packed in Britain is British bacon. EU competition laws prevent the real truth coming out on the pack, but responsible shops will often stick a Union Jack or recognisable British mark on the pack. Having said that, plenty of imported meat slips into ready meals and is never labelled as such. This matters mainly because animal welfare systems are even worse abroad than here, and some practices are still legal in other countries – even in EU member states – when they are banned in the UK. Food manufacturers do not always have to state the country of origin for fresh or processed foods, except in the case of controversial foods such as beef. The rule of thumb is this: if the country of origin is not stated, the food is probably not British. This is particularly so with fresh fruit and vegetables. Apples are plastered with Union Jacks when British are in season: otherwise they tend to be sold just as 'apples'.

The free market and fair trade

Love it or hate it, the Western world is more or less open to trade, although the term free trade is an interesting two-way street, with different rules in each carriageway. Whether free trade is right or wrong, one thing is certain: aspects of it are grossly unfair both to us and to exporting countries. We import what are, in our terms, cheap goods with abandon; the exporting countries pay through the nose to do so via export levies.

Aid agencies campaign for trade barriers to be lifted between the West and developing or 'third' countries as a cure for poverty. If barriers were lifted on both sides, however, all hell would break loose. Under our current system, the West could 'get there first', meaning it would flood the poorer countries' food supply chains with dumped goods grown under our subsidy system – it already does to an extent – negating the developing countries' need to grow their own. It would also move in and set up business for export, which would likely make the few, rather than the many, rich.

But if, as aid agencies want, the trade barrier is lifted to favour only the developing countries, then – in terms of food – we may find ourselves unwittingly buying goods made to a standard that would not be permitted in the UK. This is already happening, between the UK and other EU member states, which are permitted to use production methods denied to us for food safety and animal welfare reasons.

British farmers operate under the most stringent food production rules in the world, and yet we are importing food that could not legally be sold if it had been made here. Because the majority of shoppers buy purely on price, lifting trade barriers to allow more cheap imports could spell the end of British farming and food production. Close the free market? No, we would put an end to centuries of culinary curiosity.

This is a case for shoppers to be circumspect about what they buy – and when they buy it. The sensible choice is to support British food production where standards are higher, as with meat; buy into our gluts of fruits and vegetables when they are in – avoiding the cheaper Spanish equivalent sitting beside it; and always buy with a mind to support small food businesses.

The worldwide commodity exchange has been held responsible for some of the appalling poverty among farmers in the developing world. When oversupply pushes prices down, farmers fall quickly into debt. In 1992 the Fairtrade Foundation was formed by CAFOD, Christian Aid, Oxfam, New Consumer, Traidcraft and the World Development Movement. They were later joined by the Women's Institute. The idea of fair trade is for retailers to deal directly with farmers' co-operatives or producer groups, committing to a minimum price in spite of supply. The stories emerging about fairly traded foods are encouraging – a case where changing shopping habits has had a positive effect on the lives of Windward Island banana farmers, Rwandan coffee growers and Palestinian olive oil producers. Beware, however, the attempts currently being made by giant food conglomerates to jump on the Fairtrade bandwagon and gain certification for one product while they continue to trade less ethically with the producers of all their other foods.

It's not wholly offensive to mention in the same breath that it would be nice if some fair trading went on at home. Dairy and other livestock farms will become extinct in the UK unless a fair price is paid for milk by the main dairies and the supermarkets that buy from them. If there were no livestock farms in the UK, we would end up with a landscape that was a mixture between a national park and a weed-infested wilderness, and a diet of 100 per cent imported meat.

The workforce and other people

When travelling around fruit and vegetable farms in the UK, it is impossible to miss the flexible workforce – the pickers and labourers without whom weeding and hand harvesting would be impossible. But it is also clear that the farms that are happy for a journalist to tour their premises and talk to their staff are unlikely to have much to be ashamed of. There are some excellent schemes for students, and in Jersey the relationship between the Madeira workers and the potato growers is good: living conditions are warm, in substantially built cottages, and the families earn enough from January to June to sustain their lives on the island of Madeira during the rest of the year.

But there are gangmasters who break every rule, exploiting the desperation of workers who want a life in Britain. They pay below the minimum wage and operate no limits to working hours. As a shopper, it is difficult to know who picked your carrots. Supermarkets say they try to keep track, but in practice this is hard to do. The new gangmaster laws that came in after the drowning of the cockle pickers at Morecambe Bay in 2004 are yet to be properly tested.

The tragic reality is that the children of today's farmers are less and less likely to follow their parents into the business; indeed many are actively discouraged by their parents, and the workforce of the future is likely to be more and more made up of immigrant workers who will work for lower wages. The same workers are employed in processing plants and abattoirs, and as usual they are doing the filthy, tedious jobs. So we have a conundrum. We want to buy British, but buying British may encourage poor practice. If there is a solution, it is to seek out the vegetable box scheme or the farm that opens its doors to scrutiny. Food from such places will cost more, so it is a case of eating the cheaper-to-grow produce, choosing seasonally to get the best value from gluts, and perhaps deciding that pulses are going to play a greater part in your diet.

In exporting countries, the workforce question is also a serious matter, along with the wider impact of food production on populations. Poor monitoring of pesticide use is a much greater problem outside the UK and large numbers of people can be affected, including children – and child labour. Water supplies can be hijacked or polluted by unscrupulous industries; land is acquired from tribal populations who have only a few historical rights to it, their natural habitat subsequently flattened to make way for industrial farming. Information about such practice does filter back, however, and shoppers have a chance to boycott foods whose production causes people suffering.

Additives

Artificial additives do not turn up in food because shoppers need them but because the food industry needs them for economic reasons. While it is understandable that manufacturers should want to profit from their business, the liberal use of colourings, flavourings and preservatives has gone too far. Additives are in much of the food targeted at children. They warp the concept of natural taste, inducing ignorance of the real thing. They have been proven to alter behaviour, and some are known allergens.

Additives are divided into various categories. The largest groups are colours, preservatives, antioxidants, sweeteners, emulsifiers, gelling agents, stabilisers and thickeners. Then there is a smaller number each of acids, acidity regulators, anti-caking agents, anti-foaming agents, bulking agents, carriers and carrier solvents, emulsifying salts, firming agents, flavour enhancers, flour treatment agents, glazing agents, humectants, modified starches, packaging gases, propellants, raising agents and sequestrants.

The food industry is preoccupied with using appearance to attract customers, and also with the stability of food and its shelf life. It is unfair to blame only the manufacturers when retailers are after the same thing. Shoppers do not ask, however, for the plethora of innovations that appear on shelves on a daily basis. The food industry will always say it is supplying demand, identifying what shoppers want. I think this is rubbish. Supermarkets in particular have created a demand, identifying a weakness for novelty in bored supermarket shoppers (and especially their children), and have risen to it with some alarming imaginings. 'Meal solutions', they call them – but have you ever heard someone say, 'What I really need is a Thai spiced shepherd's pie topped with a feta cheese and ginger parsnip mash'?

Ready-made food can be great – if it is made with good-quality ingredients and nothing else. Even a sausage needs no more than salt as a preservative. However, it will have a shorter shelf life, and buying additive-free food means shopping more frequently – although I make good use of a small chest freezer for bread, sausages and baked things.

Additives are listed on labels, either in code as E numbers, with their industry name, or – if permitted – a common name. This can be confusing. For example, a label can show monosodium glutamate, flavour enhancer or E621 – these are all the same additive.

Manufacturers use different names for additives such as mono-sodium glutamate because they are controversial. Flavour enhancer sounds so great, don't you think? The flavour of your food has been enhanced. Terrific, you think, just what it needs. But it doesn't – or it wouldn't if the manufacturers used ingredients with real flavour. A ready-meal maker's greatest ambition is to put as much water and other cheap ingredients such as modified maize starch as possible into a recipe, and they get away with it by tipping in salt, flavour-ings, colour, gelling agents, stabilisers, emulsifiers, in fact anything that will hide the fact that these bulk ingredients have no texture or flavour.

The organic sector uses some additives, although nothing like as many as conventional manufacturers. Under the Soil Association's standard, organic producers can use 30 additives (the EU permits 35) including gum fillers, emulsifiers, preservatives and one colour (annatto).

There is a gaping discrepancy between parents' anecdotes about the effect of additives on their children and the constant reassurance from the industry that these additives are non-toxic. But the point is missed. The kind of reactions seen in children to certain colours, flavourings, sweeteners and preservatives are *allergic* reactions, and food additives are tested only for toxicity. In 2002 a government-sponsored study monitored 277 three-year-olds from the Isle of Wight for the effects of additives, which were given in orange juice along with placebos. Many parents of children given additives reported significant changes in mood and behaviour. The additives tested included the artificial food colourings tartrazine (E102), sunset yellow (E110), carmoisine (E122), and ponceau 4R (E124), plus the preservative sodium benzoate (E211). Test doses were well below the levels permitted in children's foods and drinks yet still the allergic reaction certain children showed was significant. But while the authorities commissioned another report, insisting this one was inconclusive, it is noticeable that manufacturers have mostly removed the 'Filthy Five' from children's food.

Not all E-numbered additives are bad. Some, such as ascorbic acid (E300), are simply vitamin C. E-numbers are additives approved by the EU and their effects on our bodies vary.

With the exception of the glutamate family (E621–633), flavourings do not need 'E' approval. With natural flavouring, this is fine but flavourings fall into three interesting categories:

❁ **Artificial** – chemical imitations of real flavours.
❁ **Nature identical** – nice euphemism, where the actual chemicals present in real flavours are extracted to make flavourings.
❁ **Natural** – real essences and dried flavours.

When shopping, bear the following in mind as you read labels: if a manufacturer has added flavourings and colourings, the other ingredients are substandard. Avoid such foods if you can.

Labels and logos

Read the labels of everything you buy. They tell you nothing and they tell you a lot. When they say little, that says a great deal; missing information is an indication of poor production standards or dubious origins. Ingredients must be listed on labels by law, in descending order of quantity, and most labels also include nutritional information – the place to spot the presence of salt, saturated fat, sugar and sometimes hydrogenated fat.

Logos say something about the food. Watch for the five British organic logos (the Soil Association one is the best known). The Demeter logo indicates biodynamic food – delightful stuff that has been grown in accordance with lunar cycles but which is basically organic. The red Lion Quality mark stamped on eggs means they came from hens that have been vaccinated against salmonella. The Fairtrade logo tells you the producer received a fair price, and the fishy-patterned Marine Stewardship Council (MSC) mark is a sign of fish from a certified sustainable source.

Other logos are more ambiguous in what they say about the food in the pack. The Red Tractor covers a wide range of production assurance but allows for intensive production. The same can be said for 'Farm Assured' and the British Quality marks for beef, pork and lamb. LEAF allows pesticide use (though under stricter controls, but I have visited LEAF farms and been impressed with successful schemes boosting wildlife). The RSPCA's Freedom Food logo indicates a vast improvement in animal welfare in intensive farming, but it does not come anywhere near the Soil Association standard of animal welfare.

I hate logos, but we need them. I would prefer to read an epistle on a label that tells me all there is to know about the food in a pack, linked through to websites with contact details. But none of this would be necessary if shops employed knowledgeable staff and trained them to talk to you about the food they sell.

Retailers

There are four main supermarket chains in the UK: Tesco, Asda, Sainsbury and Morrisons. Then there are smaller chains, such as The Co-op, Waitrose, Budgens and Booths. Much has been said about the buying power of the big chains. This book focuses on how shoppers' habits can make demands on the retailers, who have no choice but to respond to them.

I sent a detailed questionnaire to the supermarkets, asking how they source or produce most of the foods mentioned in this book. They were given a four-week period in which to reply. Of the Big Four, Morrisons declined to answer shortly after receiving the questionnaire, while Asda did not meet the deadline, pleading time poverty (they were given one month, then a further two months in all). Tesco sent only part of the questionnaire back to me, just inside the extended deadline of three months, again pleading lack of time. That these big retailers cannot put their hands on an up-to-date database in the computer age is an embarrassment on their part. The information should be available, so it appears they chose not to give it. They do have customer service lines (see below), where you can obtain lists of ingredients and sometimes information on the country of origin, but details are hard to obtain from these sources.

The results of the questionnaire are included in most sections and I have tried where possible to mention ethical options sold by supermarkets (e.g. Fairtrade bananas, organic chicken, cod from a sustainable source ...). If information from supermarkets who did respond to the questionnaire is missing, it may be because they did not answer clearly or didn't answer at all.

For up-to-date information about products, the supermarkets can be contacted on the following numbers:

Asda: 0500 100055
Booths: 01772 251701
Budgens: 0870 526002
Co-op: 0800 0686 727
Morrisons: 01924 870 000
Safeway: 01622 712 987
Sainsbury: 0800 636262
Somerfield: 0117 935 9359
Tesco: 0800 5055 5555
Waitrose: 0800 188884

But however many pounds in every ten we spend at Tesco, small shops still exist. Great butcher's shops, cheese shops, specialist food shops, bakeries, fishmonger's and even a few greengrocer's cling on in the high streets – please seek them out. They actually have shop assistants who can talk knowledgeably to you, and may even help carry bags and give cooking advice. Yep, pinch yourself, you're having a pleasant shopping experience.

Farm shops are my favourite, partly because they make superb meat and just-picked organic produce affordable. No high-street rents and no middle men mean lower prices. And you can take the car – very eco-unfriendly, but you can hardly tramp across fields with your shopping.

Low prices for fresh food are promoted by the supermarkets but before you rush to buy the free-range chicken or English asparagus at Tesco, check the price at your farm shop, butcher's or local produce stalls. Three experiments carried out by my husband, Dominic Prince, in 2004/2005, in the *Evening Standard*, the *Spectator Magazine* and on 'Tonight with Trevor McDonald' (ITV), revealed certain prices at the small shops to be up to 40 per cent lower than those at Tesco – a considerable margin.

Online shopping for home-delivered food is another way to buy the best-quality food at the right price. I still find the worldwide web a weird shop. I am unable quite to complete the transaction without phoning the online shop about something quite unnecessary, just to make sure that there are people and not Martians running the place. But mail order is great. Don't be put off by the home-delivery practicalities. Most online or mail-order companies will organise a delivery time to suit you, or bring it to your office if that helps, or give the delivery to a neighbour or hide it in the garden shed in your absence. Once you have dealt successfully with a home-delivery supplier for the first time, it's a good idea to add the clause 'leave unsigned' to the order, particularly if you have a good hiding place. Small companies are flexible about this, although some will not do it for safety reasons.

The higher price of good food

The cost of naturally reared meat, organic vegetables and good-quality, additive-free ready-made foods will always be higher than budget-priced, intensively produced, additive-heavy foods. One of the most off-putting elements in changing shopping habits, when we are so used to paying less, is the higher price. But by balancing the ratio of luxury foods to cheap, everyday items and finding out how to use cheap cuts of meat, using up leftovers so we don't waste a thing, and buying into gluts when they are at their cheapest (and most delicious), it is possible to keep the bill close to the old one. This kind of latter-day household management was the subject of my first book, *The New English Kitchen* (Fourth Estate, 2005). Many of its recipes show how the finest food will fit inside a tight budget. Think twice, for example, before you throw away the chicken carcass. Remember that stock can be made from its bones and used to make a risotto, so in the end it contributes to two meals.

Health, nutrition and functional food

In the past twenty years obesity rates in the UK have trebled, to 20 per cent of adults and 10 per cent of children. The food industry is – rightly – under fire for manufacturing and promoting unhealthy food. The industry responds by saying that, if we all took more exercise, it would not matter that we consume too many fats and sugars. I predict that the industry will wish it had not ignored its responsibility for so long. Some food manufacturers are reducing fat, salt and sugar content in the food they make; a time may even come when we laugh at the way we gave children sugar-coated breakfast cereals, in the same way our parents giggle at how their GP once offered a cigarette during a consultation. The authorities are trying to catch up on the situation, again far too late. The Food Standards Agency's suggested proposal of a red–amber–green 'Traffic Light' warning logo on food was trounced in early 2006 by the announcement that some of the biggest players in the industry plan voluntarily to change the nutritional information on their packaging, giving the RDA (recommended daily allowance) of each particular food. That the daily allowance of any particular food will be decided by the manufacturer is laughable – but it could also be seriously confusing to the consumer.

It may be true that all food is nourishment to a degree, but what we put in our bodies is now a major preoccupation. The food industry –

no slouch when it comes to fashion – has responded with 'functional foods', foods with added beneficial ingredients, such as pro-biotic yoghurt drinks (said to aid digestion) and chickens with added essential omega-3 fatty acids (for heart and tissue health). Before you throw these things in the trolley, bear in mind that, unlike those made by pharmaceutical companies or even herbal remedies, the health claims on food labelling need not be backed up. The functional food industry is also expecting that these rules will be relaxed further in the near future. Take omega-3: there is no doubt that these fatty acids are heart-healthy, but I'm sorry to say that there is just not enough evidence to prove they boost brain power *except in premature babies.* The food industry is set to make billions out of gullibility. Nutritionists all say the same thing: stick to eating, or feeding your kids, a varied diet made up of fresh foods, freshly cooked.

Packaging

Try to picture one and a half billion dustbins full of waste, inside them 12 billion carrier bags, at least one billion emblazoned with the names of our major supermarkets. Add to this a few billion glass jars, bottles and cans that missed the recycling bin. And then imagine burying the whole lot. Choose a spot. The Lake District? The Norfolk Broads? The Wiltshire Downs? It has to go somewhere and much of it, sad to say, is the debris of our dinners.

Waste Watch, a government-funded agency, reports that 28 million tonnes of waste are generated by UK households annually, of which only 11 per cent is recycled; 81 per cent is dumped in landfill sites and space is running out without more recycling. The government has said that the food and drink industry is a major source of waste, accounting for 10 per cent of all industrial and commercial waste, 'notably packaging'.

The figures for recycled waste have gone up encouragingly but there is still a problem with packaging. Most irritating is the pass-the-parcel package: cardboard cartons containing 12 boxes of cellophane-wrapped biscuits are typical. Chocolate packaging can be outrageous. Have you ever scrabbled desperately through cellophane wrapping and a triple-thickness cardboard box, then removed a sticker from a waxed paper layer to reveal another of corrugated paper, under which 12 chocolates are sitting, wrapped in foil? Some suppliers use recycled, biodegradable packaging, but less is better. Brown paper bags are a great wrapping for vegetables and fruit, newsprint good for meat and fish and, if you shop by car, it is good to take boxes from supermarkets, not carrier bags. Or use baskets. Feel superior at the checkout, putting your hand up to say 'no' to the carrier bag.

Building the Savvy Shopper directory

There is a shopping guide for each food featured in this book. Many of the suppliers were found when I was writing the Savvy Shopper articles for the *Daily Telegraph* in 2004–5 but I have also found many new sources of good food that you can buy with a clear conscience. There isn't room to feature every food, and taste is a subjective thing, so feedback from readers and suggestions for any future updates are most welcome.

I should add that I live in the south of England, so there will be a disproportionate number of suppliers from that region in the directory. Many of them, however, offer home delivery services and will bring the shopping to your door, wherever you live. Telephone numbers are provided so that each supplier can be contacted for information about stockists and mail order.

Many of the food producers included in this book can do home delivery; if home delivery isn't mentioned, contact them for details of stockists. I have not been able to include every small food shop on every high street, or farm shop in the countryside – but do keep an eye out for good independent shops. Nothing is more welcome to a shopper than a shop filled with good food, beautifully kept, run by knowledgeable assistants who are sympathetic to the needs of the shopper. With the creeping dominance of the chain retailers, these shops – and all those other food producers selling food with real integrity – need your loyalty and support. So be a savvy shopper and decide what the future of food shopping should be. There is considerable power in your wallet; put it to the best possible use.

HOW TO SHOP FOR BRITISH FOOD IN SEASON

UK-grown vegetables and fruit

New breeds, modern storage and the wider (and controversial) use of polytunnels and glasshouses mean that the season for UK-grown produce is now greatly extended. British tomatoes, for example, are available from February onwards. Supermarkets sometimes stock UK produce in preference to imports (e.g. apples, strawberries and raspberries) but unless they can buy in large quantities throughout the whole UK season for a particular vegetable or fruit, they tend to source imports, which are often cheaper. For this reason there is more chance of buying a wider variety of UK-grown produce through 'box schemes', which are more economical if bought direct from the farm where they are grown. Best value is to be had during the 'glut' – the natural window when outdoor-grown produce peaks and is at its most abundant.

Fish and shellfish

There is an optimum time to buy fish and shellfish, namely outside the spawning period of each species. This gives the fish a chance to reproduce and reduces the catch of egg-bound females. But a seasonal approach is not all a shopper needs to adopt when buying fish. Always choose large, mature fish and ask the fishmonger about the catch method: 'line caught' is preferable to trawled, for example. Fish from UK inshore fisheries, which tend to fish for shorter periods in smaller boats by more sustainable means, are the best choice.

Game

The season for game birds is short, but take advantage. Some species, such as grouse and woodcock, are rare and expensive but during the height of the pheasant shooting season there is a glut well worth buying into. Other, naturally wild game such as rabbit and wood pigeon are available fresh for most of the year. Wild venison has 'close' seasons when it can be shot but not sold; these differ between Scotland and England and Wales. The open seasons are marked on the chart that follows.

Seasonal meat and dairy produce

While most fresh meat and cheeses are now available all year round, there are still a few festive and traditional specialities that have a short season. Lamb deserves special attention. We could reduce our dependence on imports of New Zealand lamb by tapping into the supplies of the light 'upland' lamb and mutton available direct from farms and traditional butchers throughout the autumn and winter.

SEASONAL CHART

UK-GROWN VEGETABLES AND FRUIT

Apples (August to March)
Asparagus (May to June)
Aubergine (May to September)
Cabbages (all year round)
Carrots (June to April)
Cauliflowers (all year round)
Celeriac (October to February)
Cherries (June to July)
Courgettes (June to October)
Cucumber (February to September)
Curly kale (all year round)
Farmed blackberries (July to October or until the first frost)
Fenland celery (November to January)
Fennel (May to October)
Forced rhubarb (December to March)
French beans (July to October)
Fresh herbs (April to November)
Garlic (August to December)
Gooseberries (June to July)
Grapes (September to October)
Green celery (March to November)
Jersey Royal and Cornish Early new potatoes (February to June)
Jerusalem artichokes (October to March)
Kentish cobnuts (September to October)
Leeks (August to April)
Lettuce and salad leaves (January to November)
Mangetout (May to September)
Marrows (August to October)
Morels (March to April)
Mushrooms (all year round)

New potatoes (May to September)
Onions (July to May)
Oyster mushrooms (May to June)
Parsnips (July to March)
Pea shoots (May to August)
Pears (September to April)
Peas (June to September)
Plums (August to September)
Potatoes (all year round)
Puffballs, chanterelles, ceps, fairy ring and other wild mushrooms
    (September to October)
Pumpkin and squash (September to February)
Purple sprouting broccoli (November to April)
Quince (September to October)
Radishes (January to November)
Raspberries (June to October or until the first frost)
Red, white and black currants (July to August)
Runner beans (August to November)
Seakale (January to February/March)
Sloes (September)
Spinach (all year round)
Stinging nettles (March to April)
Strawberries (April to October or until the first frost)
Summer rhubarb (April to October)
Swede (November to March)
Sweet chestnuts (October to January)
Sweetcorn (August to October)
Tomatoes (February to December)
Turnips (July to April)
Walnuts (October)
Watercress (February to November but can run on in a frost-free
    winter)
Wild blackberries (August to October)
Wild garlic (March to May)

FISH AND SHELLFISH

Anchovies (September to May)
Brill (October to May)
Brown crab (February to November)
Brown shrimp (February to October)
Brown trout (March to October)
Cockles (September to May)
Cod, line-caught from Bristol and English Channel (May to
    January)
Dover sole (August to May)
Gilthead bream (January to October)
Haddock (August to February)
John Dory (May to February)
Langoustines/Dublin Bay prawns (October to April)
Lemon sole (September to March)
Lobster (April to September)
Mackerel from Bristol and English Channel (August to February)
Megrim sole (May to December)
Monkfish (July to March)
Native oysters (September to April)
Plaice (April to December)
Red gurnard (September to April)
Red mullet (August to April)
Sardines/pilchards (August to March)
Sea bass (July to February)
Sea bream (June)
Sea trout (April to October)
Spider crab (August to March)
Sprats (September to April)
Squid (April to November)
Turbot (September to March)
Venus clams (July to April)
Whelks (February to August)
Whiting (May to February)

Wild Atlantic salmon (February to October)
Witch (October to April)

SEASONAL MEAT

Christmas goose (December)
Christmas turkey (December)
Light lamb or hill lamb (September to December)
Michaelmas goose (September)
Milk-fed lamb (March)
Native grass-fed beef (December)
Salt marsh lamb (July)
Spring lamb (March)
Suckling pig (December)

GAME

Black game (12th August to 10th December)
Capercaillie (1st October to 31st January)
English and Welsh hind (doe) venison, red, fallow, roe and sika
    (1st November to 30th April)
English and Welsh red stag venison (1st August to 30th April)
English and Welsh roebuck venison (1st April to 31st October)
Grouse (12th August to 10th December)
Hare (August to February)
Mallard and other wildfowl (1st September to 31st January)
Partridge (1st September to 31st January)
Pheasant (1st October to 31st January)
Scottish fallow stag (buck) venison (1st August to 30th April)
Scottish hind (or doe) venison, red, fallow and sika (21st October to
    15th February)
Scottish red and sika stag venison (1st July to 20th October)
Scottish roe doe venison (21st October to 31st March)

Scottish roebuck venison (1st April to 20th October)
Snipe (1st September to 31st January)
Woodcock (1st September to 31st January)

APPLES

Eating apples should feel only good but now presents the conscientious shopper with myriad anxieties. On the one hand, eating fruit, any fruit, is undeniably beneficial to health; and an apple is a definite candidate for the recommended five-a-day the Food Standards Agency asks consumers to eat. But with reports that this perishable orchard fruit could be contaminated with agricultural chemicals, or that the crunchy southern hemisphere varieties snapped up eagerly by British shoppers have gobbled up an astonishing number of food miles, that oh-so-good-for-you apple can stick in your throat. Then there's the question of which apple to buy, given no ready British supply. For some, preference for, perhaps, US fruit over French, or New Zealand over Chilean, comes down to old and new loyalties; a case where the wallet becomes a voting slip.

Are there chemical residues on apples?
Yes. First, be aware that while it is in the interests of supermarkets to control the level of pesticide and post-harvest fungicide drenches applied to apples from the 'dedicated' British farms that supply them, they are less able to monitor all imports. In 2005 the government-backed Pesticides Residues Committee sampled 63 apples, finding chemical residues on all but seven. No residues were found on the four organic samples taken. Residues were found on all EU-originated apple samples. Two samples contained residues at levels unacceptably high for children. Many apples are waxed to protect them and enhance their appearance; this wax may contain fungicides, so wipe off as much as possible before eating. Concerned parents should peel imported apples before giving them to children.

Are organic apples the right choice?
Not always. Organic apples from supermarkets, organic food shops and even box schemes are often imported, and the food miles they clock up negate any environmental gain. Buying British-grown

organic apples is ideal but you will have to look hard for them. Growing a disease-free, good-looking apple without pesticides is a tough task in the British climate. Old trees that have never been treated with agricultural chemicals tend to produce abundantly without problems, but organic farmers say that new orchards can develop disease/pest problems after just a few years, which are very hard to control.

When are apples at their best?

Apples are at their best eaten just a few weeks after picking, when the sugars have developed yet the fruit is still juicy and crunchy.

Is it true that apples in shops can be up to a year old?

After picking, British apples are stored for up to six months at 2–3°C in a 'controlled atmosphere' with nitrogen gas and ammonia to reduce oxygen levels. But not all apples are stored this way. In 2005 the chemical 1-methylcyclopropene was approved for use in Europe, a gas that when pumped into cold rooms or shipping containers halts the release of ethylene, the natural hormone in fruit that ripens it. This means the apple you buy can be up to *one year old*. 1-methylcyclopropene is music to the ears of long-distance exporters (such as the US and New Zealand), because the apples retain their 'just-picked' looks, flavour and juice. Previous storage techniques would see the apples mellow in flavour and become drier in texture during storage. So that's great – crispy apples all round? Well, no. While this development could pay high dividends for exporters and retailers, there is little in it for us consumers. There is evidence that the chemical is carcinogenic in very high doses and its use is a threat to the survival of our own orchards and to the seasons themselves.

When are British apples in season?

The season for apple growing in northern hemisphere countries runs from August to March but, with the exception of a few varieties, the more unusual ones are available for only some of this time. This is either because they are in short supply or because they do not store well. Our cooler summers delay the arrival of British apples in the shops, with little but Discovery available in August and the first Cox's Orange Pippins hitting the shelves in late September. Thanks to 'controlled atmosphere' storage methods, British apples are available until March (although the supply is limited). The southern hemisphere season kicks in neatly in April, lasting through the British summer and into autumn. Savvy shoppers beware – it can encroach on the start of the British season, the time when loyalty to British farms is paramount. New Zealand apples are in shops until November.

How can I know where an apple comes from?

By law, labels on bags, trays or boxes and the shelf-edge information must carry a country-of-origin sticker. Information on those annoying individual stickers is provided voluntarily but they typically identify the apple type and, in the case of British apples, will often helpfully show a Union Jack symbol.

Is a red, shiny apple bound to be a good apple?

No! A tight, shining skin may belie woolly flesh underneath. Smell the apple – a fusty, wet-cardboard aroma is an indication of this.

Where should I buy apples?

Buy British in season, to support growers competing against lower-priced imports. The UK could be self-sufficient from the Cox harvest and supplies Bramley apples year round, but continued demand for popular imports, among them Golden Delicious, Braeburn, Gala and Granny Smith, inhibits loyalty to British orchards. Meanwhile, new nations join the fray: apples from Chile, the Czech Republic and Poland are here; the Fuji variety from China in the northern hemisphere is a particular threat to our growers. Outside the British season, it is best to choose apples that have travelled the least distance and have been shipped rather than air freighted. Customer service departments at supermarkets should supply this information if asked.

What the supermarkets say

Waitrose has a commitment to selling 70 per cent British produce when in season and stocks Cox's apples in all stores from October to March, grown on their own Leckford Farm in Hampshire. During the autumn months Waitrose sells heritage varieties from the Brogdale Horticultural Trust, plus organic apples. Leckford Farm also sells apples at the 'farm gate' in autumn – the farm is located on the A30 between Stockbridge and Sutton Scotney.

Booths sells as many British apples as it can possibly find in season and has a policy to source locally where possible. Willington Fruit Farm in Cheshire supplies specialist varieties to this northern supermarket chain and the stores host occasional apple tastings.

Budgens banned all French apples from their stores when the French stopped importing British beef after the BSE crisis and has never reintroduced them. In the British season, it buys 65 per cent British apples and no imported variety that can be grown in the UK. It also sells a number of traditional varieties, including Worcester Pearmain, Egremont and a North American-bred apple, Cameo, from a longstanding Kent supplier.

Sainsbury claims to prioritise English produce if it deems the quality acceptable. It also imports, and therefore transports by air, apples from all over the world. However, it states that it only imports apple varieties that are not grown in the UK, according to customer demand. It does offer an organic supply of apples.

Marks & Spencer imports apples from five different continents but states that it has a preference for UK-grown fruit when the quality meets customer expectation.

The Co-op sources its apples primarily from Europe and is working with UK growers to use crops whenever they are in season. The packaging is biodegradable and compostable. All apples are delivered by road and sea freight

Tesco sources apples from the UK, US, New Zealand, China, Australia and South America but states it prefers to buy UK produce if it meets their specifications. It claims to buy more UK apples than any other retailer (but this is probably due to its size). It sells organic and also claims to sell a fairly traded apple 'when available'.

Where to buy British apples

Farmers' markets are a good source of apples during autumn, and the place to find those elusive British organic ones. For details of your nearest market, check **www.farmersmarkets.net** (tel: 0845 458 8420), or **www.lfm.org.uk** (tel: 0207 833 0338) for London. Alternatively, find a source of local apples through **www.bigbarn.co.uk** – put in your postcode and apples and suppliers will be displayed on a map.

**Broomfield's Apples, School Plantation, Holt Heath,
Worcester WR6 6NF
Tel: 01905 620233
www.broomfieldsfarmshop.co.uk**
Grower Colin Broomfield will send a 5-kilo box of apples anywhere in the mainland UK. Unusual varieties include Winter Gem, Crispin, Lord Lambourn and Jupiter.

**Charlton Orchards, Charlton Road, Creech St Michael,
Taunton, Somerset TA3 5PF
Tel: 01823 412959
sally@charlton-orchards.co.uk**
Traditional good keeping types include Orleans Reinette, Ashmead's Kernel, Adam's Pearmain and Egremont Russet. They will send out a 56-apple crate (four varieties).

**Crapes Fruit Farm, Rectory Road, Aldham,
Colchester, Essex CO6 3RR
Tel: 01206 212375**
150 different apple varieties, available at different times throughout the season. Home delivery available.

Park Fruit Farm, Pork Lane, Great Holland,
Nr Frinton-on-Sea, Essex CO13 0ES
Tel: 01255 674621
www.parkfruitfarm.co.uk
Choose from 40 apple varieties, including D'Arcy Spice, George Cave
and King of the Pippins, packed carefully in layered boxes. Mail order
available.

Yorkshire Orchards, White House Farm, Bolton Lane,
Wilberfoss, York YO41 5NX
Tel: 01759 305079
www.yorkshireorchards.co.uk
A new orchard with over 60 apple types, both traditional and modern.
The website includes an Apple Chooser, which selects alternative
varieties to favourite supermarket ones. Farmer Richard Borrie
recommends Rajka, a new red apple developed in the Czech Republic
that has a hint of strawberry in it; also Topaz, an extra crisp and juicy
James Grieve. Apples can be posted to most UK locations. Apple tree
rental available – a treat for the apple-passionate who do not want to
tend their own tree. An annual fee will guarantee home delivery of all
the fruit from one well-tended mature tree or three years of fruit
from a young tree.

ASPARAGUS

Sometimes the British climate has its benefits. Our spring emerges out of winter so slowly that plants struggle to get going, battling against unexpected droughts, frosts or freak torrential rainfall. With asparagus, the outcome of growing in such crazy conditions is a vegetable with a feistier flavour than its southern European rival. But that's not the only reason to buy British . . .

Why should I buy British asparagus?

Before our season begins, the majority of our spring asparagus comes from an earlier growing season in Spain. Spanish asparagus is also grown outdoors but, while some can be very good indeed, it grows faster in Spain's warmer climate and its taste will never be as intense as that of British asparagus. All asparagus must be cooked as soon as possible after picking or the stems will become tough, so imports, which of course take time to travel to the UK shops, are at a disadvantage. Asparagus from Spain can have several centimetres of tough, inedible stalk.

Air miles can be a serious problem for exported asparagus. Spanish asparagus is transported by lorry but asparagus from other exporting countries, including Thailand and Peru, is air freighted. Environmentalists point out that this is a high fuel–oil cost for a low-calorie food – meaning is it worth the environmental cost to ship a non-essential food? I'd argue that there is more justification in shipping bananas or citrus fruit. The best line to take is to choose imported – preferably outdoor-grown Spanish – as an occasional luxury.

When does the British season begin?

Usually around the end of April, running to a cut-off point in the third week of June. Growers must leave enough stalks in the ground to 'go to seed' and so provide a good crop for the following year.

Why is boiling now better than steaming?

Newly developed breeds of asparagus have a uniform tenderness along the stalk that allows them to be snapped at the base during harvest, not cut. It was the case that the old breeds were cut, just under the ground, so the stalks were sold with a tougher end to them. Asparagus steamers were created so that the whole stalk would cook evenly.

What is the best way to prepare asparagus?

The modern breeds can be boiled for five to seven minutes, until just tender when pierced with a knife, then lifted out and laid on a tea towel to drain thoroughly (do not bruise them by throwing them into a colander). Chefs often pare away the outer skin on the lower end of the stalk to guarantee even cooking. This is a good idea that also yields extra-green cooked stalks.

Are chemicals used to grow asparagus?

It is hard to track chemical use in importing countries but Spanish growers who supply UK supermarkets may not use any more than their UK counterparts. Chemical use in the UK varies; if you want to avoid all but the organic sector's few approved chemicals, then buy organic, where all weeding is done by hand. But there are conventional suppliers – even large-scale ones – who measure the impact they have on the environment: carrying out ornithological surveys and encouraging beneficial predatory insects on crops to replace pesticides. Members of the Asparagus Growers Association (see page 40) are refreshingly transparent about pesticide use. Responsible growers are reluctant to use sprays because almost the whole plant is eaten.

The big problem for growers is weeds, so in the UK a limited number of herbicides is conventionally used before the shoots appear. After that, growers should weed by hand, but there is no rule that guarantees this. Fungicides are sometimes used during a harvest in wet weather. The point about asparagus is that the stalks are above ground for no more than 11 days, so with decent weather conditions and no pest attacks they stand a good chance of being chemical free.

Reports recording pesticide residues comfort a little. Both British and imported asparagus were tested for residues in spring 2004. Residues were found on one out of 47 samples. The sample – from Peru – contained residues of the pesticide cypermethrin below UK maximum residue levels, but obviously if other growers can produce residue-free asparagus, we do not want to see any at all.

Is asparagus good for you?

It is classed as a 'superfood', especially for pregnant women, because it contains particularly high levels of natural folic acid, plus vitamins A, C and E. It is also a good source of potassium and fibre – so eat lots during the glut.

But what about that smell?

The smell in urine after eating asparagus comes from sulphur-containing degradation products that are created as the body metabolises the asparagus. The odour, which can be nasty, gave the asparagus its old reputation, 'chambermaid's nightmare'. It is said that healthy kidney function will produce that smelly 'pee' within 15 minutes of eating the stalks, but it is also true that some people are totally unable to detect the smell, so don't panic if you eat asparagus and the air in the loo appears, er, as sweet as ever.

What other varieties are there, apart from green?

White asparagus is very popular in Belgium, France and Italy but imported stalks can be flavourless and tough. Red asparagus, which crops at the same time as green, is making a comeback in the UK and is available in May. Asparagus 'sprue' is not another breed, just thin stalks, and is very good stir-fried or cooked quickly and added to a risotto.

How do I choose asparagus?

Green asparagus is sold in two thicknesses, 'jumbo' and 'kitchen'. There is little difference in flavour; it is always the freshness that counts. Sniff the tips, which should smell fresh and fruity, not of compost. Inspect the stalks for damage and look out for very dry ends, which probably mean that the asparagus has been hanging about a bit.

Supermarkets tend to buy direct from farms, but nevertheless you need to scrutinise their asparagus for signs of age. It is possible that it has been held in a warehouse for up to three days before distribution.

For the freshest asparagus, buy direct from farms, produce markets or from local greengrocers who go to regional wholesale markets that take delivery of freshly picked asparagus from local farms every night.

What the supermarkets say

Sainsbury claims to take all the British produce that is available to it during the UK season but says that demand outstrips supply. In these cases it imports produce, from countries in Asia, the Americas, and Africa. All of this produce is transported by road and air freight. Sainsbury also stocks organic asparagus.

Tesco's asparagus is grown in Peru and Guatemala. Tesco states that it sources British when quality is at its best. It also sells an organic variety.

Marks & Spencer sources its asparagus from Peru, the UK and South Africa. It says that it has extended the selling period of British asparagus, now selling it out of season for two months longer – to great success (obviously). The asparagus is usually transported by air and road freight.

The Co-op sources its asparagus from the UK, Peru and Thailand. There is no organic option. The asparagus is transported via road and air freight.

Budgens' asparagus is sourced from the UK when in season, Peru and Spain at other times. It does not sell an organic variety.

Where to buy British asparagus

Pick-your-own farms and farm shops are the best source of asparagus during the season, and very good value. Buying from them also supports the local economy. The Asparagus Growers Association has a list of all suppliers who sell at the farm gate: look at **www.british-asparagus.co.uk** or phone 01507 602427.

Mail-order asparagus is available from the following suppliers:

C. W. Cave (Terrington) Ltd, Hall Farm, West Rudham,
Kings Lynn, Norfolk PE31 8TE
Tel: 01485 528238

Mr and Mrs J. M. Harlow, 1 Westenhanger Cottage,
Maidstone Road, Horsmonden, Tonbridge, Kent TN12 8DD
Tel: 01892 722533
www.easyasparagus.com

A. H. and H. A. Pattullo, Eassie Farm, By Glamis,
Angus DD8 1SG
Tel: 01307 840303

BABY FOOD AND INFANT FORMULA

While breast milk is the best possible baby's tipple, it appears that you are never too young to be green. The buzzword in the baby food and formula market barely needs saying, but organic it is. Ten years ago organic baby food and formula companies could be counted on the fingers of one hand. Now there are at least a dozen. Once weaned, you can be a green gourmet, too. Forget slimy purée – baby gets a menu worthy of an entry in the *Michelin Guide*. But just before you dash off to buy these Lilliputian ready meals, remember that is exactly what they are and, just like milk from the breast, freshly cooked food from fresh ingredients is always best.

Does organic mean pesticide free when it comes to baby food?

Yes, and interestingly under UK law conventional baby food is free of pesticides, too. The maximum limit for pesticides in milk formula and baby food is set at 0.01mg per kilo, a level so low it effectively means no residues are present. This is not to say there is not a problem. In 2002, when cereal-based baby foods were tested for the organophosphate, pirimiphos methyl, two out of 71 samples had detectable levels. Later that year three out of 73 samples were found to contain the same pesticide – they were withdrawn, but inexplicably cereal-based baby food was not tested the following year.

So is buying vegetable ready meals for babies a wiser buy than a fresh carrot or squash?

In terms of pesticide residues, it could provide a guarantee of safety from them, but the benefits of cooking fresh food for a baby or child are greater. It should be said that pesticide manufacturers and conventional farmers continue to argue that agricultural chemicals are safe, but there is still much debate about the so-called cocktail effect of more than one residue on one vegetable. You can always buy organic produce and make baby food with that. Organic growers and producers are permitted to use very few agricultural chemicals, whereas hundreds can be used in conventional farming.

Where do the meat, dairy and eggs in baby food come from?

Unless the label has Soil Association organic certification, or carries a statement on animal welfare and feed, the meat, dairy or egg content could derive from intensively reared livestock. Other organic marks are a good sign but Soil Association animal welfare standards are the most stringent.

Is the milk base of formula milk from cows kept in intensive farms?

Non-organic formula will have come from conventional farms, though not all conventional farms are intensive. Again, a reputable organic certificate is a sign of good husbandry. Be aware that conventional, large-scale milk production is bad for the environment (see page 247) and that animal welfare can be compromised. It is not, however, an unsafe food.

What's added to conventional formula milk?

The basis of formula milk is protein, whey and casein in a ratio as close as the manufacturer can get to that in breast milk. Fat is added, usually a mix of animal and vegetable fat, but increasingly long-chain polyunsaturated fatty acids (LCPs) are added too. These include fish-oil-based omega-3 and plant-based omega-6, which are known to benefit the heart and stimulate brain function. Vitamins and minerals are also added, along with amino acids and sometimes proteins called nucleotides, which occur naturally in breast milk and can boost immunity.

Are non-dairy (cow's milk) formulas available?

There are formulas based on goat's milk and soy for babies with a family history of allergy-based illnesses. They also contain added nutrients. If you think your child is intolerant or allergic to dairy milk, it is important to seek the advice of a paediatrician or nutrition expert before choosing any alternative.

What's the difference between conventional formula and organic?

There is little difference in the basic ingredients, but with each formula the proportions of each may vary. In organic formula, the food-based ingredients must be organically sourced.

Are the recipes for infant formulas tested?

Formulation of infant milks is under the control of UK and EU legislation. The law is designed to stop the use of untested novel substances in the manufacture of infant formulas and changes cannot be made to formula milks without proper trials.

Why are free samples of formula milk given to new mothers?

For loyalty and profit – the manufacturers want their business. It is very tempting for mothers who are struggling in the early breast-feeding days to top up with formula or even switch over to it. The same practice takes on a more sinister role in developing countries with water cleanliness problems. In 2002 Unicef estimated that 1.5 million babies would die a year from unsafe bottlefeeding. The food corporation, Nestlé, was singled out for aggressively marketing formula milk in developing countries and a worldwide boycott of their products began in 1978. In May 1999 a ruling was published against Nestlé by the UK Advertising Standards Authority (ASA). In an anti-boycott advert, Nestlé had claimed that it marketed infant formula 'ethically and responsibly'. The ASA found that the corporation could not support this or other claims in the face of evidence provided by the campaigning group, Baby Milk Action.

Can baby food and formula be contaminated with GMOs?

Livestock that produce milk, meat or eggs for the baby food and formula market may be given GM feed, unless they are only grass fed. The authorities say that since the feed passes through the gut, there will be no contamination. GM watchdogs argue that there is some evidence that DNA from GM material remains in and passes through the gut of animals. They also insist that testing and labelling of GM foods is not adequate. Organic baby food producers police for GM contamination very effectively, and the smaller producers provide exceptionally clear traceability.

Do baby foods contain colourings or other additives?

Yes. The only colours permitted are riboflavin and beta-carotene, which are vitamins with a natural colour. The government complies with EU law and 'restricts' the use of other non-natural additives. Keep an eye out for starch-based 'fillers', such as modified maize starch (corn starch) and maltodextrin, which are added to bulk out food, thus reducing the ingredient cost (water can be added for the same reason). They make food tasteless, necessitating the use of flavourings. Maltodextrin has no nutritional use. Read the labels, choosing only foods that are 100 per cent natural.

Do baby foods contain added sugar?

Yes. A survey by the Food Commission found 50 per cent sugar in Nestlé Fruit Stick and 37 per cent in Boots Teddy Bear biscuits, compared with 36 per cent in a jam tart. Traditional Farley's Rusks (29 per cent) have more sugar than a chocolate digestive (27 per cent). And so-called 'reduced-sugar' products from Farley's (21 per cent) and Hipp (21 per cent) had more sugar than a jam doughnut (19 per cent sugar). These are biscuits for children who are just getting their first teeth! Check the ingredients list for added sugar, including any mention of dextrose, glucose, corn syrup and other types of sugar.

Do baby foods contain salt?

There should not be any salt in baby food. Babies up to 12 months need 1g or less salt a day, which they will get naturally from their milk and meals without adding extra. Never add salt to food for a baby or a child under five.

Where to buy trustworthy baby foods

It is always better to wean a baby on to home-made foods prepared from good-quality fresh ingredients. Only feed ready-made foods when there is a genuine time constraint, in which case look out for the following brands:

**All Good Stuff, Chadwick House, Birchwood Park,
Warrington WA3 6AE
Tel: 01925 830500
www.allgoodstuff.com**

Not so much ready meals as simple fruit and vegetable purées, frozen in individual portions. Very good for newly weaned babies. Home delivery available.

**Baby Organix, Knapp Mill, Mill Road,
Christchurch, Dorset BH23 2LU
Tel: 0800 393511
www.babyorganix.co.uk**

Baby Organix was among the first British mainstream organic baby food manufacturers. The recipes are based on traditional home cooking. Available from most supermarkets, as well as independent shops.

**Daylesford Organic Farm Shop, Daylesford, Nr Kingham,
Gloucestershire GL56 0YG
Tel: 01608 731700
www.daylesfordorganic.com**

Organic fruit and vegetable purées for babies, cooked for a short time to retain nutrients, and free from additives, salt and sugar. Home delivery available.

Goodness Direct, South March, Daventry,
Northamptonshire NN11 4PH
Tel: 0871 871 6611
www.goodnessdirect.co.uk

Goodness Direct stocks some established imported brands, including Nanny Goat Milk Infant Nutrition and follow-on milk from New Zealand, BabyNat organic infant formula and bottled purées, Familia Swiss Baby muesli and the Hipp organic range. Home delivery available.

Hipp, 165 Main Street, New Greenham Park,
Newbury, Berkshire RG19 6HN
Tel: 0845 050 1351
www.hipp.co.uk

Hipp converted its range to organic in 1995 and sells food, infant formula milks and follow-on milks. Available from all major supermarkets, or direct from the website.

Mini Scoff, Scoff Central, Unit 3a Midlands Industrial Estate,
Holt, Wiltshire BA14 6RU
Tel: 01225 783221
www.miniscoff.co.uk

Good ideas, including organic vegetable and pasta dishes, meat recipes, and even a dish with very mild chilli to galvanise young taste buds. Home delivery available.

Mums4 (by Mothers for Children), 58 Clarendon Street,
Leamington Spa CV32 4PE
Tel: 01926 771285
www.mums4.com

Organic yoghurt sweetened only by the fruit and milk, the equivalent of one teaspoon of natural sugar as opposed to the 2–3 teaspoons of sugar added to conventional children's yoghurt. Available from Tesco, Waitrose and home delivery from Ocado.

Plum Baby, PO Box 283, Lyndhurst, Hampshire SO43 7WZ
Tel: 0845 389 0061
www.plumbabysuperfoods.com
Susie Willis's new company makes Fairtrade-accredited mango and banana purée with quinoa; spinach, parsnip and basil; and blueberry banana and vanilla.

Truuuly Scrumptious Organic Baby Food,
Charmborough Farm, Charlton Road, Holcombe,
Radstock, Somerset BA3 5EX
Tel: 01761 239300
www.bathorganicbabyfood.co.uk
Imaginative recipes, frozen in microwavable pots to retain the goodness in the organic raw materials. Puréed sweet potato or apple and raisin for young babies; sweetcorn chowder, salmon and broccoli for older ones. Home delivery available.

BACON (AND PORK)

It should be so simple. Cover a fresh pork back or belly with salt and a little sugar, leave it to cure, then mature it in a cold, dry room and you have bacon. But simple it isn't. Traditionally cured bacon is still available but the majority of commercial bacon is produced very differently – and much of it is imported from other European countries, a long way from our breakfast tables. The same issues apply to bacon's raw material, fresh pork. This ranges from slow-grown traditional breeds with sublime flavour and superb cooking qualities (meaning less shrinkage and no seeping white paste during cooking) to characterless, pale, fatless joints that are as disappointing as they are cheap. It is worth bearing in mind that, due to the poor cooking quality of such pork, the cheapest pork is not always the best value.

What methods are used to make commercially cured bacon?

Commercially made bacon is wet cured in brine with either phosphates or a derivative. Injected into the meat, phosphates encourage the absorption of water, which boosts the weight of the meat. This is the milky liquid that seeps from the bacon as it fries. Bacon cured this way will retain a higher level of salt – a matter of concern to anyone watchful of their diet.

How is traditional bacon made?

It can be wet or dry cured. The former is placed in a brine tub with salt, sodium nitrite (E250 – note nitrite not nitrate) and potassium nitrate (E252, otherwise known as saltpetre), plus the spices, sugar or seasoning that give it its character. Dry-cured bacon is placed in a mixture of dry salt, sodium nitrate, potassium nitrate, seasonings and/ or spices. Nitrates give bacon its pink colour. Ordinary salt produces very unappealing grey bacon. Organic production permits the use of both. After curing, it is hung to dry and mature. With no injections of phosphates, traditional cures are less salty and the flavour of the meat more obvious. These two methods are well suited to traditional, slow-growing pig breeds.

Should I be concerned about the preservatives in bacon?

Obviously excessive salt in bacon is not healthy but it is much better to eat bacon that has been dry cured or traditionally brined (the Wiltshire cure) than injected with brine and phosphates, as is sometimes the case with commercial cured pork. The preservative with the greater problem is potassium nitrite (E249), which is not permitted in food specifically made for infants and small children because it can affect the body's ability to carry oxygen and is therefore a danger to asthma sufferers or those with respiratory illness. Just to confuse matters further, sodium nitrate (E251) and sodium nitrite (E250) can also be used in the curing process. The latter is controversial and some retailers will not permit its use because it is potentially harmful to children.

Who makes bacon?

Britain, Holland and Denmark are major producers but bacon is also made in the Irish Republic, France, Germany and Spain. The majority of bacon eaten in the UK is imported, mainly from Holland and Denmark, and the figure is on the increase. Recently it was reported that imports have increased by 38 per cent to 300,000 tonnes, and that excludes fresh pork that is imported and cured in the UK.

Why not eat imports?

It is largely a moral choice. Welfare for British pigs, especially breeding sows, is of a higher standard. It is estimated that two-thirds of breeding sows in other EU countries (apart from Sweden, whose welfare standards are more on a par with UK ones) are kept indoors, confined individually in small stalls all their lives. In the UK, indoor-farmed breeding sows are confined during birth and for four weeks after the birth in 'farrowing crates', which measure six feet by four feet (the pigs weigh about 250 kilos). The reason given is to protect the piglets, and British pig farmers say they are trying to design a larger, more welfare-friendly crate. Once the sows have mated again – about five weeks after the last litter – they are moved to pens where they are kept in groups for the duration of the pregnancy – about five months. They may be on straw bedding, which is good, but could be on slatted floors – not good. Young indoor-reared British pigs are loose housed in pens, about half of them on deep litter straw.

In all European countries (apart from Sweden) pigs are kept in groups. Tail docking is permitted in Europe and the UK, but only under veterinary supervision, so at least farmers are not routinely carrying it out. Nose rings are permitted, but rare in the UK.

Is all British pork welfare friendly?

No. Welfare experts say standards for 70 per cent of pigs (reared indoors) could be improved. The other 30 per cent are reared out-doors, where they can behave more naturally, but they must have some sort of shelter.

What do pigs eat?

In spite of being omnivores, British and European pigs are now, in the most part, vegetarians. Meat and bone meal feed are banned (due to BSE), and so is pigswill (which by definition contains meat waste) because it is thought it can spread diseases such as foot and mouth. Pigs are permitted some fishmeal, but it must constitute no more than three per cent of their feed. Pigs can eat dairy waste, such as whey from cheese making, but this is sadly rare (the whole Parma ham/Parmesan business was founded on feeding pigs whey). Whether or not this enforced vegetarian diet affects their growth is not yet known – will the pig of the future evolve with no meat-eating teeth?

Pigs are now fed dried concentrates of cereals including soya (which can be GM derived); co-product feed from the food industry, such as biscuits (so they are snacking on lots of sugar, salt and hydrogenated fat!); or waste from the non-meat ready-meal business. Farmers can also choose to 'wet feed' a sort of nice porridge with cereals and, best of all, Greenwich Gold, the leftover 'mash' from London gin making. If I were a pig I know what I would choose from the menu. Roots are the correct natural feed for outdoor pigs, who love turnips, but best of all is the acorn and apple diet of woodland- or orchard-reared pigs. Ideally some common sense regarding pig feed needs to be applied; a return to eating fat from butchery or poultry waste could be a good thing.

Look at it this way – if the science was right, feeding meat and bone meal to vegetarians (cattle) caused a disaster; should we now be depriving natural omnivores of the small amount of flesh they would naturally eat in the wild?

When is British bacon not British?

In theory a side of Danish- or Dutch-reared pork could be cured, sliced and packed in Britain and then be labelled British (the country of origin on the pack will read 'UK'). Beware of packaging dressed up to look 'olde' – the bacon may be nothing of the sort. It must be said that supermarkets often differentiate between British and, say, Danish because consumers enjoy the taste and size of the Danish rashers. Well and good, but for me welfare remains a big issue. It is a perfect example of how uneven the playing field can be among the European member states when it comes to food production.

What's in a bacon sandwich?

It's hard to tell, but 85 per cent of bacon sold through catering outlets – such as restaurants, takeaways, cafés, motorway service stations, schools, hospitals and office canteens – is imported. No need for a label makes it easy to hide.

What the supermarkets say

None of the 'Big Four' supermarkets would reveal what percentage of British bacon they sell. **Waitrose** says 82 per cent of its bacon is British and **Budgens'** own label is 100 per cent British. Some supermarkets sell speciality bacon (including organic – look for Soil Association for ultra-high welfare standards for the pigs), which is cured in the traditional manner (seek out British bacon made from British-reared pork).

Artisan-made bacon by post

Traditionally made bacon stores well, so it makes sense to buy in large quantities to justify the price of home delivery. All the producers listed below offer a mail-order service.

Blackface.co.uk, Weatherall Foods Ltd, Crochmore House, Irongray, Dumfries DG2 9SF
Tel: 01387 730326
www.blackface.co.uk
Pork from 'Iron Age' pigs (a cross between Tamworth and wild boar), with a darker, fuller-flavoured meat.

Bleiker's Smoke House Ltd, Glasshouses Mill, Glasshouses, Harrogate, North Yorkshire HG3 5QH
Tel: 01423 711411
www.bleikers.co.uk
Smoked food experts, Jurg and Jane Bleiker, dry cure and smoke backs of 100 per cent British free-range pork, deep in the Yorkshire Dales.

Brampton Wild Boar, Blue Tile Farm, Lock's Road, Brampton, Beccles, Suffolk NR34 8DX
Tel: 01502 575246
Deep-flavoured bacon from fourth-generation purebred boar.

Denhay Farms Ltd, Broadoak, Bridport, Dorset DT6 5NP
Tel: 01308 422717
www.denhay.co.uk
Bacon from free-range pigs fed a natural diet. Denhay also make the excellent organic Duchy Originals bacon, which is widely available in supermarkets. Denhay bacon is available through mail order.

Heal Farm Meats, Heal Farm, Kings Nympton, Devon EX37 9TB
Tel: 01769 574341
www.healfarm.co.uk
Organic bacon made using traditional breeds, reared in exceptional conditions: British Lop, Tamworth, Welsh and more.

Maynards Farm Bacon, Weston-under-Redcastle, Shrewsbury, Shropshire SY4 5LR
Tel: 01948 840252
www.maynardsfarm.co.uk
Various traditionally cured styles of bacon, made with the interesting addition of spices in the cure such as ginger and caraway.

Richard Woodall Ltd, Lane End, Waberthwaite, Nr Millom, Cumbria LA19 5YJ
Tel: 01229 717237
www.richardwoodall.com
Award-winning bacon from a closed herd of Landrace and Large White pigs.

Sillfield Farm, Endmoor, Kendal, Cumbria LA8 0HZ
Tel: 015395 67609
www.sillfield.co.uk
Peter Gott's skilfully made bacon is produced from beautifully cared-for pigs that roam almost wild.

Slacks, Newlands Farm, Raisbeck, Orton, Penrith, Cumbria CA10 3SG
Tel: 01539 624667
www.edirectory.co.uk/slacks
Air-dried bacon from locally sourced, free-range, dairy-fed pigs.

BANANAS

A banana is all the more enjoyable when you are sure the growers received a fair sum, so it is well worth paying the extra 40 pence or so per kilo for Fairtrade fruit – it is a low price for a highly nutritious food. However, as the Fairtrade phenomenon gathers pace and our supermarkets commit themselves to selling some fairly traded food, concern about the production methods for conventional bananas grows. Meanwhile, a trade war is brewing that could change the banana map forever, narrowing consumer choice.

What's behind the incredible popularity of bananas?

In the first place, bananas are a 'superfood', like papaya and broccoli. They have high levels of fibre (good for the gut), vitamin C (to protect against disease) and potassium, which, apart from slashing the risk of heart disease, is an excellent hangover cure. We love them, too, as we do eggs, for their naturally built-in hygienic wrapping.

Why are bananas such an important fruit to the UK?

They've long been part of our culture, tied in with our loyalty to the once-colonised countries who supply us with them. The same countries used to be chiefly sugarcane growers, but that market began to collapse in the 1930s and 1940s, when northern European farmers started growing sugar beet (later sustained by some tasty subsidies). In other words, we wiped out the sugar business in the Caribbean, causing social unrest. To compensate, we set up Geest, a company whose name became synonymous with exporting bananas.

Do long, straight bananas come from a different plant from the small, curvy ones?

Almost every banana on sale, indeed 98 per cent of world export, is the Cavendish variety. Cavendish is high yielding and travels well, lasting up to four weeks after picking. But growing one type of banana creates a monoculture, reducing biodiversity and attracting disease even to the reasonably disease-resistant Cavendish. Banana 'shape' comes down to the farming method; small, curvy bananas tend to be Caribbean, where they use less expensive fertilisers and pick early. A London market importer likened the Caribbean banana to 'a small hungry hand' – with good reason.

Why is there a banana trade war?

Because the US companies with huge banana business interests in South America protested that under WTO (World Trade Organisation) law the Europeans can no longer offer favourable trade conditions to Caribbean exporters. The EU has now ruled that all countries should pay a single tariff, or tax. The Caribbean growers say that, due to poorer growing conditions, banana production is more costly there and with a single tariff they cannot compete. They say the US complaint was about corporate greed, and will not bring fairness. The EU stands accused of making rules without evaluating the outcome. No study has been done to check how even the playing field will become and the Caribbean countries say the future of banana growing is under threat. Around 80 per cent of the banana market is controlled by corporations, including Dole, Del Monte, Bonito and Chiquita.

Are bananas sprayed?

Bananas rank second on the 'most sprayed' list (cotton ranks first), especially on large-scale plantations that can afford the expense of agricultural chemicals. Some of these pesticides and fungicides are hazardous to growers. Workers in Honduras have just persuaded a multinational corporation to stop using chlorpyriphos after a study showed it caused skin allergies, appetite loss and fertility problems. There are compensation cases pending in Nicaragua over similar claims of horrific damage to workers' health.

Are bananas artificially ripened?

All bananas, including organic ones, need a trigger for ripening. Most producers use ethylene, a gas that is permitted even under Soil

Association rules. Ethylene is naturally produced by fruit, but for commercial purposes it is manufactured, a by-product of industry. Remember that you can ripen bananas, tomatoes and avocados by putting them in a paper bag and letting the natural ethylene enclosed get to work. Ethylene is not that harmful and the Soil Association argues that it must permit this treatment or we can forget the availability of organic bananas.

Are organic bananas more eco-friendly?

Bananas travel several thousand miles, organic or not. But both conventional and organic bananas travel by boat, not plane, and leaving the banana out of the fruit bowl would have a devastating sociological impact on producing countries so it is a worthwhile exception to make, even for those aiming to keep food miles to a minimum. Bananas are also very nutritious. Soil Association-certified bananas hail from the Windward Isles, Costa Rica and Ecuador.

Which is the ideal banana to buy?

It is best to buy organic or Fairtrade bananas; the extra is worth paying and they are still a remarkably cheap food. Be aware, however, that Fairtrade does not necessarily mean organic, and Fairtrade bananas could have been treated with agricultural chemicals unless the pack *also* says organic. Having said that, it is also the case that Faitrade bananas tend to be grown by producer groups of small-scale farmers who cannot afford the expense of pesticides and fertilisers, so minimise their use. Likewise a premium should be paid to organic banana farms, boosting their income, so there is an element of fair trade, too.

Sales of Fairtrade bananas are growing at an astonishing rate of 43 per cent per annum, increasing from sales of 18 million kilos in 2003 to 25 million kilos in 2004. Some countries need more help than others. The Windward Islands are the most needy and fairly traded bananas from there are the ones to buy. Look for the 'Windwards' label, but also for Caribbean bananas in general.

What the supermarkets say

Sainsbury sells both a Fairtrade and an organic supply of bananas. **Marks & Spencer** and the **Co-op** import their bananas from the Caribbean and sell an additional Fairtrade supply and an organic supply. **Budgens** sells bananas sourced from all over the Caribbean, including a Fairtrade and an organic variety. **Waitrose** sells Fairtrade bananas from the Windward Isles and **Tesco** sells them from the Caribbean.

It is interesting to note that at the time of writing the price of conventional bananas in the 'Big Four' supermarkets was a standard 85 pence per kilo. Could they be 'price fixing', which is illegal? No – the price is too low to accuse the stores of this. Supermarkets rate bananas as a KVI – a 'known value item'. This means they lower the price as far as it can possibly go, which works out the same for each of the Big Four. No wonder fair trade is needed.

BEEF

Burnished and juicily rich, a roast forerib of beef is as magnificent on the Christmas table as turkey or goose, and just as seasonal. Traditionally December is the time to slaughter adult cattle still fat from grazing, then slowly mature the beef, hanging it in cool winter temperatures. But while a margin of this culture continues, the beef industry in general has been turned on its head by modern farming methods, technology and, in the last decade, by consumer uncertainty over BSE.

The implementation of the Over Thirty Month (OTM) age-limit rule, a measure brought in at the height of the BSE scandal, had a devastating impact on our native breeds. Farmers crossbred pure-bred 'native' cattle with larger Continental types so they would grow to full size within the allowed time. While this beef is safe and nutritious, it does not measure up to the great flavour and texture of the British pedigree breeds so suitable for roasting. With the lifting of the OTM rule in November 2005, it is hoped that farmers will be able to afford to revive and maintain the pure native breeds and British beef will be 100 per cent British again.

What is – or was – the Over Thirty Month rule?

The OTM rule was introduced in March 1996 to restore shoppers' confidence. Under the rule, all British beef or dairy animals must be slaughtered before the age of 30 months. There is much argument about the science behind the introduction of the OTM rule, with government scientific advisors insisting that the measure would eradicate the disease and keep cattle BSE free. Farmers complained it was simply a PR initiative, there to placate consumers, and I agree with them. It led to the slaughter of over five million older animals at a huge cost to the taxpayer. The rule was implemented in the dairy industry, too. But numbers of animals with BSE in the UK have dropped to equal levels with other EU countries and the scheme is now to be scrapped. This means that the slower-growing traditional breeds will have the four or more years they sometimes need to reach optimum maturity and a return to traditional flavour and texture.

But how can we be sure British beef is risk free?
The UK will change to a testing regime once the OTM rule is dropped: any animal suspected of having the disease will be slaughtered, then tested. Meat and bonemeal feed, the suspected catalyst for BSE infection, is banned and so-called 'specified risk material' (SRM), such as heads, some offal, most of the vertebrae and all spinal cords, is not permitted for sale. With no proof that nvCJD (the human form of the disease) is spread by eating meat from cattle with the disease, the risk can never be fully assessed. The best way to be sure that beef is safe is to have a full history of the herd from which it was supplied. The new beef labelling laws provide full traceability, but there is nothing like buying from a herd that has always been closed, i.e. one where animals are never bought in.

Where's the benefit in removing the OTM rule?
Nearly a million British cattle will return to the food chain over the next two years, pushing up the percentage of beef available in shops so we can move towards eradicating the need for imported beef, specifically the forequarter beef used in cheaper burgers. This will obviously boost the incomes of British livestock farmers.

What's wrong with imported beef?
Problems with imported meat include lack of traceability and lower safety standards. Imported meat has been found to contain spinal cord, and SRM banned throughout Europe. Some beef is imported from South America, Africa and EU countries. Shops do not like to advertise this fact so it tends to find its way into the catering trade or ready meals. There are always welfare and feed issues with imported meat; most countries do not have our stricter rules on welfare and especially feed. Incidentally, beef sold by breed name can be a product of another country. Dutch Aberdeen Angus is frequently sold in the UK and is often the 'Aberdeen Angus' steak on menus.

Is all the Aberdeen Angus in shops 100 per cent Aberdeen Angus?

No – and the industry is very protective of this information. Cross breeding results in a high ratio of meat to bone, quickly – hence its appeal after the OTM rule was introduced, which saw slower-growing native breeds being slaughtered before reaching their full potential. Also, be aware that beef called 'Scottish' may be native–Continental cross. This is not so much a taste issue (the beef can be delicious if kindly reared, well fed and hung for the correct time) but it is a breed heritage and especially a welfare problem. The cross breeding of Continental cattle such as Limousin and Charentais with Aberdeen Angus is rife but the resulting meat can be called Aberdeen Angus. I have visited farms in Scotland where this practice takes place, where farmers have complained to me that mixing the breeds can cause the calves to be too big for the native-bred mothers and they can have trouble giving birth. Lastly, in my view, the larger-grained meat of fast-growing native–Continental crossbreeds is ill suited to British cooking, especially as roasting joints, and far better, I'm afraid to say, for the Continental veal market. Connoisseurs of beef prefer the small joints of tight-grained native beef. Given the choice, I would go for pure-bred native beef.

What information is on the label of beef packs in supermarkets?

Labels on beef sold in supermarkets must comply with the new labelling regulations, and butchers must display somewhere in the shop notices showing the origin of their beef. The labels or notices should show the name of the country or countries in which the animal was born, reared, slaughtered and cut. Beef labelled 'British' must come from animals born, reared and slaughtered entirely within the UK. Supermarket labels rarely carry more information; suppliers must seek approval for additional information on labels, such as 'grass fed', 'Farm Assured', or astonishingly, 'English'.

How can I be sure of buying the best beef?

* **Ask about breed** – beef from native breeds has tight-grained flesh best suited to roasting; native breeds include pedigree Aberdeen Angus, Hereford, South Devon, Welsh Black, Lincoln Red, Longhorn, Belted Galloway, Highland and White Park.
* **Ask about feed** – meat from animals grown slowly on a mainly grass/silage diet with some cereal in winter has the most flavour. Non-organically reared animals can be fed GM cereals in the UK.
* **Ask about welfare** – stress caused by long journeys to abattoirs, and thereafter overcrowded pens (lairage), and noise has been proved to change PH levels in meat, affecting tenderness and flavour.
* **Ask about hanging** – a side or quarter of beef should be hung for between three and five weeks, uncovered, at a temperature of 2–3°C.

What the supermarkets say

The Co-op sources its beef from the UK and Ireland and 95 per cent of the animals are reared outdoors, feeding on natural pasture, silage and some concentrates, as required. Although the Co-op operates a strictly non-GM policy, it states that these concentrates may contain soya that is not specified as non-GM. Journey time to the abattoir is approximately six hours.

Sainsbury sells a range of organic beef and well-hung conventional beef. It cannot guarantee the latter is not given GM feed.

Marks & Spencer sources its beef from England, Northern Ireland and Scotland. Animals are fed a forage-based diet with at least one season grazing at grass and no GM feed. The journey to the abattoir takes no longer than four hours.

Budgens' beef is reared in England. The cattle are fed on grass, silage and meal, which, although free from fishmeal and growth promoters, may contain some GM substances. The abattoir is less than 100 miles away.

Waitrose sources all its beef in the UK. The mixed breed animals are reared 95 per cent of the time outdoors on a GM-free diet that is 75 per cent forage based (grass, silage), the rest wheat, barley and soya. Journey times to slaughterhouse average nearly four hours.

Tesco beef is sourced from the UK, Ireland, Argentina and Brazil (country of origin is always labelled, so look for the small print; even if the label says Aberdeen Angus, the country of origin could be food-mile-heavy South America). The cattle are fed a forage-based diet but with other cereals ('not generally soya bean'). Tesco did not state whether the feed was GM free.

Where to buy British beef

We taste-tested beef from the farms below and, without exception, the meat was outstanding: tight grained, full flavoured and beautifully tender. Salt was never an option. Meat from these farms is produced from slowly grown cattle fed a natural, predominantly grass diet, then killed locally and traditionally matured. All the farms offer home delivery.

Barkers, Mid Torrie Farm, Callander, Perthshire FK17 8JL
Tel: 01877 330203
www.barkershighlandbeef.co.uk
Breed: Highland

Baylham House Rare Breeds Farm, Mill Lane, Baylham,
Needham Market, Suffolk IP6 8LG
Tel: 01473 830264
www.baylham-house-farm.co.uk
Breed: White Park

Blackface.co.uk, Weatherall Foods Ltd, Crochmore House,
Irongray, Dumfries DG2 9SF
Tel: 01387 730326
www.blackface.co.uk
Breed: Scottish Galloway (now aged up to four years)

Brown Cow Organics, Perridge Farm, Pilton, Shepton Mallet,
Somerset BA4 4EW
Tel: 01749 890298
www.browncoworganics.co.uk
Breed: Guernsey (beef animals are from this family farm's dairy
herd)

Donald Russell Direct, Harlaw Road, Inverurie,
Aberdeenshire AB51 4FR
Tel: 01467 629666
www.donaldrusselldirect.com
Experts in butchery (Continental and British cuts) and hanging meat.

Edwards of Conwy, 18 High Street, Conwy,
North Wales LL32 8DE
Tel: 01492 592443
www.edwardsofconwy.co.uk
Breed: Welsh Black

Gellynen Lodge, Cwmbach Llechrhyd, Builth Wells,
Powys LD2 3RP
Tel: 01982 551242
Breed: Welsh Black

Gilchesters Organic Farm, Hawkwell,
Northumberland NE18 0QL
Tel: 01661 886119
www.gilchesters.com
Breed: White Galloway (organic)

Hereford Prime Direct, Mains of Airies Farm, Stranraer,
Wigtownshire DG9 0RD
Tel: 01776 853516
www.herefordprimedirect.co.uk
Breed: Hereford

Long Ghyll Farms, Brock Close, Bleasdale, Preston,
Lancashire PR3 1UZ
Tel: 01995 61799
www.farmhousedirect.com
Breed: Highland

Lower Hurst Farm, Hartington, Nr Buxton, Derbyshire SK17 0HJ
Tel: 01298 84900
www.lowerhurstfarms.co.uk
Breed: Hereford (organic)

Pipers Farm, Cullompton, Devon EX15 1SD
Tel: 01392 881380
www.pipersfarm.com
Breed: Devon Ruby

The Somerset Meat Company, Marshalls Elm, Street,
Somerset BA16 0TY
Tel: 01458 448990
www.meatontheweb.co.uk
Breed: Red Devon Ruby

The Well Hung Meat Company, Tordean Farm, Dean Prior,
Buckfastleigh, Devon TQ11 0LY
Tel: 0845 230 3131
www.wellhungmeat.com
Breed: Aberdeen Angus and South Devon (organic)

West Country Water Buffalo, Lower Oakley Farm,
Chilthorne Domer, Yeovil, Somerset BA22 8RQ
Tel: 01935 940567
Breed: Water Buffalo

West Hembury Farm, Askerswell, Dorchester, Dorset DT2 9EN
Tel: 01308 485289
www.westhembury.com
Breed: White Park

Woodlands Farm, Kirton House, Kirton, Boston,
Lincolnshire PE20 1JD
Tel: 01205 722491
www.woodlandsfarm.co.uk
Breed: Lincoln Red

Wootton Organic, Ramshorn Farley Oakamoor,
Staffordshire ST10 3BZ
Tel: 0800 652 9469
www.woottonorganic.com
Breed: Aberdeen Angus

Welfare-friendly British veal

Veal is a by-product of the dairy industry, because obviously only females are needed for milk production and male calves are therefore unwanted. The cruel practice of confining veal calves to crates and feeding them milk only (calves need straw roughage) that is permitted in EU countries is banned in the UK. In March 2006 the EU voted to lift the 10-year ban on live cattle exports, which means that farmers can now send unwanted calves for veal production to Europe again. The more milk-fed British veal you consume, the less farmers will be encouraged in this inhumane practice. The farms below produce humanely reared veal.

Helen Browning Organics, Eastbrook Farm, The Calf House,
Cues Lane, Bishopstone, Swindon, Wiltshire SN6 8PL
Tel: 01793 790460
www.helenbrowningorganics.co.uk
Innovative system in which calves are left a long time with their mothers. The emphasis at this farm is on the humane treatment of livestock. Also produces beef.

**Little Warren Farm, Fletching Common, Newick,
East Sussex BN8 4JH
Tel: 01825 722545**

Specialist small-scale farm producing organic veal and beef. All calves are reared naturally and humanely and suckled on Jersey cows for six months.

**Welfare Friendly Veal, Higher Stavordale Farm,
Charlton Musgrove, Wincanton, Somerset BA9 8HJ
Tel: 01963 33177**

The veal calves on this farm are reared the kind way, loose in small groups in open barns with deep straw bedding, fed on a mixture of milk, straw and grains. The farm sells several cuts of meat, which is pink with a sweet, buttery flavour.

BISCUITS

Tea and biscuits being a national pastime, it comes as no surprise that the crunchy one of the duo escapes much scrutiny. In any case, the very longevity of some brands suggests that our biscuit habits are hard to break. Who, for example, remembers a time when Bourbon Creams did not exist?

However, the biscuit world may be about to change. In January 2006 new labelling laws came into play in the US that will send shock-waves through Britain's biscuit makers. The issue is the transfats in hydrogenated fat, a prime ingredient in mass-produced biscuits (and snack food) that is linked to a host of health troubles. From January packs must state the presence of transfats, a move that the American Food and Drug Administration believes will save lives. There are no plans yet for such labelling in the UK, but that may change.

Manufacturers maintain that hydrogenated fat helps biscuits store well, but the low price of the stuff is really the big attraction. However, in a nation where childhood obesity and type-2 diabetes are on the rampage, should we eat more, cheaper biscuits or relish the luxury of the occasional one packed with butter (which has fewer of the negative health implications of hydrogenated fats)? And is fat the tip of the iceberg in the biscuit debate? What else is added to biscuits in the name of innovation?

What ingredients should be in a biscuit?

A plain sweet biscuit, like shortbread, should be just butter, sugar and flour. Varying the ratio of these ingredients affects the texture: a high butter content makes the biscuit crumbly and rich – and more ex-pensive; a greater ratio of starch (from flour) delivers a harder, drier biscuit. But it's unusual to see butter on a pack's ingredients list at all. In its place will be the dreaded hydrogenated fat and a wealth of other additives designed to colour, flavour and preserve.

What's wrong with hydrogenated fat?

Plenty, and the authorities agree, though there are no plans yet in the UK to label the transfat content in foods containing hydrogenated fat. Transfats are created when fat is hydrogenated, which means that the fat is hardened and the melting temperature raised by a chemical process. Transfats raise cholesterol, reduce the nutritional value of breast milk and are linked with low birth weight. They also reduce the immune response, affect fertility, disrupt enzymes that metabolise chemical carcinogens and drugs, and increase the formation of free radicals that cause tissue damage. Transfats also raise blood insulin, a factor in the development of diabetes. In the UK, biscuits containing hydrogenated fat must mention it in the ingredients list. It will usually appear as 'hydrogenated vegetable oil'. The oil itself is often mixed and can be derived from various plants, including rapeseed, sunflower, soya, maize, coconut and palm kernel oils. Some of these oils are saturated.

Surely butter is no healthier than hydrogenated fat?

On the contrary, evidence is emerging that butter is by far the more nutritious of the two. The fat in butter is saturated, so it is not recommended that we eat large quantities of it, but it does have many benefits. It contains 'true' vitamins that are fat soluble, therefore easily absorbed and more potent. The saturated fat in butter is antiviral and antimicrobial and is burned rapidly for energy – faster than unsaturated vegetable oils, which are more readily stored by the body. It aids digestion and the lauric acid in butter helps prevent tooth decay. Butter may even help you lose weight. The calories from butter are more rapidly burned than those found in corn or olive oil. Butter from grass-fed animals contains conjugated linoleic acid (CLA), a potent anti-cancer agent that also aids weight loss and promotes lean muscle tissue. Butter contains only a fraction of the transfat found in hydrogenated fats.

What other fats or oils are used to make biscuits?

As concern about transfats increases, the industry has turned to other technology. Some labels will read 'vegetable oil and vegetable fat', which means the manufacturer has combined ordinary vegetable oils (refined palm, rapeseed or oil from another plant) or vegetable oils that have been hardened by another means. Fractionation is popular with bakers; this process separates (using a centrifuge) the saturated fat in vegetable oils from the unsaturated fat. The saturated fat, which has a higher melting point, will have the firmness that is desirable for baking. Remember, however, that you will be consuming a higher proportion of saturated fat. Lower-fat vegetable oils can be hardened using 'interestification', a more complex process in which the fatty acid molecules are altered and rearranged using enzymes. All this technology – you ask yourself, on the basis that we are not meant to stuff ourselves with biscuits anyway, why not just eat the odd butter biscuit?

What else is in a biscuit?

There's sugar, often plenty of it, and if it is refined beet sugar (see Sugar, page 388) it consists of so-called empty calories – in other words, it has no nutritional value at all. Buy biscuits made with pure unrefined cane sugar or fruit sugars; there is little nutritional value in either but the process by which they are made is environmentally sounder. Check the salt content; this may be marked as sodium, which is nearly three times the strength of salt. The recommended salt intake for adults is 6g per day – that's approximately 20 digestives. Beware innovations: wacky-flavoured biscuits will have their fair share of artificial additives and there will be industry trickery, including using plum-based jams and adding raspberry flavouring (Jammie Dodgers, for example, although the manufacturer, Burton's, has removed the unpleasant red colouring and say that plum jam makes it stretchier).

Should biscuits contain salt?

Not if they contain good-quality ingredients. Almost all manufactured biscuits contain salt, sometimes too much.

Are there genetically modified ingredients in biscuits?

The Food Standards Agency admits that if soya or maize appears on the ingredients list, a non-organic biscuit could contain up to 0.9 per cent genetically modified material – if that material exceeds 0.9 per cent of the biscuit, its presence must be stated on the label.

Which mass-market biscuits should I buy?

Read labels, looking for mention of hydrogenated vegetable oil, and do not be reassured by the words 'partly hydrogenated' – it means much the same thing. Do not be taken in by words such as 'farm-house' and 'made to a traditional recipe', especially when there are sulphate preservatives and hydrogenated fat in the ingredients list. Refreshingly, McVitie's uses no hydrogenated fat in popular biscuits such as HobNobs and Chocolate Digestives, nor does it use artificial colour or flavour in either. Scottish shortbread is also a good choice, often being made with just butter, sugar and flour.

Where to buy biscuits

**Blue Mango, 7 Lemon Market, Lemon Street, Truro,
Cornwall TR21 2PN
Tel: 01872 277116**

Delicious cheese biscuits made with unsalted Cornish butter, Doves Farm flour, Greens of Glastonbury Cheddar and a pinch of cayenne, rolled with sesame and celery seeds. Mail order, or visit the shop in Truro, where sweet biscuits are available.

**Doves Farm Foods, Salisbury Road, Hungerford,
Berkshire RG17 0RF
Tel: 01488 684880
www.dovesfarm-organic.co.uk**

Organic chocolate chip cookies and other biscuits, including raisin and honey, Cheddar cheese, lemon zest, and very good digestives.

Duchy Originals, The Old Ryde House, 393 Richmond Road, East Twickenham TW1 2EF
Tel: 020 8831 6800
www.duchyoriginals.com

Rich butter biscuits, both sweet and savoury, made with traditionally grown oats and grains.

Frank's Biscuits, Unit 12a, Holmer Trading Estate, Hereford, Herefordshire HR1 1JS
Tel: 01432 376729
www.franksluxurybiscuits.co.uk

Frank Cornthwaite bakes shortbread with pure Somerset butter and flour – so good he has succeeded in selling it to Scotland in true coals-to-Newcastle style. Mail order available.

The Gingerbread Shop, Church Cottage, Grasmere, Ambleside, Cumbria LA22 9SW
Tel: 015394 35428
www.grasmeregingerbread.co.uk

Extraordinary chewy gingerbread with no equal. Mail order available.

Honeybuns, Naish Farm, Stony Lane, Holwell, Sherborne, Dorset DT9 5LJ
Tel: 01963 23597
www.honeybuns.co.uk

Made on a Dorset farm, these biscuits are highly popular with children. Baked by the appropriately named Goss Custard family, they are made with local eggs, butter and gluten-free grain. Mail order available.

Island Bakery Organics, Tobermory, Isle of Mull PA75 6PY
Tel: 01688 302223
www.islandbakery.co.uk

Prize-winning biscuits hand baked by Joseph Reade on the Isle of Mull, using vegetable oils but never hydrogenated ones. Available online from www.realfooddirect.co.uk

Konditor and Cook, 22 Cornwall Road, London SE1 8TW
Tel: 020 7261 0456
www.konditorandcook.com
This small chain of four London shops uses superb ingredients
(free-range eggs, pure butter) in its beautifully made biscuits. Try the
lemon moons, made with ground almonds and topped with a thin
layer of meringue.

Lavender Blue, 1 Sandway Cottage, Bourton, Gillingham,
Dorset SP8 5BH
Tel: 01747 821333
Somerset butter is used in these grown-up biscuits: white chocolate
and lavender, cranberry and walnut, orange and cardamom. Mail
order available.

Macgregors Original Oatcakes, Highland Avenue,
Dunoon, Argyll PA23 8PB
Tel: 01369 704858
www.macgregorsoatcakes.co.uk
Very thin, high-baked biscuits – the best biscuits for cheese on the
market. Mail order available.

Popina, Unit 3, Sleaford Industrial Estate, Sleaford Street,
London SW8 5AB
Tel: 020 7622 3444
www.popina.co.uk
Isadora Popovic's biscuits are made with entirely natural ingredients,
using imaginative recipes from all over Europe.

BREAD

Shop for bread and the choice is clear. There are the unmistakable sliced loaves in their wrappers or the crusty, slowly made 'craft' loaves of old. I cannot dwell on the thousand or so different types of bread sold all over Europe but a comparison between sliced and wrapped bread and craft bread is inevitable. Bread became adulterated so that baking could be mechanised. The industry will argue that it has brought cheap bread to millions, and it has, but this has been at the cost of the integrity of traditionally made bread from wholesome flour. Interestingly, over the last 40 years we have almost halved the amount of bread we eat at home, while the sandwich market has grown 50 per cent. So, if we cannot be bothered to make our own sandwiches, will we ever again make our own bread?

Who makes our bread?

In the UK, 81 per cent of bread sold is made by 11 large 'plant' bakeries, 17 per cent by supermarket in-store bakeries and the remaining 2 per cent by smaller 'craft' bakeries. Over half the bread is produced by two companies, Allied Bakeries and British Bakeries. There are approximately 3,500 craft bakeries in the UK, compared to nearly ten times that in France.

How is most of our bread made?

The majority of bread sold in the UK is 'sliced and wrapped', a soft bread that keeps for up to seven days, but there is a trend towards craft breads. Most bread is made using a high-speed process known as the Chorleywood Process, with the usual base of flour, yeast, water and salt but also plenty of additives. The dough is made within three minutes, using intense, high-speed mixing. Yeast levels of up to 1.75 per cent are used in high-speed bread making, compared to 0.5 per cent used in commercial bread before World War II. The wheat gluten network in bread differs when bread has been made at high speed, a factor that many suspect contributes to wheat intolerance.

Is our bread too salty?

Yes, a slice can contain up to 0.5g of salt and, with the average daily salt allowance for adults at 6g and for four to six year olds at 3g, that's too high. More flavoursome, stoneground flour would negate the need for so much salt.

Which artificial additives are used to make sliced and wrapped bread?

By law, the flour in sliced and wrapped bread must have minerals and vitamins added to it to replace the nutrients lost in the milling process. One of them, calcium carbonate, is derived from chalk. Ascorbic acid, E300 (vitamin C), is added to 'improve' the flour, strengthening it so it rises well. There will be preservatives, either vinegar (acetic acid, E260) or calcium propionate (E282), which it is claimed prevent the absorption of added calcium in the bread. Emulsifiers (E471 and E472) stabilise the dough, improve the crumb structure and keep the bread soft.

Are all the additives listed on labels?

No. Sliced and wrapped bread may have amylase enzymes added, which soften the loaf, but as they are destroyed during baking they do not need to be listed on the label.

Does bread contain fat?

Yes. Bakers have found that fats, too, give bread a long shelf life (as if there were not enough other additives in there to keep the stuff going until next year). The fats are either fractionated (processed using centrifugal force) or hydrogenated (which contain transfats, see page 222).

Are there GM ingredients in bread?

Bakeries, even the big guys, do their best to keep any GM ingredients out of bread because they know shoppers hate the idea of it. Soya, which is widely used in sliced and wrapped bread to whiten it, and soya lethicin, an emulsifier, are also used. Soya lethicin could be GM contaminated but the quantity in the bread will not exceed the set limit for ingredients in food, so you will not see it on the label. By law, labels must indicate if a product contains more than 0.9 per cent GM ingredients. Not reassuring, but the bread companies would be crazy not to track the soya content in their bread for fear of being caught.

What is sourdough bread?

Any bread that has been made using a slow fermentation process, where slow-acting wild yeasts are used, can claim to be a sourdough. Even baguettes and ciabatta are sourdoughs but it is more pronounced in breads such as Poilâne (see page 79). Beware fakes. Olive oil is sometimes used to darken ciabatta to the greyish colour associated with sourdoughs. You can always tell by the taste, which should be rounded and ripe.

Is yeast a natural product?

Not exactly. Yeast for the commercial bread industry is 'grown' on non-organic molasses (a by-product of sugar production). The yeast itself is natural but environmental campaigners say the production process pollutes the environment. The waste products from yeast production include sulphuric acid, phosphoric acid, magnesium sulphate, cleaning agents and disinfectants – all pollutants if released into the water supply. Organic bakers are permitted to use this yeast but many craft bakers now use 'wild' yeasts, grown on bases of flour and fruit, which do not leave a by-product. Wild yeast gives bread a ripe, nutty flavour – hence sourdough bread.

How can I avoid bread with additives?

That's easy – choose bread that is made with the original basic ingredients: flour, water, yeast and salt. A little vegetable oil or butter is fine, a little sugar gets the bubbles going. Read labels.

Are there additives in organic bread?

Yes – organic bakers can add vinegar and ascorbic acid flour improvers but not all d..

Are there pesticide residues on bread?

In surveys in 2002, residues were found on over 50 per cent of loaves tested (although stated to be at safe levels). Residues were found on 26 per cent of speciality breads. No residues were found on organic loaves.

But surely sliced and wrapped bread is a victim of snobbery? After all it is cheap and long lasting?

It is true that plenty of cheap bread will feed and nourish, even if it is adulterated. But if sociological change is the job of the baking business, why not reopen the thousands of small bakeries that once kept high streets alive? Regional distinctiveness would be revived – which has proved excellent for local economies.

Is the bread business good for the environment?

Not great. It is said that 50 million polythene wrappers are used each week to wrap bread, and that carbon emissions from the bread factories are high. How this compares to the days of the local bakeries is not known.

What is the difference between the bread from supermarket in-store bakeries and other commercially made bread?

At least 20 per cent of our bread comes from supermarket in-store bakeries. These bakeries are owned by the supermarkets or franchised out to larger bakeries. Either the loaves are baked from bread mixes that are made into dough on site, or frozen unbaked or semi-baked loaves are delivered to the in-store bakery and finished off in the oven. Many of these bakeries add dough conditioner to the bread mix. This is known as activated dough development and gets the dough rising at a faster rate than normal fermentation. The styles of bread made in the part-cooked culture tend to be Continental in appearance (baguettes etc) but in fact taste nothing like the crisp-crusted sourdough bread made traditionally in France. As to the comparison between this and craft-made bread – there isn't one. It is a wasted opportunity, though.

Where to buy good bread

**Artisan Bread, Unit 16/17, John Wilson Business Park,
Whitstable, Kent CT5 3QJ**
Tel: 01227 771881
www.artisanbread.ltd.uk
Several varieties of hand-crafted bread made using traditional grains
and wild yeast. Products include rye and spelt bread; spelt pizza bases
and pumpkin bread. Mail order or contact for stockists.

Baker and Spice, 75 Salisbury Road, London NW6 6NH
Tel: 020 7604 3636
www.bakerandspice.com
Choose from a long list of hand-made breads that includes various
naturally leavened 'levain'-style loaves, pain de mie (a soft white that
children love), caramelised garlic and poppy linseed.

The Celtic Bakers, 42b Waterloo Road, London NW2 7UH
Tel: 020 8452 4390
www.thecelticbakers.co.uk
Extra-environmentally friendly bread made with traditional flours.

**Ditty's Home Bakery, 44 Main Street, Castledawson,
Northern Ireland BT45 8AB**
Tel: 02879 468243
www.dittysbakery.com
Typical Northern Irish griddle-cooked potato farls.

**The Flour Station Bakery & Confectionery Supplies,
22–34 Gwynne Road, Battersea, London SW11 3UW**
Tel: 020 7223 5656
Artisan breads made with traditionally milled flour at this wholesale
bakery, established by Jamie Oliver.

Hobbs House Bakery Ltd, Unit 6, Chipping Edge Industrial Estate, Hatters Lane, Chipping Sodbury, Bristol BS37 6AA
Tel: 01454 321629
www.hobbshousebakery.co.uk
Award-winning bakery specialising in organic breads. Mail order available.

Judges Bakery, 51 High Street, Hastings Old Town, East Sussex TN34 3EN
Tel: 01424 722588
Josephine Fairley and Craig Sams (the founders of Green & Black chocolate), together with an award-winning baker, recently opened this bakery specialising in slow, overnight-leavened breads of every type from rough Granary to French baguettes.

Lighthouse Bakery, 64 Northcote Road, London SW11 6QL
www.lighthousebakery.co.uk
Tel: 0207 228 4537
Small, traditional bakery run by Rachel Duffield and Elizabeth Weisberg (who bakes the bread). Several speciality loaves, including an outstanding sourdough and interesting breads from all over Europe.

Long Crichel Bakery Ltd, Long Crichel, Wimborne, Dorset BH21 5JU
Tel: 01258 830852
www.longcrichelbakery.co.uk
Organic breads and cakes baked in a specially built wood-fired oven in a converted stable. Sourdough breads and English breads using traditional craft skills are specialities.

McPhies Bakery, 1527 Shettleston Road, Glasgow, Strathclyde G32 9AS
Tel: 0141 778 4732
Traditional craft breads made with stoneground flour.

Neal's Yard Bakery, 6 Neal's Yard, London WC2H 9DP
Tel: 020 7836 5199
Wonderful sourdough breads to match the amazing Neal's Yard cheeses.

Poilâne, 46 Elizabeth Street, London W1W 9PA
Tel: 020 7808 4910
www.poilane.fr
The London branch of a Parisian bakery started by Pierre Poilâne in 1932. Signature breads are their huge wheels of stoneground wheat sourdough, rye bread and dense fruit bread. The large loaves can be sliced or cut and bought by weight. Mail order available.

St John Bread and Wine, Spitalfields, 94–96 Commercial Street,
London E1 6LZ
Tel: 020 7247 8724
www.stjohnbreadandwine.com
Huge, truly rustic, traditionally made loaves from Fergus Henderson's charismatic bakery.

Staff of Life Bakery, 2 Berrys Yard, off Finkle Street,
Kendal LA9 4AB
Tel: 01539 738606
Artisan breads made by a true craft-bread enthusiast using local, traditionally milled flour. During the season there is a damson sourdough using the fermented yeast of the fruit, sourced from the Lyth Valley. Also, ask for his snail-decorated loaves. Home delivery available.

True Loaf Bakery, Mount Pleasant Windmill, Kirton-in-Lindsey,
North Lincolnshire DN21 4NH
Tel: 01652 640177
www.trueloafbakery.co.uk
Thirty different breads made from organic wheat flour, wheat seed and malt flours traditionally milled on the premises.

BREAKFAST CEREAL

So what would you and the rest of the family like for breakfast? A tablespoon of refined white sugar, a few vitamin pills, a couple of grams of salt – oh yes, and some milled grain? The latter on its own would be better. A bowl of oats needs little embellishment but this great and simple idea has given birth to an extended family of hybrid cereal breakfasts: quick to prepare, easy to store and supposedly good for you. But are they? Why do they need added vitamins and salt and why so much sugar? Packaging that is super attractive to children, free gifts and chocolate-coated goodies inside have made some cereals the X-rated, top-shelf mag of food. One to keep out of the reach of children ...

When I buy breakfast cereal, am I buying a health food?

Don't be dazzled by the 'fortified with vitamins' statement on the pack; it is spin. The vitamins are added because much of the goodness is lost when milling the grain (see Flour, page 181).

Is muesli a better option?

The original Bircher muesli is a great option. Soak oats and almond slivers in a mixture of water, milk and lemon juice overnight, then in the morning add grated apple (or other fresh fruit) and serve with honey. Substitute yoghurt for the milk, if you wish. Be wary of some modern commercial mueslis, though, which can contain added sugar, and even chocolate. Those packed with masses of nuts and dried fruits can also have quite a high calorie count. They are at least wholefoods, though, and are a better option than many of the sugary milled cereals on offer.

Why is salt added to breakfast cereals?

Because many of those grains have no flavour, thanks to the total removal during milling of the outer layers of grains that provide their fibre and their flavour – the germ in wheat, for example. Grains such as maize have very little flavour anyway. Kellogg's cornflakes were judged by the National Food Alliance to be nearly as salty as seawater and to contain 0.87g of salt per serving, which is nearly a third of a three-year-old's daily allowance. A high-salt diet is said to be a cause of high blood pressure, heart attacks and kidney failure and has even been linked to stomach cancer, asthma and osteoporosis.

Why so much sugar?

It is inexplicable why some cereals need to be coated or glued together with something as pointless as refined white sugar but most brands contain between 30 and 50 per cent. Take Quaker Sugar Puffs: the box says 'nutritious' and 'fortified with vitamins and iron', but this breakfast cereal contains 35 per cent sugar, nearly two teaspoons of sugar in every 30g serving. Surely the manufacturers are not trying to lure children into pestering parents for sugary breakfasts rather than wholefood ones? Sugary cereals give the breakfaster a burst of energy, which quickly diminishes, leaving no other nutritional benefit.

Which breakfast cereals are low in sugar?

Of course, pure oats and bran don't contain any sugar. Of the manufactured brands, Shredded Wheat has no added sugar and Weetabix and Rice Krispies are low in sugar. While sugar is an obvious addition to cereals such as Frosties and Frosted Shreddies, it is also added to some of the more 'natural-looking' cereals, including Kellogg's cornflakes and Cheerios. The Food Commission has criticised Nestlé for the high sugar and salt content of most of its cereals.

Are there chemicals in my breakfast?

In some cereals, yes. The worrying aspect of this is that in spite of the intensive milling of the grain, pesticide residues are regularly detected in 10–30 per cent of conventional corn-based cereals. Residues of fumigants, which are used to keep pests away from cereals while in storage, have also been found on breakfast cereal.

Could there be GM ingredients in cereal?

Not at present but contamination remains a risk while GM technology is supported in the US and some South American countries. Kellogg's products in Europe are reportedly free from proteins from GM soya or maize. Nestlé, whilst it doesn't use GM ingredients in the UK, is not unsupportive of the use of gene technology. Weetabix Ltd stated that no GM ingredients, additives or derivatives are used in any of its processes. Quaker Oats Ltd says it does not use ingredients containing GM material in any Quaker product. The company tests all soya-based lecithin (E322), an emulsifier used in its products, to ensure freedom from GM material.

Which cereals are GM free?

Apart from the brands mentioned above, organic cereal manufacturers best police the ingredients in their cereals for GM material.

Are cereal bars as wholesome as they look?

Check the labels. Despite their earthy wrapping, they can contain a lot of sugar, salt and flavourings. According to the Food Commission, some cereal bars are very unhealthy. For example, a Kellogg's Coco-Pops bar was found to contain a greater proportion of calories from sugar than milk chocolate, and there were saturated fats in a Kellogg's Rice Krispies bar forming 29 per cent of its calories. The Food Commission concluded that many breakfast cereal bars had higher levels of sugar than nutritionists recommend for a healthy breakfast such as a bowl of cereal with semi-skimmed milk. Ten had higher fat levels.

You would imagine, given that cereal bars are popular with children, that pesticide levels would be carefully monitored. In 2001 cereal bars were tested for residues for the first time and they were found in over 70 per cent of them.

How environmentally friendly are breakfast cereals?

The packaging is often mainly recycled but it is a problem nonetheless. There's too much of it, with too little inside. It is possible to buy known brands of cereal loose by the kilo from 'weigh' shops. This is a good and inexpensive avenue to take, providing you trust the source.

Where to buy good breakfast cereals

Perhaps, given the above information, it would be better if we all ate porridge, but the following sell good-quality breakfast cereal. Do read labels, however. These companies usually sell a range and there may be salt and sugar added to some of their products and not to others.

Alara Wholefoods, 110–112 Camley Street, London NW1 0PF
Tel: 020 7387 9303
www.alara.co.uk

Imaginative organic muesli-based breakfast cereals, including a fairly traded muesli and a range specially designed for the needs of certain age groups: children ('Growing'), expectant mothers ('Blooming') and older people ('Prime' – forgive the pet-food connotations, this one is very good). The company has a strong ethical policy, sourcing locally (British) where possible. Home delivery available.

Dorset Cereals, Beverill Avenue East, Poundbury, Dorchester DT1 3WE
Tel: 01305 751000
www.dorset-cereals.co.uk

Mueslis made with good-quality cereals and fruit, most of which contain no added sugar. All but one of the mueslis contain no added salt. The high-fibre muesli is recommended.

Jordans Ltd, Holme Mills, Biggleswade, Bedfordshire SG18 9JY
Tel: 0800 587 8901
www.jordans-cereals.co.uk

Good organic porridge oats and multigrain (non-organic) porridge oats.

Nature's Path, Community Foods, Brent Terrace,
London NW2 1LT
Tel: 020 8450 9411
www.naturespath.com
Excellent range of organic cereals from an ethically minded Canadian company, including Heritage Bites and Heritage Flakes (made with traditional grain breeds) and puffed millet rice. For children there is the Envirokidz range, including Gorilla Munch, cinnamon-flavoured Orangutan 'O's and cocoa-dusted Koala Crisps. The only sweetener used in the children's range is evaporated cane juice.

Sharpham Park, Glastonbury, Somerset BA16 9SA
Tel: 01458 844080
www.sharphamparkshop.com
Launched in 2005, a range of breakfast cereals made from spelt, one of the world's most ancient cereal plants. Puffed spelt, plus five types of muesli. Mail order available.

Southern Alps Ltd, Unit 14, West Yoke Farm, Michael's Lane,
Ash, Near Sevenoaks, Kent TN15 7HT
Tel: 01474 871275
www.southern-alps.co.uk
Delicious hand-made mueslis prepared from excellent-quality ingredients.

Whole Earth, Combe Lane, Wormley, Godalming,
Surrey GU8 5SZ
Tel: 01428 685100
www.wholeearthfoods.com
Cornflakes sweetened with cane sugar and no added salt.

BROCCOLI (AND OTHER BRASSICAS)

With its long British growing season and high nutrient content, broccoli has become an essential in almost every shop, and, for a vegetable that comes with the flower attached, it stores well too. Then to add to its merits, there is the beauty of green broccoli's more sophisticated cousin, purple sprouting broccoli – a vegetable that when eaten freshly picked has as much quality as asparagus. Best of all, broccoli's sweetness and lack of sulphur flavour mean that children do not wrinkle their noses at it as they traditionally do with unfairly maligned cabbage and Brussels sprouts. So is broccoli all good news for shoppers? Not quite – chief among concerns are the use of pesticides on the crop and a suggestion that this oh-so-healthy vegetable is not quite as good for you as it used to be ...

Is broccoli in season all year round?

It may always be on shop shelves but the British season for green broccoli ends with the first frosts of October or November. Most of our broccoli is grown outdoors in Lincolnshire, with the first crops harvested in May. November sees the first harvest of cold-loving purple sprouting broccoli, which should be available until early April, so in theory, if you switch from one to the other you can eat British-grown broccoli all year round.

If it's not British, who else grows it?

Out-of-season green broccoli is imported from Spain, France and Italy. The broccoli is packed in ice boxes, which keep it 'fresh' but the nutrient value is reduced. Broccoli from southern Spain clocks up a weighty 900 food miles. The Spanish also make heavier use of agricultural chemicals. In 2000 the government reported that 14 per cent of sampled imported broccoli contained pesticide residues and half of these were over the maximum recommended level. One sample of British broccoli, however, contained residues of a pesticide banned in the UK. Broccoli was tested again in 2005 but so far results have been published only for broccoli grown in southern European countries. In this instance, residues of the pesticide, chlorothalonil, were found on one sample. Chlorothalonil is permitted in the UK but pesticide watchdogs, the Pesticide Action Network (PAN UK), have listed this agricultural chemical as a 'bad actor' – a pesticide that is a probable carcinogen. The reduction in residues found on all the samples is generally to be welcomed, though broccoli's popularity should see it tested more frequently than every five years.

Why is broccoli described as a 'superfood'?

It contains high levels of sulforaphane, a cancer-fighting antioxidant. These nutrients were found occurring naturally in a Sicilian wild relative of the plant, which was then crossbred with commercial species, giving modern broccoli an increased nutritional value with 100 times the level of sulforaphane. Broccoli also contains high levels of calcium, although according to scientists its calcium levels have dropped by 75 per cent since 1940. In his book *We Want Real Food* (Constable, 2006) Graham Harvey explains that not just broccoli but *all vegetables* have lost vitamins and minerals. Explanations for this include the over use of fertilisers on crops and, conversely, the breeding of modern hybrids that crop early, resist disease and have a long shelf life. You cannot, therefore, go too wrong if you eat lots more broccoli.

How can I be sure of choosing pesticide-free broccoli?

Of the samples tested for residues in 2005, seven were organic and none of these contained a single residue, making organic the best choice. Organic farms are permitted to use six agricultural chemicals, while conventional farmers have hundreds at their disposal.

Should I buy loose or wrapped broccoli?

The wide expanse of the flower head on broccoli means it oxidises quickly, giving unwrapped broccoli a short shelf life of three days.

Wrapped and refrigerated, it will keep for five days or more. If you prefer to buy vegetables without packaging, you must buy fresher broccoli more frequently (or buy it unwrapped and wrap it in cling film before storing).

Is a hole in the stalk a bad sign?

Not in nutritional terms. British broccoli often has holes – a sign of erratic growth caused by our climate. Holey broccoli deteriorates quicker than broccoli with a solid stalk, but it is still worth buying rather than imported for its freshness, low food-mile scale and high nutrient value.

Does GM broccoli exist?

Yes, but it is not yet permitted for sale. Scientists are developing a super-broccoli with 80 times more cancer-fighting ability (not to be confused with the one crossbred with a Sicilian wild plant, above). The plant is expected to be ready in three years' time and will raise tricky questions about where the line should be drawn between food and preventative medicine.

What is calabrese?

Calabrese is an Italian brassica similar to broccoli but with a pale green, pointed, looser-packed flower head. It is grown in the UK but, since it is a more tender plant, you are unlikely to find those not grown under glass before their season in August and September.

Do the other brassicas share similar issues with broccoli?

Yes. Cauliflowers and cabbages can be grown in the UK all year round, so it is always best to ask for British if you want the freshest produce. Cauliflower is a precarious crop for farmers, who are unable to sell it during hot weather, when the sun turns the white flower yellow. At this time, acre upon acre of crop can be grubbed and wasted because apparently neither supermarkets nor their customers want a yellowed cauliflower, even though the taste and nutrient quality are the same as for pure white ones. So don't turn your noise up at hot-weather cauliflowers: eaten raw, thinly sliced, with a dressing, they are a revelation. Cabbages and cauliflowers have similar pesticide issues to broccoli, so you may prefer to choose organic. Brussels sprouts have recently undergone quite a change in flavour. New breeds taste much less sulphurous than those in my Seventies' childhood and they – and sprout tops – now join purple sprouting broccoli as a seasonal winter vegetable to look forward to.

What's in the supermarkets?

All chains, large and small, should sell UK-grown green broccoli and purple sprouting in season. If there is no indication on the price tag, look at the side of the packing cases (if it is not in those green plastic ones) for evidence of country of origin. If no UK-grown broccoli is available during the season, don't be afraid to ask a manager or customer services; your demands will be noted. Organic broccoli is available in some supermarkets.

Where to buy British broccoli in season

Fresh, locally sourced broccoli can usually be bought at farmers' markets and farm shops. To find the ones nearest to you, check **www.farmersmarkets.net** (tel: 0845 458 8420), or **www.lfm.org.uk** (tel: 020 7833 0338) for London. For details of farm shops, look at **www.farma.org.uk** or **www.bigbarn.co.uk**.

Box schemes can deliver both green and purple sprouting broccoli to your door. They are listed in the directory on the Soil Association website (**www.soilassociation.org**) or your nearest local scheme can be found on the local food network (**www.localfoodworks.org**).

The following retailers specialise in organic vegetables:

Abel & Cole, 8–15 MGI Estate, Milkwood Road, London SE24 0JF
Tel: 0845 262 6262
www.abel-cole.co.uk
Home delivery nationwide.

Farmaround Organic, Office B143, New Covent Garden Market, Nine Elms Lane, London SW8 5PA
Tel: 020 7627 8066 (home delivery in London)
Tel: 01748 821116 (home delivery in the north of England)
www.farmaround.co.uk

Fresh Food Company, The Orchard, 50 Wormholt Road, London W12 0LS
Tel: 020 8749 8778
www.freshfood.co.uk
Home delivery nationwide.

Growing Communities, The Old Fire Station, 61 Leswin Road, London N16 7NY
Tel: 020 7502 7588
www.growingcommunities.org
Collection only, reducing the price for London customers. There are three collection points, including this one; call to find the nearest.

Organic Connections, Riverdale, Town Street, Upwell, Wisbech, Cambridgeshire PE14 9AF
Tel: 01945 773374
www.organic-connections.co.uk
Home delivery nationwide.

Riverford Organic Vegetables Ltd, Wash Barn, Buckfastleigh, Devon TQ11 0LD
Tel: 0845 600 2311
www.riverford.co.uk
Home delivery in London, Midlands and the Southwest.

Solstice Home, Unit 851–2, New Covent Garden Market, London SW8 5EE
Tel: 020 7498 7700
www.solstice.co.uk
Home delivery nationwide.

Sunnyfields Organic, Jacobs Gutter Lane, Totton,
Southampton SO40 9FX
Tel: 02380 861266
www.sunnyfields.co.uk
Home delivery in Hampshire, Dorset, Surrey and Central London.

BURGERS

Burgers are almost synonymous with the BSE cattle disease scandal, yet there's no denting our passion for them. A rough estimate reports that we consume nearly a million tonnes of burgers a year, yet in spite of new labelling laws that tell us more about the burger in the shop than ever, many commercial burgers are only partially beef (or other meat) and in some types of burger, only part of that need actually be muscle. The rest? Well, well, try fat, gristle and mechanically recovered meat . . .

Is the burger in the shop a bargain?

No! Frequently the price of lean minced beef is below that of ready-made burgers, which may contain added ingredients.

What do the various burger names on the packs mean?

UK regulations governing the labelling of burgers divides them into three types:

* **Burgers** – must contain at least 80 per cent of the meat or food named in the title, e.g. beef or chicken. Some 65 per cent of the meat must be lean.
* **Economy burgers** – must contain at least 60 per cent of the meat or food named in the title. Some 65 per cent of the meat must be lean.
* **Hamburgers** – the meat used must be pork, beef or a mixture and the burger must contain at least 80 per cent meat, with 65 per cent of that being lean meat.

So what else is in burgers?

Fat can be added, and you will know it is there because much will run, or render, during cooking, leaving a very thin burger. If offal is added, it must be itemised on the label, but you are unlikely to find it in shop-bought burgers. Mechanically recovered meat (MRM) may be present. This is a deeply unpleasant paste made up of meat scraps recovered by suction from the carcasses of beef, lamb and pork. However, public revulsion for products like MRM makes it a more likely ingredient in caterers' burgers. Until 1996 MRM could contain beef spinal cord but since BSE any material that could pose a risk to humans is removed.

Where does the beef in the burger come from?

Most burgers are made from beef, although lamb, venison and pork burgers are also available, often from specialist butchers. The beef in commercial burgers is likely to be from the 50 per cent consumed in the UK that is derived from the dairy industry. Male calves, clearly unwanted at dairy farms, are reared for beef, although they will never match the specialist beef breeds in quality. They will often be reared indoors or in yards, and grow quickly on a diet containing high levels of concentrated feeds and silage. They are finished (fattened up) as quickly as possible. Transport to slaughter may well involve long journeys in close confinement, increasing stress and the risk of infectious diseases such as pneumonia.

Does the welfare of livestock affect the flavour of beef burgers?

It is nothing like as important as it is with beef that is reared to be the Sunday roast, because the beef is minced, doing away with the need to take steps to ensure tenderness, a good 'marbling' of fat or good-sized roasting joints. It has been proven, however, that poor standards of welfare and increased stress levels in livestock alter the PH balance in the meat, which affects both flavour and tenderness.

Can I tell from the label how the animal was reared?

Beef labelled 'naturally reared', 'free range', 'grass fed' or 'organic' should hail from welfare-friendly systems. If no information of this kind is given on labels (or on posters and leaflets in butcher's shops) you can surmise by their omission that the burger you are buying has come from an intensive bull-beef system. All shops need to provide more information at the point where beef is sold. The Soil Association logo is a guarantee of good welfare but conventional farms can have excellent systems, too.

Is the beef in the burger British?

It is good to know that it usually is, because intensive systems in exporting countries fall short of our standards. Beef labelling laws insist that the country of origin is marked on packs – but watch out for some clever marketing. Some exporting countries are rearing British breeds such as Aberdeen Angus and mark this on labels to make the burgers look British. Turn the pack over and you will see the words 'Britain, Ireland and South America' in the country of origin box on the official label, indicating that the Aberdeen Angus breed was reared abroad.

Where does imported beef for burgers come from?

We import about a third of the beef we eat, including beef from Ireland, which most UK consumers feel is British. But we also import from other European countries, especially Holland. Outside the EU, the main exporting countries are Brazil and Argentina, plus some African countries. They have to pay a levy to export, so the economics do not always work well for them, and supply is erratic.

Burgers can contain a mixture of British and imported meat. In 2005, inspectors from Quality Meat Scotland (a trade organisation that promotes Scottish meat – it must be said) found traces of low-grade beef in burger samples taken from retailers. They also DNA-tested samples on sale in Scotland, revealing that all contained Zebu genetics – meaning the beef is from Bos Indicus cattle, which are specially bred for tropical climates but whose meat has a low eating quality.

Are there GMOs in beef burgers?

UK-reared livestock can be given GM feed and this does not need to be declared on the label. The manufacturers argue that the GM feed travels through the body of the animal and no genetic material is absorbed. The environmental sector remains very uncomfortable with this.

What else is in burgers?

All burgers, especially economy burgers (see above) can be bulked out with cereal. There would be nothing wrong with adding a pure cereal – in the Middle East, lamb patties are made more delicious with the addition of cracked bulgar wheat – but the cereal bulk in most burgers is either tasteless rusk or breadcrumbs, and both contain additives. These include yeast extract (very popular among burger makers) as a flavouring, wheat protein, wheat flour, pea fibre, onion powder, soya protein isolate, fat (usually beef), plus sodium metabisulphite (E223), sodium sulphite (E221), neither of which is recommended for children, and the stabiliser sodium phosphate (E339) (which can be used as a laxative). Burgers may also contain hydrolised vegetable protein (HVP), a plant-based flavouring (usually soya) that has been chemically altered to imitate the flavour of meat. HVP has been found to contain the carcinogen chloropropanol, sometimes called 3MCPD.

What the supermarkets say

Waitrose stocks both organic and conventional burgers, both made using forequarter cuts of meat sourced from the UK. The beef content of each product varies from 92 to 99 per cent. The cattle that supply the beef are fed a GM-free diet.

Tesco's beef burgers are 82 per cent beef and made from forequarter trim cuts from beef sourced from the UK and the Republic of Ireland. It did not indicate if the cattle are fed GM material. Tesco does not sell an organic range.

Marks & Spencer sells burgers made from forequarter beef sourced from Scotland, England and Northern Ireland. Their burgers are 94 per cent beef. The meat comes from suckler herds naturally reared on their mothers for six months, then fed on a forage-based diet.

Sainsbury sells burgers made from forequarter cuts of beef sourced from the UK and Ireland. They sell hand-pressed burgers made with 93 per cent Scottish beef. The cows are indoor reared and fed a diet comprising cereals, grass and potentially GM soya meal. Sainsbury also sells organic beef burgers.

The Co-op's beef burgers are made using forequarter cuts and trim flank of beef sourced from the UK and Ireland. Their burgers are 85 per cent beef. The cattle are reared mainly on grass and are housed only during poor weather. They are fed on natural pasture with additional concentrates when required, which could include GM material. The Co-op also sells organic beef burgers under the Big Sky brand.

Budgens uses hindquarter trim of beef sourced from the UK to make its burgers. This meat represents 85 per cent of the final product. The cattle are fed on a diet free from any growth promoters, antibiotics or fishmeal. Budgens does not sell organic beef burgers.

Where to buy burgers (and minced beef)

The following suppliers specialise mainly in pure native British breeds, reared slowly and naturally. All will deliver meat to your door. It is more economical to order burgers either in bulk or as part of a mixed box of meat cuts. Many of these suppliers make burgers with meat from their other livestock, too, so ask about ones made from lamb, venison and pork.

Barkers Highland Beef, Mid Torrie Farm, Callander, Perthshire FK17 8JL
Tel: 01877 330203
www.barkershighlandbeef.co.uk
Breed: Highland

Baylham House Rare Breeds Farm, Stowmarket, Ipswich, Suffolk IP6 8LG
Tel: 01473 830264
www.baylham-house-farm.co.uk
Breed: White Park

Brown Cow Organics, Perridge Farm, Pilton, Shepton Mallet,
Somerset BA4 4EW
Tel: 01749 890298
www.browncoworganics.co.uk
Breed: Guernsey (beef from this family farm's dairy herd is surprisingly good)

Daylesford Organic Farm Shop, Daylesford, Nr Kingham,
Gloucestershire GL56 0YG
Tel: 01608 731700
www.daylesfordorganic.com
Breed: Pedigree Aberdeen Angus

Donald Russell Direct, Harlaw Road, Inverurie,
Aberdeenshire AB51 4FR
Tel: 01467 629666
www.donaldrusselldirect.com
Crossbred, mainly with Aberdeen Angus, but this is a company that
has made its name maturing beef and a wide range of cuts.

Edwards of Conwy, 18 High Street, Conwy,
North Wales LL32 8DE
Tel: 01492 59443
www.edwardsofconwy.co.uk
Breed: Welsh Black

Gilchesters Organic Farm, Hawkwell,
Northumberland NE18 0QL
Tel: 01661 886119
www.gilchesters.com
Breed: White Galloway (organic)

Long Ghyll Farms, Brock Close, Bleasdale, Preston,
Lancashire PR3 1UZ
Tel: 01995 61799
www.farmhousedirect.com
Breed: Highland

Lower Hurst Farm, Hartington, Nr Buxton,
Derbyshire SK17 0HJ
Tel: 01298 84900
www.lowerhurstfarm.co.uk
Breed: Hereford (organic)

Mains of Airies Farm, Stranraer, Wigtownshire DG9 0RD
Tel: 01776 853516
www.herefordprimedirect.co.uk
Breed: Hereford

Penmincae Welsh Black Beef & Lamb, Gellynen Lodge,
Cwmbach Llechrhyd, Builth Wells, Powys LD2 3RP
Tel: 01982 551242
Breed: Welsh Black (organic)

Pipers Farm, Cullompton, Devon EX15 1SD
Tel: 01392 881380
www.pipersfarm.com
Breed: Devon Ruby

Red Poll Meats, Cherry Tree House, Hacheston, Woodbridge,
Suffolk IP13 0DR
Tel: 01728 748444
www.redpollmeats.co.uk
Breeds: Red Poll and Welsh Black (organic beef available)

The Somerset Meat Company, Marshalls Elm, Street,
Somerset BA16 0TY
Tel: 01458 448990
www.meatontheweb.co.uk
Breed: Red Devon Ruby

Well Hung Meat Company, Tordean Farm, Dean Prior,
Buckfastleigh, Devon TQ11 0LY
Tel: 0845 230 3131
www.wellhungmeat.com
Aberdeen Angus and South Devon (organic)

West Country Water Buffalo, Lower Oakley Farm,
Chilthorne Domer, Yeovil, Somerset BA22 8RQ
Tel: 01935 940567
Breed: Water Buffalo (UK reared)

West Hembury Farm, Askerswell, Dorchester, Dorset DT2 9EN
Tel: 01308 485289
www.westhembury.com
Breed: White Park

Woodlands Farm, Kirton House, Kirton, Boston,
Lincolnshire PE20 IJD
Tel: 01205 722491
www.woodlandsfarm.co.uk
Breed: Lincoln Red (organic)

BUTTER AND SPREADS

Butter bad, margarine good, or so the mantra went throughout 70 years of spreads made using hardened vegetable oils. But recent scientific evidence claims that the transfats in spreads, margarines and lard-based shortenings are more harmful than butter, and that dairy fat wins the nutrient quality stakes despite being a saturated fat.

Could it be possible that, after years of being considered the bad apple of fats, butter is a safer and more wholesome food? It may be, but that does not stop it having a number of other drawbacks, notably animal welfare and pollution issues.

What is so bad about transfats?

Dr Mary G. Enig, a US-based nutritional scientist and biochemist who has studied fats for over 30 years, says the evils of transfats are numerous. They raise cholesterol levels, reduce the cream content of breast milk, lower immunity to disease and raise blood insulin levels, thus heightening the risk of diabetes. Moreover, she has linked their consumption to low birth weight in infants and says they can pose cancer risks. Enig's evidence is controversial, but in the US claims like these are now taken very seriously, and a food containing transfats must indicate their presence on the label. This is not yet law in the UK, but if the authorities in the US are concerned about it, it should be. The Food Standards Agency states that there is a problem with transfats (see below) and may yet change the labelling laws. At present, British manufacturers need only indicate if there is hydrogenated fat in the product. Transfats don't have to be included in the nutritional information provided on a food label unless a specific transfats claim has been made, such as 'low in transfats'.

Which is better for you, butter or 'spread'?

Spreads contain varying levels of transfats. Those made with hydrogenated oil will have the highest levels, but transfats are formed when all vegetable fats are refined. The transfats in butter, dairy foods and other animal fats are naturally occurring and do not share the harmful properties of the synthetic transfat that results from hydrogenation. For example, conjugated linoleic acids (CLA), which are found in animal fats, are healthy.

Transfats raise the type of cholesterol in the blood that increases the risk of coronary heart disease and the Food Standards Agency admits that the effects of these transfats may be worse than that of the saturated fat found in both butter and spreads. Transfats 'are harmful and have no known nutritional benefits', it says.

Apart from their transfat content, the refined oils used to make spreads go through a number of processes, most involving heat but also deodorisation. By the time they get to the breakfast table, they are a thoroughly adulterated food.

Are low-fat spreads and olive oil spreads the answer?

They still can contain transfats and a lot else besides. Bertolli 'Lucca' Olive Oil Spread, for example, contains 21 per cent olive oil (Bertolli's own), plus rapeseed oil, vegetable oil, buttermilk, water, emulsifiers, preservatives, thickener, flavourings, colouring and vitamins. (I love the Lucca in the name – this spread is manufactured outside Italy, using predominantly Spanish olives!) Watch out for the use of the term 'vegetable oil': 'vegetable' may say 'carrots' to you, but it is more likely to be palm oil, a saturated fat that carries serious environmental concerns but that manufacturers like to use because it has a high melting point – i.e. it is naturally hard (like butter) and they do not need to hydrogenate it.

Can fat be hardened by other means than hydrogenation?

Yes. Vegetable oil may also be 'fractionated' refined rapeseed oil, made using a process that splits the unsaturated part from the saturated part – you get the saturated part of the oil which becomes solid. The oils in low-fat spreads undergo interesterification, a process that rearranges the molecular structure of the fats. The fatty acids are rearranged at low temperature by adding enzymes – just as you would when digesting fat; so you are eating a kind of pre-digested fat. Flora contains interesterified fat.

So should I choose processed fat over natural fats like olive oil and butter?

I'd go for the wholefood. The question is this: do you want to spread this amalgam of hi-tech processed foods and additives on your toast, even if it is low in fat? Why not just dip your bread in some good extra virgin oil? Or use butter, comparatively a much purer food, in sensible quantities?

What's so good about butter?

Butter may contain saturated fat but it has plenty of natural goodness. Butter made from cow's milk contains unique acids that protect the body against viral illness, fight tumours and guard the gut from pathogenic bacteria and the negative effects of microbes and yeasts. Butter is also rich in vitamins A and D, which aid the absorption of calcium, benefiting bones and teeth. However, do not ignore warnings about overeating saturated dairy fats – enjoy butter in moderation.

Whichever way you look at it, surely butter is fattening?

In fact, evidence is emerging that eating a bit of butter helps with weight loss. The short- and medium-chain fatty acids (such as butyric and lauric acid) contained in butter are used rapidly for energy – faster than those in other oils, including olive oil. That means that calories from butter are more rapidly burned than those in long-chain fatty acids, such as those found in corn or olive oil. The medium-chain lauric acid in butter actually raises metabolism.

While the arguments rage between the pro-butter lobby and their counterparts who make the spreads, eating small amounts of butter is a wise choice.

Which foods contain transfats?

To check for the presence of transfats in pastry, biscuits, cakes, confectionery and savoury snacks, look for the words 'hydrogenated' or 'partially hydrogenated' on labels. There is no law as yet to show the presence of transfats themselves, but the Food Standards Agency would like to see transfats labelling. By the way, the words 'low in transfats' denotes their presence, not absence.

So are the problems with fat purely about health?

Sadly not. The production of palm oil – a cheaply priced favourite of the food industry, which hides it in manufactured foods – has had a devastating impact on the eco-system of Southeast Asia, where large tracts of natural forest have been cleared to make way for palm plantations. Palm oil, incidentally, is a very highly saturated fat.

And is butter innocent?

Butter troubles abound. There is the poor quality of life for cows in large-scale, intensive dairy farms, and the effluent from such farms can poison the local environment and water supply (see Milk, page 247). Cheap imports of butter (or cream for butter-making) have put economic pressure on farmers, causing them to increase herd sizes – sometimes up to a 1,000 head – keeping the dairy cattle indoors all their lives so they never graze in fields.

Does it matter what Daisy the cow eats?

The most nutritious butter with the best cooking qualities is made with cream from cows grazed on grass (which makes the most nutritious, most vivid yellow butter) or fed silage and haylage. Large-scale commercial farms often use compound feed based on GM cereals.

What is the difference between British and Continental-style butters?

British butter tends to be churned from fresh cream and then salted. Cream for Continental butter is ripened, developing lactic acid, which preserves the butter without salt. Many people, especially chefs, prefer lactic butter – understandable for its creamy melt and the tang it adds to baking. The best compromise for shoppers is to be loyal to pure British farmhouse butters – but why not enjoy a little French butter, too? It may nudge British farmers to try making butter the Continental way.

Can I buy good butter in the supermarket?

It's worth paying a little more for decent butter. **Sainsbury** and **Waitrose** use only British cream in their own-brand 'British butter' (a labelling loophole allows butter made with imported cream to be marked the same). **Marks & Spencer** sells 85 per cent British butter; other supermarkets sell approximately 50 per cent British. Good Continental butters include Bridel Organic, Languetot and Lescure.

Some supermarkets sell good farmhouse butter, occasionally from local farms. Scan the shelves for this, or for British-sourced organic butter – both are a safe choice. Good British organic butters include Rachel's Organic Dairy (which does an unsalted butter) and Yeo Valley.

Where to buy real farmhouse butter

The following butters are made on farms where good welfare and a high-quality, mainly grass, diet are a priority. All can be delivered to your door.

Barwick Farm Organic Dairy Products, Tregony,
Truro, Cornwall TR2 5SG
Tel: 01872 530208
Organic farm-made butter from a 60-strong Jersey herd.

Definitely Devon Ltd, Rolle Road, Torrington, Devon EX38 8AU
Tel: 01805 622018
www.definitelydevon.co.uk
A co-operative of 24 Devon farmers, producing slightly salted butter the traditional way.

Grivan, 27 New Covent Garden Market, Nine Elms Lane,
London SW8 5LL
Tel: 0207 627 9666
Email: sales@grivan.co.uk
Mail-order top-quality French butter.

Valerie and Alan Kingston, Glenilen Farm, Co. Cork
Tel: 0353 (0)283 1179
Sweetcream butter churned the traditional way using milk from the
Kingstons' own farm. Glenilen have recently been given permission
to make butter from raw cream. Contact for stockists.

Pengoon Farm, Nancegollan, Helston, Cornwall TR13 0BH
Tel: 01326 561219
www.pengoon.co.uk
Family-run farm with a Jersey herd producing clotted cream and
butter.

Pam Rodway, Wester Lawrenceton Farm, Moray IV36 2RH
Tel: 01309 676566
Unsalted lactic cultured butter made with milk from Rodway's 25
Ayrshire cattle – a beautiful butter to cook with. Local availability
only.

Somerset Local Food Direct, Unit 1, Thomas Way,
Glastonbury NA6 9LU
Tel: 01458 830801
www.sfmdirect.co.uk
Organic butter from the West Country.

Pure-butter ready-to-cook pastry

Much of the fresh, frozen (and cooked, for that matter) pastry on sale
is made with hydrogenated fats. The following West Country food
producer has pioneered the UK's first organic, pure-butter, ready-to-
use pastry:

Dorset Pastry Ltd, Unit 8D Hybris Business Park,
Warmwell Road, Crossways, Dorset DT2 8BF
Tel: 01305 854860
www.dorsetpastry.com
Seven varieties of pure-butter pastry, including puff, shortcrust, sweet
vanilla and cheese. Mail order available.

CANNED VEGETABLES AND FRUIT

'4,000 jumbo jets or 132 Eiffel towers' is an oft-quoted fun statistic representing the estimated equivalent of steel tinplate food cans recycled each year in Western Europe. That's good news, surely? Er, no. While there are recycled glass mountains awaiting use, the British are notoriously poor at recycling the far more essential material, steel. Canning is an enduringly popular way to preserve foods, surviving in spite of fridge-freezers, modified-atmosphere packaging and chemical preservatives. The attachment is almost affectionate: how many late-night hunger pangs have been solved by the opening of a tin? It would be good to say this age-old preservation technique is 100 per cent free of troubles, but sadly a thing or two must be confronted when reaching for the can opener . . .

What process is used to can vegetables and fruit?

The vegetable or fruit is put in the can, covered with either water, juice, brine or syrup and sealed. The can is then heated, briefly cooking or pasteurising the contents and preserving the food in the process.

How long does canned food keep?

The official line is two years, but canned food can keep much longer than that. There will be a 'best before' date stamped on the can – usually on the lid or base. If you use canned food past the best-before date, the safety advice is to cook it, making sure it simmers for five minutes.

Is there any difference in the nutritional value of canned and fresh food?

Very little, say nutritionists. Some canned vegetables and fruit lose a little of their folic acid, and vitamin C levels also diminish, but other nutrients and fibre remain intact.

Is there anything in the can apart from the vegetable or fruit?

With vegetables, there will almost always be salt, and you should check the levels on the label if you are concerned about this. The recommended daily salt allowance for adults is 6g. Canned fruit and some vegetables (notably sweetcorn) may contain added sugar, although it is possible to buy canned fruit in natural juice. Some manufacturers make a virtue of adding neither salt nor sugar and this will be displayed prominently on the can. Colourings and flavourings may be added; be especially watchful when buying canned mushy peas. If they are bright green, they will almost certainly contain added colour (see Peas, page 287). Other colourings to watch out for are tartrazine (E102), sunset yellow (E110), carmoisine (E122) and ponceau 4R (E124). During a government-funded scientific study, children fed these additives suffered changes in behaviour, becoming hyperactive and having difficulty settling down to sleep. Ultimately the authorities said the study was inconclusive but there is a huge body of anecdotal evidence from parents showing that these and other additives adversely affect children. It is essential to read labels if you want to avoid additives.

Is canning a safe packaging?

The big problem is bisphenol-A. Many cans are lined on the inside with a coating that prevents metal corrosion and therefore contamination but which is mainly there to prevent a tinny flavour migrating into the food. The coating is usually plastic, but it can contain bisphenol-A, a chemical shown to have hormone-disrupting properties as it mimics female hormones. Friends of the Earth (FOE) and the World Wide Fund for Nature (WWF) have campaigned against its use. In 2001 a Food Standards Agency study found that the liquid in most canned food is contaminated by bisphenol-A, with the highest levels in cans of peas. The chemical was also found in cans of artichokes, beans, mixed vegetables and corn but they were not tested for contamination. Be wary when you see this coating; it has been used on tins of baby food and also fruit. The chemical is thought to be especially harmful to babies. The Food Standards Agency reports that the chemical can remain in use so long as no more than 3mg per kilo migrates into the food. 'Any exposure is too much,' say FOE campaigners. FOE insists that companies should take a precautionary approach on the issue of bisphenol-A. They believe around 80 per cent of cans still contain it and consumers are none the wiser, as no information is given on labels.

Is there a safer way to can or bottle food?

Some organic producers use a coating of epoxy phenolic – safer, they say, than bisphenol-A.

Are cans environmentally friendly?

It would be better if we recycled more. Recycling cans means that the steel industry can use scrap steel, thereby reducing the amount of energy (up to 75 per cent) required to make steel from virgin material. Think about the 4,000 jumbo jets. Some local authorities recycle cans from conventional rubbish bags, but not all. Your local authority recycling officer will tell you if this is the case in your area. To find a can recycling bank, telephone Save-A-Can on 01495 334521 or search **www.recycle-more.co.uk** or **www.wastewatch.org**

Are there pesticide residues in canned fruit and veg?

Recent testing showed residues on canned fruit and vegetables to be low but in 2003 samples of citrus fruit were found to contain the fungicide azoxystrobin and also methamidophos, an organophosphate insecticide classified as highly hazardous. Pesticide residues are more prevalent in canned fish products.

I buy mainly canned tomatoes; should I be concerned about where they come from?

Yes. Canned tomatoes in the UK are sourced from Europe, the world's largest producer cultivating 8.5 million tonnes of tomatoes a year (the UK does not grow tomatoes for canning). European tomato growers (except UK growers!) are subsidised to the tune of £280 million each year by the EU (funded by taxpayers). One and a half million tonnes of Europe's tomato crop are sold fresh, the rest are processed: either canned, made into ketchup or pasta sauce. In 2004 the EU reported that of those seven million tonnes of tomatoes, 40 per cent of it was wasted during processing. Even so Europe over-produces tomatoes, and this can have a detrimental effect on poorer developing countries that also grow tomatoes. For example, in the 1990s Ghana was forced to open its market to tomato imports as a condition of loans and aid from developed countries. Inexpensive canned tomatoes originating from subsidised European farms were then 'dumped' there, undermining Ghanaian tomato farmers. Two out of Ghana's three tomato processing plants closed. While there has been subsidy reform in other areas of agriculture with new systems of payment to farmers, reform in the tomato sector has not been carried out along the same lines. So we are paying for overproduction, and it's mainly big business that is getting the benefit.

Where to buy safe, ethically traded canned vegetables and fruit

Most supermarkets stock a range of organic canned fruit and vege-tables, including tomatoes and baked beans.

Brindisa, 32 Exmouth Market, Clerkenwell, London EC1R 4QE
Tel: 020 7713 1666 (or call 020 8772 1600 for stockists)
www.brindisa.com
Pioneers who brought wood-roasted piquillo peppers, fine-quality cooked chickpeas, pulses and other canned and bottled vegetables to the UK. Their suppliers are small-scale artisan producers, hand picked by the company.

Carluccio's, 12 Great Portland Street, London W1W 8QN
Tel: 020 7580 3050
www.carluccios.com
Sun-dried tomatoes, artichokes, peppers and excellent passata (pre-served puréed tomato). Mail order available.

Goodness Direct, South March, Daventry,
Northamptonshire NN11 4PH
Tel: 0871 871 6611
www.goodnessdirect.com
Online delivery service that stocks Biona canned tomatoes.

Kelly's Organic Supermarket, 46 Northcote Road,
London SW11 1NZ
Tel: 020 7207 3967
Very good range of organic bottled vegetables, including the Mon Jardin and Delizie d'Italia ranges.

Suma Wholefoods, Lacy Way, Lowfields Industrial Park, Elland,
West Yorkshire HX5 9DB
Tel: 0845 458 2290
www.suma.co.uk
Large range of organic canned vegetables.

CHEDDAR CHEESE

A glance at the supermarket cheese section is enough to confirm that Cheddar dominates. But how did the name of a small place in the West Country end up stamped on cheese made in every Western country where a cow can thrive? The answer lies in 'Cheddaring' – the cheesemakers' technique that gives cheese a smooth, dense texture and, crucially, a long shelf life. We exported a great idea, and now 60,000 tonnes of that idea come back to us from various countries including Australia, Canada, New Zealand and the US. We eat more imported Cheddar than our own, but does it matter? Cheddar is simply milk, transformed by a process with its roots in tradition, a wholesome and often inexpensive food. But there is a type of Cheddar that should not be forgotten. Still made on farms close to the famous gorge, it waves the flag for authenticity, small-scale dairy farms and, above all, subtlety of taste.

How is Cheddar made?
Cheddaring – kneading the curds with the salt – gives the cheese a smooth density. After Cheddaring, the cheese is chopped, then pressed, wrapped and matured. It develops flavour as it matures.

Is there anything wrong with mass-produced cheese?
Mass-produced 'block' Cheddar, shrink-wrapped and matured in plastic, is nutritionally and chemically the same as artisan Cheddar (except organic) but it will never possess the fascinating, many-layered flavours of cloth-wrapped, hand-made Cheddar. While it arguably benefits struggling British dairy farmers who need a wider market for their milk, mass-market cheese production supports predominantly intensive dairy farming and consequent problems with animal welfare and substandard feed.

What does 'farmhouse' mean?

Farmhouse cheese and cheese made on-farm refer to cheese made in an on-farm dairy. Or at least this is usually the case but there is currently no restriction on the word 'farmhouse' on labels. The Food Standards Agency would like to curtail this kind of marketing speak if the cheese is made in a factory and not on a farm. The use of the term, Farm Assured, or the Red Tractor logo on meat and dairy products, refers to a set of standards for British farming. These standards, while more stringent than those of other European member states, still permit livestock to be kept indoors, rather than grazing in fields. They also allow for GM feed.

What's good about artisan Cheddar?

Comparing mass-market Cheddar to Cheddar hand-made on the farm is like comparing fizzy pop to fine wine – both are enjoyable but only one possesses complexity of flavour. You will find the rounded, sweet aroma and taste of orchard fruits and nuts in great Cheddar, especially one that has been made from raw rather than pasteurised milk and used traditional 'starters' to activate the cheesemaking process. Artisan cheesemaking generally supports small dairy farming and local sourcing, and you can be certain of the standard in all its stages of production.

Is Cheddar safe when made with raw, unpasteurised milk?

Yes. The bacterial 'starters' used in cheesemaking effectively suppress harmful pathogens in milk. The risk element is further reduced if cheesemakers use their own cow's milk, or milk from a trusted source with a record of consistent good hygiene in the dairy – hence there is no such thing as mass-market Cheddar made from raw milk, because large producers buy in milk from lots of different sources. It is not in the small-scale artisan cheesemaker's interest at all to put anyone at risk, and small dairies go to extreme lengths to be safe when using raw milk. As the cheese matures, its acidity rises, reducing the risk element further.

The pack says British – but is it?

Dairies could use imported milk and label the cheese British because it is made in the UK. The practice is discouraged but labelling correctly is a voluntary, not a legal, requirement.

What's wrong with imported cheese?

Much of our imported cheese travels long distances (although it is likely to be sea not air freighted) and there are inherent problems with milk traceability and animal welfare. Cheddar imported from the US could be made using milk from cattle fed the hormone rBGH, which boosts their milk production. The use of rBGH is banned in EU countries.

How old is the cheese I buy?

The longer Cheddar is matured, the more powerful and well developed the flavour. Mild Cheddar is matured for about five months, while really mature Cheddar can be 12 months old.

What is vegetarian Cheddar?

Cheddar is made using rennet (an ingredient that curdles milk), which contains rennin, a digestive enzyme. Non-vegetarian rennet is taken from the stomach of an unweaned calf but vegetarian rennet is sourced from plants or fungi.

Which Cheddar should I buy?

For authentic, traditional Cheddar, choose the West Country Farmhouse (WCF) brand (sold pre-packed and sometimes ready to cut in Waitrose and Booths supermarkets). This guarantees that the cheese is made entirely by hand from locally sourced milk in a designated geographical area. WCF cheeses include Keen's, Montgomery Cheddar, Westcombe, Brue Valley Vintage, Parkham, Denhay, Greens of Glastonbury, Coombe Farm, Kingston, W. H. Longman, Tower and Ashley Chase. See **www.farmhousecheesemakers.com** for other stockists. Some WCF cheeses are made with raw milk. Specialist cheese shops tend to store and care for cheese better than supermarkets because they keep it at a higher temperature, perfect for maturation. You will see more moulds on the surface of the cheese and it will have a heightened aroma and flavour.

Cathedral City brand (available in supermarkets) is a good, inexpensive mass-market Cheddar made by Dairy Crest using all British milk sourced in the southwest of England.

What's in the supermarkets?

All the supermarket chains sell Cheddars hailing from other countries but they are gradually beginning to stock lines of traditional British cheese, too. Some are more loyal to British Cheddar than others. Over 90 per cent of the Cheddar **Sainsbury** sells is UK sourced and it sells Quickes Traditional Cheddar and 'So' organic farmhouse Cheddar. **Marks & Spencer** sources 95 per cent of its Cheddar from the UK. **The Co-op** sources 85 per cent from the UK. **Waitrose** sells WCF Cheddar, including Keen's, which can be cut to the size you want.

Where to buy farmhouse Cheddar

All the cheeses listed below are available by mail order.

Daylesford Organic Farm Shop, Nr Kingham, Gloucestershire GL56 0YG
Tel: 01608 731700
www.daylesfordorganic.com
Daylesford Cheddar is a beautifully made organic cheese that rings with the flavours of apples and hazelnuts. Made with milk from a Friesian herd.

Denhay Farms Ltd, Broadoak, Bridport, Dorset DT6 5NP
Tel: 01308 458963
www.denhay.co.uk
Denhay Cheddar is a pasteurised West Country Farmhouse cheese that has won multiple awards. There are five herds of cows at Denhay and their milk is used to make both cheese and cream. Each cow is even given its own mattress to lie on during the colder months when they are housed indoors

The Fine Cheese Company, 29 and 31 Walcot Street,
Bath BA1 5BN
Tel: 01225 483407
www.finecheese.co.uk
This shop has an efficient mail-order service offering a good choice of
cheese that has been perfectly matured.

Hamish Johnson, 48 Northcote Road, London SW11 1PA
Tel: 0207 738 0741
This expert specialist cheese shop will deliver anywhere in the UK. It
stocks five Cheddars: Montgomery, Keen's, Denhay, Isle of Mull and
vintage Lincolnshire Poacher (a new cheese classified as Cheddar).

La Fromagerie, 2–4 Moxon Street, London W1U 4EW
(tel: 020 7935 0341) and
30 Highbury Park, London N5 2AA
(tel: 020 7359 7440)
www.lafromagerie.co.uk
These shops stock a good range of English Cheddars plus countless
other cheeses, beautifully cared for.

I. J. Mellis, Head Office: 78 Albion Road, Edinburgh EH7 5QZ
Tel: 0131 661 9955
www.ijmellischeesemonger.com
Carefully matured UK and Irish cheeses. Shops in Edinburgh,
St Andrews, Glasgow and Aberdeen. Contact for location.

Neal's Yard Dairy, 17 Shorts Gardens, Covent Garden,
London WC2H 9UP
Tel: 020 7645 3554
www.nealsyarddairy.co.uk
A huge range of Cheddar, hand picked by Randolph Hodgson, who
was instrumental in the revival of many of the West Country
Farmhouse Cheddars.

Turnbulls, 9 High Street, Shaftesbury, Dorset SP7 8HZ
Tel: 01747 858575

Turnbulls is a deli and café that specialises in maturing local, British and Continental cheeses to perfection. It also sells unusual relishes to accompany the cheeses, notably one made with lemon zest and a lovely sticky red and yellow sweet pepper pickle. No website yet, but delivery service commencing in 2006.

Other farmhouse cheeses

The renaissance of traditional Cheddars has spread to other British cheeses. Both new and traditional cheeses that have been hand-made on the farm abound in specialist food shops and some supermarkets stock them, too.

There are cheeses made with goat's, ewe's, even buffalo milk and many are original, newly created cheeses made with such skill that they could easily take on the French. The same issues of milk quality and animal welfare apply; many of the 400 or so cheeses are made with raw milk and consequently have wonderfully diverse character and flavour.

The range of hand-made and naturally matured Double Gloucester, Stilton, Red Leicester, Wensleydale, Lancashire and Caerphilly cheeses is now enormous but here are a few names among the best of the modern, newly created cheeses:

Celtic Promise (Supreme Champion at the 2005 British Cheese Awards), Mrs Bell's Blue, Caws Cenarth Caerffili, Aged Cerney, Golden Cross, Ashmore Farmhouse Cheese, Shropshire Blue, Oxford Blue, Beenleigh Blue, Devon Blue, Berkswell, Bishops Kennedy, Coolea (Irish), Gubbeens (Irish), Durras (Irish), Flower Marie, Gubbeen, Lord of the Hundreds, Malvern, Saval, Somerset Rambler, Stinking Bishop, Wigmore and Waterloo.

In March 2006 the Food Standards Agency announced plans to cut the salt content of Stilton from 2.3 per cent to 1.9 per cent, thereby showing its ignorance of the careful art of cheesemaking. If you want to eat less salt, eat less Stilton; but don't mess with a recipe developed and perfected over hundreds of years.

CHERRIES

Mid July, and the short season for British cherries is in its glut. If it is a good year and the crop lush, there is a sweet fortnight when cherries are not only affordable but, more importantly, local. At other times of year, greengrocers source less tender but roadworthy fruit with a price tag relative to first-class travel. However, while French fruit can inoffensively supplement the diminished supply from our depleted orchards, there's no excuse to buy into the cherry jet set – the North American import that gobbles fossil fuel to ensure that the soft fruit season never ends.

How long is the British cherry season?

Our cherry season runs from mid June to the end of July but there is a glut moment of two, sometimes three, weeks within this time. Growers cultivate many varieties, whose staggered harvesting time stretches the season. The names of old varieties often relate to the sensuous shape of cherries – Alba Heart, Smoky Heart, Strawberry Heart among them. Other popular varieties include Merchant, Bing, Lapins and Napoleon. Not all are necessarily British in origin. All cherries stem from two different types, either sweet or sour, and can be grown anywhere with a temperate climate. Rainier are yellow with a reddish tinge and Picota are stalkless, often sold at a budget price.

Why are there so few British cherries around?

Most supermarkets stock cherries during the season but, with less than 1,000 acres of cherry orchards left in Britain (there were 18,000 in 1951), cherries are quite scarce. Competition and the global market are partly responsible for the decline, but the large trees in the old cherry orchards of Herefordshire and Kent have become unmanageable. There is a new initiative to plant smaller trees, and DEFRA predicts an upturn for the British industry.

Where do supermarket cherries come from?

Between May and July, cherries are imported from Turkey, Greece, Italy and Spain. These cherries are rarely air freighted and are therefore less of a fossil fuel problem. Not so the cherries from the US, Canada, Chile and Argentina that supplement the summer season. Cherries are also grown in France, but these are rarely on sale in supermarkets (though they are available from greengrocers). In November, a new tranche of southern hemisphere cherries hits the shops. Priced up to four times that of British ones in season, they are a luxury whose texture and taste often disappoint.

Are cherries sprayed?

Farmers treat cherries with a number of agricultural chemicals. In 2004 the Pesticide Residues Committee (PRC) tested 26 cherry samples from various countries for 95 pesticide residues. Residues were detected in 20 of the samples but the PRC says the levels were not high risk. Environmentalists claim, however, that the 'cocktail' effect of multiple residues is still unknown and that maximum residue levels set by the government are too high.

Are dried cherries safe to eat?

Cherries are often dried with the aid of sulphur dioxide gas, which preserves the colour and protects against pests and bacterial growth. Sulphur dioxide (E220 and derivatives E222, 223, 224 and 225) is produced from coal tar. In high concentrations it is toxic, and its use in fruit drying has been linked to the onset of asthma (see Dried Fruit, page 170).

Why are glacé cherries so red?

Glacé cherries are dyed with erythrosine (E127), a chemical colouring derived from coal tar that is banned in Norway and the US. It is suspected of affecting thyroid activity and can be carcinogenic. It is possible to buy undyed glacé cherries in wholefood shops.

Who are the cherry pickers?

All fruit growers are dependent on migrant workers, but working conditions and pay vary from country to country. The US cherry farms came in for particular criticism in a 1999 report that claimed Washington State pickers were living in squalor or sleeping without shelter, earning as little as two and a half dollars per crate picked. This was in spite of strict migrant workforce rules and it was noted that while wages and conditions remained poor, the price of cherries continued to surge upwards.

So, should I buy imported cherries?

While the British market picks up, French are the next best thing – but cherries are best during their home season. The sheer anticipation of it makes them taste twice as good and you won't have to pay through the nose.

What the supermarkets sell

Supermarkets operate an almost never-ending season, sourcing from all over the globe. All, however, sell British cherries when in season, so take advantage. They tend to over package the fruit in irritating plastic cartons; brown paper bags are nostalgically more pleasing (and environmentally friendly) and if the fruit is freshly picked there shouldn't be any leaks.

Where to buy cherries

Look for cherries at farmers' markets in season. To find the ones nearest to you, look on **www.farmersmarkets.net** (tel: 0845 458 8420), or **www.lfm.org.uk** (tel: 020 7833 0338) for London. Alternatively, find details of farm shops on **www.farma.org.uk** or **www.bigbarn.co.uk**.

Brogdale Horticultural Trust, Brogdale Road, Faversham,
Kent ME13 8XZ
Tel: 01795 535286
www.brogdale.org
At Brogdale, 220 varieties of cherry are preserved as part of the National Fruit Collection. Buy cherries from their shop when in season.

Warborne Farm, Warborne Lane, Boldre, Lymington,
Hampshire SO41 5QD
Tel: 01590 688488
George and Kate Heathcote's superb farm shop sells cherries among other award-winning organic produce.

Where to buy undyed glacé cherries
Wholefood shops usually sell undyed glacé cherries sourced from Provence. From the supermarkets, Waitrose sells undyed glacé cherries and Sainsbury sells undyed glacé cherries from Billington's.

CHICKEN (AND OTHER POULTRY)

CHICKEN

Quick-to-cook, cheap-to-buy, easy-to-like chicken; surely the perfect food for the new millennium? Busy people need wholesome, fresh ingredients that they can deal with quickly after they return from work. Yet those same busy people are not always so comfortable with the newspaper headlines that have accompanied the emergence of cheap, intensively produced chicken. The rise in popularity of free-range and organic birds is due solely to concerns about factory farming. But rumblings about, or even an outbreak of, avian influenza (AI) strain H5N1 threaten the free chicken, as it were. With the disease in the UK, we can expect to see birds back in the shed or, worse, mass slaughter similar to that witnessed during the foot and mouth outbreak of 2001. The irony is that disease spreads fast when animals are densely stocked.

Irrespective of this, the common issues relating to chicken continue to pose the same big question: should chicken be a cheap dish for every day or should we go back to the 1935 ethos, when the *Daily Telegraph* carried an advert showing a chicken to cost more per pound than sirloin steak?

Why do some chickens cost £3 and others £20?

The price reflects the farming method. It is possible to rear a chicken in only 38 days, and hence sell it for under a fiver, but traditional, slow poultry rearing (which can take up to six months) pushes up the farmer's costs and therefore the shelf price.

How are broiler-house birds produced?

Chickens bred specially for fast growth are reared indoors, on a diet specially designed to get them up to size in the minimum time. Welfare troubles are endless – but here's a few:

❧ While muscle growth is fast, the chickens' bones are often too weak to support their weight, and they are also susceptible to painful infections in the pads of their feet.

❧ Sheds are often overcrowded – 38 kilos live weight per square metre, a difficult measure for inspectors to audit, given the constant growth of the birds, the addition of new ones and the slaughter of others. (The Farm Animal Welfare Council, which advises the government, recommends no more than 34 kilos per square metre as the maximum.) Added to this, birds suffer stress caused by excessive heat and almost constant artificial lighting.

❧ Rough handling followed by long journeys in packed lorries at extreme temperatures sees over a million birds die on their way to slaughterhouses every year.

❧ Birds can actually 'live' through the automated slaughter process, reaching the plucking stage alive.

In short, the life of a broiler-house bird is horrendous, if mercifully short. Hope for change is remote; an EU directive to change standards is under discussion but nothing is likely to happen until 2010.

Is a chicken what it eats?

No doubt about it. For the traditionally reared chicken, a cereal diet supplemented by forage in pasture, picking up the odd grub, will produce flavoursome meat with a well-exercised, muscular texture and well-calcified bones that make rich, gelatinous stock. Shoppers often complain that chicken tastes of fish: feed in the broiler house is also cereal-based but high-protein feed for fast growth, based on fishmeal, can be used. Farmers usually say they only feed it to the hens early in life – but then, why the fishy flavours in the meat, and in stock made from the bones? Soya (which can be GM derived) is often fed to the chickens, along with oils and additives, including vitamins, enzymes and antibiotics. All are for high-speed growth. Antibiotics that are 'prescribed' by vets help keep the birds disease free – a necessity when they live in such cramped conditions. Antibiotic residues in meat are a huge consumer problem. A government inquiry found the

presence of antibiotics in meat to be responsible for 50 per cent of
people's decreased immunity to infections, yet control of their use
remains voluntary.

Are free-range chickens the most welfare friendly?

Not always – free-range farms can be overcrowded and handling
of the birds on farms, during transport and at slaughter can be just
as rough as for the broiler-house bird. To carry the free-range label, a
bird has only to spend half its life with access to outdoors. Unless
labelled organic, the bird's feed is also in question. Look for the words
'traditional free range' or 'free range – total freedom' on the labels, as
these indicate higher welfare standards.

Is organic the highest standard?

The strictest standard, in terms of welfare and feed, is the organic Soil
Association mark, which strictly and properly governs housing, outdoor conditions, welfare and feed. Depending on the type of housing,
organically reared birds are stocked at different densities:

* **Organic (mobile housing, e.g. arks)** – 30 kilos per square metre.
  This is the stocking density permitted when birds are outside for
  most of the day and shut in the ark at night only. Less room in the
  ark also encourages birds to spend more time outside during
  the day, foraging and taking exercise. Their meat tends to have
  the best muscular texture.
* **Organic (fixed housing, e. g sheds)** – 21 kilos per square metre.
  This is the maximum stocking density for birds that have access to
  outdoors all day. However, a lower number of birds per square
  metre means they are less likely to spend all day outdoors.

Note that 'traditional free-range' non-organic birds are also stocked at
a higher density when they are kept in mobile housing. Like organic
birds, these are a good choice.

What additives can be found in fresh chicken meat?

The vile practice of 'injecting' meat with water and proteins (sometimes from other animals) to boost weight is banned in the UK but not in the EU, which exports chicken for UK consumption in ready meals and the takeaway trade.

What about those circular chicken slices in bubble packs?

Avoid them – this is 'formed chicken' and contains only a percentage of chicken plus various additives and gelling agents to bind the water that manufacturers add to them. They are an industry money-making ruse, and often aimed at children. They can contain hefty quantities of salt to pep up their non-flavour.

My ready meal says 'UK produced' – is it?

Not necessarily – it may have been cooked here but the meat could have come from any country permitted to export to the UK (see below). If an imported raw material undergoes a substantial change, such as cooking, smoking or curing, the manufacturer can say the finished ready meal or smoked chicken is UK produced. The Food Standards Agency (FSA) encourages 'best practice' and would prefer such a product to be labelled 'made in the UK from Brazilian chicken'. 'Best practice' is a naïve hope when faced with the cunning of some sectors of the food industry. They know consumers are put off by imported meat and would perhaps prefer not to confront these issues. The FSA nevertheless advises the industry not to mislead consumers.

Which countries export chicken to the UK?

Brazil exports the most and Thailand was a large exporter, too, until 2005, when there was an outbreak of H5N1 avian flu. Other sources include South America (Chile, Argentina, Uruguay) and Croatia. It's unnerving to realise how huge the distance travelled for a product that is so popular all over Europe.

How are chickens reared in Europe?

France and Italy farm poultry intensively, too, but they have also always had a large, thriving market for the slow-reared farmhouse bird – a food that has *always* been regarded as a luxury and has a price to match. There has been no need for them to revive this bird, so to speak; it never went away, as it did in the UK. Such is the value of these creatures that they are sold with head and feet on (they are hung, non-eviscerated, for a day or two to allow the flavour to develop) and the precious giblets inside are always a bonus. Delicious breeds such as the poulet de Bresse have enormous gourmet value and are sometimes available in the UK.

Can you catch avian flu from eating chicken?

The following advice was issued by the Food Standards Agency in December 2005: 'The risk of acquiring avian influenza through the food chain is low, and there is no direct evidence to support this route of infection. Evidence from human infection indicates that direct contact with infected birds is the main risk factor, and that consumption of infected chickens has not been identified as a risk factor.

'Several factors will contribute to preventing or limiting infection following ingestion of viruses, including lack of appropriate receptors, and non-specific defences such as saliva or gastric acid. Proper cooking will destroy any virus present in meat or eggs.'

Is H5N1 bird flu a threat?

Many believe a pandemic of AI H5N1 in western Europe a strong possibility, and think the disease will be active for about five years. If the virus arrives in the UK, the authorities (DEFRA) will carry out a mass slaughter of domestic poultry in the area where the disease is identified. All domestic poultry will be shut in, including those in free-range systems. DEFRA say free-range and organically reared birds will still be sold under that name. This is not a comfort to that industry, which prides itself on the welfare of poultry.

The Soil Association, in support of high standards of animal welfare, recommends a vaccination policy to stop the spread of H5N1.

It claims that this will save the all-important free-range and organic industry. But while Holland, France and Spain have stockpiled vaccine, the UK has ordered vaccine only for zoological, rare and endangered species of poultry.

Are we importing chicken from countries with a bird flu outbreak?

No. When an outbreak occurs, poultry exports from that country will be banned. In the case of an outbreak in an EU country, trade restrictions will only be imposed on the region where an outbreak has occurred. For export to the UK, EU poultry will have to carry certification; proof that it is free of disease. A risk will remain from illegally imported diseased poultry or any missed by veterinary inspectors at ports.

Is jointed or filleted chicken a less wasteful buy than a whole bird?

Quite the opposite. If you buy jointed or filleted chicken, you are paying for discarded material such as the central carcass, which could be used to make a delicious stock for soup and risotto if you buy the whole bird. Drumsticks are cheap, though, because the price of the popular breast fillets is hiked up. Chicken fillets are at polar odds with the valuable, slow-grown farmhouse chicken – a symbol, if you like, of post-War food production. But they exist and they are occasionally useful for quick cookery, so go for free range or organic and try thigh fillets, which are in fact better for curries and stir-fries.

Which chicken should I buy?

For total piece of mind, buy chicken with the Soil Association logo, but if you visit a good butcher or use a mail-order service where you can discuss the welfare and feed of the birds you buy, non-organic farms can be fine.

But organic chickens are so expensive

They cost up to three times the price of a broiler-house bird. There are two ways of looking at it: either think of chicken as the treat it once was and have it only occasionally, or make more of the bird, using up leftovers and making stock from the carcass. Shamelessly, I should say that my book, *The New English Kitchen* (Fourth Estate, 2005), has an entire chapter devoted to making and cooking with stock. It is not as time consuming as you might think.

What the supermarkets say

Note that all except the organic chickens sold by supermarkets are given antibiotics in their feed in the event of an outbreak of infection. Every retailer states that these are given only under veterinary supervision but this is not a consolation. Infection is a sign of poor welfare.

Sainsbury sells standard indoor-reared British chicken, stocked at a density of 34 kilos per square metre. It also sells free-range and organic chickens reared in the UK at a stocking density of 27.5 kilos per square metre. These are not fed antibiotics or feed containing GM soya. However, the chickens are sometimes given starter diets that contain small percentages of fish.

Marks & Spencer sells Oakham chickens, a breed exclusive to its stores. These UK-sourced chickens are fed a GM-free vegetarian diet. They are reared indoors, stocked at a density of 34 kilos per square metre. The free-range chickens are given 27 kilos per square metre and, as a bonus, one square metre of ground on which they are 'free to roam' – a long way from a bird with access to an entire field.

The Co-op chickens are sourced from the UK, Germany, Poland, Holland and Italy. They are fed on a cereal-based diet with no fishmeal, plus non-GM soya. The use of growth promoters is prohibited. The chickens are stocked at a density of 38 kilos per square metre. The Co-op also sells free-range chicken.

Budgens sells British chickens but not free range. It says, 'Stocking densities are in compliance with ACP [DEFRA's Assured Chicken Production scheme] requirements' – which means a maximum of 38 kilos per square metre, although ACP standards prefer farmers to stock at no more than 34 kilos per square metre. The birds are killed after 40 days. No other information was given.

Waitrose sells four ranges of chicken: Select Farm (which is standard indoor reared), free range, organic and traditional free range. All the birds are fed a cereal-based diet, with GM-free soya, and none are given growth promoters or fishmeal. Indoor-reared birds are stocked at 34 kilos per square metre, free range at 27.5 kilos per square metre, organic at 21 kilos per square metre, traditional free range at 32 kilos per square metre but with plenty of freedom to roam outdoors. Waitrose also sells the wonderful Sheepdrove chickens (see below).

Tesco sells chickens farmed in the UK and Holland, which it says are approved by an 'independent assurance scheme', whatever that means. Indoor-reared chickens are stocked at 38 kilos per square metre; free range at 27 kilos per square metre; organic at 30 kilos per square metre but with freedom to roam outdoors. Indoor-reared and free-range birds are fed on a diet containing cereals, fishmeal and non-GM soya meal. Chickens are slaughtered at seven to eight weeks.

Worryingly, **Asda** and **Morrisons** did not supply information about the chicken they sell.

Where to buy chicken

The following mail-order suppliers respect the highest standards of welfare and feed:

Creedy Carver Ltd, Merrifield Farm, Upton Hellions, Crediton, Devon EX17 4AF
Tel: 01363 772682
www.creedycarver.co.uk
From a Devon co-operative of 10 traditionally run poultry farms. Jointed birds available. Good value and a good welfare system.

Higher Hacknell Farm, Burrington, Umberleigh, Devon EX37 9LX
Tel: 01769 560909
www.higherhacknell.co.uk
Exceptionally high organic standards, from a beautiful mixed farm.

Label Anglais, Temple Farm, Roydon, Harlow, Essex CM19 5LW
Tel: 01279 792460
www.labelanglais.co.uk
Traditional, French-style varieties reared in a totally free-range system. Home delivery.

The Real Meat Company, Warminster, Wiltshire BA12 0HR
Tel: 0845 762 6017
www.realmeatco.sageweb.co.uk
Master Gris breed, specially developed for slow growth and free range. High standards of welfare and additive-free feed.

Sheepdrove Organic Farm, Warren Farm, Lambourn,
Berkshire RG17 7UU
Tel: 01488 71659
www.sheepdrove.com
Outstanding animal welfare standards for these Soil Association-certified chickens reared on a state-of-the-art farm on top of the Berkshire downs. There is an on-farm abattoir and the farm cleans its own water supply through a reed bed system. These chickens are excellent value for money, given the high production standards, and wonderful flavour.

The Somerset Meat Company, Marshalls Elm, Street,
Somerset BA16 0TY
Tel: 01458 448990
www.meatontheweb.co.uk
Slow growth plus good feed and welfare result in extra-muscular chickens, with strong bones for stock.

OTHER POULTRY

Poussin

Poussins are a special breed of chicken designed to be slaughtered when immature – a pointless system that restaurant chefs seem to find irresistible but that cannot be justified in terms of animal welfare standards.

What the supermarkets say

Two supermarkets provided information about the poussins they sell:

Waitrose's British poussins are indoor reared. The chain says it is working on 'an extensive trial involving creative perches for poussins made out of balls and bales of hay'. The birds are fed on a cereal-based diet, which does contain small percentages of fishmeal. However, the meal is non-GM and the birds are fed no growth promoters. The birds are killed after 28 days.

Tesco sells British poussins that are reared indoors and fed a cereal-based, non-GM diet that does not contain fishmeal or soya meal. The breed is a slow-growing one and growth promoters are not used. Poussins are transported to an abattoir with what Tesco's describes as 'a maximum total journey time of eight hours' – i.e. the same as from London to France by van. Tempted?

Duck

Ducks share many of the same welfare issues as chicken and in their case there is a particular problem. The farms that supply the mass market can be very industrial, with ducks unable to access water (for wading or swimming) throughout their lives.

What the supermarkets say

Sainsbury's duck is indoor reared with access only to drinking water. Small percentages of fish are contained in the duck's starter diet, reducing as the duck ages. The diet contains non-GM soya.

Waitrose stocks free-range Peking ducks that have access to water to 'bathe' in (they do not use the word 'swim'). They are fed a non-GM cereal and wholegrain diet, containing no fishmeal. The birds are slaughtered after 49 days in an abattoir less than a mile away.

The Co-op's ducks have no access to water except for drinking. The birds are fed a non-GM diet with no fishmeal.

Marks & Spencer stocks a Peking breed. The ducks are housed on straw, in open-sided barns. Access to water is for drinking only, although the ducks can submerge their heads. The feed is GM free.

Where to buy welfare-friendly duck

Creedy Carver Ltd (for contact details, see page 128)
Reared in open pens with access to water for swimming, and fed a natural diet.

T. and S. C. Herdman & Son, Clyro Hill Farm, Clyro, Hereford HR3 6JU
Tel: 01497 820520
www.clyrohillfarm.co.uk
Organically reared ducks, kept in family groups and fed on grass and an organic wheat supplement. Home delivery available.

Home Farm Shop, Tarrant Gunville, Dorset DT11 8JW
Tel: 01258 830208
Superb outdoor-reared ducks from Marlene and Rodney Belbin's small farm. Call in advance to check stock.

Traditional Devonshire Meats, Locks Park Farm, Hatherleigh, Okehampton, Devon EX20 3LZ
Tel: 01837 810416
www.traditionaldevonmeats.co.uk
Organic ducks grown slowly with the emphasis on minimum stress. Home delivery available.

CHOCOLATE

Before delving into the blissful world of chocolate, I should stress that there is good news with the bad. The essential sin of eating too much chocolate at Easter and Christmas need not necessarily be diminished by guilt. Good-quality chocolate has much going for it as a food; the bad is, well, bad.

British chocolate consumption can only be described as astonishing. Each year, we buy £3.7 billion worth of chocolate. That includes a mind-blowing 53 million kilos of chocolate confectionary bars, 77 million kilos of boxed chocolates, 70 million kilos of chocolate bars and 22 million kilos of top-grade couverture chocolate melted into puddings and cakes.

Chocolate contains more than 400 compounds that affect your mood, stimulating the release of the happy hormone, serotonin, plus endorphins and the amino acid, phenylathamine. All this is the reason for chocolate's notoriously addictive 'feel-good factor', although studies show it is not the cocoa but the sensual pleasures of it in the mouth that really create the cravings. Twice as many women crave chocolate as men, by the way. But if feeling good is to extend to how you shop for chocolate, be aware that, while delicious issue-free chocolate of all types is available to those in the know, there is also a dark side.

What is in a bar of chocolate?

A bar of milk chocolate should contain cocoa mass, which is a combination of dry cocoa solids (the basis of cocoa powder) and cocoa butter, milk solids, sugar, and little else. Plain chocolate should contain the same but without the milk solids. In reality, though, and in order to make huge profits, confectionery manufacturers adulterate 90 per cent of chocolate sold in the UK with vegetable oils – some of them highly saturated – and occasionally starch.

What does the label reveal?

British labelling law defines the minimum quantity of cocoa solids permitted in each type of chocolate. Some of these 'minimums' are very minimal indeed, allowing the addition of lots of vegetable oil. Note also the odd nifty euphemism when it comes to naming the categories:

* ❈ **'Family milk chocolate' or 'milk chocolate'** – need only contain a minimum of 20 per cent dry cocoa solids and cocoa butter, and 20 per cent milk solids. The bulk will be sugar, vegetable oil and other non-chocolate ingredients.
* ❈ **'Chocolate a la taza'** – low-grade chocolate (like 'family milk', above) that has an allowed minimum of 18 per cent flour or starch.
* ❈ **'Chocolate'** – must contain at least 35 per cent cocoa solids, including not less than 18 per cent cocoa butter. Really good chocolate will contain a lot more than this, which is why good manufacturers label with the actual percentage – say, '40 per cent cocoa solids'. Sugar will also be added.
* ❈ **'Couverture'** – the chocolate for melting and baking. Must contain a minimum of 35 per cent cocoa solids, of which 31 per cent is cocoa butter. Sugar is added.
* ❈ **'White chocolate'** – contains not less than 20 per cent cocoa butter and 14 per cent dry milk solids.

Which other fats are added to chocolate (apart from cocoa solids)?

Permitted vegetable oils include palm oil (which has high levels of saturated fat and is a problem in environmental terms), coconut oil, mango kernel oil, illipe oil and kokum oil. If chocolate contains vegetable oil, it must be labelled 'contains vegetable fats other than cocoa butter'.

The ingredients list on the pack often includes soya lethicin – what is it?

Soya lethicin (E322) is an additive used in the blending process to emulsify the other ingredients in the chocolate, preventing any separation. It is used in both commercial confectionery and gourmet chocolate. Soya lethicin is deemed safe for consumption by the World Health Organisation. However, since this additive is a soya product, it has GMO implications: GM soya is now a widely used ingredient and, while no more than 0.9 per cent of any food sold in the UK is permitted to contain GM ingredients without labelling, the small amount of soya in your chocolate bar could be GM unless it is a completely organic product. This is not to say that all conventional chocolate contains GM soya lethicin, but the organic sector polices for GM the most effectively.

Any other additives I should watch out for?

Confectionery bars often contain flavourings, including vanillin, a chemical imitating vanilla that is toxic in large quantities. Filled confectionery bars contain a lot else besides. One look at the ingredients list on a Mars Bar will confirm this.

Are there pesticide residues in chocolate?

It is very hard to say because there is no up-to-date information. The last time chocolate was tested nationally was in 2002, when 48 samples of *white* chocolate were examined! Before that, Continental chocolate was tested in 1999, cooking chocolate in 1997 and ordinary chocolate (confectionery bars etc) in 1994. Eleven years ago for the most popular type! Not only is such infrequent testing a real cause for consumer concern (some vegetables, for example, are tested at least once a year) but residues of lindane (Gamma HCH) were found in six of the white chocolate samples. The Pesticide Residues Committee (PRC) assessed that none of the levels detected were of concern for human health but lindane is a known carcinogen, an endocrine disruptor (affecting fertility) and one of the Dirty Dozen agricultural chemicals targeted by the UN for worldwide elimination. What is worse is that there is no Maximum [pesticide] Residue Level for chocolate; this is 'decided on an individual product basis'.

So is chocolate bad for you?

Chocolate with a high (at least 40 per cent) proportion of cocoa solids has a lot to recommend it. It is rich in flavonoids, which are compounds that promote the activity of cancer-fighting antioxidants in the body. Both flavonoids and the procyanidins that are found in chocolate are also good for cardiovascular health; it is said that chocolate has a positive 'aspirin effect' on blood platelet function. Paradoxically, though chocolate can contain a lot of sugar, it is not necessarily the bad guy in the Western world's obesity epidemic. The Swiss consume the highest quantity of chocolate in Western Europe (9.9 kilos per person each year) but have the lowest rate of cardiovascular illness and obesity.

What's in my cup of drinking chocolate?

Cadbury's drinking chocolate contains cocoa powder from Ghanaian beans, plus sugar, salt and vanilla flavouring. The salt level is 0.25g per 200ml serving. Ordinary cocoa powder (Cadbury's again) contains 100 per cent pure cocoa, and is a better choice because you can avoid the salt and add your own cane sugar. Chocolate drinks are another matter: Cadbury's Highlights contains hydrogenated fat and artificial sweeteners.

Both Fairtrade and organic (and fair-traded organic) hot chocolate drinks are available.

Where does chocolate originate from?

Ninety per cent of UK chocolate is sourced from Africa's Ivory Coast, the rest from South America and the Caribbean.

Why does Fairtrade chocolate exist?

Because most dealings between growers and manufacturers are very unfair to the growers, who are essentially the little, vulnerable guys. There is appalling poverty among growers. Virtually all chocolate growers are smallholders, and vulnerable to price change on the free market when chocolate is traded on the exchanges. The farmers' reaction to a price drop is to eke more, lower-grade beans from their land, flooding the market with yet cheaper produce and making matters worse.

What's so good about Fairtrade chocolate?

The Fairtrade Foundation has certified several chocolate manufacturers, offering a stable price to farmers, which allows them to plan ahead, buy vehicles, improve equipment and roads, build community projects and protect and clean the water supply. Because Fairtrade chocolate passes through fewer hands, consumers can track their chocolate back to the farmer and be better aware of such issues as pesticide use. Be aware, however, that Fairtrade chocolate is not necessarily organic.

How can I recognise good chocolate?

Good chocolate with a high ratio of cocoa solids should break with a nice 'snap' when cool enough. No snap is the sign of a high vegetable oil content. A glossy surface indicates that the chocolate is well made and, like wine, there should be plenty of 'notes' in the aroma. Chocolate melts below body temperature at 33°C, which is why it becomes liquid on the tongue. It should have a smooth mouth feel, with no graininess. White 'blooming' on chocolate is caused by moisture or temperature fluctuation – chocolate that looks like this has been poorly handled and stored. Take it back to the shop.

Do the supermarkets sell ethically traded chocolate?

Certified Fairtrade brands to look for in supermarkets include **the Co-op** own-label, Divine and Dubble (from the Day Chocolate Company), Green & Black Maya Gold (owned by Cadbury's) and **Tesco**'s own-label Fairtrade Milk and Dark Chocolate.

From the Aid Agency shops

Oxfam sells Traidcraft, Chocaid and Conscience products. Traidcraft chocolate is also available online from **www.traidcraft.co.uk**.

Where to buy Fairtrade Easter eggs

Certified brands include Divine, Montezuma (see next page) and Co-op own label.

Where to buy artisan chocolate that is ethically traded

Chococo, 'Cocoa Central', Commercial Road, Swanage, Dorset BH19 1DF
Tel: 01929 421777
www.chococo.co.uk
Chocolates and chocolate bars made with cocoa beans from Venezuela, Tanzania and Ghana, using ethically and fairly traded ingredients 'wherever possible' and fresh local Dorset produce. Mail order available.

The Chocolate Trading Company, Chorley Hall Lane, Alderley Edge, Cheshire SK9 7EU
Tel: 01625 592808
www.chocolatetradingco.com
For Mora Mora, a high-grade, single-origin chocolate created from Criollo, Trinitario and Forestero cocoa beans co-operatively farmed in Madagascar. The chocolate is made and packed in Madagascar, too. Also for Malagasy Sambirano, another Madagascan, equitably traded chocolate – very dark and earthy, for bitter chocolate fans. Mail order available.

Rococo, 321 Kings Road, London SW3 5EP
Tel: 020 7352 5857
www.rococochocolates.com
All chocolate used by Rococo is fairly traded. The range is truly outstanding, including the exquisite artisan bars with dozens of natural flavours, from sea salt, to ginger, to chilli.

Where to buy artisan or hand-made chocolate

Artisan du Chocolat, 89 Lower Sloane Street, London SW1 8VA
Tel: 020 7824 8365
www.artisanduchocolat.com
Extraordinary chocolates and Easter eggs, flavoured with essences of
everything from tobacco, to basil, to salt.

The Booja-Booja Company Ltd, Howe Pit, Brooke,
Norfolk NR15 1HJ
Tel: 01508 558888
Award-winning organic truffles, sold in fun packaging at Easter.

Montezuma's Chocolate, 15 Duke Street, Brighton BN1 1AH
Tel: 01273 324979
www.montezumas.co.uk
Spiced gourmet bars, made with chocolate containing 73 per cent
cocoa solids.

Seventypercent.com, 57 Farmillo Road, London E17 8JL
Tel: 0870 446 0770
www.seventypercent.com
Exciting online chocolate shop specialising in gourmet chocolate, with
a keen interest in burgeoning fairly traded, but very good-quality
chocolate. Look out for Grenada, Amadei and Bonnat.

COD

Its pearl-white flesh, large flakes and gentle, marine flavour have made cod one of the world's favourite fish, but its popularity has also become a symbol of a marine environmental disaster. Overfishing and climate change have seen numbers of cod in the North Sea drop so low that a crisis is predicted that will mirror that of Newfoundland's Grand Banks in 1981, when the fishing grounds closed and thousands of fishermen and their families lost their livelihoods.

There are, though, sustainable sources of cod. Depending where and how it is harvested, careful shoppers can still enjoy their favourite fish. But remember that these sources themselves are vulnerable because of cod's convenience-food factor. While it is served as a luxury in top restaurants, most cod comes as a cheap meal from the chippy, and we eat a jaw-dropping 450 million Birds Eye fish fingers a year. The answer to the dilemma, sad to report, is either to lay off the cod suppers and eat it only as a rare treat, or to find an alternative white fish to enjoy.

Are there any cod left in the sea?

Numbers of cod in the Northeast Atlantic are judged by the International Council for the Exploration of the Seas (ICES) to be overfished. According to national statistics published by the government, the spawning stock biomass of North Sea cod fell from 157,000 tonnes in 1963 to 38,000 tonnes in 2001, a decrease of 76 per cent, although it has since increased slightly to 46,000 tones in 2004. Stocks of cod are depleted in other areas of the North Atlantic, too. Numbers are low in the Irish Sea, off the West Scotland coast, Eastern Baltic, Northeast Arctic and Norwegian coast. Healthier stocks of cod are to be found in Icelandic and Faroese waters, where management of the stock has been responsibly handled.

How did it happen?

The collapse of cod numbers is a result of a vast and complex series of events and factors but, to simplify, the blame can be laid at the feet of technology, failed EU Common Fisheries Policy and, later, its marine conservation policy. Huge trawlers carrying vast nets and state-of-the-art tracking devices mean that fishing has become a 'harvesting' rather than a 'hunting' exercise. The policy to control overfishing by awarding fisheries a quota and total allowable catch (TAC) for each species is not only inadequate protection but wasteful and open to abuse – and abused it is by a sector of fishermen who do not accurately report what they catch, illegally landing fish.

Is overfishing the only problem?

No. Global warming has sent up the temperature of the North Atlantic and some species are being found further and further north, where the sea temperatures are right for the type of fish. Cod is no exception.

How can numbers be restored?

ICES recommends that large areas of known spawning grounds be closed indefinitely. This means, effectively, that fishermen must be paid not to fish in order for the cod to recover. The remedy comes at an enormous price to the taxpayer, but it is a cost that will have to be paid in the future anyway if nothing is done and cod disappear completely. The EU has so far not taken up ICES' advice. Its own advisory board has the power to overrule ICES, despite its status as the oldest international marine science agency, with vastly improved means to count and track species. Recent policy has seen the quota for North sea cod catches once again reduced.

So which cod can I eat?

Either go for Icelandic or Faroese cod (the former is often available in supermarkets) or buy from fishmongers who have access to fish from the inshore fleet, which fishes in smaller boats using more traditional means. The British inshore fleet fishes in waters between the shore and a six-nautical-mile limit where foreign boats are prohibited. They may use nets but there is a growing trend for fish caught by hook and line, the method that does the least damage to the seabed. Cod caught by the day boats (small boats that go out and return in a day) is the best choice for freshness (it can be up to two weeks' fresher than that on supermarket fish counters) and sustainability, but be prepared to pay up to twice as much for it.

Is farmed cod the answer?

Cod farming (in tanks) is still at an early stage, so farmed cod is not yet widely available. Environmental concerns should be taken into account – among them effluent pollution and the use of the wild fish population for feed (see Salmon, page 345).

I have found worms in cod – should I throw it away?

Translucent worms, about 2–3cm long, are a natural occasional phenomenon in cod flesh. They are harmless; unless you are squeamish, simply remove them and cook the fish anyway.

Should I eat cod's roe?

Not if you value the future of the species. Eat roes from fish whose numbers are healthy. Check the Marine Conservation Society website, **www.fishonline.org**, for information and download it or ask for a free copy of the *Pocket Good Fish Guide* (tel: 01989 566017).

What are the white fish alternatives to cod?

Alaskan pollack certified as sustainable by the Marine Stewardship Council (MSC) became available in spring 2006. For stockists, see the MSC website, **www.msc.org**. The MSC is an independent organisation, set up with funding from Unilever, makers of Birds Eye fish fingers. I have, however, visited various MSC-certified fisheries and am convinced their initiative is creating good, if slow-moving, progress.

Sainsbury sells skinless boneless MSC-certified hoki fillet and MSC-certified ready-to-cook South African hake. Youngs Bluecrest offers MSC-certified hoki fillet and breaded pollack for children (Fishysaurus and Flipper Dippers), while Birds Eye does hoki fish fingers. Choose also from the various delicious, white-fleshed flat fish that are available from British waters, including megrim sole, Dover sole and dab. Keep in mind, though, that over-enthusiasm for these species will see them go the way of the cod. I like to eat lots of North Atlantic prawns (see Prawns, page 316); the sea is packed with them because they are the food of the absentee cod!

Can I eat my favourite fish finger brands?

Birds Eye does not use North Sea cod for its fish fingers but cod from Russia, Norway and Alaska. Birds Eye's Russian-based suppliers have recently been criticised for irresponsible fishing activity. Greenpeace report that between 20 and 30 per cent of fish landed in the Barents Sea is illegally caught. Unilever, who own Birds Eye, say they are unable to control its ultimate suppliers far down the chain.

What the supermarkets say

Asda sources cod from Iceland and Norway for English and Welsh stores and the North Sea for Scottish stores. To its credit, it has de-listed certain endangered species, such as trawled ling, Dover sole and skate, from its counters. These changes were made after Greenpeace gave Asda the lowest rating of all supermarkets for responsible sourcing in October 2005.

Sainsbury's cod is mainly Icelandic and it will not stock when the fish are spawning. It buys seasonally – good for them.

Booths stocks cod from the Irish sea. Around 2 per cent of cod sold by **Tesco** is from the North Sea, the rest from other areas of the North Atlantic. **Waitrose**'s cod is 100 per cent Icelandic. **Marks & Spencer**'s cod is 100 per cent Icelandic line caught; they have an admirable fish-sourcing policy overall. Note that Icelandic fisheries are well managed but bear in mind that they have resumed whale culling in their waters, to protect their fishery.

Where to buy sustainably caught cod
(and pollock or other species)

The following online fishmongers provide well-run overnight delivery services and will tell you all you need to know about the fish you are buying:

Andy Race Fish Merchants Ltd, Mallaig, Inverness-shire, Scottish Highlands PH41 4PX
Tel: 01687 462626
www.andyrace.co.uk

Andy Race's smokehouse in the West Highland coastal town of Mallaig is famous for its delicious haddock and kippers, but this ethically minded fishmonger also buys cod from local boats when supplies are good.

The Fish Society, Freepost, Haslemere, Surrey GU27 2BR
Tel: 0800 279 3474
www.thefishsociety.co.uk

Cod from carefully managed Norwegian and Icelandic waters.

Fishworks Direct, 17 Belmont, Bath BA1 5DZ
Tel: 0800 052 3717
www.fishworks.co.uk

Shops in Bath, Bristol, Christchurch (Dorset) and four in London (see below). Netted cod from small trawlers and short-trip boats.

Matthew Stevens & Son Ltd, Back Road West, St Ives, Cornwall TR26 3AR
Tel: 01736 799392
www.mstevensandson.co.uk

Wonderfully fresh, line-caught cod is available from this environmentally responsible fishmonger, who specialises in fish caught by local boats. Be prepared to buy an alternative, as Matthew sources fish seasonally and only when he can buy a good size.

Shops that sell sustainably caught cod

If you are lucky enough to have access to a good local fishmonger, always ask where and when the fish on the counter was caught, and by what method. Good fishmongers will be happy to discuss this with you.

Andy Race Fish Merchants Ltd

For contact details, see page 143.

Fishworks
www.fishworks.co.uk

Netted cod from small trawlers and short-trip boats, Fishworks operates seven shops, with restaurants attached, in Bath, Bristol, Christchurch (Dorset), Chiswick, Islington, Marylebone and Harvey Nichols, Knightsbridge – see the website for details.

Matthew Stevens & Son Ltd

See page 143 for details.

Moxon's, Westbury Parade, Shop E, Nightingale Lane, London SW4 9DH
Tel: 020 8675 2468

Robin Moxon buys fish caught by sustainable methods from inshore fisheries as much as possible, and sources cod from Iceland where numbers are at safe levels.

Rex Goldsmith, The Chelsea Fishmonger, 10 Cale Street, London SW3 3QU
Tel: 0207 589 9432

Perhaps the freshest fish available in London, sourced direct from Cornwall. Goldsmith's clients include the local French and Spanish community, so expect to find less familiar species such as octopus, gurnard and unusual flat fish on the counter in this welcome, reopened fish shop.

Other sources of sustainable fish

Graig Farm Organics, Dolau, Llandrindod Wells, Powys LD1 5TL
Tel: 01597 851655
www.graigfarm.co.uk
Home delivery service offering sustainably caught fish from the unpolluted waters of St Helena Island in the South Atlantic. All fish is caught by rod and line. Yellow fin and albacore (white) tuna, wahoo, chubb mackerel, grouper (which has a cod-crayfish texture) and bullseye.

COFFEE

The story of coffee bridges two worlds. In one we drink coffee, spending nearly £2 a cup; in the other, farmers receive a fraction of that for one kilo of coffee 'cherries'. It is also a story that highlights only too well the unfairness of the free market. While Western farmers are protected by the subsidies and trade import levies that effectively keep out imported food from developing countries, farmers in non-temperate climates can grow very little for the West that it cannot grow for itself.

Fairtrade, the system whereby more of the price paid by the consumer finds its way back to the primary producer, the farmer, is the obvious answer. But the impact of Fairtrade remains miniscule. To make progress, World Trade rules must change.

What is the heart of the problem?

The problem is that the world produces too much coffee, encouraged by an industry well able to store the mountain and also, it must be said, by well-meaning organisations that funded new coffee-growing nations in the 1990s. In 2002 coffee prices dropped to an all-time low. Central to the crisis is the fact that the industry is controlled by a few conglomerates – 'giants' whose own survival in the marketplace depends on selling the lowest-priced coffee to make greater profits, and never mind the chaos it creates for the coffee-growing nations. Retail prices for coffee in the UK have dropped since the crisis began.

Just who is big in coffee?

Nestlé, Sara Lee, Proctor & Gamble and Kraft (now Altria) are the big-time roasters. They not only make the familiar brands – Nescafé, Kenco, Maxwell House and Douwe Egberts – but own scores of brands of both instant and packaged fresh coffee.

What can be done?

Top-level change is essential – Oxfam says the big players in the industry and Western governments need to put their heads together, destroy the coffee mountain and change the way coffee is traded on the global market. Cynics may smile, but the industry is becoming uncomfortable as it shoulders the blame. A positive development occurred in 2004, when the US rejoined the International Coffee Organisation, which works to improve the economies of coffee-growing nations and also the quality of the 'raw' coffee itself. The price of coffee has risen slightly – tentatively suggesting the crisis is abating.

Will buying Fairtrade help?

Savvy shoppers who disapprove of the mainstream coffee trade face a dilemma. On the one hand, buying Fairtrade sends a positive message to the industry generally. It makes a significant difference to farmers' lives – not only improving incomes, helping them, say, to send their children to school, but enabling them to produce better-quality coffee – it is known that the lowest-paid farmers produce the lowest-grade coffee. However, boycotting ordinary coffee lowers consumption, giving no help at all to the majority of coffee farmers.

I want Fairtrade coffee but none of it tastes as good as conventional

At the outset, the feel-good factor of Fairtrade coffee was put before the flavour somewhat. Not even a clear conscience will see shoppers return to buy disappointing coffee. But steady growth of the sector has turned this around and there are now some fascinating fairtraded coffees, either blended or from single estates, that have been expertly roasted.

Which coffee is in the double skinny latte?

Coffee chains that serve Fairtrade coffee include Starbucks (Starbucks makes claims about corporate responsibility, but just one of its coffees has a Fairtrade logo – Fairtrade Blend), Costa Coffee (Café Direct brand), Marks & Spencer Café Revive (all coffee) and Pret (all filter and decaffeinated coffee – Pret a Manger claims its other coffees are ethically sourced but none carries the Fairtrade logo). All coffee sold at AMT shops and Slug & Lettuce pubs has the Fairtrade logo. Expect to pay a little more for Fairtrade coffee.

What makes good coffee?

❋ The finest coffee should be freshly roasted – no more than one week old. This is available from specialist coffee stores; if you can smell the roasting, you are in the right place.

❋ The aroma of vacuum-packed coffee diminishes quickly once the bags are opened, but storing opened bags in the freezer will help retain the fresh flavour. You can store beans or ground coffee this way; there is no need to defrost it and it can be used straight from the freezer. Beans will obviously have the fresher taste, if ground just before use.

❋ Blends can be as good as single bean coffees.

❋ Organic coffee benefits from being grown without the use of pesticides and chemical fertilisers.

What the supermarkets say

All the supermarkets say shoppers are buying more and more fair-traded coffee, with Budgens reporting a sales increase of 17 per cent year on year.

Sainsbury stocks two own-brand Fairtrade coffees, plus Percol. All **Waitrose**'s own-brand coffee is Fairtrade; it also sells four other brands. **Budgens** stocks Café Direct and Percol. **Tesco** sells an own-label Fairtrade coffee and **Marks & Spencer** coffee carries the Fairtrade mark.

Note also that Nestlé has brought out a Fairtrade coffee, to justified cries of 'Cynics!' from the fair-trading companies who pioneered the movement. Look at it this way – the few coffee growers who benefit from the scheme cannot compensate for the many who still struggle to make a living within the conventional market.

Where to buy coffee

Nearly all the companies listed below will post their coffee to you. Buying coffee by post makes sense; it is light and carriage costs are low. There are some interesting home-delivery specialists.

Glo Coffee, PO Box 844, Camberley GU15 4WD
Tel: 0845 241 6809
www.glocoffee.com
A wide range of beans and blends, roasted no more than 24 hours before dispatch.

Monmouth Coffee Company, 2 Park Street, London SE1 9AB
Tel: 020 7645 3560
www.monmouthcoffee.co.uk
All coffees are bought through one shipper, not through commodities exchange. They are roasted on the premises.

The Roast and Post Coffee Company, Bridgeview House,
Redhill Lane, Elberton, Bristol, South Gloucestershire BS35 4A
Tel: 01454 417147
www.realcoffee.co.uk
Freshly roasted organic and Fairtrade coffees.

Union Coffee Roasters, Unit 2, 7a South Cresent,
London E16 4TL
Tel: 020 7474 8990
www.unionroasters.com
Coffee bought direct from the Rwandan war widow farmers. The Rwanda Maraba bourbon coffee has a wonderful flavour; also good is the Revolution Espresso blend.

World Coffees Ltd, The Old Forge, Denman's Lane, Lindfield,
West Sussex RH16 2LB
Tel: 01444 482140
www.worldcoffees.demon.co.uk
A large range of coffees roasted on the premises, from a company with a superb fair-trading reputation.

CRAB AND LOBSTER

Sweet and firm, the white-pink meat of crab and lobster can be the most divine of all shellfish but also the most disappointing. They are often sold overcooked, the claw meat withered and flabby. The flavour of mass-market crustaceans evaporates as the lobsters and dressed crabs eke out their shelf life in the supermarket chiller cabinet. Many are not from our own waters but flown across the Atlantic, to be dressed and packed here – an extravagant waste of fossil fuel for a food that does not deserve its jumped-up price.

When is the season for crab and lobster?

Lobster is in season in June, July and August, while the brown crab season runs from spring to mid winter. Male (cock) crabs are scarce during hot weather, as they head for deeper, cooler water, but there are plenty of smaller female (hen) crabs in August. Spider crabs are abundant in spring.

Are crabs and lobsters overfished?

The Marine Conservation Society reports that stocks of lobster are at a quarter of their potential level but that the species is not endangered. Likewise crabs. It is better not to buy crabs that are less than 13cm at the widest part of the shell, or lobsters that measure less than 9cm from the eye to the beginning of the tail section. Never buy lobsters or crabs that are carrying eggs. At a local level, many fisheries have implemented conservation methods to protect stocks – using only traditional pots and returning egg-bearing females to the sea or to hatcheries.

Do they have to be cooked alive?

No, but they should be cooked the moment they die or their flesh swiftly withers inside the shell. They can be killed humanely before boiling, but commercial fish sellers tend not to do this. Instead they put crabs in cold water and bring it to the boil, which slowly suffocates them. Putting a crab in boiling water will stress it so much it will lose its claws. Lobsters tend not to do this, so are put in boiling water.

If you buy live lobsters or crabs, deep-freeze them for at least two hours before cooking to make them comatose, then plunge them into a large quantity of boiling water. Alternatively, ask the fishmonger to show you how to kill them by piercing. Putting crustaceans in cold water and bringing them to the boil is not humane.

Why do lobsters change colour during cooking?
The red pigment in their shells is stable but the blues and greens disappear when the shells are heated.

What is the dark-green liquid found in some cooked lobsters?
It is harmless, a residue of the lobster's diet, and considered a great delicacy. It is offputting to the squeamish, however, and you can wash it off if you prefer.

Is there such a thing as farmed crab and lobster?
No, but lobster hatcheries – nurseries where vulnerable young can be reared away from predators before they are released back into the ocean – are proving a success. The hatchery in Padstow, Cornwall, is open to the public.

Are crabs and lobsters safe to eat?
Yes, but if you buy cooked crustaceans, eat them within 24 hours of purchase and never eat after the 'best before' date. They are scavengers, feeding on other shellfish and sometimes fish, and are less vulnerable to the contamination that can affect 'filter feeders' such as clams and oysters.

Where should I buy crabs and lobsters?

Always ask the fishmonger about the origins and catch method: they should be caught in pots, not trawled in nets, which damages the seabed and brings up a by-catch of other fish that may have to be thrown back. Choose lobsters or crabs that feel heavy for their size and live ones that seem active. Be aware, however, that if they are on ice they will be naturally sleepy. Never buy raw dead lobsters or crabs and only buy lobsters whose tails are curled underneath them – a sign that they were alive right up to the point of cooking.

Coastal fish sellers are the best source of the freshest, locally caught crustaceans, and a few will send them live via courier. If you are near the coast, seek out fishermen who will sell to you direct. Cromer in Norfolk is famous for crab, and there is a sustainable fishery on the Isle of Wight. The lobster fishery on the South Wales Pembrokeshire coast is also well managed – all egg-bearing or 'berried' females are tagged and returned to the sea.

Should I buy crabs and lobsters from the supermarket?

Yes, if they are of British origin and in season. Many, however, are imported from the US or Canada, where overfishing issues add to the environmental problem of air-freight food miles. Supermarket 'dressed' or picked crabmeat is often pasteurised, ruining its flavour.

Two honourable exceptions are **Marks & Spencer** and **Waitrose**. Both sell clawless Western Australian rock lobsters from a sustainable source, and the Waitrose ones are stamped with the Marine Stewardship Council (MSC) logo. These lobsters are deep-frozen, then freighted by sea and road – a lot of food miles but more economical than fossil fuel.

Marks & Spencer also sells wild, pot-caught crabs originating from Canada, Norway, England and Scotland. These are sold, cooked, in the delicatessen. It also stocks cooked wild, pot-caught lobster from the UK and Canada and a wild Australian lobster that carries the MSC logo.

The Co-op does not sell lobster but it does stock pot-caught wild Northeast Atlantic crabs whenever available.

Where to buy sustainable crab and lobster via home delivery

Caledonian Connoisseur, Ettrick Riverside, Selkirk TD7 5EB
Tel: 01750 505100
www.caleyco.com
Scottish lobsters from Willie Little, a fish merchant buying direct from the boats.

Fishworks Direct, 17 Belmont, Bath BA1 5DZ
Tel: 0800 052 3717
www.fishworks.co.uk
Cornish lobsters and crabs sent direct from the coast, or visit their shops in Bath, Bristol, Christchurch (Dorset) and London (check the website for details).

Isles of Scilly Shellfish, St Martins, Isles of Scilly TR25 0QL
Tel: 01720 423898
www.scillyshellfish.co.uk
A company with exceptional environmental standards and some good-value 'boxes'.

Matthew Stevens & Son Ltd, Back Road West, St Ives, Cornwall TR26 3AR
Tel: 01736 799392
www.mstevensandson.co.uk
Matthew Stevens will not sell 'berried' females and buys only from fishermen who take them to the Padstow hatchery. Lobsters are available live or cooked and he sells superbly fresh, hand-picked crabmeat. Picked spider crab meat also available.

Seafood Direct, Henderson Street, Fish Docks, Grimsby, South Humberside DN31 3PZ
Tel: 01472 210147
www.seafooddirect.co.uk
Lobsters from the east coast of England and North Sea crabs caught by local boats.

Selective Seafoods, Ffridd Wen, Tudweiliog, Pwellheli,
Gwynedd LL53 8BJ
Tel: 01758 770397
www.selectiveseafoods.com
Crab and lobster from South Wales.

CREAM

Evil and yet so desirable, it would seem sensible to approach cream with restraint. But go the way of the French and add small quantities to sauces or a little whipped cream to a weightless profiterole? Not us. We wildly pour it all over healthy foods like strawberries or squirt it into doughnuts. It is a somewhat dysfunctional relationship, thrown into relief by a contradictory fear of the fat content in whole milk (which is in fact very low). Both cream and milk have undergone a sea change over the years. They now emerge from the dairy conglomerates' factories largely as dull, standardised foods with little flavour and no detail of provenance. Just a handful of dairies fight on to produce the full-tasting cream of the past – one that is not only worth rediscovering for gastronomic reasons but also, controversially, for good health.

Why does some cream have more flavour than others?

Traditionally cream was collected from milk that had been left to stand, unrefrigerated, in the dairy, naturally ripening with the help of 'safe' bacteria. The mellow, ripe-tasting cream that rose to the surface of the milk would be skimmed off. Food safety precautions now ensure that dairy milk is chilled within moments of the cow being milked; cream collected from this milk will have a rich but bland taste. Some modern creams are ripened during refrigeration, using live bacterial cultures, to give a tangy flavour.

How does each type of cream differ?

The various creams on sale are made using a range of methods and have different fat contents:

* **Double cream** – has at least 48 per cent butterfat and is skimmed from milk that has been allowed to sit unstirred.
* **Single cream** – the same method as for double cream but with a standard 18 per cent fat. Both single and double cream are

conventionally homogenised after collection to give a consistent thickness.

* **'Extra thick' cream** – both single and double creams that have undergone a special homogenisation process to thicken them. Neither can be whipped and both lose thickness with heat. Extra-thick single cream is useful as a lower-fat spooning cream.
* **Whipping cream** – 35 per cent fat, but left non-homogenised to help it whip up to a thick consistency. A good cooking cream.
* **Crème fraîche** – cream with a 22 per cent fat content, thickened and 'ripened' with an added bacterial culture similar to yoghurt, then pasteurised again to stop the process.
* **Clotted cream** – crustily thick cream with a 55 per cent fat content, skimmed from milk that has been heated to 82°C. Both clotted and crème fraîche have a longer shelf life than double and single cream.
* **Reduced-fat cream** – contains thickeners to boost its texture. It contains half the fat of double cream (24 per cent) – so you may as well enjoy natural single cream or crème fraîche instead.
* **UHT cream** – double or single cream that is heated, then cooled very quickly for a long shelf life. It has a slightly cooked flavour and a greasier texture.
* **Aerosol cream** – UHT cream, under pressure. Better to spend five minutes whipping the natural stuff.
* **Soured cream** – like crème fraîche but further soured with a bacterial culture.

So is cream that bad for you?

When balanced with plenty of fruit, vegetables, grains and other proteins, the butterfat in cream is good for your bones, enhances your immune system, helps retain omega-3 in the tissues and is directly absorbed, releasing quick energy. Controversially, this means that eating cream is less likely to cause weight gain than eating olive oil. It is now acknowledged that refined and hydrogenated vegetable fats are very unhealthy (see pages 68 and 99), although consuming large amounts of saturated fats in dairy foods is still accepted as a contributing factor to heart disease.

Are there pesticide residues in cream?

The last time cream was tested for residues by the authorities, none was found at unacceptable levels. Pesticide 'watchdogs', however, claim that residues of DDT, now a banned pesticide, remain in our environment generally and accumulate in animal (and human) fat, including products such as cream, because the chemical is fat soluble.

Should I eat only pasteurised cream?

Raw, unpasteurised cream is the most delicious of all. Made by smaller dairy farms, which have excellent welfare standards and consequently a low incidence of animal disease, raw cream is available at some farmers' markets and specialist dairies. Raw-cream producers take extra care with hygiene – such small businesses cannot afford not to. Pregnant women and other vulnerable groups (such as young children, the elderly) are advised to avoid it, however.

Which is better, organic or conventional cream?

For a guarantee of good animal welfare, organic is best, especially when certified by the Soil Association. Organic cream is skimmed from milk produced on organic dairy farms. Animal welfare on organic farms is exemplary, although it must be said that this is often the case, too, on small-scale conventional farms. On organic farms the livestock graze on organic pasture, untreated with agricultural chemicals (although a few are permitted even by the Soil Association). Organic farms can be big or small but no animal is pushed to produce overly large quantities of milk. Large-scale dairy farms sometimes keep their cattle indoors full time, and feed them only concentrates. This means the animals never graze on grass. There is evidence that a fresh grass diet increases the nutrient value of milk, and therefore cream. The good thing is that organic and artisan dairy products from small farms are very affordable. For more on the condition of dairy cows and the problems faced by some dairy farmers, see Milk, page 247.

Where to buy traditionally made cream

Farmers' markets can be a good source of traditionally made cream. To find the market nearest to you, check **www.farmersmarkets.net** (tel: 0845 458 8420), or **www.lfm.org.uk** (tel: 020 7833 0338) for London.

Longley Farm, Holmfirth, West Yorkshire HD9 2JD
Tel: 01484 684151
www.longleyfarm.com
Beautiful, yellow cream – the double cream has an interesting inconsistent texture, part runny, part thick.

Manor Farm Organic Cream, Manor Farm, Godmanstone, Dorchester, Dorset DT2 7AH
Tel: 01300 341415
www.manor-farm-organic.co.uk
Pam and Will are organic dairy pioneers who produce beautiful, non-homogenised double and single cream.

Neal's Yard Dairy, 17 Shorts Gardens, Covent Garden, London WC2H 9UP
Tel: 020 7240 5700
www.nealsyarddairy.co.uk
Lightly ripened with buttermilk cultures, a superb organic crème fraîche you can feel good about eating. The farm is part run by wind power, the water filtered through a reed system and washing-up water provided by solar power.

Pengoon Farm, Nancegollan, Helston, Cornwall TR13 0BH
Tel: 01326 561219
www.pengoon.co.uk
Traditional clotted cream available by post.

Rachel's Organic Dairy, Unit 63, Glanyrafon, Aberystwyth,
Ceredigion SY23 3JQ
Tel: 01970 625805
www.rachelsorganic.co.uk
Crème fraîche and double cream from welfare-friendly British farms,
where the cows are fed a 100 per cent organic diet.

Rookery Farm, Northwick Road, Mark, Highbridge,
Somerset TA9 4PG
Tel: 01278 641416 or 07798 935246
Traditionally made clotted cream (plus yoghurt using fresh milk and,
wherever possible, fresh local fruit).

Where to buy unpasteurised cream

Beaconhill Farm, Nash End Lane, Bosbury, Herefordshire HR8 1JY
Tel: 01531 640275
Raw organic cream, available from Tewkesbury, Cheltenham and
Winchcombe farmers' markets.

Ivy House Farm, Berkley Lane, Beckington, Frome,
Somerset BA11 6TF
Tel: 01373 830957
Thick, full-tasting raw Jersey cream made in Somerset. Contact for
stockists.

Olive Farm, Babcary, Somerton, Somerset TA11 7EJ
Tel: 01458 223229
Family-run farm producing beautiful, yellow-tinted raw cream from
their herd of 80 Guernsey cows. Available from Frome, Henley and
Islington farmers' markets.

CURED PORK

One huge attraction of the continuing love affair with all things southern European is the ever-changing menu of cured pork. There seems to be no end to the glories of charcuterie. Just when we have become well initiated in the appreciation of genuine Parma hams, along comes the fennel-scented *finocchiona* of Rome. Right now the hot new legs in town are Iberico hams, with their buttery fat and dark, tender meat. *Lardo di colonnata* will be next. Wafer-thin strips of this peppery cured pork fat, melted over toast, are a revelation.

A positive outcome of the 1990s food scares is growing consumer curiosity about provenance: where and how livestock are reared and what they are fed. Just because the salami has a rustic, parchment-look label, however, it does not mean it contains pork from a happy pig.

What hides behind the rustic labelling on prosciutto, salami, pancetta and co?

Like all pork products, cured meats have a major animal-welfare issue. The automatic assumption is that imported cured meats are bound to be made on cute farms set on oregano-scented hillsides. Artisan charcuterie does exist but, like all specialist meats, it is available in specialist shops and markets, especially in the country where it is produced. The vast majority of generic cured meats sold in the UK – although based on traditional recipes – are made using factory-reared pigs. Welfare standards in European countries are lower than in the UK. Mass-produced British pork comes from factory farms, too, but with marginally kinder methods than those in Europe.

How should pigs be reared?

All pork should be from part-outdoor-reared pigs fed a natural, GM-free diet. See Bacon (and Pork) on page 48 for detailed information about welfare and feed.

Is all Italian ham Italian?

Labelling law allows it not to be. The generic Italian cured meats can be a product of more than one country. Don't be fooled by the oh-so-Italian red, green and white packaging on prosciutto (air-dried ham), pancetta and many salamis. The majority of mass-produced prosciutto is made in Italy but from pork reared in northern Europe – specifically from those intensive pig farming experts, Denmark and Holland. Incidentally, while the legs travel down to Italy for the cure, the backs take their place in the lucrative British bacon market.

What is gammon?

Gammon is a pork leg that has been cured in brine with salt (or other preservatives). After curing, it needs boiling or roasting, when it becomes ham.

Other terms for cured pork are collar, which is cured shoulder, and hock, which is the end, or shin, of the shoulder cut. Some hams are dry cured in salt granules.

Is there such a thing as traceable Continental air-dried or cured meat?

Look for the specialist brands marked with a PDO (protection of designated origin) or PGI (protected geographical indication). Protected cured pork products include genuine Parma ham made under the rules of the *consorzio del prosciutto di Parma* (identifiable by a three-pointed ducal crown logo on the rind or packaging), and Culatello and San Daniele hams, which can only be named as such if they are made in the region. In Tuscany a group of farmers has reacted to the dullness of generic prosciutto by reintroducing the Cinta Senese pig, a small, wild-looking animal that loves woodland. The hams and salami are outstanding, and just arriving in the UK. Italians are also experts in curing wild boar, a meat that is not only welfare friendly but necessary, as the Italian countryside is over-run by wild pigs. From Spain there is the lovely, buttery Iberico ham, and interestingly there are now a few British producers of air-dried meat.

So what are those oval, round or square slices of 'ham'?

This stuff is re-formed meat, and is a horror that can contain up to 37 per cent added water and up to 40 additives, including gelatine, colours and flavourings, plus a heap of salt, which 'fixes' the water into the stingy amount of 'ham' pulp. This is then moulded into a laughable ham shape, sliced and often canned. Hammy is the right word. Not one of these products has anything to recommend it. And there are poultry versions, too. Re-formed chicken even turns up in children's lunchbox meals, such as Dairylea Lunchables (see Lunchbox Foods, page 238) and has a high salt content. The manufacturers' excuse for this muck? That it provides cheap food (patronising) and that it provides a tasty, succulent food (why not try home-cooked gammon?). In a 2005 survey Ye Olde Oak was the wettest meat, with 37 per cent water; Bernard Matthews wafer-thin cooked ham had 28 per cent water, Princes ham 27 per cent water, Tesco Value cooked ham 21 per cent water. I could go on. Sainsbury, Tesco, Marks & Spencer, Asda and Morrisons all make watery ham. And there are different grades among the brands: Ye Olde Oak Premium – ha! – contains 'only' 21 per cent water. No thanks.

What's in the supermarkets?

The overwhelming majority of supermarket hams and salamis are undistinguished, to say the least. However, there are some exceptions. **Tesco** sells genuine Parma and San Daniele ham. **Sainsbury** and **Waitrose** stock genuine Iberico ham from Spain, although not equivalent in quality to Joselito Iberico (see page 163). Sainsbury stocks no other cured foods made with pork from free-range farms. It does, however, sell organic ham.

Waitrose's own-brand Italian prosciutto, salami and pancetta are made with 'farm assured' pork from inspected Italian farms – an improvement in the information stakes and reassuring in terms of animal welfare, although this standard does not mean totally free range. Waitrose also stocks ham and salami made with Iberico pork.

Marks & Spencer stocks a small range of organic ham.

Where to buy cured pork products made with naturally reared meat

Brampton Wild Boar, Blue Tile Farm, Lock's Road, Brampton, Beccles, Suffolk NR34 8DX
Tel: 01502 575246

Air-dried ham made with meat from naturally reared Suffolk wild boar. The pigs are kept in two family groups, headed up by the farm's boars, Mordred and Cedric; they are slaughtered on the farm to reduce stress. Feed is vegetable, cereal and fruit based.

Brindisa, 32 Exmouth Market, London EC1R 4QE
Tel: 020 7713 1666
www.brindisa.com

Excellent Spanish-sourced, artisan-made Joselito Iberico ham from outdoor-reared pigs that feed on acorns. Also chorizo sausage from naturally reared free-range pigs.

Denhay Farms Ltd, Broadoak, Bridport, Dorset DT6 5NP
Tel: 01308 422717
www.denhay.co.uk

Air-dried ham made with pork from free-range pigs reared in East Anglia on a GM-free diet and slaughtered in a small abattoir in Norfolk. The ham is cured in salt, Bramley apple juice, Dorset honey and herbs, then lightly smoked and air dried for up to a year. Mail order available.

Gorno's Speciality Foods Ltd, Unit 3, Fairfield Industrial Estate, Gwaelod-y-Garth, Cardiff CF15 8LA
Tel: 029 2081 1225

Franco Gorno used to run a *salumeria* in central Cardiff, supplying local pizzerias with Welsh–Italian authentic pepperami (made with free-range Welsh pork). Now he sells air-dried salami of every kind, plus prosciutto. Mail order available.

Islay Fine Food, Rockside Farm, Bruichladdich,
Isle of Islay PA49 7UT
Tel: 01496 850 350
www.islayfinefood.com
For non-pork eaters, cured (smoked) beef made by Mark and Rohaise
French using meat from their own livestock reared on a remote island
farm. Mail order available or contact for stockists.

Machiavelli, Unit F, Hewlett House, Havelock Terrace,
London SW8 4AS
Tel: 020 7498 0880
www.machiavellifood.com
Salamis made with pure Italian pork, flavoured with rosemary or
sage, plus hand-made prosciutto, pancetta and capocollo (tender meat
from the neck). Mail order available.

Savoria, 229 Linen Hall – CKp, 162–168 Regent Street,
London W1B 5TB
Tel: 0870 242 1823
www.savoria.co.uk
Wide range of artisan prosciutto, pancetta and salami from Umbria
and Tuscany, including *finocchiona* (fennel-scented salami), *lombetto*
and *lombone* (Umbrian cured pork loin) and prosciutto made from
the recently revived Tuscan Sinta Cenese pig. Savoria also sells *lardo
del Leone* (similar to *lardo di colonnata*) and a good Umbrian pancetta.
Mail order.

Sillfield Farm, Endmoor, Kendal, Cumbria LA8 0HZ
Tel: 015395 67609
www.sillfield.co.uk
Peter Gott makes wild boar prosciutto from 18-month-old animals
that are slaughtered on the farm. Also wild boar pancetta,
Cumberland speck and air-dried salami. Mail order available.

DRESSINGS

A splash of oil and a dash of lemon juice – does a salad need more? Well, you could emulsify these essential components with mustard, a pinch of sugar and a touch of garlic to make classic French vinaigrette but hey, why bother? Great tracts of space on shop shelves are devoted to the food industry's vinaigrette imaginings. Only, on top of the base ingredients, or often in place of them, some hideous creativity takes place. Food technologists are at their most inventive when challenged with the task of producing a cheap emulsion. It's no holds barred with dressings – this is a product that begs for labelling regulations simply to limit the adulteration.

What should a dressing contain?

Approximately three-quarters good, cold-pressed olive, sunflower, hemp or rapeseed oil (see Vegetable Oils, page 434) and one-quarter vinegar (from wine or another liquor) or lemon juice. Mustard binds the two together temporarily and salt will bring out the flavour. Good-quality ingredients make non-aggressive, fruity dressings that enhance the taste of the salad. The best dressings are a mixture of virgin oils, well-matured vinegar, additive-free mustard made with good wine vinegar and real seasonings such as fresh herbs.

What additives are found in dressings?

Many commercial dressings are bulked out with cheap starch (usually modified maize). The ingredients are homogenised with the help of emulsifiers, then 'set' into an unctuous slime with stabilisers. A virtual palette of colourings pink up the Thousand Island dressing or give the so-called honey mustard dressing a yellow hue and that's just the start of it. Remember, none of these additives actually taste of any-thing, so flavourings and salt are tipped in to compensate. Ingredients must be listed on labels in order of quantity, with the largest amount first. It is interesting to note that in many dressings, water is the main ingredient. Do you really want to spend your hard-earned cash on flavoured, thickened water?

❂ **Emulsifiers, stabilisers, thickeners and gelling agents** – most emulsifiers are deemed natural and therefore safe. Many commercial dressings use the emulsifier xanthan gum (E415) to hold the bond of vinegar and oil, which would otherwise separate. Xanthan gum is a gluten-free carbohydrate produced by fermenting glucose with micro-organisms. It is often used with various other emulsifiers, including the marine plant, carageenan (E407), and cellulose (E460), neither of which should cause concern.

❂ **Colours** – the industry has mainly stopped using the 'Filthy Four' colourings – allergens that cause hyperactivity in children. These are tartrazine (E102), sunset yellow (E110), carmoisine (E122) and ponceau 4R (E124). Usually in their place you will find annato (E160b) (which many parents also believe to be an allergen), curcumin (E100) and plain caramel (E150a).

Why are these additives in dressings?

Because they allow manufacturers to ease up on using expensive natural ingredients. What is guaranteed is that you would not want to eat a teaspoon of any single ingredient (apart from the added water) on its own, or guzzle a plate of maize starch for that matter. And the added ingredients can be substantial. One 'vinaigrette' label showed that just 25 per cent of the ingredients were made up of oil. Since the oil content of natural vinaigrette should be at least 75 per cent of the total ingredients, and vinegar/mustard/seasonings are always minimal, that's a lot of added water and thickeners.

Is the oil good quality?

Unless the label says that cold-pressed virgin oil has been used, the dressings will contain refined 'vegetable oil' (usually canola), which has been through various high-temperature treatments that remove much of its goodness and create unhealthy transfats (see pages 99 and 222). Canola (rapeseed) oil is very high in transfats. Oils such as soya and palm are not eco-friendly and, if only a small quantity is present in the dressing, soya oil could derive from GM soya.

Does it matter what type of vinegar is in a ready-made dressing?

Vinegar, or acetic acid (E260) as it will sometimes appear on labels, need only be an issue for allergy sufferers or food intolerances. Coeliacs or those who are gluten-intolerant often prefer not to eat vinegars derived from grain (such as malt), although evidence shows there is little to be concerned about if the vinegar is made from a distilled alcohol (as malt vinegar is). Fortunately there are others: wine, rice, sherry and apple-based vinegars. Though a filtered liquid, there will always be a percentage of solids, either derived from the apple, wine or malt base, but mostly the by-products of the metabolised Acetobacter (the bacteria, or 'mother culture' added to the alcohol that changes it to acid, or vinegar). It is thought that it is these solids, and not the acetic acid, that can cause a sensitive or allergic reaction in some people. Acetic acid is often added to many commercial ready-made dressings or 'vinaigrettes'. If used in undiluted form – the vinegar sold in shops is always diluted – these dressings have a very aggressive flavour. But do check labels; by law the type of vinegar must be marked on the list of ingredients.

Of some concern is the vinegar used by the food industry as a preservative in other ready-made foods. One estimate calculates that a person who eats a lot of convenience food will consume over 6 teaspoons of (diluted) vinegar a day.

Balsamic vinegar is not diluted but – put simply – made over a long period of time using a 'mother culture', a bacterial starter that is reused and 'fed', sometimes over centuries. As the culture metabolises the alcohol, often in barrels, the liquid gradually evaporates, leaving a thick, dark, sour-sweet condiment.

If there is a film star on the label, does that mean the dressing will be any good?

Wholesome as he is, Paul Newman puts quite a few additives in his dressings – xanthan gum, flavours and colours galore. These mostly come under the 'natural ingredient' tag, but the Family Recipe Italian Dressing contains hydrolised soy protein, a nasty additive and possible carcinogen with a meaty flavour. Keep in mind that most celebrities and famous restaurants endorse foods to make money, not because they want the world to eat xanthan gum (though Paul Newman doesn't make a penny from his business, giving the profits to charity).

Where to buy additive-free dressings

Essential Dressings, 21 Eston Avenue, Malvern, Worcestershire WR14 2SR
Tel: 01684 576150
www.essentialdressings.co.uk
Hand-made and no recourse to emulsifiers, despite the thicker character of these good, honest dressings: sweet mustard and dill, lemongrass and ginger, balsamic vinegar and more.

Forum Cabernet Sauvignon Vinegar, Brindisa, 32 Exmouth Market, Clerkenwell, London EC1R 4QE
Tel: 020 7713 1666
Unique, gentle but fruity vinegar made in Catalunya, Spain. Mosto (unfermented grape juice) is blended with red wine and left to acidify slowly. The vinegar is then decanted into oak and chestnut casks.

Spanks, Pound Barton, Sutton Veny, Warminster, Wiltshire BA12 7BT
Tel: 01985 840880
www.spankslimited.co.uk
Imaginative dressings, adventurous and yet still simple enough to work with food.

Womersley Fine Foods, 18 Beastfair, Pontefract WF8 1AW
Tel: 01977 797924
www.womersleyfinefoods.co.uk
Unusual dressings based on fruit vinegars – highly recommended for
eating with grilled meat, poultry and game.

If you are persuaded to make your own dressings, see the shopping
guides in Vegetable Oils (page 437), Olive Oil (page 269) and Mustard
(page 256).

DRIED FRUIT

Something of a revolution has taken place with dried fruit recently. Having spent years on the shelves next to flour and baking powder, these former baking ingredients can now be found in snack packs. These might turn up near the fresh fruit, or occasionally, when a supermarket is feeling virtuous, near the tills instead of confectionery. These dried fruit snacks are not just small packs of raisins but juicy mango and pineapple that has been slowly air-dried in ovens. The standard of this new-generation dried fruit is so high it merits a place on the table at dinner with the cheese. But, as with all food imported from far-away shores, you should buy dried fruit with care.

Can any fruit be dried?

Yes, almost any, but the range in our shops seems restricted to orchard and vine fruits plus a few exotic fruits. Newer methods using warm ovens have shown that fruits like strawberries can be dried, too. Breakfast cereal manufacturers frequently use freeze-dried raspberries and strawberries, which, once reconstituted in the milk, become strange-textured fruity chews.

How is fruit dried?

Fruit was traditionally dried in the sun, darkening and developing a strong sweetness. To prevent bacterial growth and inhibit mould, while keeping some of the juice, colour and an element of the fresh fruit flavour, modern non-organic producers treat fruit with the chemical, sulphur dioxide (E220), or a derivative (E222, 223, 224). Sulphur dioxide is produced from coal tar and is used to preserve fruit juice, cordials, wine (including organic wine), beer and potato crisps. The use of sulphur-based additives in food is restricted. Asthma sufferers are warned that there is a slight risk that they can provoke a reaction and they can be hard to metabolise for people with poor kidney function.

Does that mean that organic dried fruit is safer to eat?

Yes, but be careful. Moulds can grow on non-treated fruit and may be harmful. Always keep dried fruit in a cool, dry place. *Aspergillus flavus*, which can be an allergen, can develop on it. Producers check the skin of fruit for moulds, using UV light.

Because organic suppliers do not use sulphur-based preservatives and prefer to dry the fruit naturally in the sun or in ovens, some fruits (apricots in particular) will have a darker appearance that may be off-putting, especially to children. But the flavours are wonderful, so persuade yourself (and the kids) to try them. With raisins, prunes and sultanas, this is less of an issue.

Can I buy dried fruit that is both colourful and additive free?

Some producers are drying additive-free fruit in ovens, producing crisp, colourful slices of apple, strawberry and pineapple. These can be delicious, but if you prefer softer fruit you will have to soak them in cold water, dab with kitchen paper and eat them quickly.

How can I tell if the fruit used is good quality?

I would trust the quality of dried fruit rather more than that of imported fresh fruit because drying is an age-old means of giving value to tree-ripened fruit that would otherwise go off. It also tends to be a very artisan trade; the producers are too small scale to afford the expense of agricultural chemicals. I have seen grape pickers in Greece lay ripe fruit directly on to cloths by the vines to dry them during the picking season. It is good, too, to witness fruit whose slight visual flaws would render it fit only for compost in the fresh fruit market be utilised as dried fruit.

What should I look for when buying dried fruit?

Ideally the fruit should have been tree-ripened. This allows the sugars to develop and makes for a softer fruit with a sweeter flavour. The sugared, dried cubes of fruit sold as snacks are inferior to sun- or oven-dried as the sugar, a powerful preservative, covers and alters the fruit's natural flavour.

All dried fruit is imported – is it right to buy it?

Dried fruit stores well and travels to the UK by ship – eco-friendly transport compared to air and road freight. Remember, it is vital trade on which farming communities in poorer countries depend. The fair-trade stories associated with some fruits can be very heartening (see below).

The snack packs can be expensive; is this justified?

Quite why tiny packs of snack fruit have to cost £1.50 in supermarkets is a mystery. Bulk bags of fruit are inexpensive and there's a hint that retailers are taking advantage of the good intentions of parents who want to put something healthier than a chocolate bar in their child's packed lunch.

What are sunblush tomatoes?

These are ordinary tomatoes, cut, then slowly dried in ovens. They are then preserved in rapeseed or sometimes olive oil, flavoured with herbs. They contain no other additives (although it would be nice if the oil was higher quality) and give recipes a genuine sun-ripened flavour. (More information on tomatoes can be found on page 412.)

What the supermarkets say

All sell additive-free, organic dried fruit, but none has a supply of dried fruit that carries the Fairtrade logo. **Waitrose**, however, buys excellent mango strips and pineapple slices sourced from the Mango Trading Company, who buy tree-ripened dried fruit from South African farms where the minimum wage and age requirements apply. The company also runs a water and sanitation project adjacent to the farm.

The other supermarkets offered little further information, although **Tesco** said most of its range originates from Turkey, Greece and England (by which I suspect it means English companies!).

Where to buy fairly traded or additive-free dried fruit

Brindisa Shop, 32 Exmouth Market, London EC1R 4QE
Tel: 020 7713 1666
www.brindisa.com

Succulent dried peaches, apricots and, best of all, fat Malaga raisins from Spain's artisan suppliers. Contact for stockists.

Carluccio's, 12 Great Portland Street, London W1W 8QN
Tel: 020 7580 3050
www.carluccios.com

Individually wrapped Doni figs stuffed with orange zest and dipped in chocolate, sourced from a family-run artisan supplier in the Marches, Italy. Carluccio's also stocks *pallone di fichi* – figs from Cosenza in Calabria, oven dried, then packed in a ball, covered with fig leaves and baked again. A wonderful present to take to Christmas hosts, to eat with cheese. Mail order available.

Crazy Jack, PO Box 3577, London NW2 1LQ
Tel: 020 8450 9419
www.crazyjack.co.uk

Good-quality organic fruit bought direct from farms and co-operatives. Prunes from Agen and the US, apricots from Malta, figs and sultanas from Turkey, and raisins from California – all additive free. Ready-to-eat soft dried fruit, such as apricots, figs and prunes, are pasteurised in bags and are also additive free. Available online from **www.goodfooddelivery.co.uk**.

Merchant Gourmet, 2 Rollins Street, London SE15 1EW
Tel: 0800 731 3549
www.merchant-gourmet.com

Sells mis-cuit plums from Agen – additive-free, sweet, tree-ripened plums cooked for 12–16 hours at 80°C, then packed in plastic bags and pasteurised. Also SunBlush tomatoes, manufactured in France and sold in good-value 1-kilo or 240g packs, plus Tomatade, a chopped version to add straight to sauces. Available online.

Southern Alps Ltd, Unit 14, West Yoke Farm, Michael's Lane, Ash, Near Sevenoaks, Kent TN15 7HT
Tel: 01474 871275
www.southern-alps.co.uk
Air-dried, additive-free fruit in small packs that are ideal for the lunchbox, car or picnics: strawberries, pineapple, Middle Eastern figs and apples.

Traidcraft, Kingsway, Gateshead, Tyne and Wear NE11 0NE
Tel: 0870 443 1018
www.traidcraft.co.uk
A wide range of Fairtrade fruits from seven sources around the world, among them apricots from northern Pakistan, Indian sultanas and mixed dried fruit.

Tropical Wholefoods, 7 Stradella Road, Herne Hill, London SE24 9HN
Tel: 020 7737 0444
www.tropicalwholefoods.co.uk
Fair-traded dried apricots, pineapple, banana, mango and papaya sourced from Uganda, Burkina Faso, Zambia and Pakistan and sold in small packs. (The company also specialises in dried wild mushrooms from Africa.) Mail order available.

EGGS

From the simple boiled breakfast egg to the catalyst that puffs air into a quivering soufflé, no food is more versatile – or controversial. The increasing number of free-range eggs on sale in supermarkets indicates that shoppers are more and more aware of the cruelty of caging hens in batteries. It's a trend to celebrate, but it goes only partly towards solving all our egg troubles. In spite of new labelling laws that require shop-sold eggs to be stamped with detailed information, eggs are still not a safe food, especially those used in ready-cooked dishes.

Which eggs are safe to eat?

British eggs, individually stamped with a 'red lion' logo, are laid by hens that have been vaccinated against salmonella. The scheme means that 90–95 per cent of British shop-sold eggs are safe and it has had a dramatic impact on salmonella-poisoning figures. These eggs are the ones to use when making mayonnaise, but seek out free-range eggs with the red lion logo if you are concerned about hen welfare, too.

Which eggs are unsafe?

The Food Standards Agency reports a serious problem in the catering trade with the use of imported eggs – Spanish eggs in particular – that are contaminated with salmonella. Salmonella infection is directly connected to poor husbandry and intensive systems, and fatal outbreaks have been traced back to these eggs. It is a mystery why a law does not exist to force caterers or those that make ready meals to provide consumers with information about the eggs they use in the same manner as retailers of fresh eggs. British egg farmers are currently lobbying the catering trade, demanding that they stop using imports.

What do the stamps on eggs mean?

Aside from the red lion, there are letters and figures stamped on every shop-sold egg. Only farm shops and farmers selling eggs direct at the farm gate or farmers' markets are exempt from the legislation on this.

By law, there must be a 'best before' date, preceded by the letters BB, then a code. The first digit of the code defines the farming method: 0 for organic, 1 for free range, 2 for barn (loose housed) and 3 for cage or battery. The letters show the country of origin, e.g. UK. The last five numbers are the farm ID.

How old are eggs in shops?

The laying date of a stamped egg will be three weeks before the 'best before' date. Shops may not sell eggs that are more than three weeks old, although they may still have plenty of life in them. Some people test eggs by putting them in a glass of water. If the egg seems very buoyant and full of air, it is too stale to eat. When cracked open on to a plate, the membrane surrounding an egg's yolk should be thick and strong, allowing the yolk to stand high above the white.

What is the price difference between organic, free-range and battery eggs?

Organic eggs cost about twice as much as battery eggs but they are still an inexpensive, good-quality protein that is much cheaper than good meat or fish. British battery eggs cost around 61 pence per half dozen, standard (higher stock density) free range 81 pence, totally free range £1.20 and certified organic £1.60.

Do I always have to pay double for welfare-friendly eggs?

Not at all. Bought at the farm gate, eggs from welfare-friendly, free-range farms usually cost just a few pennies more than British battery eggs in supermarkets. Look out for signs along the road.

Does free range really mean free range?

Free range means no more than 11 uncaged hens per square metre indoors, or 1,000 hens per hectare outdoors. A lower ratio is preferable but only 3 per cent of commercial free-range farms allow their hens to roam totally free. Soil Association standards for organic eggs insist on no more than six hens per square metre, as does the Organic Farmers & Growers certification standard; look for boxes with either logo. Aim to buy eggs from suppliers that provide plenty of information on the boxes – some show photographs of the hens on their farms, although you should not perhaps be too easily taken in by this. Ideally hens roam in large grassy fields, sheltering in wooden arks, but very few enjoy this standard of living.

Are eggs a disease threat in the event of an outbreak of avian flu?

The Food Standards Agency advice goes that while we do not have the disease in Britain, British eggs pose no threat of passing the virulent strain of avian influenza, AI H5N1, to humans, if cooked. The EU, however, is swift to ban egg exports to Europe from any country with an AI H5N1 outbreak, which indicates it believes there to be at least a possibility of the disease being passed into our bird population.

Are fresh eggs washed before sale?

No. It is permitted to wash eggs in EU countries but they cannot be classed Grade A – in other words the retailers will not touch them, as they can only sell Grade A eggs. Washing is perceived as a hygiene risk, and farmers of caged hens install special equipment to catch the egg as soon as it is laid, while it is in the interest of free-range and organic farmers to keep their hens clean with plenty of fresh bedding. Some sophisticated organic hen arks have sloping chutes to catch eggs soon after they are laid.

Should I buy cracked eggs?

No. The shell is a protective waterproof, germproof covering and the safety of the egg is compromised if it is sold with a crack. That's why egg boxes are always annoyingly open in shops – it's the customers having a peep.

Do dark yolks mean a better flavour?

No. The colour of the yolk relates to breed or feed and has no bearing on flavour. Good flavour is dependent on a balanced diet that includes vegetable, not meat or fish, protein.

Are eggs enriched with omega-3 better than ordinary eggs?

IQ-boosting eggs containing high levels of omega-3 are the latest lure for parents anxious to improve their child's focus. The hens are fed quantities of flaxseed, which is high in omega-3. It's no bad thing but don't forget that eggs contain cholesterol, so feeding a child three a day to boost their brain power may not be the answer.

What's in the supermarkets?

Aside from the large quantity of battery eggs sold in supermarkets, you will usually find free-range and organic eggs, and sometimes eggs from specialist breeds, such as Cotswold Legbar, Araucana, Burford Browns, Ebony Penhale, Chaucer Gold, Black Rock, Speckledy and Columbian Blacktail. Some supermarkets sell duck eggs and the same issues of welfare and feed apply as for hens. Ducks, however, need access to water for swimming, not just to drink, so look for evidence of this on labels or buy from a source where you can ask questions about welfare. Standards of welfare, feed and farming systems should be made clear on the box – the more details the better.

Marks & Spencer operates an ethical egg policy, selling only eggs from free-range hens and using them in its ready meals and other foods – excellent. Its hens are fed on a GM-free, cereal-based vegetarian diet; there's one metre of floor space for every 11 birds but the organic variety has more space.

Sainsbury sells free-range and organic eggs. It also sells free-range duck eggs. All the birds are fed on a non-GM, vegetarian diet free from artificial colorants. It has not banned the sale of battery eggs.

Budgens sells organic, free-range and conventional eggs, plus eggs produced by Old Cotswald Legbar hens. All eggs are UK sourced.

Waitrose sells a variety of eggs produced for them by Stonegate Farms and has even developed its own breed ideally suited to life in the free-range or organic system, the Columbian Blacktail.

The **Co-op** sells 66 per cent UK-sourced eggs from hens whose welfare complies with the RSPCA's Freedom Food standards (loose requirements compared to Soil Association-certified organic systems). Feed for the hens is GM free and the diet consists of cereals, grass and meal. The Co-op has not banned the sale of battery eggs but is admirably honest in labelling products containing 'eggs from caged hens'.

Tesco, Morrisons and **Asda** did not supply information about the eggs they sell. With such a controversial food, this omission is one that should not instil trust in shoppers.

Reliable supermarket and independent-shop suppliers
Clarence Court (tel: 01386 858007 for stockists)
Farmhouse Freedom Eggs (formerly Martin Pitt; tel: 01291 673129
    for stockists)
Munson's Poultry (tel: 01206 272637 for stockists)
Stonegate Farms (tel: 01249 730700 for stockists)
Yorkshire Farmhouse Eggs (tel: 01845 578 376 for stockists).
Yorkshire Organic Earth (tel: 01385 901215 for stockists)

Where to buy welfare-friendly eggs
Buy eggs at farmers' markets and you can quiz the stallholders on their farming practice. To find details of your local markets, check **www.farmersmarkets.net** (tel: 0845 458 8420), or **www.lfm.org.uk** (tel: 020 7833 0338) for London.

'The Chicken Came First', Lynton Mead, Outwoods, Newport, Shropshire TF10 9EB
Tel: 01952 691418
Clare Draper keeps free-range hens fed on a GM- and chemical-free diet, in an unusual mix of breeds.

The Chicken Rescue Centre, Roosters Range, Bildeston Lane, Wattisham, Suffolk IP7 7JT
Tel: 01449 741626

Martin Hudspith takes on abused and neglected battery hens and teaches them how to be chickens again. He now has 250 healthy hens happily laying eggs, who had all been discarded for no longer producing eggs in financially viable quantities. The eggs are available direct from the farm.

Kintaline Farm, Benderloch, Oban, Argyll PA37 1QS
Tel: 01631 720223
www.kintaline.co.uk

Eggs from Black Rock hens and other breeds.

FLOUR

The characteristics of a country's breads and baking should relate to the flour that can be grown in its fields, but in the UK, distinctiveness has gone somewhat awry. Most of our bread-making flour is imported, so it is up to cooks in their home kitchens to keep authentic British baking, with home-grown ingredients, alive.

Big business rules the flour industry, and pesticides are a major concern. But a small and thrusting artisan industry thrives: traditional mills filling paper sacks with flour milled from local wheat, much of it organically grown. Even with its higher price, it provides an economic source of good food.

Is the flour in the shops British or imported?

Eighty-five per cent of the non-organic ordinary white flour sold in our shops derives from British farms but most 'strong' white bread flour is made from imported wheat. This is a change from the 1970s, when only half the wheat for our flour industry was imported. The two largest millers in the UK now account for 50 per cent of production. Most of the flour milled in the UK is wheat. Rye, spelt and other grains make up only a tiny proportion.

Where does our imported wheat come from?

Nearly a million tonnes are imported, of which three-quarters come from the US and Canada.

Is all flour milled in the same way?

No. Most commercial flour is roller milled – literally put through a series of rollers – but some is stoneground, a traditional method that rubs the grain between two stones. The advantage of the traditional method is that the natural and highly nutritious oils in the flour are retained.

My children insist on white flour in their bread – can you buy a stoneground version?

Yes, but you will probably have to order it direct from a traditional mill (see below). Stoneground white flour is sifted and retains more nutrients, but it is a darker colour and the kids will have to learn that not all white bread is whiter than white. I would guess that the full flavours of stoneground will have them choosing it over ordinary white flour in the end.

Is there anything in the pack apart from flour?

Yes. By law, calcium carbonate (E170), iron, thiamine and niacin must be added to white and brown flour in controlled quantities, although this need not be declared on the label. The modern commercial roller-milling process removes wheatgerm (the heart of the wheat kernel), and with it valuable vitamins, especially vitamin B. In a vain attempt to restore the flour to its former wholesome goodness, a proportion of the vitamin B is added back to it with fortifying thiamine and niacin. Artificial fortification with calcium carbonate (which is chalk) is said by the industry to contribute to 14 per cent of adults' and 20 per cent of children's daily calcium intake.

What is the difference between strong flour and plain flour?

Strong flour is made from harder varieties of wheat, which help it to hold up during the leavening process, while ordinary flour, made from softer wheat, is suitable for cakes, pastry and biscuits.

Which other types of flour can I buy?

* **Self-raising flour** – plain white soft wheat flour with added raising agents.
* **Wholemeal** –100 per cent of the grain, milled with no additives and no grain removed.
* **Brown flour** – 80–85 per cent of the grain, with some of the wheat bran and wheatgerm removed.

* **Malted wheatgrain (Granary)** – brown or wholemeal flour with added malted whole grains.
* **00** – plain white soft wheat flour milled extra fine, the traditional flour for making cut pasta, like tortellini and flat ribbons such as tagliatelle. It is not suitable for making the kind of pasta that is extruded through machinery, such as spaghetti, or short pasta tubes like rigatoni; durum wheat (semolina) flour is used for this purpose.

What is spelt flour?

Spelt is an ancient relative of modern common wheat that contains more protein, fat and fibre than wheat. Nutrition experts say it also contains special carbohydrates called muco-polysaccharides, which play a role in stimulating the body's immune system, helping to increase its resistance to infection.

Should I take talk about so-called allergies to wheat seriously?

Sometimes. Some people are dangerously intolerant to gluten in wheat and should never eat it. Nutrition experts advise that hyper-active children should avoid wheat, too. Wheat intolerance is otherwise a grey area. There are a lot of dieters 'avoiding wheat and dairy'. Atkins dieters swear they have never felt better but inevitably go back on to the pastry and doughnuts. Do not dismiss anecdotal evidence, however. Recently leading toxicologists and toxi-pathologists have said that it is necessary to reassess toxicity in humans after 20–40 years of exposure to agricultural chemicals, and that means taking into account allergic reaction. The same scientists are especially concerned about the effects a combination, or 'cocktail', of pesticides is having on adults, and principally on children. This could mean that those who complain about the mildly irritating effects of wheat in the diet may have a genuine cause.

What are the differences between organic and conventionally grown wheat?

It is basically the seed and the level of chemical use. Different seeds have been developed for organic and conventional wheat crops. Conventional wheat varieties are developed to grow in conjunction with agricultural chemicals, including pesticides, herbicides, fungicides and fertiliser. The producers claim to be seeking, through technology, a pest-resistant, disease-resistant wheat. Some organic farmers say they have that plant and it is a hybrid closely related to early-twentieth-century wheat, needing minimal chemical use (six treatments are permitted by the Soil Association but are often not used at all). Some organic farms are experimenting with taller plants and have evidence that they shade out the weeds, reducing the impact of weed competition, produce strong stems with waxy leaves, thus avoiding the need for any crop protection, and rarely fall over.

If traditional wheat breeds need minimal chemicals to grow, why don't all farmers grow them?

They are not convinced they can profit from it, as it has a lower yield. Flour would become more expensive in the shops – but organic flour is still good value for money when you think of its bulk and nutrient quality. Don't forget that it is in the petrochemical industry's interest for wheat species to be dependent on the chemicals they manufacture.

Is any GM wheat sold in the UK?

No. Farmers are not permitted to grow it. However, flour that accidentally contains more than 0.9 per cent of EU-approved GM ingredients or 0.5 per cent non-approved GM ingredients need not be labelled, so there is risk of contamination from imported flour.

What chemicals are used on wheat crops?

Plenty can be used but I hasten to say that small-scale farmers find these treatments expensive. Wheat once grew to over a metre high, but the introduction of nitrogen fertiliser made the wheat 'straws' unstable, causing them to fall over before harvest. The chemical growth regulator, chlormequat (CCC), was introduced to strengthen the straws and it is still used. In 2003 the government tested 144 samples of bread for residues of chlormequat, finding residues 'at safe levels' in just under 50 per cent of samples, but there are no maximum residue levels set for CCC. Farmers spray with pesticides, fungicides and herbicides and may spray up to eight times from seed to harvest.

How dangerous are agricultural chemical treatments to humans?

The manufacturers say they have all been tested for toxins and prove harmless in specified quantities but a report in 2005 by the Royal Commission on Environmental Pollution (RCEP) warns about the potentially damaging effects of pesticides on local residents' and bystanders' health and criticises the government's failure to take this seriously. The RCEP says there is a need to overhaul the risk assessment of pesticides, which it believes to be currently inadequate.

What is the environmental impact of the flour industry?

Little is wasted in the processing. The lost wheatgerm goes to the pharmaceutical industry and much of the oil is used in face creams, even though it would be better for our whole body, including our skin, to eat the stuff. Fuel is obviously used for milling (some delightful water mills are still in operation, however) but the real environmental threat is to wildlife. The habit of planting high-yield winter wheat just after harvest time disturbs stubble fields that provide essential cover and food for wild birds. Chemical sprays also kill birds. Some farmers have signed up to the stewardship schemes that reward them for protecting the environment.

Can I buy good flour in the supermarkets?

All major supermarkets sell organic flour and Waitrose stocks particularly good flour from its own Leckford Estate farm in Hampshire.

Where to buy flour milled from traditional wheat breeds

Gilchesters Organic Farm, Hawkwell, Northumberland NE18 0QL
Tel: 01661 886119
www.gilchesters.com
A farm that has experimented with growing pre-War breeds organically, with great success. Its flour is milled at the Watermill, Penrith.

Where to buy traditionally milled flours

We made bread with flour from the following mills. Each had its own character; some made lighter bread, some heavier, protein-rich bread. None needed much salt, or any additives apart from yeast and water.

Burcott Mill, Wells, Somerset BA5 1NJ
Tel: 01749 673118
www.burcottmill.com
Superb flours from a rare working watermill, one of just 28 fully working, water-powered flour mills left in Britain today.

Bursledon Windmill, Windmill Lane, Bursledon,
Southampton SO31 8BG
Tel: 02380 404999
www.hants.gov.uk/museum/windmill
Restored working windmill, selling stoneground wholemeal flour made from local wheat and specialising in strong wholemeal flour to use in bread-making machines.

Doves Farm Foods Ltd, Salisbury Road, Hungerford,
Berkshire RG17 0RS
Tel: 01488 684880
www.dovesfarm.co.uk
Over a dozen flours (including several gluten-free ones) from a larger-scale producer with integrity. Available from all major supermarkets, or check the website for other stockists.

Lurgashall Watermill, Weald and Downland Open Air Museum, Singleton, Chichester, West Sussex PO18 0EU
Tel: 01243 811022
www.wealddown.co.uk
Stoneground wholemeal flour from a seventeenth-century watermill.

Sarre Windmill, Ramsgate Road, Birchington, Sarre, Kent CT11 0JU
Tel: 01843 847573
Again, a truly traditional mill, producing flour from mainly local wheat.

Shipton Mill Ltd, Long Newnton, Tetbury, Gloucestershire GL8 8RP
Tel: 01666 505050
www.shipton-mill.com
Specialist flours made from cereals that have been individually selected from Britain's top growers. Online shop.

N. R. Stoate and Son, Cann Mills, Shaftesbury, Dorset SP7 0BL
Tel: 01747 852475
www.stoatesflour.co.uk
Truly excellent flour from a small watermill, with all the goodness of the wheatgerm left in, even in the white. Produces a heavy, savoury white bread that is hard to imitate with any other flour.

Sunflours, The Hutts Mill, Grewelthorpe, Ripon, North Yorkshire HG4 3DA
Tel: 01765 658534
www.sunflours.com
Millers and wholesalers of organic wholemeal flours.

The Watermill, Little Salkeld, Penrith, Cumbria CA10 1NN
Tel: 01768 881523
www.organicmill.co.uk
Very small-scale mill using waterpower to mill organic and bio-dynamic flour. Mail order available.

FRENCH BEANS (AND OTHER FRESH BEANS)

Let's say for starters that this is the greatest vegetable misnomer since Brussels sprouts. The constant supply of thin green beans sealed in little bags or cartons in your local supermarket comes to you from much further away than France. These are the air-freighted fillers for winter supermarket produce sections. French, 'fine' or 'dwarf', beans share their cargo space in the jumbo jets with sugar snap peas, mangetout, shelled garden peas, broad beans and runner beans and, due to the fossil-fuelled air miles they gobble, are the *bêtes noirs* of environmental campaigners. But is the Kenyan bean quite the villain we have been led to believe? Or are more than a few farmers in developing countries desperately grateful for the trade?

What is the definition of a French bean?

The nomenclature is pretty vague but the *Oxford Dictionary of Plants* identifies the thin green bean that can be eaten whole as a 'French' bean and also, confusingly, as a 'kidney' bean. In fact, what we call French beans, dwarf beans, 'fine' beans or string beans (though new breeds are no longer stringy) are hybrids. These beans grow on small bushes and are picked when tender, green and about 10cm long. Scarlet runner beans are the large beans that crop in the UK in August; yard beans are long green beans that grow in Thailand; bobby beans are fat green beans that grow mainly in the UK; and 'haricots' refer to the various types that can be dried and boiled for cassoulet.

Where are French beans grown?

The season in northern Europe runs from June to October. While supermarkets stock European beans in summer, regular supplies of the same bean are harvested throughout our winter months in Africa, mainly Kenya and Gambia. (Other beans, including runner and yard beans, are grown in South Africa and Thailand.) While the European bean glut is one to be welcomed, as these beans travel relatively short distances to our shops, those from Africa are more controversial.

How do fresh beans from Africa get to the UK?

Via air freight. Flamingo, a company that supplies beans, other vegetables and flowers from Africa to several UK supermarkets, including Sainsbury and Tesco, has stated that 20 planes a week take off with its produce. These include jumbo jets. Each year, it says, 100 million packs of vegetables, many of them beans, are flown to the UK. The vegetables are blast-chilled immediately after picking and processing (shelling, topping and tailing etc). The company says that produce can get from field to plate in 48 hours. It must be said that these beans, however fresh, can be tough compared to the tender beans harvested during the European glut.

Are fresh beans food-mile friendly?

No. Beans fly over 3,600 miles to the UK from Kenya, at a massive cost of fossil fuel. Sea freight is the most environmentally friendly form of overseas transport for food – air freight the least.

But how do bean crops affect the environment in exporting countries?

This is a subject for debate. The environmental campaigners say that growers in Kenya are responsible for depleting the water supply, and that large areas of historic natural landscape have made way for acre upon acre of plastic sheeting and glasshouses. This, they say, affects the lifestyles of indigenous people, as has the arrival of a large immigrant workforce that uses more than a sustainable supply of trees for domestic fuel. The companies that operate their own farms and employ smallholders dispute this, saying they take great care to clean and keep the water supply high. Near Mount Kenya, a major area for French beans, Flamingo says it takes water from a reservoir rather than from the mountain streams; it also says it belongs to a scheme that pipes water direct to 'subsistence' farmers who grow food only for themselves.

Are there pesticide residues on beans?

The news is good and bad. While there are large companies increasingly developing bio-controls for pests (predatory insects are released on to crops to kill spiders and aphids), pesticides are still widely used. In 2005 the Pesticide Residues Committee reported residues exceeding the maximum allowed residue levels (MRL) on samples of beans from Marks & Spencer (grown in Kenya), although the supermarket chain disputes the finding. Residues exceeding the MRL were also found on samples from Safeway–Morrisons (grown in Egypt) and Asda (grown in Egypt.) No residues were found on beans from Sainsbury, Tesco and Waitrose. But remember it is not just British consumers who should be concerned – some pesticides are extremely toxic and workers, unless properly trained, are also at risk from their effects in high concentration. Incidentally it is worth noting that residues exceeding the MRL have been found on several samples of Thai yard beans and edamame beans (fresh soya beans, sourced in China).

Who farms and picks beans?

In Africa there are large farms employing thousands, and small former subsistence farmers who work to the large exporters' (and British supermarkets') specifications. Since they are a cash crop (i.e. one that the Africans eat little of themselves), beans are good for the local economy. The larger exporters claim they provide schooling for local children as well as the children of those they employ; they also provide medical care, including teaching HIV/AIDS awareness, family planning and hygiene. Fairtrade-accredited beans do not yet exist, however. Nor do we know how much pressure supermarket chains put upon the exporting companies and those that supply them to keep prices as low as possible.

Is bean farming a monoculture?

No, many other crops are grown besides beans. In fact you could identify a large quantity of the fresh produce from your local supermarket as it boards its plane to the UK: baby vegetables, including leeks and carrots; runner beans, mangetout, sugar snap peas; podded garden peas, podded broad beans, packed selections of any of the above, plus many flowers, especially roses (the reason the glasshouses of southern England are now empty). All this is in the name of crop rotation – keeping the soil healthy. No bad thing. Yet it rankles, somehow.

Do beans need all that packaging?

The air-freighted produce would not survive the journey loose in boxes but it would be better if it were only packed in plastic bags, not hard plastic trays. Few local authorities will accept these for recycling and they are bulky for landfill. Avoid beans packed this way and encourage supermarkets to use less packaging.

So should I buy Kenyan beans or not?

You decide, after looking at the argument both ways.

Kenya (and other developing countries that air freight to the UK) is undergoing an agricultural revolution, gaining the same opportunities as we have to export cash crops and finally boost their economy. With this will come the displacement of indigenous people, negative effects on their environment and a loss of innocence that visitors to these beautiful countries will find hard to accept. But many of the people involved, especially those working for certain UK supermarkets (see below), can educate their children, use medical facilities and even have some disposable income. In return, the argument goes, we get a supply of crunchy greens throughout our root-vegetable-dominated winters.

On the other hand, there is concern about the chronic use of fossil fuel to transport vegetables with negligible nutritional value (compared to bananas, mangoes and avocados) that we could quite easily do without in the UK. Anyway, it's not all roots here in January. What's wrong with eating exciting European winter gluts of purple sprouting broccoli, forced rhubarb, seakale, blood and Seville oranges? Would it not be better for Africa to export a more sustainable crop? And how much are they really gaining? Everyone knows the British retailers use pressure to get the lowest prices, so this type of farming may not have a real future.

It's a tricky one, but it is certain that food crops from Africa are here to stay and much must be done to eradicate the use of pesticides and audit the claims about environment and social welfare made by exporting companies. Me? I eat the odd bean dinner.

What the supermarkets say

Sainsbury says its beans are sourced from Africa (Kenya, Zambia, South Africa and non-government farms in Zimbabwe), Morocco and Egypt. Beans from the latter two countries are sea or road freighted, while beans from the other African countries are air freighted. Sainsbury's suppliers have a good record for pesticide use and Flamingo, which supplies Sainsbury's Kenyan beans, amongst other products, uses biological controls and claims it has almost eradicated pesticide use.

Waitrose also sources its beans from dedicated farms, which are involved in social welfare schemes, use non-chemical biological pest control and are sensitive to the local environment.

Tesco sources beans from Kenya and Egypt and says it is currently investigating a fair-traded variety.

Where can I buy French beans during the European season?

Fresh, locally sourced French and other beans, including broad beans, runner beans and tougher 'bobby' beans, can be bought at farmers' markets and from farm shops. To find the one nearest you, contact **www.farmersmarkets.net** (tel: 0845 458 8420) or **www.lfm.org.uk** (tel: 0207 833 0338) for London. Check **www.farma.org.uk** or **www.bigbarn.co.uk** for details of farm shops and pick-your-owns.

Organic French and other beans can be ordered from the following vegetable suppliers, subject to availability:

Farmaround Organic, Office B143, New Covent Garden Market, Nine Elms Lane, London SW8 5PA
Tel: 020 7627 8066 (for home delivery in London) or 01748 821116 (for home delivery in the North of England)
www.farmaround.co.uk

Organic Connections, Riverdale, Town Street, Upwell, Wisbech, Cambridgeshire PE14 9AF
Tel: 01945 773374
www.organic-connections.co.uk
Home delivery nationwide.

Riverford Organic Vegetables Ltd, Wash Barn, Buckfastleigh, Devon TQ11 0LD
Tel: 0845 600 2311
www.riverford.co.uk
Home delivery in London, Midlands and the Southwest.

Solstice Home, Unit 851–2, New Covent Garden Market, Nine Elms Lane, London SW8 5EE
Tel: 020 7498 7700
www.solstice.co.uk
Home delivery nationwide.

Sunnyfields Organic, Jacobs Gutter Lane, Totton, Southampton SO40 9FX
Tel: 02380 861266
www.sunnyfields.co.uk
Home delivery in Hampshire, Dorset, Surrey and Central London.

FRUIT JUICE

The expectation, when drinking our per-capita average of 13 litres of orange juice a year, is that it does us nothing but good. The reality is that many types of fruit juice come with baggage: preservatives, diminished vitamin content and pesticide residues. Some even come with a small dose of animal protein, derived from the swim bladder of a fish. Yummy. But if you know your juices, choosing it is no problem.

What's the difference between the various types of juice?

* **Pure fruit juice** – juice that is pressed 'direct' from the fruit, or 'not from concentrate', and often labelled as such. In the case of the 'freshly squeezed' or 'pressed' juices, it may or may not be pasteurised during packing. This juice is 100 per cent juice and has the purest flavour. However, the preservative, citric acid, can be added, and salt can be added to tomato juice for flavour enhancement.
* **Juice from concentrate** – juice from fruit that has been squeezed or pressed, concentrated by evaporation of up to 50 per cent of the natural water in the juice, then pasteurised. The flavour is altered by the process, which should be indicated on the label although it is often not immediately clear.
* **Concentrated fruit juice** – where more than 50 per cent of the water has been removed; this juice is rarely sold on its own but is added to fruit juice drinks.
* **Juice drinks** – watch out for these: they're based on fruit juice but also other ingredients including sugar, sweeteners, colours and preservatives. Sunny Delight, sold in the chiller cabinet (see below), contains only 5 per cent juice, plus other ingredients not beneficial to a child's diet. Some juice drinks are carbonated.
* **Fruit 'nectar'** – a syrupy juice with added sugar.

Why are some juices sold from the chiller cabinet, others not?

Pasteurised pure fruit juice keeps for two to six weeks; 'freshly squeezed' or 'pressed' juice has a shelf life of a few days. Both must be kept in the refrigerator. But some 'juice' is sold unnecessarily from the chiller, as it gives it a 'freshly squeezed' look even when not. Long-life juices that have had more pasteurisation keep for up to nine months out of the fridge.

Is fruit juice as good for you as we are led to believe?

The vitamin content is diminished by pasteurisation, especially in long-life juice, but mineral and beta-carotene levels are left un-affected. The real problem is sugar. Fruit sugars held in the structure of whole fruit are less damaging to teeth than those released during processing (diluting juice before giving it to children is recom-mended). Pasteurisation also damages natural enzymes in juice that aid absorption into the body.

Can it contain pesticide residues?

Yes, although the Pesticide Residue Committee is satisfied with levels. Environmentalists are not, however. Residues include bupirimate (considered immunotoxic) and carbendazim (dangerous to both humans and the environment and on Friends of the Earth's 'Dirty Dozen' list).

Does our love of fruit juice benefit the environment?

No. Most UK-sold fruit juice is imported or made from imported fruit. The New Economic Foundation says 25 tonnes of materials are expended to produce and transport just one tonne of imported orange juice. The importing of fruit juice from the Americas rather than Europe significantly increases the fuel consumption—food mile aspect. Glass bottles, while less eco-friendly to produce, are easier to recycle than card packaging such as Tetra Pak. This is made from six-layer, three-material, poly-coated packaging, which takes a long time to break down in landfill sites. It is possible to recycle Tetra-Pak successfully, given the right facilities, so ask your local council about this or contact **www.drink-cartons.com**.

Who makes fruit juice – and where?

It is often hard to tell on labels, and many juices are blends of varied-quality frozen concentrate. But 80 per cent of orange juice sold in the UK is from Brazil, reported by *Ethical Consumer* magazine to have high workers' rights abuses. Their 2000 report criticised Del Monte in particular but praised Just Juice and Stute for good ethical working practice.

Can we be sure that the juice we buy is safe and non-adulterated?

No. Juice can be adulterated with enzymes (taken from animal material) that help with filtration; isinglass, a gelatine made from the swim bladders of sturgeon fish; and beef blood. 'Animal-free' juices (listed by *Vegan Shopper* magazine in 2005) include Libby's (apple, grapefruit, orange, tomato); Co-op (apple, pineapple and grapefruit); Marks & Spencer (apple, apple and mango, Florida grapefruit, Florida orange, Jaffa orange, organic apple, organic orange, pineapple, lime and passionfruit) and Safeway–Morrisons (all). Most juices contain citric acid, a safe preservative. It is also used as an 'acidity regulator', to sharpen flavour to popular taste – often to the detriment of the real fruit flavours.

Which is the healthiest juice?

The one you make yourself. Invest in a juice extractor or citrus juicer, use as many home-produced fruits as possible (or European fruits for citrus juice) and chuck the waste on the compost heap.

If the carton says a donation is made to a charity with each sale, are the contents extra good for you?

Not necessarily. While it is great for the charity to have more income, the juice inside may not be a fresh-pressed juice but rather a pasteurised juice drink with added vitamins and debatable nutrient quality.

Where to buy the most nutritious, environmentally friendly, unadulterated juice

Bensons, Stones Farm, Sherborne, Gloucestershire GL54 3DH
Tel: 01451 844134
www.bensonsapplejuice.co.uk
Hand-pressed English fruit juices, including apple and rhubarb or pear. Their three-litre bag-in-a-box is an excellent idea. Home delivery available.

Copella Fruit Juices Ltd, Hill Farm, Boxford, Sudbury, Suffolk CO10 5NY
Tel: 01787 210496
www.copellafruitjuices.co.uk
Pressed Suffolk apple juice plus good local mixes, such as apple and blackberry or apple and elderflower.

Heron Valley Cider Ltd, Crannacombe Farm, Hazelwood, Loddiswell, Kingsbridge, Devon TQ7 4DX
Tel: 01548 550256
Fresh juices from a family farm, including apple and root ginger.

Luscombe Organic Drinks, Colston Road, Buckfastleigh, Devon TQ11 0LP
Tel: 01364 643036
www.luscombe.co.uk
Fruit juices from a gorgeous Devon farm, claiming total freedom from all preservatives and acidity regulators, GMOs, animal by-products and pesticide residues.

Where to buy fairly traded juice

Chegworth Valley, Waterlane Farm, Chegworth, Harrietsham, Kent ME17 IDE
Tel: 01622 859272
www.chegworthvalley.com
Single-variety juices including a refreshing Bramley and a mellow Russett, plus interesting combinations with other home-grown fruit, including rhubarb and raspberry; and pear juice is also available. As well as selling litre bottles, Chegworth sell a useful, good-value-for-money five-litre fruit juice box – so you can have it on tap.

Fruit Passion, Gerber Foods Soft Drinks Ltd, 78 Wembdon Road, Bridgwater, Somerset TA6 7QR
Tel: 01278 441600
www.fruit-passion.com
Orange and tropical fruit juice direct from Cuba's farmers (but in conjunction with the Cuban government), who have been able to set up a mechanical workshop and plant a tree nursery with the proceeds. Available from Oxfam and from major supermarkets.

Grove Fresh Organic, Saxley Court, 121–129 Victoria Road, Horley, Surrey RH6 7AS
Tel: 01293 820832
www.grovefresh.co.uk
Fresh organic fruit and vegetable juices for the mass market.

Park Fruit Farm, Pork Lane, Great Holland, Frinton-on-Sea, Essex CO13 0ES
Tel: 01255 674621
www.parkfruitfarm.co.uk
Fresh, completely untreated, single-variety apple juice. Yeasts develop on the juice after five days as the juice begins to ferment. It's still drinkable and nutritious and can be stored in the freezer.

HERBS

It only takes a leaf or two for the varying aniseed-fruit aromas of basil, coriander, dill and tarragon to infuse a dish beautifully. Stews are lifted by a handful of chopped parsley, salads brightened by a number of herbs. Indeed, modern British cooks must wonder how food could ever have been delicious without the triangular packs that swing so invitingly on supermarket gondolas. But are herbs purely a force for good? Yes, but not without troubles – including a packaging mountain and a price tag that sets them among the industry's top-ranking rip-offs.

Why are herbs rarely sold in sizable bunches, like those you see in European markets?

Because herbs make great margins for retailers. For example, putting 10g of herbs into a plastic pack and selling it for 65 pence, as some supermarkets do, earns the supermarket a whopping £65.00 a kilo – *and we often throw away the stalks*. A larger bunch may cost less from the supermarket (80g can cost £1.60, a relatively lowly £20 per kilo) but an enormous bunch of gleaming fresh herbs from an ethnic food shop costs about 80 pence. It is clear what is going on here – so much for *'every little helps'* and *'good food costs less'*. The consumer loses out heavily with herbs and every little leaf helps the shareholders. Supermarkets would argue that herbs are perishable, but the footfall in their shops is enough to ensure that herbs are not on shelves for long.

Are herbs sprayed with chemicals?

Farmers use both pesticides and herbicides when growing herbs. Recently the retailers, fearing the consequences, have insisted that their suppliers (both in the UK and abroad) work within a protocol that is independently audited. Use of biological controls (natural pesticides) is on the increase. When tested in 2002, residues were detected in 26 out of 51 samples; residues on one sample exceeded government safety levels. Organic farmers can use a limited amount of chemical pesticides. They tend, however, barely to use them, and many use biological controls such as releasing beneficial predatory insects.

Who picks herbs?

Although only small areas are needed to grow a lot of herbs, they are labour intensive. Farmers in the UK employ immigrant labour to help and, while bad practice is a problem, again the supermarkets say their suppliers must conform to strict rules regarding their workforce. New laws to control the gangmaster element in food production are on the way, but until they are implemented and seen to be properly working you cannot be certain the herbs you eat have been grown without cruelty to people.

Are herbs environmentally friendly?

Packed herbs create a lot of unnecessary rubbish. Polytunnels are unpopular in rural areas for aesthetic reasons but when farmers heat them to extend the growing season and use lighting they are also costly on fossil fuels. Herbs destined for supermarkets are refrigerated *and* transported long distances – yet more fuel. Locally grown herbs can be bought from farmers' markets and there are a surprising number of herb farms that operate farm-gate sales.

How can I get the best value from fresh herbs?

Buy them in big bunches and wrap them in damp newspaper, then a plastic bag – they will keep in the fridge for days like this. Alternatively, buy a mature plant.

What is in herb tea?

The herbs in herb tea could have originated anywhere in the world, where pesticides and workforce issues will be uncertain. Buying Fairtrade brings peace of mind, and choosing organic with an accreditation from the Soil Association (or another British certification body) means you can trace exactly how the herbs were grown. The same advice applies to dried herbs.

Do ready-meals really contain fresh herbs?

Labelling may say 'herbs, oil', meaning that the meal can contain herb-infused vegetable oil. It is cheating, but the product is reasonably natural. Because the oil has no leafy bits in it, manufacturers may well add a few leaves for effect. Hmm.

Are dried herbs safe?

Compared to spices, which can become infested with moulds and pests (and are often treated with chemicals), yes.

What's in the supermarkets?

Depending on the time of year, herbs come into the UK mainly from Israel, Spain and France. Some Southeast Asian herbs, such as Thai basil, are air freighted to the UK, a wasteful exercise when they could be grown closer to home. These are unlikely to turn up in supermarkets. During the British season (April to November/December), the UK's prolific herb growers make up approximately 50 per cent of the supply.

The best deal from supermarkets is pot herbs, which are usually British, grown all year round, and are the most economic option in terms of waste and value. If you are a gardener, separate out the shoots (there will be dozens) and re-pot them. You will have a virtual herb farm at the end of the exercise for very little money.

All the supermarkets surveyed said they always buy British, when in season.

Where to buy fresh herbs

Many of the following suppliers sell at farmers' markets. To find the markets nearest to you, check **www.farmersmarkets.net** (tel: 0845 458 8420), or **www.lfm.org.uk** (tel: 020 7833 0338) for London. Call for dates or other stockists. If there is no local supplier listed, Jekka's Herb Farm (see page 202) does home delivery.

Arne Herbs, Limeburn Nurseries, Chew Magna,
Bristol BS40 8QW
Tel: 01275 333399
www.arneherbs.co.uk
Farmer Anthony Lyman Dixon grows a huge variety of culinary
herbs.

Eggleston Hall, Eggleston, Barnard Castle,
County Durham DL12 0AG
Tel: 01833 650553
www.egglestonhall.co.uk
Herbs from a walled garden.

Huntly Herbs, Whitestones, Gartly, Huntly,
Aberdeenshire AB54 4SB
Tel: 01466 720247
Around 150 different herbs, grown by Scottish experts.

Jekka's Herb Farm, Rose Cottage, Shellards Lane, Alveston,
Bristol BS35 3SY
Tel: 01454 418878
www.jekkasherbfarm.com
Experienced growers who can mail herb pots all over the country.

Laurel Farm Herbs, Main Road, A12 Kelsale, Saxmundham,
Suffolk IP17 2RG
Tel: 01728 668223
www.theherbfarm.co.uk
Herb plants especially packed for shipping: 'Our herb plants are
grown without heat and remain outside in the winter, so you buy a
truly hardy herb plant and all herbs are sent out to you in pots 15cm
round.'

Where to buy dried herbs

Culpeper, c/o Napiers, 35 Hamilton Place, Edinburgh EH3 5BA
Tel: 0870 950 9001
www.culpeper.co.uk
Excellent blends, including a good bouquet garni, plus single herbs.
Phone for details of shops or buy online.

Norfolk's Finest Herbs, Home Farm, Riddlesworth, Diss,
Norfolk IP22 2TD
Tel: 01953 681075
www.norfolksfinestherbs.co.uk
Eighteen types of carefully dried English herbs, plus some useful
blends, all hold their flavour and green colour in storage exceptionally
well.

Steenbergs Ltd, PO Box 48, Boroughbridge, York YO51 9ZW
Tel: 01765 640088
www.steenbergs.co.uk
New company with a reputation for fair trading (but no logo) and a
long list of pungent dried herbs.

Where to buy herb tea

Daylesford Organic Farmshop, Daylesford, Near Kingham,
Gloucestershire GL56 0YG
Tel: 01608 731700
www.daylesfordorganic.com
Daylesford has a tea bar at its farmshop in the Cotswolds, serving a
range of unusual herbal and green teas; it can also send eight of its
organic teas via home delivery.

Duchy Originals, The Old Ryde House, 393 Richmond Road,
East Twickenham TW1 2EF
Tel: 0208 538 9991
www.duchyoriginals.com
Organic, powerfully scented chamomile, peppermint and fennel tea.

Fairtrade companies producing herb tea

Clipper Tea, Beaminster Business Park, Broadwindsor Road,
Beaminster, Dorset DT8 3PR
Tel: 01308 863344
www.clipper-teas.com

Equal Exchange Trading Ltd, Suite 1, 2 Commercial Street,
Edinburgh EH6 6JA
Tel: 0131 554 5912
www.equalexchange.co.uk

HONEY

Take honey on toast for granted at your peril. One statistic says that one in three teaspoons of food we consume could not exist without bees. And bees are under threat. The wild population is at risk because of agricultural pesticides, and kept bees more so from diseases that could wipe them out. No bees, no pollination, no food plants – less food for livestock and humans. The average beekeeper is not young, and those that harvest our imported honey are chronically underpaid. Choose which honey you buy with great care.

Why is honey production important?

Honey itself makes a small contribution to the economy, about £12.5 million a year, but a government study conservatively judged the spread of pollen by kept bees to be worth £120 million to the farming economy. The same government is currently threatening to cut the spend on honey disease monitoring by inspectors – an essential service. It is an irresponsible position to take, and ministers (or prime ministers) should take steps to avoid the environmental disaster it will cause. Most beekeepers are enthusiasts who work for no profit, with honey as a by-product. They are just as much at risk as the bees, and trade associations are desperate to attract young beekeepers.

If bees are diseased, is honey safe to eat?

Yes, on the basis that the diseases that kill bees pose no risk to humans. On the other hand, bees can be treated with antibiotics to control disease and honey from these hives can contain residues. British and imported honey is checked for residues and ones that exceed safe levels should never be sold. Honey cannot be guaranteed free from residues, however. Chinese honey imports were banned for two and a half years when high levels of chloramphenicol, an antibiotic known to cause cancer in humans, were found in it. The ban was lifted in July 2004. Note, though, that honey contains natural antibiotics.

How can I tell where the honey in the jar is from?

By law, honey should be labelled with the country of origin. If blended, it should say whether it hails from inside or outside the EU.

Should I choose imported honey over British?

Choose British, as we need to support our honey industry and there are few food miles involved. Over 40 per cent of honey sold in the UK is imported and much of our honey contains blends from all over the world. Bear in mind that imported honey is much cheaper, less traceable and often not fairly traded. There is a growing market for fair-traded honeys, many of which are single variety, undergo less processing and taste delicious.

Is honey a completely natural food?

That is the impression, but honey can be processed like any other food. It can be heat treated (or pasteurised) to preserve liquidity and destroy pathogens; homogenised or filtered to remove pollen. Heat treatment also diminishes honey's natural benefits. Labels must identify filtered honey – pollen in honey is valued by hayfever sufferers. Raw honey is available (see page 208) and contains the highest levels of pollen.

Is organic honey 100 per cent pure?

There is always a risk that the bees have collected pollen from food plants that have been sprayed. The prevalence in the UK of oilseed rape crops, an especially attractive flower for bees, means the bee may travel more than the usual two kilometres to collect pollen. This concern is compounded by GM oilseed rape trials. Farmers are not obliged to warn local beekeepers of trials.

Can imported honey be contaminated with GM?

Yes, but the sale of it is banned in the UK. Without regular testing, and bearing 'bee travel' in mind, a risk remains. The effects of GM pollen on human health are unknown, hence the concern.

Should I feed honey to a baby?

The Food Standards Agency says no, because there is a risk of the infant contracting botulism.

Why are some honeys clear, some set and opaque?

It is down to the sugar content in the nectar collected by the bees; some honey is naturally set but all others, including pasteurised runny honey, will eventually set, albeit in rough crystals.

What are the health benefits of honey?

They are numerous but the most significant ones are the natural anti-bacterial elements and healing properties. Bear in mind that filtration and heat treatment reduce these. Manuka honey has the greatest 'healing' reputation. Sugars in honey are nutritionally fairly pointless, although we need to consume some sugars to survive and they may as well be those that occur naturally in food rather than refined ones.

What the supermarkets say

Tesco states that all its own-brand honey is made in England or France, despite its list including items described as 'Australian eucalyptus honey', 'Mexican honey', 'Greek honey' and 'New Zealand clover honey'. It also sells a Fairtrade Chilean honey made by Rowse.

Marks & Spencer sells a Chilean Fairtrade honey. It does not sell British-made honey.

Waitrose sells English honey and Scottish heather honey. It also sells organic honeys from New Zealand and Australia and an interesting fairly traded honey from Zambia, harvested from wild bees by local beekeepers, then packaged and shipped by Tropical Forest.

The Co-op is working on launching its first range of own-brand honey. It also sells a Fairtrade Chilean honey made by Rowse, as does **Sainsbury**.

Where and how to buy honey

Go for local – and that includes when travelling. Single variety, or honey produced within a defined geographical area, is the best choice – take a similar approach to buying good wine. Farm shops and farmers' markets are good sources of local honey. To find the markets nearest to you, check **www.farmersmarkets.net** (tel: 0845 458 8420), or **www.lfm.org.uk** (tel: 020 7833 0338) for London. For details of farm shops, look at **www.farma.org.uk.**

Cotswold Honey Ltd, Avenue Three Station Lane, Witney, Oxfordshire OX28 4HZ
Tel: 01993 703294
www.cotswoldhoney.co.uk
Fairly traded imported, English and raw honeys. Mail order available.

Duchy Originals, The Old Ryde House, 393 Richmond Road, East Twickenham TW1 2EF
Tel: 020 8831 6800
www.duchyoriginals.com
Pure organic honey from hives on the Balmoral Estate.

Equal Exchange Trading Ltd, Suite 1, 2 Commercial Street, Edinburgh EH6 6JA
Tel: 0131 554 5912
www.equalexchange.co.uk
Organic certified Fairtrade honey from Nicaragua, supporting 40 beekeepers who treat bees for disease naturally. Mail order available.

The Hive Honey Shop, 93 Northcote Road, London SW11 6PL
Tel: 020 7924 6233
www.thehivehoneyshop.co.uk
Extraordinary range of honeys, including a good Manuka with a high index of medicinal properties, plus other bee produce. The shop also sells a local honey collected in Wandsworth and another London honey from beehives in Hampstead. The diversity of the flowers grown in the capital's gardens and roof terraces lends an especially interesting flavour to these honeys. Mail order available.

Maison du Miel, 74 rue Vignon, 75009 Paris
Tel: 0033 1 47 42 26 70
www.maisondumiel.com
France's finest honey shop, with a huge range of single-flower honeys and very special AOC Corsican honey. Worth a visit.

Quince Honey Farm, North Road, South Molton,
Devon EX36 3AZ
Tel: 01769 572401
www.quincehoney.co.uk
Family-run honey farm founded in 1949, which operates 1,500 hives over 2,500 square miles of Devonshire hills and moors. The Exmoor heather honey is especially good.

Rowse Honey, Moreton Avenue, Wallingford,
Oxfordshire OX10 9DE
Tel: 01491 827400
www.rowsehoney.co.uk
Organic honey from Australia and New Zealand and Fairtrade honey from Chile.

ICE CREAM

One of the first jobs carried out by the young scientist, Margaret Thatcher, was to discover ways to 'inflate' ice cream with air and boost its value – to some a neat analogy for later activities. Now there are new reasons to beg for a countrywide revival of ice cream, with poorly paid dairy farmers in desperate need of fresh ways to add value to their milk. Novice farmhouse ice-cream makers have brought gastronomy back to ice cream, and are well worth seeking out – not because they need encouragement but in order to shove the frozen whipped palm oil that poses as ice cream out of the marketplace. Ice-cream wars – commence!

Is all ice cream made from dairy cream?

No. Manufacturers of commercial ice creams use vegetable fat. In pots labelled 'ice cream', any fat that is not dairy cream or milk can simply be listed as 'vegetable fat'. The problem is that manufacturers go for cheap fats such as palm kernel oil, which may sound exotically healthy but is highly saturated and not environmentally friendly. This is the most common fat used in the whipped ice cream sold out of vans.

What's in 'dairy ice cream'?

All the fat used in dairy ice cream must be dairy fat, milk or cream derived from cows. This may mean just milk powder. The label need not specify cream, but if there is any in there the manufacturer will most likely boast about it. Eggs may be added to traditional mixes to emulsify them but commercial ice cream will contain cheaper glycerides made from partially hydrogenated fat. There are serious health issues connected with hydrogenated fat (see Butter and Spreads, page 99) and, while dairy cream is not exactly a slimmer's meal, it is an altogether more natural product. Ice cream made with ewe's, goat's or buffalo milk will always be labelled as such.

What else is in ice cream?

All other ingredients in ice cream must be listed. Watch out for colourings, especially chemical reds and oranges, which can have adverse effects on children. Beetroot-derived reds are okay. Cane sugar is preferable to refined beet sugar, as it is marginally more nutritious and environmentally friendly, but starches are a problem for the gluten allergic. Emulsifiers are added to help 'fix' the fat and water content, while stabilisers are added to preserve it. Polysaccharide stabilisers thicken the water in the milk and stop the formation of ice crystals. These are the additives that make some ice creams disgustingly chewy. Gelatine is a more natural alternative but because it is animal based, makers prefer to use plant-based gums, such as guar gum. Carageenan, a seaweed thickener, is the best natural alternative. Some ice creams contain starch fillers, such as modified maize starch – cheap, tasteless bulk that makes more profit for manufacturers than it benefits the consumer.

Last but not least, there will be a good amount of air in ice cream, whipped in for bulk.

Is ice cream safe to eat?

With very few exceptions all the dairy fats in ice cream are pasteurised, killing bacteria, harmful or not. Do not, however, refreeze and eat ice cream that has melted, as it could be contaminated with bacteria.

What's so good about artisan ice creams, apart from the taste?

Buy British ice creams, made locally with whole milk and cream from British dairy farms and you will do much to boost the beleaguered dairy business – and they are utterly, utterly delicious.

Where to buy ice cream

Most large supermarkets stock some good-quality ice creams such as the ones listed below. Read the label, looking for 100 per cent natural ingredients, but expect to pay more. It must be said, however, that solid, traditionally made ice creams without the Thatcher 'air legacy' are good value.

Hill Station, Stanier Road, Calne, Wiltshire SN11 9PX
Tel: 01249 816596
www.hillstation.co.uk
Not too sweet, exotic flavours including mango and lime, coconut, cinnamon and coffee.

Kelly's Cornish, Lucknow Road, Walker Lines Industrial Estate, Cornwall PL31 1EZ
Tel: 01208 77277
Made in Bodmin with whole milk and cream or clotted cream from a local farm, combined with real fruit and sauces.

Rocombe Farm Fresh Ice Cream Ltd, The Mendip Centre, Rhodyate, Blagdon, Nr Bristol BS40 7YE
Tel: 01761 462798
www.rocombe.com
Another in the family of newly sophisticated ice-cream makers, Rocombe, which used to produce ices more along the jolly lines of raspberry ripple and chocolate, now makes after-dinner 'Editions', including Far Eastern Stem Ginger, Rich Pralines and Columbian Coffee. Never mind.

Home-delivered ice cream
We found only one:

September Organic, Unit 5, Whitehill Park, Weobley, Herefordshire HR4 8QE
Tel: 01544 312910
www.september-organic.co.uk
Elderflower cream, apple crumble and brown bread are among the flavours made by this imaginative dairy, unique in its ability to sell direct via mail order.

Small-scale ice-cream makers worth seeking out

Cornish Legend, 1 Rundle Court, Station Road, Liskeard, Cornwall PL14 4DA
Tel: 01579 345777
www.cornishlegend.co.uk
Prize-winning organic, naturally flavoured ice cream made in Liskeard.

Hadley's Dairy Products Ltd, Home Farm, Colne Engaine, Essex CO6 2HU
Tel: 01787 220420
True artisan ice cream made by Jane Hadley, with milk from cows reared to exceptionally high welfare standards. The ice cream is flavoured with fresh fruit, Valhrona chocolate, real vanilla and honeycomb. The Farmer Bill brand was created specially for children.

LaBelleRouge, Ty Mawr, Llanon, Aberystwyth SY23 5LZ
Tel: 01974 202906
www.labellerouge.com
An unusual, ripe-flavoured ice cream made with fresh Welsh water buffalo milk, egg yolks, sugar and a pinch of salt. The company, which also makes mozzarella, is proud of the simplicity of this ice cream, which is delicious eaten simply with honey and almonds or hazelnuts.

Shepherds Ice Cream, Cwm Farm, Peterchurch, Hereford HR2 0TA
Tel: 01497 821898
Hand-made sheep's milk ice cream flavoured with blackberries, damsons and tayberries. Look out for it at festivals, such as Glastonbury, the Big Chill, the Larmer Tree and Hay-on-Wye literary festival, or buy from the farm's own ice-cream parlour in Hay-on-Wye.

LAMB

Lamb has flavour, shock horror. This is a recent revelation as mutton and meat from older lambs have finally entered the consciousness of British meat eaters. For a long time it seemed only that British lamb was tenderly sweet and pale, then, when stocks ran low, in came New Zealand lamb – tenderly sweet and, yes, pale. My, how boring – it's the perpetual spring lamb. Genetic modification couldn't come up with one this good. And all the while that 100,000 tonnes of NZ lamb was coming into ports, it passed boats crammed with live sheep from the UK going on hellish journeys to southern Europe – 50,000 head of them a year. Only these were the interesting ones: tasty, slightly older lambs with the flavours of wild grasses from fell, dale and highlands. Destination slow cooking, with garlic, tomatoes and wild marjoram. Meanwhile, we chomped through another plate of bland ... pale ... tender – you got it. If one good thing came out of the foot and mouth epidemic of 2001, it was the shrill wake-up call that told of this crazy swap, and manic transportation scandal.

So what kind of lamb is in season, when?

* **March–April** – spring lambs, young and newly weaned. These are the lambs born around Christmas. Most are specially bred for this season and the practice of getting them up to this weight for spring is fairly unnatural. Many are reared indoors and are fed concentrates, which pushes their weight up quickly.
* **May–July** – British lamb will still be in shops, larger lambs born in early spring who have fed on the new grass. This is fine-tasting young lamb, often superior to 'spring' lamb and cheaper, too. June and July are also the season for salt marsh lamb – interesting, stronger-flavoured meat with a herby taste, from smaller hill and moorland lambs, brought down to the salt marshes to graze.
* **August–October** – hogget (or shearling). These are lambs (usually hill breeds) that have reached a year old or more; their meat is

stronger flavoured and delicious. Light lamb – so called because the animals are smaller – is also in season. These are hill lambs, normally destined for southern Europe, and they have bags of taste, though less meat on the bone. They can be bought by mail order direct from farms. Two reasons to eat light lamb: by selling direct to you, the hill farmers get a much-needed better price; and the sheep will not have to suffer long journeys across Europe in trucks.

✤ **November–spring** – New Zealand lamb arrives. It's nice stuff, and I am glad the sensible New Zealand farmers, who never receive subsidies, have an outlet. But in the modern world, with climate change put down to excessive oil use, there is no getting away from the fact that this shipped-in lamb has a food-mile sickness.

What is mutton?
Mutton is from sheep that are slaughtered at over two years old. You may be offered wether, which is the same thing – a castrated sheep more than two years old. Older sheep have more flavour and, although a really aged animal will need a lot of slow cooking in order to be tender, most mutton animals produce beautiful tender meat.

Is lamb farmed intensively?
Apart from those rushed to muscle up for the Easter season, most lamb is farmed relatively naturally, fed mainly on a grass diet whose flavour is reflected in the meat. Concentrated feeds can be given, which will be based on soya and could be genetically modified. It must be said, however, that most farmers would prefer to avoid the expense.

Do sheep have stressful lives?
The worst aspect of a sheep's life is transport. They are moved often, from grazing areas to farm, along motorways care of agents, and stopping at livestock markets where more are added to the truck. Finally to the abattoir. Long-distance transport raises stress levels. The livestock markets are losing out to the supermarkets, however, who are

tending to buy direct from farms. This, in spite of the loss of tradition, is something of a relief.

How long should lamb or mutton be hung for?

All lamb and especially mutton should be matured on the bone for two to three weeks to develop flavour and tenderness. You can always tell poorly hung lamb by the way you have to saw at the meat of a relatively young animal when carving. Sadly, most supermarket-sold lamb, while often naturally reared, is poorly hung.

Is organic lamb superior to conventional?

A high-grade conventional lamb is as good a choice as organic; choosing organic in the case of lamb is more about the environment. It is good to know, for example, that the animal was fed a GM-free diet and grazed on land that is not treated with chemicals. This is not to say that all conventional lamb is; hill farmers in particular rear lambs on untreated land and are not 'organic' simply because they cannot afford the cost of going organic (i.e. certification and three years of conversion).

What the supermarkets say

Waitrose sources lambs from Welsh upland and mountain farms and from mountain breeds. It does not sell mutton, as all its lamb is under a year old. It sells New Zealand lamb in the winter only. All its British lambs are reared outdoors and fed predominantly on grass, which is sometimes supplemented (when grass is less abundant or not a consistent quality) with forage-based supplementary feeds (e.g. hay, silage, grain). Growth promoters and fishmeal are prohibited.

Marks & Spencer sells UK-reared lamb from June to December; it sells New Zealand lamb in winter but for some of that time there is also Brecknock Welsh lamb available, sourced from 45 farms in the Brecon Beacons. It also sells salt marsh lamb between June and October. Animals are approximately nine months old when slaughtered.

Tesco does not sell light lamb, mountain lamb or mutton. Its British lamb is sourced from suppliers all over the UK and it sells regional lamb products in Northern Ireland, Wales, Scotland and the Southwest. The lambs are generally reared outside, with some exceptions during the winter months. Their diet can include grass, silage, cereal and turnips. Tesco sells New Zealand lamb all year round.

The Co-op sells Welsh hill lambs as well as standard lamb, and New Zealand lamb between January and May. It sells an own-brand mince that contains a proportion of mutton. All its British lamb is outdoor reared and fed grass and some concentrates. Ewes are occasionally given fishmeal during pregnancy.

Sainsbury does not sell hill or light lamb but it does put mutton in some mince. It sells New Zealand lamb between January and June. Its British lamb is reared mainly outdoors, although some animals will have been born indoors and housed indoors during inclement weather.

Budgens does not sell light lamb or mutton. Its British lamb is sourced from Cumbria, Northumbria, Lancashire and Yorkshire. The lambs are reared part indoors, part outdoors and are fed on a mixture of grass and cereals. Budgens also sells New Zealand lamb.

Where to buy naturally reared lamb and mutton

All types of sheep meat are most economically bought in boxes containing a half or whole lamb in several cuts, ready to store in the freezer, although some farmers will send individual cuts. All the producers listed below do home delivery unless otherwise stated.

Blackface.co.uk, Weatherall Foods Ltd, Crochmore House, Irongray, Dumfries DG2 9SF
Tel: 01387 730326
www.blackface.co.uk
The self-sufficient Scottish Blackface ewes lamb in late April out on the Scottish hills, then stay with their lambs until the last week of August, grazing the heather, blaeberries, mosses and grasses that contribute to the delicious flavour of the meat. Two-year-old wether and five-year-old ewe mutton also available.

Borrowdale Herdwick, Rosthwaite, Borrowdale, Cumbria CA12 6XB
Tel: 01768 777675
www.borrowdaleherdwick.co.uk
Meat from these sheep, native to the fells, is darker and more flavoursome than any other. The fat is yellowish but pleasant and has a high omega-3 content. The meat arrives in a good-looking box, insulated with Herdwick wool which the farm advises stuffing into your gumboots to keep your feet warm!

Fornside Farm, St John's in the Vale, Keswick, Cumbria CA12 4TS
Tel: 017687 79173
www.fornside.co.uk
Robert and Pam Hall rear Herdwick sheep, the traditional hefting breed (meaning they stay in an area though unfenced) with its blue-grey wool from the Lake District. Sweet, very full-flavoured meat.

Hazel Brow Farm, Low Row, Richmond, North Yorkshire DL11 6NE
Tel: 01758 886224
www.hazelbrow.co.uk
Swaledale lamb grazed on a unique farm in the Pennine Dales, whose 93 hectares of grassland is divided into 94 fields by 15km dry stone walls. The Calvert family farms totally naturally, producing all silage and hay for their livestock on the farm.

Holker Food Hall, Cark-in-Cartmel, Nr Grange-over-Sands,
Cumbria LA11 7PL
Tel: 015395 58328
www.holker-hall.co.uk
Wonderful salt marsh lamb that grazes on Morecambe Bay. The
supply begins in June or July. No mail order.

North Highland Fine Lamb, Midfearn, Ardgay,
Sutherland IV24 3DL
Tel: 01863 766505
www.finelamb.co.uk
Chas Brooke farms in Sutherland, northern Scotland. He puts the
denser texture and aromatic flavour of his lamb down to the region's
climate and vegetation – and it has earned its place on Jeremy Lee's
menu at the Blueprint Café in London and Michel Roux's at Le
Gavroche.

Sheepdrove Organic Farm, Warren Farm, Lambourn,
Berkshire RG17 7UU
Tel: 01488 71659
www.sheepdrove.com
Lamb and mutton from Peter Kindersley's exemplary organic farm
on the Wiltshire Downs. The sheep are from predominantly Shetland
stock, and the farm, which has its own scientific research centre for
organic farming, pays special attention to animal health and welfare
and the related benefits of their modern organic system.

Snowdonia Lamb, Rhiw, Llanbedr, Gwynedd LL45 2NT
Tel: 01341 241469
www.snowdonialamb.f9.co.uk
Brian MacDonald runs a co-operative of nine farms within the
Snowdonia National Park, specialising in meat from Welsh mountain
sheep. On the menu at the River Café in London last year, this dark-
coloured lamb has a rich flavour that the farmers attribute to the
mountain-maritime environment of North Wales. Organic meat
available.

The Thoroughly Wild Meat Company, Bratton House,
Bratton Seymour, Wincanton, Somerset BA9 8DA
Tel: 01963 824788/07770 392041
www.thoroughlywildmeat.co.uk
Somerset salt marsh lamb prepared locally and hung for at least seven days before being cut.

Traditional Devonshire Meats, Locks Park Farm, Hatherleigh,
Okehampton, Devon EX20 3LZ
Tel: 01837 810416
www.traditionaldevonmeats.co.uk
Paula Wolton's flock of hardy Whiteface Dartmoor sheep thrive on high grassland in Devon, yielding beautifully juicy meat known locally as 'angel meat' because of its special flavour.

Welsh Organic Aran Lamb, Maldwyn and Margaret Thomas,
Cwmonnen, Llanuwchllyn, Bala, Gwynedd LL23 7UG
Tel: 01678 540603
www.aran-lamb.co.uk
The Thomases are fiercely and proudly Welsh, and passionate about lamb, as the farm's eccentric website demonstrates. These are lambs grazed on the Aran Mountain, certified by the Organic Centre Wales.

LARD AND DRIPPING

Use lard in pastry and it promises to be endlessly crisp. Spread dripping on toast, top it with cress and have a filling little meal. Both fats produce fabulous roast potatoes, and it was once the norm to cook chips in animal, not vegetable, fats. In spite of the high vitamin content, our doctors don't approve, because these are saturated fats. But a little at a time is a pleasure, and at least these fats do not go through the horrendous refining process that diminishes the goodness of most vegetable oils – indeed, makes them potentially harmful.

What is lard?

Lard must be pork fat or it cannot be labelled as such. The fat is heated, which reduces most of it to a liquid. This is then filtered and cooled, leaving a white, naturally hard fat with a high melting point. Because it undergoes no further deodorising, lard retains a porky taste, which is great for cooking. Unlike many spreads and margarines, the lard you find in shops is not hydrogenated (see page 68) but do read the label, just in case. Lard keeps in the fridge for up to 12 months.

How harmful are animal fats?

Animal fat is saturated and health experts recommend we limit the amount we consume. But animal fats have many good, rarely mentioned properties, and there is controversial evidence that the good in them may outweigh the bad. First of all they are a whole, natural food. Lard, dripping and also dairy fat (see Butter and Spreads, page 99) are antiviral and antibacterial, and they can play a part in fending off disease, including cancer. The palmitic and stearic fatty acids in meat fats are important for energy metabolism and normal growth. The conjugated linoleic acids (CLA) actually help *reduce* body fat. Meat fats contain a good balance of omega-3 and omega-6, although in small quantities. They contain naturally occurring transfats.

What are transfats?

Transfats occur naturally in animal fat but are *made* when other (vegetable) fats are refined or hydrogenated (hardening fat using a chemical process to lower the melting point). Transfats in vegetable oil raise cholesterol, reduce the nutritional value of breast milk and are linked with low birth weight. They reduce the immune response, affect fertility, disrupt enzymes that metabolise chemical carcinogens and drugs, and increase the formation of free radicals that cause tissue damage. They also raise blood insulin, a factor in the development of diabetes.

Transfats in animal fats, however, are naturally occurring and do not share the harmful properties of synthetically produced transfats in hydrogenated fat such as margarine. The World Health Organisation (WHO) recommends that we reduce our intake of both trans and saturated fat. The US Department of Agriculture estimates that transfats found naturally in meat, milk and other dairy produce constitute 15–20 per cent of our total transfat intake, while other nutrition experts claim natural transfats are consumed at much lower levels.

Is there anything else in lard?

Because the melting point has not been raised higher by hydrogenation, the antioxidant, E321, is often added to commercial lard to prevent it becoming rancid. Rancidity gives lard a cheesy, unpleasant smell, which lingers in food that has been cooked with it. E321 is a synthetic preservative, also known as butylated hydroxytoluene (BHT), and is due to be restricted in the EU over the next few years. Taken in large doses, it has been found to cause liver damage, and in some people, migraine.

Where does lard come from?

Most of the lard you see wrapped in white paper in chiller cabinets hails from the slaughterhouses of Denmark, Holland and Belgium. Animal welfare standards are much lower in these countries – for example, stalls and tethers and routine tail docking are still legal practice. Although such practices are banned in the UK, up to 70 per cent of our pigs are still indoor-reared (see Bacon (and Pork), page 48). Lard from free-range pigs is a rare commodity, but very easy to make yourself if you buy pork fat from a butcher you trust and melt it at home. Equally it makes great economic sense to strain and keep the fat from slow roasts like pork belly, store it, then cook with it later.

Is the lard in processed foods the same as that on the shelf?

No – it is often further refined to remove the residual pork taste so it can be added to foods without affecting their flavour.

What is dripping?

Like lard, dripping is simply fat that is rendered from slow-cooked meat. Commercial beef dripping, sold in a paper wrapper, is usually a buff colour with a very high melting point and will be rock solid when taken from the fridge. When made at home from a fabulously fat joint of traditionally reared beef, then cooled, dripping will have a delicious layer of jelly underneath. Sadly this is not the case with most bought drippings.

Is beef dripping safe to eat?

In terms of BSE, beef dripping comes under the same rules as beef, and may not enter the food chain unless it can be traced back to the farm. That is not to say illegal dripping does not slip through the net. In 2004 the Food Standards Agency ordered a sale withdrawal of Nortech 'Finest Beef Dripping' when it was discovered to contain material that was not fit for human consumption. It is unlikely to have posed a risk to human health, but when you buy any meat or related product it is better to know where it has come from. Saving dripping from Sunday roasts is the best possible source.

Is there such a thing as vegetarian lard?

Yes, Trex, made by Pura Foods, is a 'vegetable shortening'. It may be all vegetable oil but it is refined and contains the dreaded hydrogenated oil. Flora makes one, too, using interesterified fat, mainly rapeseed and palm oil (see Butters and Spreads, page 99).

Is suet the same as dripping?

Suet should be grated beef fat, and non-rendered, therefore not heat treated, but all commercial suet has added hydrogenated fat. Vegetable 'suet' is also based on hydrogenated fat. The best source of suet is your local butcher. Ask for beef fat and grate it yourself. It will be a small amount of trouble for the best dumplings on the planet.

How are duck and goose fat made, and can I use them in the same way as lard and dripping?

Duck and goose fat are made by slowly rendering the fat from the duck or goose skin, then straining it. It is a traditional product of Southwest France, where it is used to make confit, or preserved meat. It is also used in cassoulet. It makes roast potatoes with the loudest crunch, but it is not so suitable for pastry. Do experiment, however, with adding it to savoury breads.

If hydrogenated vegetable fats are preferred by manufacturers for making pastry etc, does that mean there is a shortage of meat fat?

No! Too much fat is wasted, taken to rendering plants – and the butcher or cutting plant has to pay for this service. Manufacturers add hydrogenated fat to products because it gives them a longer shelf life. You will be doing your butcher a favour financially if you ask him for fat, and it will reduce traffic on the roads and fuel oil consumption. What is more, you can buy – at what should be a very low price – pork fat from naturally reared livestock. You do not have to render it, but place a piece in the roast potato tin and it will render to cook them beautifully. Some butchers sell their own ready-made dripping and lard.

What the supermarkets say

Few were forthcoming on the subject but the **Co-op** told us its lard derives from Belgian pigs.

Where to buy British welfare-friendly lard and dripping

The Real Meat Company, 10 Silver Street, Bradford on Avon, Wiltshire BA15 1JY
www.realmeatco.sageweb.co.uk
Tel: 01225 309385
Butcher Paul McEvoy will supply British lard to order. Home delivery available.

Where to buy goose and duck fat

Goose and duck fat are available from specialist food shops and delicatessens. Catusse Grasse d'oie goose fat is available from Waitrose.

Lard as an art form

In Italy lard has escaped the disapproval of health officials and is celebrated, not denigrated. Cured in salt, flavoured with herbs or creamed with truffles, it is best eaten melted over the hottest toast.

Savoria, 229 Linen Hall – CKp, 162–168 Regent Street, London W1B 5TB
Tel: 0870 242 1823
www.savoria.co.uk
Four fabulous lard treats, including creamed with truffles; home delivery available.

LETTUCE AND SALAD LEAVES

With the forever-summer availability of lettuce and bagged salads, everyone except kitchen gardeners forgets there is a British season for edible leaves. Before the imports began to flood in, you would hardly see an outdoor-grown lettuce on a table between October and April. But the evolution of salad has had its significant moments. The popularity of Iceberg in the 1970s, a salad with a loud crunch but little flavour. Frisée was the only leaf to be seen eating in the 1980s. Then, in 1992 came the bagged salad. A few small leaves, cunningly packed in modified-gas-filled, acetate pillows. Ruinously expensive, and disinfected with water 25 times more chlorinated than that in the local Lido. Remove the chlorine, say the salad magnates, and you'll get a dose of food poisoning. Once we questioned whether eating lettuce was worth the calories burned to do so; now we wonder if we should eat this once-great symbol of good nutrition at all.

What's good about lettuce and baby leaf salad?
There's little energy value. You would have to eat a kilo – that's about a carrier bagful – to get 130 calories. What's more, the phytochemicals found in all lettuce contain a mild sedative, so crunching through a kilo may not make you feel like a jog round the park. Mature lettuce has greater nutritional value than baby leaves, and the greener and more fibrous your leaves the more vitamins and fibre they contain.

What chemical residues can be found on lettuce and leaves?

❈ **Nitrate fertilisers** – green leafy vegetables contain a lot of nitrates, both naturally but also from nitrate fertilisers. There is a theoretical link between ingesting high levels of nitrate in vegetables that have been sprayed and stomach cancer; in the meantime a study backed by the Food Standards Agency claims that high levels of nitric oxide in the body act as anti-microbactcrial agents, so perhaps they are not so bad for you after all. On both questions, the jury remains out. The EU and UK authorities say our daily dietary intake of nitrates should be limited to 219mg – how we are expected to measure this is a mystery.

❖ **Pesticide residues** – higher levels of pesticides are sprayed on to field-grown lettuce than any other vegetable crop, averaging over 11 applications of spray each year. Residues of inorganic bromide, a potentially ozone-depleting chemical, and iprodione, a potential carcinogen, have been found on British-sold lettuce. In 2004 the Pesticides Residues Committee found that 23 out of 73 samples tested contained residues. Out of these, nine had multiple residues but the government agency says levels were not high enough to affect human health. Pesticide residue watchdogs believe the rules regarding pesticide usage are frequently broken, and maximum residue levels are set too high.

Where will my lettuce or bag of leaves come from?

In our season – April to November – there should be British salad in every supermarket and greengrocer's but you will see a lot of whole lettuces from Spain and leaves from Holland, France and Italy, where they can be grown outside – a cheaper method, lowering the price of lettuce, that the retailers favour. Be wary of imports on the basis that pesticide applications are less easy for our retailers to monitor, and they may be heavily disinfected so they can survive long-distance transportation and shelf-life requirements at their destination.

It is also good to try to buy vegetables from a source that boasts ethical trading standards, since scandalous stories about poor treatment of pickers and packers have emerged. Of the supermarkets, Waitrose holds the highest reputation for ethical treatment of workers, with Marks & Spencer a close second

If salad leaves are already washed, should I wash them again?

It's better to wash all lettuce and leaves, then dry them in a salad spinner. But be warned that bagged leaves have already been washed with water chlorine disinfectant and may become soggy if you wash them again. Fresher leaves should survive a wash and spin in the salad spinner. The heavy use of chlorine is extremely controversial. Not only does it remove flavour but it has been linked to birth defects. *The Ecologist* magazine reported that levels of around 50mg (but occasionally up to 100mg) of chlorine are used to one litre of water (2mg of chlorine per litre of swimming-pool water is the norm). Manufacturers claim that they are under pressure from retailers to produce totally pathogen-free leaves. Overall it is safer to eat whole mature lettuce than bags of loose leaves, because the outside leaves will have taken the brunt of most of the spray and can be removed.

Is organic a better option?

Yes, but be aware that organic growers are permitted to use a limited range of six pesticides. Virtually all strive to manage without, using natural predators and 'beetle banks' to attack other pests and spraying with fatty acids to kill aphids. They fertilise naturally, sometimes adding seaweed nutrients to the soil. They say rotating a variety of plant species removes the 'monoculture' element of lettuce farming.

How can I buy a wider variety of salad leaves?

Demanding variety will go a long way to ensuring that retailers encourage farmers to grow something other than Iceberg and Cos. Among the edible leaves on offer, seek out red purslane, Italian red dandelion, red amaranth, gold mustard, mizuna, red orach, tatsoi, Chinese water pepper, salad burnet, burdock and takinogawa.

It is very easy to grow your own baby leaves in windowsill pots or growbags. Cut and use the larger leaves and they will keep coming. Some will even grow in winter, under fleece.

What the supermarkets say

The Co-op sources its lettuces from the UK, Spain and France, although it states it uses British crops when in season. There is no organic supply of lettuce at the Co-op.

Marks & Spencer imports its lettuces and leaves from Europe, America and Africa but states that it has a defined British season from April to November. It sells a range of organic lettuce leaves.

Sainsbury buys its lettuce from the UK and Spain, and its bagged leaves are sourced from Kenya and Portugal. It uses spring water rather than chlorinated to wash its salad. It also sells an organic variety.

Budgens states that its lettuces are transported via lorry from 'more than one country'. It stocks British when in season. It does sell an organic variety but it is more expensive, as this lettuce is apparently harder to grow.

Tesco sources its lettuce from various European countries as well as the UK and America. It stocks an organic supply, too.

Supermarkets selling the 'cleanest' leaves

Waitrose washes its conventional salad leaves using water and chlorine but rinses them twice in tap water afterwards to remove residues. Its organic leaves are washed in a solution of water and fruit acid.

Where to find British organic lettuce and salad leaves

During the season, farmers' markets will often feature growers who sell organic leaves and lettuce. To find the markets nearest to you, check **www.farmersmarkets.net** (tel: 0845 458 8420), or **www.lfm.org.uk** (tel: 020 7833 0338) for London. Or check **www.farma.org.uk** or **www.bigbarn.co.uk** for details of your nearest farm shop selling produce.

Home delivery

Local vegetable box schemes will send a selection of vegetables to your door and many specialise in salad leaves.

Secretts, Hurst Farm, Chapel Lane, Milford, Godalming, Surrey GU8 5HU
Tel: 01483 520529
www.secretts.co.uk
Will send beautiful leaves anywhere in the country, packed in a polystyrene box to keep them crisp.

Where to buy lettuce and salad leaf seeds

Future Foods, Luckleigh Cottage, Hockworthy, Wellington, Somerset TA21 0NN
Tel: 01398 361347
A wide variety of rare edible leaf seeds to grow in pots yourself. Mail order available.

Nicky's Nursery, 33 Fairfield Road, Broadstairs, Kent CT10 2JU
Tel: 01843 600 972
www.nickys-nursery.co.uk
Specialist in oriental leaves. Mail order available.

LONG GRAIN RICE

Along with risotto rice, specialist long grain varieties of rice such as basmati have boomed in the UK over the last decade. We now import 175,000 tonnes of fragrant basmati grains a year, mostly from Southern Asia, but it is still the case that 96 per cent of the world's long grain rice harvest is eaten in the countries where it was grown. The current generation has never known a supermarket shelf without basmati but 20 years ago it was a very exotic ingredient indeed; for anyone who had not tapped into the traditional Asian community shops, only the very slightly fragrant American long grain rice was widely available. The issue now is to protect the traditional breeds of rice, and their growers. Many countries can grow long grain, and some would like to use high-tech farming methods to grow more, which could ease the traditional rice growers out of the trade. With rice, the global market has the potential to be very brutal.

What is the difference between the various types of long grain rice?

Breed is the main difference. The two best-known types sold in the UK are basmati and American long grain. Basmati, which originated from the grasses growing close to the Himalayas, is very fragrant and keeps its scent and flavour during cooking. The rice grain is very long, and the genuine type lengthens further to a needle shape when cooked; if you look closely you will see the surface also has a ridged appearance. Basmati is now grown mainly in India but also in Pakistan.

American long grain rice is starchy and less flavoursome. Geologists believe that American rice originated in Africa, more specifically in Madagascar, and was brought to Carolina with the slaves, who taught US farmers how to grow and mill it. Long grain rice is also grown in Africa, Southeast Asia and South America – basically anywhere warm where there is water.

How is rice grown?

The juxtaposition between the methods of growing the two main types of long grain rice sold in the UK is interesting:

* **Asia** – the rice seedlings are grown in a 'nursery'. Meanwhile, the paddy fields are ploughed by water buffalo 'power' and fertilised with muck, then logs are dragged across the fields' surface to smooth it ready for planting. The paddy fields are flooded with river and rain water before the seedlings are planted by hand. The rice crop is harvested and threshed (the grain separated from the stem) by hand once the water has been drained from the fields.
* **North America** – highly specialised equipment, including lasers and computers, is used in rice farming. Irrigation is artificial, as there is no reliance on the seasonal rains. Land 'planes' level the land with heavy equipment employed to create even fields that slope gently, so that the paddy will flood in a uniform manner. Laser guidance systems decide the position of the water control levees. The seed is drilled direct into the soil, or cast over dry or flooded fields by aeroplane. Fresh water is pumped from deep wells, nearby rivers, canals or reservoirs to maintain the water depth during the growing season. Fertilisers are applied from the air and combines are used for the harvest.

Which is the most environmentally friendly rice?

It barely needs saying but the Western method uses a lot more fuel oil. Urea is sometimes used as a herbicide on basmati crops but Asian farmers generally use few chemicals because they are too expensive. In both nations, flooding also prevents weed growth and keeps certain pests away; in India snakes and amphibians, attracted by the flood-water, act as a natural pesticide.

What happens after harvest?

The rice is threshed, then the husk is completely removed, leaving behind the bran. At this stage the rice is called 'brown'. To produce white rice, the grains are put through a mill and polished until the bran is removed. This final stage is much the same for Western- and Eastern-grown rice. Much Eastern-grown rice destined for the UK market is milled in the UK, close to the ports where the rice ships dock. This is because there is a trade levy on fully milled basmati rice. Milling it in the UK is better for our economy, if not so good for the Indian rice trade.

Why is some rice parboiled?

The US brand, Uncle Ben's, is always parboiled before packing, and there is an alternative parboiled basmati. Parboiled rice is suitable for dishes such as biryani, where the rice needs to remain firm.

Are there pesticide residues on rice?

Yes, although not so much crop spray as residues from fumigants that are used to kill burrowing rodents and weevils in cargoes or warehouses. When rice was last tested by the Pesticide Residues Committee in 2000, hydrogen phosphide residues were found on 39 out of 72 samples. Residues of inorganic bromide, an ozone-depleting chemical also used to fumigate rice, have been found, too. The PRC did not assess the levels they had found to be dangerous.

Is it true that not all basmati on sale is pure?

Yes, and the problem is such that five years ago the Food Standards Agency encouraged the industry to act. It has done, and Tilda, the UK's biggest supplier, takes samples for DNA testing from every sack of rice. If the rice does not match one of the 20 recognised basmati breeds, the farmer must take it back. The reason for all this fuss is economics. Basmati is a slow-growing rice, the Gloucester Old Spot pig of the rice world. It costs a lot to grow and sells for a premium in the West (the UK, US, Middle East and northern Europe). It is barely eaten in India, except by those who can afford it, so it's a cash crop, originally grown for the benefit of ex-pat Indian and Pakistan communities, but now for a wider audience of addicted curry lovers. So the more unscrupulous rice packers were popping in up to 40 per cent of cheap, swift-growing long grains but still selling them at the premium price.

Can I tell by reading the label if the rice is pure?

A pack labelled basmati can contain up to 7 per cent of another rice – any more and it must state that it is a blend. If it contains more than 97 per cent basmati, the country of origin will be stated on the pack – either 'produce of India' or 'produce of Pakistan.' There are recognisable good brands, such as Tilda.

The basmati in the pack looks damaged – why?

It is just a lower-grade rice. Budget basmati will contain 10–20 per cent broken grains, but more than 20 per cent broken grains and the rice must be called 'basmati and broken grains'. If you have access to traditional Asian shops or supermarkets you can buy broken grains, which are used to make traditional Asian rice puddings.

Is rice fairly traded?

Rice is traded on the world commodity market, so growers are vulnerable to price fluctuation. In the case of basmati, recognised brands such as Tilda in India have very good relations with farmers, who by law must sell their rice at auction and not direct to the millers (compare this to the workers' stories in the tea business, page 399). At the *mandi* (the market), farmers can turn down the price set at auction and demand a second one later in the day just so they can get more money. But not all Asian or Western-grown long grain rice is fairly traded, and you should be wary when little information is offered, especially with supermarket own-brand rice.

Small communities of growers can be damaged in the global 'free' market. Haiti, one of the world's poorest countries, was once almost self sufficient in rice. Within ten years of opening its economy, the country was dependent on imports, leaving large numbers of poor at the whim of rising grain prices.

Should I be loyal to Eastern or Western rice?

Both have a role in our diets but there is no doubt that basmati is the 'gourmet' rice, thanks to its light, needle-shaped grains and aromatic flavour. Its low-tech production is also worth championing, and it's a cash crop that is very important to the economy of the region. American companies have shown palpable envy of basmati and other Asian rices. The Texan firm, Rice Tec, attempted to patent an American long grain variety using a fragrant basmati seed. The Indian government fought against this attempt by a US company to control a food staple, and fortunately won. Rice Tec was, however, allowed to register three hybrid versions of basmati – Texmati (brown), Jasmati (Thai style) and Kasmati (Indian style) *and* permitted to claim that its brands are 'superior to basmati'.

Does GM rice exist?

Yes. Experiments with pest-resistant GM rice have been going on in China for years and in 2005 Greenpeace reported that illegally sold GM rice had entered the food chain when it had not been approved. China has been chomping at the bit to grow GM crops, but so far the poor image of GM technology in Europe has prevented approval. In 2000 Monsanto promised to 'donate' its vitamin-A-enriched Golden Rice seeds to poorer countries in a quest to reduce the numbers of children affected by blindness due to vitamin deficiency. The cynical among us wondered why the image-conscious biotech firm didn't just hand out food. The project stalled after further research revealed that the poorly fed cannot use the vitamin-A-rich beta-carotene in the rice unless they are eating a varied diet with lots of leafy vegetables! Further trials are taking place.

How do the various types of long grain rice differ in flavour?

❋ **American long grain, non parboiled (i.e. not 'easy cook')** – when cooked, this rice is white and sticky, with little flavour. Its blandness is just right, however, with Chinese stir-fries and Thai curries.

❉ **American long grain, parboiled ('easy cook')** – the rice of British 1970s and 1980s childhoods: creamy-coloured grains that do not stick and a slight 'wet paper' taste.

❉ **Pure basmati** – long white grains with an earthy flavour and strong fragrance when cooked. The boiled grains will be light and fluffy. It is possible to buy 'broken' basmati grains; these will cook to a more solid, starchy mash and are traditionally (and successfully) used for rice puddings.

❉ **Easy-cook basmati** – when cooked, the rice grains are off-white and firmer textured and less fragrant. This basmati is traditionally used in twice-cooked dishes such as biryani.

❉ **Thai Homali 'fragrant'** – white and slightly sticky, slightly fluffy when cooked, this rice breed is naturally very fragrant. You can achieve a similar effect if you add a Thai lime leaf to the pan when cooking basmati.

Rice brands to watch out for

Graig Farm Organics, Dolau, Llandrindod Wells, Powys LD1 5TL
Tel: 01597 851655
www.graigfarm.co.uk
Organic white and brown basmati rice. Mail order available.

Tilda Ltd, Coldharbour Lane, Rainham, Essex RM13 9YQ
Tel: 01708 717777
www.tilda.com
This family-run business was set up to provide high-quality pure basmati for the UK's Asian community and is now Europe's largest basmati supplier. Tilda does much work protecting the basmati breed. It has a good reputation among the community in Haryana Province north of Delhi, where basmati is grown, buying a large school, building an eye clinic and offering free technical advice to farmers. It produces white, brown, and parboiled 'easy-cook' rice. The pure white is sold in various bag sizes but large bags are very good value and come with a zip that keeps mites out.

Traidcraft, Kingsway, Gateshead, Tyne and Wear NE11 0NE
Tel: 0870 443 1018
www.traidcraftshop.co.uk
Fairly traded white and brown basmati rice sourced from about 20 small family farms in Haryana Province in India. As well as a better price, farmers get free help with farm development and are encouraged to develop sustainable agriculture. Note that this rice does not have the internationally recognised Fairtrade logo. Mail order available.

Veetee Rice Ltd, Veetee House, Neptune Close,
Medway City Estate, Rochester, Kent ME2 4LT
Tel: 01634 290092
www.veetee.com
Established in 1987, Veetee sells pure basmati and other long grain rice, sourced from India, Pakistan, Guyana, the US, Italy, Spain, Surinam and Thailand. Available from Asian shops and some supermarkets.

White Pearl, Map Trading, 2 Abbey Road, Park Royal,
London NW10 7BS
Tel: 020 8965 0193
www.maptrading.co.uk
Pure basmati rice from Pakistan that is a favourite with the Muslim community. Available in Asian stores.

LUNCHBOX FOODS

For many parents, the reaction to the horrors revealed in 'Jamie's School Dinners' was to apply DIY. Surely it's best to send the kids to school with a lunchbox in order to lift the school-dinner blues? Not so. Health officials are just as worried by the food that parents choose for children as they are by the efforts of school cooks. Meanwhile, ranges of 'lunchbox' ideas have mushroomed on shelves, most of them 'enhanced' by additives, many of them potentially harmful. To list them all would fill a fat book. The best advice when shopping for suitable foods is to read those labels, and use the guide below not just to feed but to nourish your child.

What hides behind the labels of so-called 'lunchbox' foods?

Additives, additives . . . watch out for them in the following foods:

* **Meat** – those characteristic round slices of ham, chicken or turkey are known in the business as 'formed' meats. They contain water and usually starches, sugars, milk, salt, flavouring, stabilisers, antioxidant and the preservative sodium nitrite (E250), which is not recommended for children. There's not much meat in them: one sample tested (from Dairylea 'Lunchables') contained just 79 per cent chicken.
* **Cheese** – look closer. The popular Golden Vale 'Cheesestrings', renamed a 'cheese food snack', are made from cheese with added salted cheese powder, and their flavoured versions contain colour and flavourings.
* **Yoghurt and fromage frais 'tubes'** – often contain maize starch, sugars, emulsifiers, acidity regulators and preservatives, as well as colour and flavourings.

What's so bad about the additives?

Additives are problematic in degrees but parents tend to be most concerned about the ones that cause hyperactivity. In 2002 a government-funded study identified the worst of them and advised parents to watch out for the following colours: sunset yellow (E110), tartrazine (E102), ponceau 4R (E124), carmoisine E122 and the preservative, sodium benzoate (E211). Since then manufacturers have noticeably replaced these artificial colours with so-called natural ones. But annatto (E160b), now used in place of tartrazine, is believed by the Hyperactive Children's Support Group (HACSG) also to be an allergen. Cochineal and carmines (E120), iron oxide (E172) and caramels (E150) are frequently used in today's lunchbox foods. There is a long list of additives that are also believed to aggravate asthma.

But would manufacturers dare to put dangerous additives in their foods?

The manufacturers of colourings and preservatives say their products undergo toxicology testing but food watchdogs point out that such tests cannot tell if an additive causes hyperactivity or allergic reactions.

Why are problem additives permitted in foods?

The government says the 2002 report is still inconclusive, and so their use remains legal. The Food Standards Agency has commissioned another study but we have to hold out until 2007 for the results, firing scepticism that the FSA listens more to the food industry than it does to the consumers it was set up to protect. The authorities should listen to concerned parents, who unwittingly carry out experiments with additives every day, many of them reporting negative results. Teachers also report improvements in behaviour when children's lunches are freshly cooked from natural raw materials.

What other bad ingredients are found in manufactured children's foods?

The worst offenders are salt, hydrogenated fats (transfats) and sugars.

❉ Salt content is shown on the label, but note that manufacturers often list the 'sodium' content, which is the same thing. There are 2.5g salt to every gram of sodium, however, and the label can mislead you into thinking you are giving a child less salt. The Food Standard Agency Guidelines are as follows:

1–3 years: 2g salt a day (0.8g sodium)
4–6 years: 3g salt a day (1.2g sodium)
7–10 years: 5g salt a day (2g sodium)
11 and over: 6g salt a day (2.5g sodium)

❉ Hydrogenated fats, which contain unhealthy transfats, are added to pastry, biscuits, cakes and many other snacks to replace butter, which is a far more natural and healthy fat (see Butter and Spreads, page 99).

❉ Crisps and other crunchy snacks are often fried in palm oil, a saturated fat whose production causes serious environmental trouble in Southeast Asia where the oil palm is farmed.

❉ Soya is used in many bread products and in the emulsifier, soya lethicin. It is a potential allergen and can be derived from GM ingredients.

Could manufacturers leave out the additives?

Yes, at a cost of long shelf life, jolly colours, powerfully 'tempting' aromas and the hideous prospect of having to use more expensive 'real' ingredients.

Are commercial lunch kits a good choice?

Lunch kits featuring favourite cartoon characters and offering a fruit drink, a cracker or similar, some cheese and meat seem cute but they can have a high salt content, and the ingredients are not exactly the whole foods children deserve. Dairylea Lunchables contain re-formed chicken (made with just 79 per cent chicken, see above), which is not as wholesome as real chicken and contains salt and other additives. On checking with Kraft Foods, which manufactures Lunchables, I discovered that the re-formed chicken derives from Spanish indoor-reared birds and the cheese slices are made with milk from German cows – how international! Kraft admits it does not 'specify that they [their suppliers] use particular types of feed'. So, although asked, it did not answer questions about GM feed (for livestock), antibiotics in feed, fishmeal in feed and it ignored my request to visit the farms that supply it. As a parent, I would prefer to know much more about these meal kits than is on the label. I would want less salt in them too. Kraft defends the salt content, saying that these foods are aimed at older children 'as an occasional treat'. On the basis of what we do not know about them, avoid these meals.

Are organic lunchbox items the answer?

Organic foods can contain certain additives, so read the labels, but they are generally responsibly made.

How should I prepare a lunchbox?

It is better to do your own thing. It's a little more work, but buy plain or wholemilk cottage cheese, cut up Cheddar or other hard cheese and use naturally reared or organic cold meats and salami. Look for traditional bread (see page 73) and never forget fresh fruit. Water down your own fresh juice to avoid buying expensive, diluted, artificially flavoured 'juice drinks' (see page 194). For more colourful lunches, Fiona Beckett has written an imaginative book on the subject, *The Healthy Lunchbox* (Grub Street, 2005). Be careful of supermarket ranges for kids; few of the foods are real or pure. For treats, though, you could try the items listed below.

Where to buy good lunchbox items

Duchy Originals, The Old Ryde House, 393 Richmond Road, East Twickenham TW1 2EF
Tel: 020 8831 6800
www.duchyoriginals.com
Duchy Originals biscuits are made with real butter, and each biscuit contains only a trace of salt. They also make good chipolatas and ham suitable for children.

Eastbrook Farms Organic Meat, The Calf House, Cues Lane,
Bishopstone, Swindon, Wiltshire SN6 8PL
Tel: 01793 790340
www.helenbrowningorganics.co.uk
Exceptional welfare-friendly ham slices and (raw) chicken drumsticks. Mail order available.

Honeybuns, Naish Farm, Stony Lane, Holwell, Sherborne,
Dorset DT9 5LJ
Tel: 01963 23597
www.honeybuns.co.uk
Child-friendly home-made cakes from a Dorset Farm, including flapjacks, shortbreads and cookies. Mail order available.

Yeo Valley Organic Dairy, Mendip Centre, Rhodyate, Blagdon,
Somerset BS40 7YE
Tel: 01761 462798
www.yeovalleyorganic.co.uk
Strawberry Jumble & Fruit Tumble yoghurts, made with all organic
ingredients – good for younger children.

Other suitable items for lunchboxes include:

Apples (see page 30)
Bananas (see page 54)
Bread (see page 73)
Cheddar Cheese (see page 111)
Cured Pork (see page 160)
Fruit Juice (see page 194)
Noodles (see page 258)
Potato Crisps (see page 302)
Sushi (see page 393)
Tomatoes (see page 412)

MAYONNAISE

In the case of mayonnaise, the mass-market sauce overtook the real thing in the popularity stakes long ago. The pale gloop that comes out of jars bears little relation to the yellow emulsion beaten in a bowl at home, yet millions of Hellmann's buyers cannot be wrong when they claim how good it is – especially, it must be said, with chips. But the inventor of the original mayonnaise, a French chef who substituted oil for cream in an egg sauce, would be horrified to see what it has become: a global sauce with an uneasy link to animal cruelty. If bottled mayo's fans felt the same way, the use of battery eggs in the big-brand sauces could become a thing of the past . . .

Where are the eggs in commercial mayonnaise from?

Around 80 per cent of processed foods containing eggs use eggs from caged or battery hens, and the same statistic can be applied to bottled mayonnaise. Hellmann's still uses battery eggs, supporting a system that sees a hen eke out a short life in a cage with a floor space no bigger than an A4 sheet of paper. With no room to behave naturally – pecking, foraging, taking dust-baths – the life of a hen in a cage is utter misery. They are slaughtered as soon as their egg-laying ability is exhausted. The treatment of worn-out battery hens can be compared to that of a slowing PC: cheaper for the owner to replace than to mend.

Given the EU labelling law that allows the words 'British' or 'UK Origin' to be used on anything *made* in this country but not necessarily using British ingredients, you can deduce that the eggs in mayonnaise could have come from anywhere. The UK is a major importer of liquid egg, and unless the producer marks the real origin on labels, assume that your bottled mayonnaise has at least a food-mile problem and at most serious animal welfare issues – UK animal welfare standards, while far from perfect, tend to be higher than those of exporting countries.

Are the eggs used in bottled mayonnaise safe?

Yes. The eggs, both yolks and whole eggs (many manufacturers use whole eggs to provide cheaper bulk), are pasteurised to safeguard against salmonella. Be aware, however, that eggs from British hens, vaccinated against salmonella and stamped with the 'Lion' mark, are available to manufacturers, who could use them to make a natural mayonnaise that, while not risk free, would be 'safer' than that made with fresh eggs from non-vaccinated hens.

What additives are used to manufacture mayonnaise?

Various emulsifiers and stabilisers are added and, while they are not on the 'dirty' list of additives, it is a question of whether we really want xanthan or guar gum in what should be a natural amalgamation of eggs and olive or sunflower oil, with the added acidity of lemon or vinegar. Sugar may also be added.

What sort of oil is used in bottled mayonnaise?

Ideally extra virgin olive oil or sunflower oil, or a combination of both. Most commercial mayo uses only the cheaper sunflower, but beware mayonnaise made from 'vegetable oil'. This could be anything: maize, canola, palm, soya ... at least olive and sunflower oil are low in saturates, so marginally better for your health. Oils sourced outside Europe (palm, canola, maize) have both food miles and fair-trading issues.

What's in reduced-fat mayonnaise?

Reduced-fat mayonnaise is usually bulked out with modified maize starch and water, and is bolstered by extra emulsifiers (gum, lethicin). It contains about 2g fat per serving as opposed to 10g for regular mayonnaise – but given the ingredient profile, it is probably better to eat two teaspoons of conventional mayo rather than ten teaspoons of a highly unnatural food.

Is organic mayonnaise better?

Organic producers allow the above additives (although they must be of organic origin), going against the promotion of good natural food. They have the edge on animal welfare issues, though. Certified organic eggs are from hens kept to high welfare standards: free ranging and naturally fed.

What's in the supermarkets?

Marks & Spencer's mayonnaise excels. Made from free-range eggs and a combination of extra virgin olive oil and sunflower oil, with no additives, it is a steal at 99 pence for 200g.

Waitrose sells organic mayonnaise.

Selfridges and **Harvey Nichols** use free-range eggs in their own-label mayonnaise.

The Co-op should be applauded for its honesty, marking its conventional mayo as containing eggs from 'caged hens'. It also sells mayonnaise made with free-range eggs.

Tesco's mayonnaise is made with eggs sourced from France, Belgium and Holland. It could provide no more information concerning its mayonnaise, the eggs used to make it or the hens that laid them.

Where to buy welfare-friendly mayonnaise

Farmhouse Freedom Eggs Ltd, Great House Farm, Gwehelog, Nr Usk, Monmouthshire NP15 1RJ
Tel: 01291 673129
www.freedomeggs.co.uk
Good mayonnaise made with eggs from free-roaming hens. Home delivery available.

Pollen Organics, Three Firs House, Bramshott Chase,
Hampshire GU26 6DG
Tel: 01428 608870
www.pollenorganics.com
Made with a mix of extra virgin olive oil and sunflower oil, organic eggs and other natural ingredients. Pollen also makes a good hollandaise sauce.

Simply Delicious, Baxters Food Group, Fochabers,
Scotland IV32 7LD
Tel: 01343 820393
www.baxters.com
Organic, sharp-flavoured mayonnaise made with sunflower oil, eggs, cider vinegar, sugar and mustard flour, plus organic dextrose (avoid the 'light' alternative, which is full of the usual stabilisers and emulsifiers).

MILK

There's been a revival of dry-cured bacon and a partial hand-back of the crust on the loaf but where did the top of the milk go? Milk has somehow escaped foodie-revisionism. But while the over thirty-fives who stoically put up with warm bottled milk for their school elevenses have good reason for not joining the lament, milk is a food despised by many for the wrong reasons. It also drums up a lot less concern than beef. Nevertheless, the simple carton of milk that you put in the fridge is top-heavy with issues, sadly not with cream ...

Is there such a thing as fair-trade milk?

Very little of it, yet British dairy farmers do not earn enough from milk production and urgent action is needed. In 2000 there were 15,219 dairy farmers in the UK, according to the NFU. In 2004 the union reported that there were 13,264, that is a loss of nearly 2000 dairy farmers. It's a vast number, even taking into account foot and mouth disease. It is still declining at a rate of almost four farms a week. The national dairy cattle herd is, however, still the same size; the farms are just consolidating. Seventy-five per cent of UK-produced milk is sold to the Big Four supermarkets. Quitting dairy farmers claim they cannot profit from the low prices they are paid for the milk they produce.

What can be done to halt the crisis?

Supermarket chains, via processors, must pay more to the farmer or British dairy farming will head for extinction. The NFU reports that farmers are increasing the size of their herds – consolidation supported by that slave to supermarket pressure, DEFRA. The average British herd is 95, large by European standards, and 250 head are deemed just profitable. Big herd sizes can decrease welfare standards. Milk inspectors privately report the highest standards to be on smaller farms. Neighbours of consolidated dairy farmers have grave concerns about the effects of increased amounts of effluent in the water supply and local environment.

So let's just import milk?

Imported milk has murky traceability. Policing the use of illegal hormones and poor welfare is difficult and imported milk has a shorter shelf life. Standards of welfare on conventional farms in the UK are high compared to the rest of the world, but the Soil Association's organic dairy farming standard is the one to aim for.

But is all British milk welfare friendly?

No. Many dairy cows suffer almost permanent lactation, mastitis infections and rough handling. Some large herds are permanently housed and never get to graze on pasture. Farmers defend this, saying their welfare is not in question – but even so, these animals, like caged hens and pigs in stalls, are denied a fundamental freedom. These systems are more common with large herds, and the trend is moving more and more towards this as farms consolidate, increasing the volume of milk in an effort to make a profit.

How much do supermarkets profit out of milk?

Dairy farmers receive about 18 pence per litre, depending on the season. It costs the farmer 21 pence to produce the milk. Profit-margin fog lies over the processing. An insider reported that it can cost the milk processor just 5 pence per litre to collect, process, pack and deliver milk, meaning supermarkets pocket a handsome 100 per cent profit. Even doubling the processing cost adds terrific élan to a food that stays on the shelf an average six hours.

If it's necessary to skim fat from milk, is it healthy?

Even whole milk is skimmed to provide a uniform drink. The pity is that the fat gets a bad press when the actual, quite innocent 4.5 per cent fat content in whole milk provides essential vitamins to aid the absorption of all-important calcium. Mothers and middle-aged women, who need a healthy calcium ration, take special note – skimmed milk is nutritionally a pretty pointless drink (if you prefer skimmed, however, ask your doctor about supplements). Whole milk is not fattening: it has just 4.5 per cent fat compared with double cream, which contains 48 per cent fat.

Which is healthier, organic or non-organic milk?
The healthiest milk hails from the cow fed the healthiest diet. It seems cruel to hold up the organic standard when so many conventional farmers are in crisis, but organic feeding regimes are more wholesome; GM feed and many fertilisers are banned. In 2005 the Danish Institute of Agricultural Research reported that organic milk has 50 per cent more vitamin E, 75 per cent more beta-carotene and extra omega-3 and antioxidants. Organic milk also contains high levels of conjugated linoleic acid (CLA), which helps you burn the fat you eat.

Conventional milk contains these elements too, albeit at lower levels, but if supermarkets paid more for milk, ending the current financial crisis, conventional farmers might have the confidence to re-employ the natural feeding regimes of traditional dairy farming and the organic farmers. Note, however, that organic farmers profit little more than conventional ones in spite of the higher price tag their milk attracts.

Is milk safe?
Contamination of fresh milk is rare. Almost all milk is pasteurised (heat treated) to kill pathogens. The spread of diseases such as tuberculosis and brucellosis is contained by pasteurisation.

Is raw milk safe?
Many devotees believe so. Raw, untreated milk (green top), available from the farm gate from licensed suppliers, can be judged a safe food because the farmers must take extra care with hygiene in order to keep their licence. Raw milk tends to be produced on farms with small herds, where welfare is paramount and the milk is totally traceable. Contact with disease such as brucellosis is not completely

unavoidable, however. The health authorities advise pregnant women, very young children and the elderly not to drink it but its fans (I am one) are militant in their support for it. It is a delicious whole food. Its protein structure is unaffected by the heat treatment, or homogenisation, that has given milk a major makeover. Many people who are milk intolerant claim that non-homogenised unpasteurised milk is easier to digest.

Does milk contain pesticide residues?

Whole and semi-skimmed milk are tested frequently for pesticides, but skimmed very rarely because the residues tend to be held in the fat. The last reported samples were taken in 2004, when 55 samples of fresh milk, including organic, were tested for the presence of 11 organochlorine pesticides – none were found. Environmental groups claim, however, that the fat in milk still contains traces of the banned pesticide, DDT.

Where's the top of the milk gone?

Most milk is homogenised to break up and distribute the fat particles evenly. Homogenised milk deteriorates faster and lacks the silky feel of non-homogenised (for suppliers of non-homogenised milk, see below).

Do we need so many types of milk?

The industry is constantly trying to find new ways to market milk. Some are good ideas, but be sceptical. Beleaguered dairy farmers would perhaps fare better if they turned surplus milk into cheese, yoghurt or ice cream. Obviously this comment sounds patronising, but I am yet to meet a maker of good farmhouse cheese who can produce enough to supply demand.

Below are listed a few of the milks you will find in supermarkets:

* **Single-breed milks** – milk from specific breeds, such as Channel Island (Guernsey) or Ayrshire.
* **Night-time milk** – from cows milked in the early morning, when

their natural melatonin (sleep-inducing hormone) levels are high. Correct me if I am wrong, but I have never known a cow milked late in the morning.

❈ **Nutrient-enriched milk** – with added nutrients such as vitamins or omega-3, which is known to boost heart health.

❈ **Filtered milk** – this has been put though a fine filter to remove even more bacteria than pasteurisation, so it keeps longer. Not really a whole food, despite its claims.

❈ **UHT** – ultra-heat-treated milk that keeps even when out of the fridge. Organic is also available.

❈ **Dried milk powder** – this often contains added vegetable fat and sometimes added vitamins.

How can I shop to help British dairy farmers?

❈ Buy from local co-operative milk rounds that pay farmers a fair price and offer them ownership of the industry. Dairy Farmers of Britain (tel: 0800 834823; **www.dfob.co.uk**) includes the brands Yorkshire Milk, Cadog (Wales) and Dairygate, and can deliver nationwide. Milk Link (tel: 01752 331800; **www.milklink.com**) delivers across the south of England.

❈ Buy milk from supermarkets that trade fairly with farmers. During research for this book, I asked all the supermarket chains about the price paid to farmers. The Big Four claim that this information is commercially sensitive. Of the smaller chains, only Waitrose and Marks & Spencer revealed the sum: 21–22 pence per litre to farmers.

❈ When buying organic milk, look for the OMSCo logo on the carton, even on supermarket milk. OMSCo (Organic Milk Suppliers Co-operative) states that the average price paid to organic farmers for their milk is 26–29 pence per litre. Organic milk is on supermarket shelves at 60–70 pence per litre.

❈ Buy specialist brands, because farmers tend to earn more from them and most are produced in a sustainable way. They include Duchy non-homogenised (most supermarkets), Manor

Farm organic (Waitrose and Fresh & Wild stores), Bowland fresh non-homogenised (Booths), English Select Farm Milk non-homogenised (Marks & Spencer), White and Wild (major supermarkets), Rachel's Organic Dairy (major supermarkets) and Horizon non-homogenised (independent healthfood shops.)

❧ Buy British veal. It is a by-product of milk, and welfare standards are high (see page 65).

What the supermarkets say

Sainsbury states (rather vaguely) that it works actively with both dairy farmers and milk processors to help improve their efficiency and reduce their costs. It sells Gold Top Jersey and Guernsey milk, Highgrove Breakfast milk, Taste the Difference Guernsey milk, and White and Wild semi-skimmed milk, all of which are good-quality products. It also stocks Delemere goat's milk and Rachel's Organic.

Marks & Spencer sells milk produced in England, Wales, Scotland and Northern Ireland. It currently pays 21.48 pence per litre for conventional milk and 26 pence per litre for organic. Its 'English whole milk' is non-homogenised.

The Co-op had nothing to report beyond selling UK-sourced conventional and organic homogenised milk.

Waitrose sells both organic and non-organic varieties of milk. Its Select Farm semi-skimmed milk is homogenised; the rest of the range is not. It also sells Duchy Originals and Manor Farm organic non-homogenised milk.

Budgens' milk is standard homogenised British milk.

Where to buy welfare-friendly 'whole' milk

Duchy Originals, The Old Ryde House, 393 Richmond Road,
East Twickenham TW1 2EF
Tel: 020 8831 6800
www.duchyoriginals.com
Duchy Originals fresh organic milk comes from the Ayrshire cows at
Highgrove. It is pasteurised but not homogenised.

Manor Farm Organic Milk Ltd, Manor Farm, Godmanstone,
Dorchester, Dorset DT2 7AH
Tel: 01300 341415
www.manor-farm-organic.co.uk
Lovely milk from a multiple-award-winning farm with a Friesian
herd.

Park Farm Dairy, Matthews Lane, Hadlow, Tonbridge,
Kent TN11 0JG
Tel: 01732 851843
A small, family-run dairy processing its own milk and fresh cream
products.

St Helen's Farm, Seaton Ross, York YO42 4NP
Tel: 01430 861715
www.sthelensfarm.co.uk
The UK's leading producer of goat's milk, located in more than
300 acres of land where the goats are milked twice daily.

Where to buy raw milk

Old Plaw Hatch Farm, Sharp Thorne, East Grinstead HR19 4UL
Tel: 01342 810652
Small, biodynamic farm, selling unpasteurised milk, cream and its
own award-winning cheeses.

MUSTARD

The well-worn joke goes that it is the mustard we didn't eat that made the mustard barons' millions. And it's true. Being keen as mustard for the condiment sees more of it disappear down the drain than down our throats – greed that fuels big business. The cliché, incidentally, derives from the eighteenth-century mustard company, Keens. In Dijon, however, mustard is not only eaten in large quantities (families consume up to two kilos a week, say producers) but applied to the chest in compresses to heal coughs and colds. Mustard comes in many guises: seedy, smooth, flavoured with almost anything from honey to hops. But beware. In spite of its natural preservative properties, it can also contain some nasty additives.

Why is mustard hot?

The heat in mustard comes from an enzyme reaction that takes place when liquid is added to the pounded seed. The name mustard comes from 'must' – the leftovers from the winemaking, whose strained juice was added to the early mustards.

What else is in mustard?

The 'heat' is preserved with the addition of acid, usually vinegar. The finer the vinegar the better the mustard – hence the fame of Dijon mustard made in Burgundy with vinegar from its great wines. Some English mustards are made with ale. Non-gourmet, basic mustards are made with malt or spirit vinegar.

There are two basic types of mustard seed – yellow and oriental or brown seed – and 95 per cent of mustard is made with a blend of both. The bran is removed from the outer seed, which is ground, then pounded before the liquid is added. Sugar, salt, spices and wheat flour are often added to the mix.

Does mustard contain synthetic additives?

Some does. Turmeric root (E100) is often added for colour but it is an additive that is actually healthy, and especially good for the digestion. Scientists believe turmeric may have anti-cancer properties. Many mustards (including Colman's) contain the preservative, citric acid, which is also problem free.

However, controversial colourings can be used. Check labels for tartrazine (E102), the most allergic of all yellow food dyes, said to cause hyperactivity in children (not that they eat much mustard), migraine and blurred vision. Other additives include the sweetener, aspartame (E951), which has unproven links to cancer; potassium metabisulphite (E224) and sodium metabisulphite (E223). Asthma sufferers are advised to avoid foods containing sulphites, which can be allergens. Note also that wasabi, the Japanese horseradish paste eaten with sushi, wrongly supposed to be a type of mustard, often contains blue, green and yellow colourings (see list of suppliers below).

Can mustard in the UK contain GM ingredients?

The seeds of the best known, Colman's and French's (American), are not genetically modified (Colman's seed is grown in the UK and guaranteed non GM). Most mustard seed, including that in some 'French' mustards, is non GM and grown in Canada. But be careful if soya flour is listed among the ingredients – it could come from GM soya.

Is mustard good for you?

Yes, mustard oil (and horseradish) is antibacterial, protecting against listeria, E. coli and other food pathogens because it contains allyl isothiocyanate (AITC). Mustard oil has 93 per cent AITC, while horseradish contains 60 per cent.

How long does mustard keep?

Heat affects mustard, so buy small quantities and keep the jar in the fridge after opening (this is why mustard was originally stored in earthenware jars, incidentally now very collectible). For the same reason, if you cook with mustard, add it at the last moment.

Where to buy mustard

Check the ingredients list on every jar to ensure there are no problematic artificial additives. The mustards below are all recommended.

**Goodness Direct, South March, Daventry,
Northamptonshire NN11 4PH
Tel: 0871 871 6611
www.goodnessdirect.co.uk**
This online shop sells Mitoku natural wasabi powder you can mix yourself – a good alternative to artificially dyed wasabi. Contains ground horseradish, wasabi leaves, roots and stems and mustard.

**Island Mustard, Rosemary Vineyard, Smallbrook Lane, Ryde,
Isle of Wight PO33 2UX
Tel: 01983 567600**
Seven types of mustard, including wholegrain and chilli, made on the Isle of Wight by Victoria Gregg.

**Maille, 6 Place de la Madeleine, Paris 76008
Tel: 0033 14 01 50 600
www.maille.com**
Moutarde Fine de Dijon and Moutarde à l'Ancienne (with grains), based on a 300-year-old recipe and made with fine wine vinegar. The mustard is made with mainly Canadian seed, although the company is trialling French crops once more, a fact to be celebrated. Available from specialist food shops and some supermarkets. Real mustard enthusiasts should visit the Maille shops in Paris (address above) and Dijon, where dozens of mustards, made with individual Burgundy wines and flavoured with everything from cassis to hazelnuts, are sold fresh on tap.

**The Merchant Farmers Mustard and Preserve Company,
Newbury Lane, Cousley Wood, East Sussex TN5 6HB
Tel: 01892 783430
www.themerchantfarmer.co.uk**
Excellent mustard made in Sussex by artisan mustard maker Jonathan Ffrench, using English wine vinegar.

Mount Fuji International Ltd, Felton Butler, Nesscliffe,
Shrewsbury SY4 1AS
Tel: 01743 741169
www.mountfuji.co.uk
Similar to English mustard, sold in tubes, this Japanese mustard
makes a good sauce for fish tartare or grilled steak. Mail order available.

Shaken Oak Farm, Old North Leigh Lane, Hailey, Witney,
Oxfordshire OX29 9UX
Tel: 01993 868043
www.shakenoak.co.uk
Award-winning 'hot and smooth' mustard, plus others flavoured
with black pepper or ginger and honey.

The Tracklement Company Ltd, The Dairy Farm, Pinkney Park,
Sherston, Wiltshire SN16 0NX
Tel: 01666 840851
www.tracklements.co.uk
Good, wide range of pungent mustard with no artificial additives.
Mail order available.

NOODLES

The two personalities of the noodle phenomenon could not be culturally further apart. There's the pot noodle, an instant snack that deliberately cultivates a downmarket image to appeal to 16–24 year olds. And there is the newer sensation of city high-street noodle bars. Five years ago they barely existed; now it's easy to grab a bowl of ramen or rice vermicelli, swimming in a steaming broth with vegetables – authentic, healthy food for sophisticates who have travelled to the Far East for their holidays.

The immense popularity of the instant pot noodle in the UK is not, as it is in Japan, because it provides a solution to the blue-collar workforce's need to eat a working lunch in a hurry, but a direct result of canny marketing. Unilever's vast Pot Noodle sales are largely attributed to spontaneous, unplanned snacking, eased along by the installation of hot-water dispensers in convenience stores. In February 2005, however, Pot Noodle's slogan, 'It's dirty, and you want it', spectacularly backfired when three varieties were withdrawn from sale in the illegal dye Sudan 1 scandal; junk snacking suddenly looks less cool.

What's in a cup or pot noodle?

The specks of meat and shrivelled vegetables in your noodle cup could have originated anywhere – there is no obligation for manufacturers to provide information. If you or your children are allergic to monosodium glutamate (MSG), be careful. Look on the label for the words 'flavour enhancer' – permitted word usage for MSG-type flavourings, which are also identified as E620–637. Intolerance varies but some people show consistent symptoms. Hyperactive children are vulnerable to its effects, which range from rages, anxiety attacks and mood swings to heart palpitations, migraine, sweats, depression and dizziness.

Packs can also contain hydrolised vegetable protein (HVP), a flavouring processed using hydrochloric acid that yields an artificial meaty taste and excuses the manufacturer from adding plenty of real meat to the stock powder, boosting profit. HVP can contain the contaminant, 3MCPD, a chloropropanol that has been found to be carcinogenic when given to rats.

What's in authentic noodles?
Almost all dried packet noodles are made from natural ingredients. Rice noodles are bound with water, while wheat noodles – which include soba (buckwheat) – are bound with water, or water and eggs. It is possible to buy noodles made with maize or millet.

Why do Chinese egg noodles cook quicker than Italian pasta?
Oriental noodles have already been cooked. After the dough is mixed, rolled and cut, wheat noodles are boiled and rice noodles steamed before drying. They reconstitute quickly when added to boiling water and, in the case of rice noodles, they only need to soak in hot or cold water.

Are all noodles made in the Far East?
All rice noodles are made in the Far East but wheat noodles can be made anywhere. Sharwood's wheat noodles are made in Belgium, so travel less far.

Do noodles contain GM ingredients?
Genetically modified ingredients must be listed on the labels of food sold in the UK, and consumer distaste for GM foods has so far prevented manufacturers changing policy. Most wheat flour for UK-sold mass-market noodles is sourced in Europe and Canada, neither of which currently grows GM wheat. Biotech firms are lobbying hard to get pesticide-resistant wheat into Canada and Europe. Japan does not grow GM crops, and the Chinese are resisting growing GM rice for the time being, since they recognise the importance of exporting rice-based foods to GM-wary nations. It is predicted, however, that 20 per cent of their crop will be genetically modified by 2010.

Where to buy naturally made pot or cup noodles

Goodness Direct, South March, Daventry,
Northamptonshire NN11 4PH
Tel: 0871 871 6611
www.goodnessdirect.co.uk

Online shop selling Clearspring buckwheat soba noodles, wheat lomein noodles and organic bifun rice noodles; also Sakurei organic jinenjo soba noodles made with buckwheat and mountain yams.

Harvey Nichols, 109–125 Knightsbridge, London SW1X 7RJ
Tel: 020 7235 5000
www.harveynichols.com

Stocks Madam Pum's all-natural instant coconut and green noodle Thai-type soup. Mail order available.

Wing Yip Ltd, 375 Nechells Park Road, Nechells,
Birmingham B7 5NT
Tel: 0870 608 8800
www.wingyipstore.co.uk

Wing Yip sells Hama udon noodles and soup (no artificial colourings, flavourings or flavour enhancers). Available online or at their shops in Birmingham, Croydon, Cricklewood and Manchester.

Where to buy traditionally made noodles

Atari Ya, 7 Station Parade, Noel Road, London W3 0DS
Tel: 020 8896 1552 (also at 595 High Road, North Finchley,
London N12 0DY; tel: 020 8446 6669, and 15–16 Monkville
Parade, Finchley Road, London NW11 0AL; tel: 020 8458 7626)
www.atariya.co.uk

Sanchi organic somen, the noodles to serve cold with a soy dressing and blanched vegetables; there is a choice between wheat flour and barley flour (thinner) somen. Home delivery available in the M25 area.

Goodness Direct Ltd (see above for contact details)
Sakurai soba and udon noodles in various thicknesses, plus a quick-cooking ramen variety. Mail order available.

Harvey Nichols (see above for contact details)
Annie Chun's extra-good-for-you natural wheat and rice flour noodles. The wheat noodles are made only with egg white, so are cholesterol free, and the rice noodles are the best pad thai noodles available.

Here Organic Supermarket, Chelsea Farmers' Market, 125 Sydney Street, London SW3 6NR
Tel: 020 7351 4321
'Here' is one of the best London organic stores and stocks a wide range of organic noodles, including Blue Dragon organic egg noodles and a choice of plain egg or spinach and egg noodles from The Noodle Company. It also sells fresh noodles, including a good chick pea noodle.

Wing Yip Ltd (see above for contact details)
Stocks Earth brand noodles made very traditionally using the rolling and folding method. They cook beautifully and are highly recommended. Also sells nice and chewy fresh udon noodles. Available online or at their shops in Birmingham, Croydon, Cricklewood and Manchester.

NUTS

The globally sourced nut bowl is a Christmas given, yet nuts are an everyday food taken for granted and rarely considered. The overall image of nuts may be a healthy one, but there are dangers for those who are allergic, and parents should watch the high salt content in nutty snacks. And how circumspect should nut shoppers be, when there is the planet to consider?

Do farmers get a good deal when we buy nuts?

No, according to the Fairtrade Foundation, which has accredited only a few suppliers. Nuts often hail from countries that desperately need the trade but individual farmers do not necessarily profit well. When prices are forced down, farmers will often grow more, depressing prices further and compromising the quality of nuts. Having said this, some nuts may not carry the Fairtrade mark but still be ethically traded.

Are there pesticide residues on nuts?

Residues were found on 29 out of 48 non-organic samples of various nuts taken by the Pesticide Residues Committee (PRC) in 2004. The residues were inorganic bromide – a result of the use of the fumigant, methyl bromide, which is applied to kill rats, mice and other pests during storage.

But should we worry about chemical residues on a food that has a shell?

While the PRC says that levels in the samples were not dangerous and that low levels of inorganic bromide occur naturally in some foods, methyl bromide is an ozone-depleting chemical whose use has already been stopped in some countries. It is also a dangerous chemical to apply. In the United States, more days are spent in hospital receiving treatment for methyl bromide accidents than for any other agricultural chemical. There has been trouble, too, with the use of

Savoria, 229 Linen Hall – CKp, 162–168 Regent Street,
London W1B 5TB
Tel: 0870 242 1823
www.savoria.co.uk
Online shop selling food-mile-friendlier nuts from Italy, including
almonds and pistachios from Sicily, hazelnuts from Piedmont and
pine nuts from Pisa.

Suma Organic, Lacy Way, Lowfields Industrial Park, Elland,
West Yorkshire HX5 9DB
Tel: 0845 458 2291
www.suma.co.uk
Organic cashews, Brazil nuts, ground almonds, hazelnuts, peanuts
and pine nuts.

Kentish cobnuts

The season for these delicious English nuts runs from mid-August to
October; they are available from farm shops and via home-delivery
services. To find suppliers, contact the **Kentish Cobnuts Association, Apple Trees, Comp Lane, St Mary's Platt, Sevenoaks, Kent
TN15 8NR**
Tel: 01732 882734
www.kentishcobnutsassociation.co.uk

OLIVE OIL

Like wine, olive oil attracts connoisseurship and snobbery. Every single-estate extra virgin oil is subtly different, yet with olive oils on the market costing over £40 for 200ml, you know that someone is being taken for a ride – you. Don't be too concerned about owning a supply of oil pressed from so-called rare olives when it is perfectly possible to find very high-quality olive oil for around £12 for 750ml. Even lower-grade extra virgin possesses olive oil's most exciting feature – its health properties. Scientists have reported that the oleic acid in olive oil acts against the gene that triggers breast cancer. And olive oil is kind to your heart, too, being exceptionally high in monounsaturated fats and helping to lower blood cholesterol. So many oils now line the supermarket shelves, it is easy for anyone to buy in, but beware of misleading labels – not all olive oil is as healthy as it appears . . .

Why do some olive oils taste fresh and fruity, others mellow, others bland?

The variety of olive used gives the oil its character and flavour, but method is vital. Oils made swiftly after harvest, using the 'cold pressing' method with gently handled, unbruised olives, have a low acidity that will allow these flavours to sing. Ripeness also counts. The greener the olive, the fruitier the oil; black olives make mellow oil.

What is the difference between virgin and extra virgin oils?

Producers can label their oil extra virgin if the acidity is low – no more than 8 per cent. It must also be tasted and approved by an internationally accredited panel. Virgin oil is made in the same way, but higher acidity indicates slightly less care in handling the olives and pressing the oil, hence its lower price.

Is olive oil as safe and healthy as we are led to believe?

Extra virgin and virgin olive oils are all as healthy as can be but there have been troubles with olive pomace oil, which is refined from the residue of the first oil making, using heat and chemicals. Refined olive oil is made using a similar method. Cancer-causing chemicals have been found in Spanish and Greek pomace oils; consequently the Trading Standards Institute routinely tests them. No contamination has been recorded since 2001, but tracking is difficult.

Can I tell which oil has been used in a ready-made pasta sauce, spread or ready meal?

Yes, in theory – the grade of oil should be marked on the label but I remain sceptical. Where olive pomace oil is used as an ingredient, it should not contribute more than 2 micrograms per kilo of benzo(a)pyrene, or BaP (BaP is a polycyclic aromatic hydrocarbon (PAH), a chemical that is known to cause cancer by disrupting genetic material). The Food Standards Agency says that if olive pomace oil is used, pasta sauces, antipasti and ready meals should show its presence on their labels.

Is my Italian olive oil definitely Italian?

No. It is legal to label oil made with imported oil or olives Italian if it is bottled in Italy. Generic Italian-style oils, such as Berio and Bertolli, are not made with exclusively Italian olives. It is no longer permitted to label with the regional identity, say, Tuscan, except descriptively, e.g. 'typically Tuscan'. Choose 'single estate' or 'estate bottled', which indicate that harvest and pressing have taken place locally. Don't go by the visuals. A picture of an olive on packaging is legal with just 50 per cent olive oil inside.

The greener and cloudier the oil, the better?

No. Green oil is just a result of using greener olives. Some of the best Ligurian oils are delicately pale. Cloudy oil is unfiltered and, although it's strongly characterful, it could have a shorter shelf life.

Does frying with olive oil diminish its healthy properties?

High heat causes small amounts of trans fatty acids, or transfats, to form (transfats are harmful to health – see Butter and Spreads, page 99) but usual frying temperatures (150–175°C) and cooking times of no more than five to ten minutes are thought to have a negligible effect. Ordinary cooking, roasting and baking will diminish the flavours of olive oil, so use lower-priced, good commercial extra virgin for cooking, and keep your single-estate EV for eating raw.

What should I spend on single-estate, cold-pressed extra virgin olive oil?

500ml of the best can cost as little as £7 and up to £17. Spend more and you are into the realms of olive oil über-snobbery – but enjoy it all the same.

Is organic oil superior?

Not always. Many estates producing oil are not certified organic but never use chemical farming methods. They sometimes do not apply for accreditation because there is a cost involved. But organic oils will hail from groves that may have been untouched for centuries, so there is a feel-good factor here. Organic does not mean the oil will taste better, however. Low-acidity, fruity oil has more to do with skill and the variety of olive.

What's in olive oil spread?

Not much olive oil, even in the organic ones, plus other, often un-specified, vegetable oils including refined rapeseed (which contains transfats) or soya (an allergen risk). Then there's salt, emulsifiers, thickeners, preservative, flavouring, colour ... mmm, how delicious. See Butter and Spreads on page 99 for more on olive oil spreads.

How should olive oil be stored?

In a cool, dark place, so away from the hob. Since olive oil improves with age only in the first three months, it is best to buy it a good way from its 'best before' date, which is usually two years after bottling.

Do supermarkets sell decent olive oil?

Read labels in the supermarket, looking for the extra virgin among the ordinary olive oil. There are hundreds of oils available, many of them from single estates whose labels can carry a lot of detail.

Where to buy olive oil

Serious olive oil shoppers should approach trusted importers, such as the ones below. Buy in bulk for better value.

Elanthy, PO Box 227, Chipping Norton, Oxfordshire OX7 9AH
Tel: 0800 169 6252
www.elanthy.com

A well-made, good-value oil (sold in three-litre cans) from olives picked and cold pressed in southern Greece, with herbaceous, green apple flavours. Home delivery available.

Mortimer & Bennett, 33 Turnham Green Terrace,
London W4 1RG
Tel: 020 8995 4145
www.mortimerandbennett.co.uk

This delicatessen and online shop stocks Manni olive oil, made from the rare Olivastra Seggianese olive grown on the Tuscan mountains. Huge snob appeal, and fabulous price and packaging; the shop stocks other exciting oils, too.

The Oil Merchant, 47 Ashchurch Grove, London W12 9BU
Tel: 020 8740 1335

Expert Charles Carey has been importing oils from all over the world since 1985, and has some of the best on his mail-order list. He also sells to Harvey Nichols, Selfridges and Fortnum's. Try Ravida from Sicily, with its flavours of artichoke and meadow; Morgenster from South Africa, a great 'New World' oil; or the herbaceous, evergreen, toned organic Tuscan Badia a Coltibuono.

Olives et Al Ltd, Unit I, North Dorset Business Park,
Sturminster Newton, Dorset DT10 2GA
Tel: 01258 474300
www.olivesetal.co.uk
Giles and Annie Henschel have been importing olives and oil for 12 years and sell four excellent, good-value olive oils. One in particular, Naturvie from Spain (three types from a 200-year-old family-owned olive farm), Giles describes as the most amazing oil he has ever tasted. Mail order available.

Vom Fass, 21 High Street, Chalfont St Giles,
Buckinghamshire HP8 4QH
Tel: 0870 750 0962
www.vomfassuk.com
Several extra virgin olive oils, originating from Tuscany, Crete and Andalusia. Mail order available; also sold on tap, straight from the cask, at Selfridges.

Zaytoun, Statfold Seed Oil Developments Ltd, Unit 8,
Graycar Business Park, Barton-under-Needwood,
Burton-on-Trent, Staffordshire DE13 8EN
Tel: 01283 713866
www.zaytoun.org
An ethical business importing olive oil made by Palestinian farmers from some of the oldest olive trees in the world, at Fairtrade prices. Zaytoun invests all its taxable profits to help create a sustainable future for Palestinian farmers. It has applied for organic accreditation. Check the website for stockists.

ORANGES (AND OTHER CITRUS FRUIT)

If a banana's secret weapon is its ability to ripen off the tree, the orange is the fruit with the winning attire. The tough, water- and germ-proof protection of its deliciously scented skin is its enigma; without it the UK would consume few oranges, and without citrus in our diet we'd be a sorry lot. The closest orange groves regularly supplying the UK are in Spain, but the Spanish are by no means the world's biggest growers. Look to Brazil and Florida for that, where fields of citrus trees never seem to end. However, while oranges make a vital contribution to our health, dosing us with vitamin C, their cultivation gives the planet quite a bit of stress. The most important question is this: are we eating more oranges than we need?

Where do oranges come from?

Originally from the Far East but they are now grown in Brazil and the US, the Middle East, Asia (China predominantly), southern Europe, Central America, South Africa and Indonesia. Oranges from the US and Brazil are grown mainly for the juice industry, while Spain, the fourth largest grower, grows mainly for the fresh fruit markets.

Where should we buy oranges from?

In theory it is best to buy from the country nearest to you, because the distance travelled is the shortest and therefore the least greedy on food miles. The UK imports a good proportion of oranges from Spain, 90 per cent of which travel here via road freight. Buying Spanish oranges is also the better, although not ideal, choice in terms of ethical farming practice. After that it is better to buy oranges from other southern European countries or the Middle East. Italy, Morocco, Israel and Egypt also produce oranges for the UK. Italy is the main producer of blood oranges, the delicious red-pigmented oranges that have a short season in February and March.

How are oranges grown?

In Spain, orange farming is becoming more intensive as farms increase in size, but there is a move to reduce the amounts of agricultural chemicals used. Until 1980, 80 per cent of Spanish orchards were less than three hectares in size. Methods were based on traditional ones, using natural fertiliser and 'flood' irrigation techniques (oranges need a lot of water), with most weeding, harvesting and pruning done by hand. But now, as farms get larger, irrigation is by automatic drip feed, which reduces labour costs, and there can be heavy use of artificial fertilisers and pesticides (see below). Farmers grow only a few popular varieties of orange, mainly Navels and Navelinas. In the height of the season these flood the market, pushing the price down and bringing poverty to farmers.

Are there pesticide residues on my orange?

There was a shocking report in 1999 revealing that, when over 66 samples of oranges from all over the world were taken (by UK authorities), a cocktail of chemicals was found on each. While none exceeded the maximum residue levels set by the government watchdog (too high, environmental groups claim), there were some nasties there, including 2,4-D, a herbicide that is toxic to humans and which easily leaches into soil and water, polluting the environment.

Until quite recently, Spanish growers have used far too many fertilisers and pesticides. A 1988 study of 300 *parcelas* (plantations) in the Valencia region showed that over 70 per cent of groves had excessive levels of phosphate and potassium in the soil, more than was needed by the plants. The water supply was shown to contain concentrations of nitrogen much higher than the maximum amount permitted for drinking water under European Commission Regulations.

Overspraying was blamed, and the British retailers insisted the Spanish growers join a scheme in which chemical use could be more strictly audited. Only half signed up, and pesticides on *all* non-organic oranges remain a problem.

What about sprays on other citrus fruits?

The latest surveys showed residues on the majority of samples of limes, grapefruit and lemons, and on all the satsumas tested. Obviously if you are not eating the peel, there is less to worry about, but do wash citrus fruit if you are using the zest.

How can I avoid eating oranges that have been sprayed?

You can't entirely, but organic growers limit the amount of spray they use, making organic oranges a good choice. Organic growers can apply a mixture of fish and kelp products to provide adequate quantities of nitrogen, phosphorous, potassium and micronutrients to the trees. They are permitted the restricted use of copper sulphate spray against pests and fungus but little else. Wash oranges in hot running water if you are going to use the zest.

Why are some citrus fruits sold 'unwaxed'?

Citrus fruit has a fairly long shelf life compared to other fruits but it is usually sprayed with a harmless wax-like coating to extend this. You can do much to remove it by scrubbing the fruit with a soft brush in warm water. Seville oranges (the bitter 'marmalade' oranges) and some lemons are sold unwaxed. Organic producers are permitted to use the coating.

Are there pesticides in my marmalade?

This has been a huge problem but Spanish farmers have taken steps to reduce the use of chemical spray. In 2004 48 samples of marmalade (including two organic ones) were tested for 33 types of pesticide residue. None contained residues of those sought. Organic marmalade will have been made from oranges grown with little or no spray and is now becoming much easier to buy.

Should I worry about who picks my oranges?

Child labour is a problem in Brazilian and Mexican orange farms, whose oranges are used mainly for juices that are sold in the UK. Working conditions can be very poor, with children working 14-hour days at 21 cents (US dollars) per hour. Recently the main Brazilian association of orange growers collaborated in a campaign to eradicate child labour on farms so more children could attend school. Broader social and economic changes are needed for this to take effect and it is estimated that it could take some years. Your concern about these issues can speed this up – consumer boycotts encourage the authorities to act more quickly.

What the supermarkets say

Sainsbury states that it buys citrus fruit from all over the world but that it insists farmers, students and local adults pick the fruits. It sells a Fairtrade equivalent of every citrus fruit.

Waitrose sells organic bitter Seville oranges from the Ave Maria farm in Andalusia for about two to three weeks from the second week in January, plus other organic citrus all year round.

Some **Co-op** stores sell Fairtrade organic oranges, lemons, satsumas, clementines, Navels, Navel lates and Valencias.

Some **Tesco** and **Booths** stores sell Fairtrade oranges, lemons, satsumas and Valencias. **Budgens** does not sell Fairtrade citrus fruit.

If you see the Fairtrade logo on oranges they will have been produced on Sun Orange Farms in the Sunday's River Valley in the Eastern Cape of South Africa. Workers become co-owners of the fruit farms.

Where to buy marmalade and lemon curd

Duchy Originals, The Old Ryde House, 393 Richmond Road, East Twickenham TW1 2EF
Tel: 020 8831 6800
www.duchyoriginals.com
Organic Seville, blood orange or clementine marmalade, and a lemon curd made with untreated Sicilian lemons.

Kitchen Garden Preserves, Unit 15 & 16 Salmon Springs Trading Estate, Cheltenham Road, Stroud, Gloucestershire GL6 6NU
Tel: 01453 759612
www.kitchengardenpreserves.co.uk
Award-winning organic orange marmalade (and five other types, including a choice between rough and fine cut), plus lemon curd. All these preserves have a genuine home-made flavour and appearance. Mail order available.

OYSTERS, MUSSELS, SCALLOPS (AND OTHER BIVALVES)

During the winter, a season of rich food, there is something very appealing about the light, fresh charms of shellfish. A gentle wine and shallot broth with a few mussels and langoustines is an ideal antidote to the big roasts of Christmas, and few things can be more refreshing than oysters washed down with an uplifting glass of champagne. But while many of the species currently in prime condition are abundant and sustainable, finding them is the trick. Furthermore, after the tragedy of the Morecambe Bay cockle pickers, shoppers need reassurance that shellfish are harvested by responsible companies.

When are oysters and other bivalves at their best?
During winter. Wild or rope-grown mussels, scallops, oysters, cockles and the various clam species are excellent during the winter months.

Are bivalves endangered?
All the above are at safe biological limits (except native oysters in some areas) but it is how each type is caught that matters, so check the details given with the species listed below. Both oyster and mussel farming are environmentally sound; neither method produces marine-polluting sediment.

Who harvests shellfish?
Licensed fishermen, fisheries (fishing businesses) and shellfish farms are the backbone of the shellfish industry, but there is also the issue of beach shellfish such as cockles, which can be harvested by less skilled workers. The deaths of 23 Chinese cockle pickers in Morecambe Bay in February 2004 threw light on an underground culture of illegal workforces operated by 'gangmasters'. Since then new legislation has

been brought in to curb bad practice. Locally in Morecambe Bay there's a new permit system, and a dedicated police officer gathering information on any illegal practice on the sands.

How do I know if shellfish are from clean water?
Seawater is graded A, B or C, according to purity. Bivalves from Grade A water can be eaten straight from the sea but those harvested from Grade B or C must be purified in clean water on shore.

Which shellfish should I avoid?
Providing you are satisfied with the catch method and source of the fishery, go for it. Oysters are best bought when there is an R in the month – from September to April, but farms can produce certain types all year round. Always look for shellfish from the UK or Europe. Green-lip mussels (which are sold cooked and frozen or defrosted) lare imported from New Zealand. They may be large and good for stuffing but they are not a patch on fresh mussels harvested in Scotland.

Which shellfish should I buy?
All bivalves should be cooked alive. If they don't reopen after cooking, throw them away.

* **Mussels** – wild mussels grow in the strong tidal waters of estuaries and have the finest texture and flavour. They are hand dived and a good supplier will rest them after cleaning, to reduce the stress caused by harvesting. Rope-grown, farmed mussels are an excellent source of delicious, inexpensive, environmentally friendly shellfish. Choose mussels with smooth shells and sharp edges.
* **Oysters** – wild natives have a powerful marine flavour and plenty of meat in them until May, when their season ends. A top-quality, mature native oyster is a real delicacy but expect to pay more. In some areas, numbers of native oysters are low – ask about the stock if you are concerned. Good-sized farmed oysters from very clean waters are also a good choice.

❧ **Scallops** – large, diver-caught scallops are the best, but very much subject to availability. It is essential to buy scallops harvested from Grade A waters.

❧ **Cockles** – as with other bivalves, the water is tested for levels of pollution and a moratorium imposed if it is found to be contaminated. Some fisheries have complained that the authorities are overzealous in this respect, closing fisheries unnecessarily. As for the workforce issue, buy cockles and other beach-harvested shell-fish from a fishmonger you trust, or ask where they were picked and who by.

❧ **Clams** – there are several types: full-flavoured venus clams, commonly used in *spaghetti a la vongole*; carpetshell or palourdes, tender and delicate tasting; cherry clams – big clams to eat raw with lemon; and little paparazzi from Italy – so called because their shells open and shut in full view of sunbathers on Italian beaches. Razor clams have large amounts of sometimes quite powerfully flavoured flesh.

What's in the supermarkets?

Supermarkets sell few live shellfish, although some will sell mussels and occasionally oysters. Most scallops are previously frozen; the green-lipped mussels that have travelled all the way from New Zealand will have been previously cooked and frozen.

Sainsbury sells good-quality mussels and oysters from the Hebrides and Northern Ireland respectively, which are farmed in Grade A waters and bought seasonally.

Marks & Spencer sells Scottish mussels, rope grown in Shetland. These are then sold cooked and pre-packed with dressings, to be reheated by the customer.

The Co-op sells wild Northeast Atlantic mussels (dredged) and farmed oysters subject to availability.

Where to buy shellfish from a sustainable source

Some coastal fish merchants who buy from the day boats and local inshore fisheries will send shellfish that has barely been out of the water a few hours to your door. Be warned that weather conditions can affect availability. Live shellfish keeps longer than you think – oysters will live for five days in the fridge.

Farmers' markets can be good places for shellfish. To find the ones nearest to you, check **www.farmersmarkets.net** (tel: 0845 458 8420), or **www.lfm.org.uk** (tel: 020 7833 0338) for London.

Andy Race Fish Merchants Ltd, Mallaig, Inverness-shire, Scottish Highlands PH41 4PX
Tel: 01687 462626
www.andyrace.co.uk
Scottish hand-dived scallops (shucked), mussels farmed in Grade A waters, and an intermittent supply of palourdes, razor clams and other clams.

Butley Orford Oysterage, Market Hill, Orford, Woodbridge, Suffolk IP12 2LH
Tel: 01394 450277
www.butleyorfordoysterage.co.uk
Oysters from the traditional oyster beds at Butley Creek.

Cuan Oysters, John McElreavey, Cuan Sea Fisheries Ltd, Sketrick Island, Killinchy, Newtownards, Country Down, Northern Ireland
Tel: 028 97 541461
www.cuanoysters.com
Oysters farmed in Grade A waters.

Falmouth Bay Oysters Ltd, The Docks, Falmouth, Cornwall TR11 4NR
Tel: 01326 316600
www.falmouthoysters.co.uk
Native wild oysters, harvested by traditional day sailing boats from protected Cornish waters, from October to April.

Loch Fyne Seafood, Clachan, Cairndow, Argyll PA26 9BL
Tel: 01499 600264
www.lochfyne.com
A company that takes sustainability seriously. Very high-quality rock oysters from the company's own beds, rope-grown mussels, and scallops caught by divers and small boats.

Matthew Stevens & Son Ltd, Back Road West, St Ives, Cornwall TR26 3AR
Tel: 01736 799392
www.mstevensandson.co.uk
Wild mussels from Exmouth, local cockles, razor clams, wild oysters from River Yealm, wild native oysters from Colchester.

Richard Haward's Oysters, 129 Coast Road, West Mersea Island, Essex CO5 8PA
Tel: 01206 383284
www.richardhawardsoysters.co.uk
Colchester native and Gigas oysters, grown in the shallow creeks leading from the Blackwater river towards the west of Mersea Island in Thames Estuary. Haward also supplies his wife's restaurant on the island, the Company Shed.

The Whitstable Shellfish Company, Westmead Road, Whitstable, Kent CT5 1LW
Tel: 01227 282375
www.whitstable-oysters.co.uk
Wild native oysters from Whitstable, plus farmed oysters cultivated on the shores of the Kilbrandon Estate, Scotland.

PASTA

You can mark the moment when pasta became a global fast food with a technological invention. It was Braibanti's first fully automated production line that kneaded, shaped and, crucially, dried the pasta – making it the perfect food for export. But while tonnes and tonnes of pasta are joyfully consumed every day in the UK, the inbuilt cultural snobbery that Italians employ when buying pasta is absent. In Italian supermarkets the majority of space is taken by old and trusted brands. In the UK we buy significantly more supermarket own-brand pasta of uncertain origin and – a phenomenon virtually unknown to Italians – long-life 'fresh' pasta. Every time the pasta we buy disappoints, we blame our supposed poor cooking skills but often it's the pasta that is at fault . . .

Why are there two types of pasta, fresh and dried?

Traditionally it was down to the wheat. The hot climate of southern Italy was suitable for growing hard durum wheat, while in the north they grew a softer species that yielded flour with little strength, like our own plain flour. In the south the durum wheat flour needed only water to make a stiff dough that could stand up to being extruded through the presses – the 'dyes' that create the shapes. In the north, eggs were added to the flour to give strength to the dough and the pasta was either rolled and cut into ribbons (e.g. tagliatelle and fettuccine) or cut and wrapped around fillings (e.g. tortellini and ravioli).

Is packaged durum wheat pasta a pure food?

Pasta has not lost its integrity, in spite of mechanisation. It contains durum wheat, water and nothing else. Compare this to white sliced bread, which needs help in the form of added enzymes, preservatives and flour improvers to survive high-speed manufacture. As to pasta's nutritional content, Italian scientists claim it provides a dripfeed of energy and is therefore a perfect food. Pasta's detractors – the Atkins camp – say it makes you sluggish; an attitude shared by the 1930s Futurist poet, Marinetti, who said Italians would never be anything but a peasant nation unless they gave up pasta. Marinetti, incidentally, was much admired by Mussolini.

Does pasta contain chemical residues?

Non-organic durum wheat is sprayed with fertilisers, pesticides and fungicides. In 2003 tests for chemical residues were carried out on 144 samples of dried pasta. Only one sample contained a residue of chlorpyrifos, but it was under the maximum residue limit. Tests in 1999 found no residues. Pasta is therefore low risk, but the organic sector would like to see more control of chemicals to protect the wider environment.

Why can mass-market 'fresh' pasta be disappointing?

So-called 'fresh' pasta, sold vacuum packed in supermarket chiller cabinets, has a shelf life of up to six weeks. It is made with durum wheat rather than soft wheat flour, which can be pasteurised along with the eggs that bind it. Pasteurisation hardens the pasta to a chamois-leather texture. Check the ingredients list for stabilisers and preservatives in fillings, and for starches that provide cheap 'bulk'. Note that little or no information is given about the quality of any meat used.

Is it true that you get what you pay for with pasta?

This is where you must tune into the Italian attitude. Snobbery regarding pasta does not necessarily mean buying the most expensive. Some 'artisan' dried packaged pasta can be very disappointing. Avoid budget pasta, costing 40–50 pence per pack. Made with inferior-quality wheat, it is sticky and heavy, even when cooked *al dente*. Look closely at the pasta you buy. It should be smooth, with no cracks. Black grains in the pasta are a sign of poor-quality durum wheat.

Should I trust the generic Italian brands?

The big brands are trusted in Italy because they make much of the quality of the wheat they use. Brands such as Barilla, Buitoni and Di Cecco use good-quality wheat. Di Cecco has the added advantage of a source of pure mountain water for making pasta at its Abruzzo factory. This means you can eat good pasta at little over £1 for 500g dry weight. Spend more if labelling indicates that the pasta was extruded through bronze 'dyes', which give it a rough surface that sauce adheres to nicely. With practice, you can tell if bronze dyes have been used by checking the surface of the pasta for a slightly mottled look.

How should I cook pasta?

If you follow this method and the pasta splits during cooking, or is heavy and floppy with no bounce, you are a good cook but you have bought poor pasta. So, lots of water – use a five-litre pan – brought to a rolling boil. Don't add oil to it. Add salt a second before you add the pasta; it will momentarily keep the water temperature high so it continues to boil after the pasta is added. Cook for the time specified on the packet (this tends to be accurate on big-brand pasta) but test a minute or so before the time is up. Dried durum wheat pasta should be *al dente* ('to the bite'), meaning that a small, opaque dot is visible inside the string, shape or wall of a tube when cut or bitten. Egg pasta, such as tagliatelle and ravioli, should be quite soft, not *al dente*, but drained before any sign of disintegration. Always dress and serve pasta immediately after draining.

Which pasta shape goes with which sauce?

Of course all pasta goes well with any favourite sauce but many shapes were developed to eat with certain textures and flavours:

* Smooth tubes, such as penne, maccheroni, bucatini and sigaretti – eat with oil and garlic, cream sauces, fish (tuna, anchovies, sardines), and wild mushrooms.
* Ridged tubes, such as sedani/sedanini and rigatoni – eat with

chunky sauces such as tomato, aubergine and ragu (game, beef, sausage or lamb sauces); also good in baked pasta dishes.

* **Short cut, such as farfalle** – eat with creamy sauces or fresh ricotta.
* **Long cut, such as tagliatelle, pappardelle, fettuccine** – eat with meat and game sauces.
* **Small pasta, such as filini, capelli d'angelo, vermicelli, avemarie and paternosti** – eat in minestrone (soups with chunks of vegetable) or in simple broths.
* **Twisted pasta, such as fusilli, gemelli, eliche** – eat in thin sauces, oils and cream.
* **Shells, such as conchiglie and orecchiette** – eat with fried bread-crumbs and garlic, or lentils, peas or pine nuts.
* **Long pasta, such as spaghetti or linguine** – eat with tomato and shellfish sauces.

What's in the supermarkets?

With very few exceptions, supermarket own-brand dried pasta tends to disappoint, being made of lesser-quality wheat than di Cecco, Barilla and the smaller-scale Italian brands. Limited ranges of these brands are available in many supermarkets – but you would do better shopping in a genuine Italian food shop where there is more choice and often better value. The generic Italian brands cost more than the supermarket ones but still provide a source of good, cheap convenience food.

So-called fresh pasta (including ravioli and tortellini) takes up plenty of supermarket aisle space, with new innovations arriving all the time. It's a question now of what *can't* be put inside tortellini, not what can. These foods have a long shelf life, and the accompanying preservatives that make that happen. They have also become big business, so be very wary of cheap fillers (starches) that are added to keep costs down for the producer. These fillers are usually tasteless, so extra salt will be added to compensate. The provenance of the meat in these filled pastas is usually a mystery. **Marks & Spencer** deserves a mention for its policy of using only free-range eggs in its egg pasta, both fresh and dried.

Sainsbury and **Tesco** sell pasta made by the Cipriani group in Venice (**www.cipriani.com**), the family that founded Harry's Bar. This is very finely rolled (100 times!), traditional 'cut' egg pasta, tagliolini and linguini. Once cooked, it has a true home-made taste and is highly recommended.

Where to buy dried pasta

Carluccio's, 12 Great Portland Street, London W1W 8QN
Tel: 020 7580 3050
www.carluccios.com
Twelve types of pasta sourced from artisan suppliers who still make the traditional shapes. Available from Carluccio cafés and shops, or to order online.

Daylesford Organic Farm Shop, Daylesford, Nr Kingham,
Gloucestershire GL56 0YG
Tel: 01608 731700
www.daylesfordorganic.com
Pale, beautifully made pasta that cooks well, packaged in elegant black boxes. Mail order available.

Savoria, 229 Linen Hall – CKp, 162–168 Regent Street,
London W1B 5TB
Tel: 0870 242 1823
www.savoria.co.uk
Online shop stocking fragrant, vitamin-rich pasta from Gina & Sofia made from durum wheat or barley (orzo), plus 20 per cent egg pappardelle ribbons and metre-long spaghetti from Giovanni Perna.

Seggiano, Peregrine Trading, 3 Wedmore Street,
London N19 4RU
Tel: 07041 450110
www.seggiano.co.uk
Organic dried pasta, made in the hilly region of southern Tuscany using durum wheat: penne (quills), chitara (a cut spaghetti with a good rough surface) and linguine (flat extruded spaghetti).

Where to buy fresh pasta

The Fresh Pasta Company, Units 5–6, Lon Parcwr Business Park,
Ruthin, Denbighshire, North Wales LL15 1NJ
Tel: 01824 707020
www.thefreshpastacompany.com
Outstanding, authentic pasta made by Mark Garcia-Oliver with 400g
eggs to 1 kilo '00' flour. Mail order available.

I Sapori di Cavallini, 146 Northcote Rd, London SW11 6RD
Tel: 020 7228 2017
Pasta made by the former Michelin-starred chef, Stefano Cavallini,
who now supplies restaurants as well as running his own shop.
Delivery service (London only).

Machiavelli, Unit F, Hewlett House, Havelock Terrace,
London SW8 4AS
Tel: 020 7498 0880
www.machiavellifood.com
Ninai Zarach imports pasta twice a week from Montecatini near
Florence. Mail order available.

Vittorio Maschio, 22–26 Northcote Road, London SW11 1NX
Tel: 020 7228 1813
With a small list of chef-clients that includes Giorgio Locatelli and
Martin Lam (of Ransome's Dock), Maschio is the best fresh pasta
supplier in London. He works with two assistants in Battersea and
will make pasta to order, collection only.

PEAS

In 2004 Sainsbury claimed it had come up with the pea that would not fall off the fork. Into the supermarket's greens section came 'pea shoots', the live pea plantlings previously thrust into the zeitgeist by their appearance in influential restaurants. Grown indoors on a West Sussex farm, these pea shoots, which are eaten raw, are available all year round and have proved to possess more than novelty value; like all peas, they are rich in fibre plus vitamins A, B12 and C. But a threat to the popularity of the frozen pea? Never. We are still guzzling nearly 100,000 tonnes of those a year – not that there is much wrong with that. Our favourite brands boost British farm incomes and are relatively safe and unadulterated. Imported fresh peas, however, pose troubling debates that environmentalists, aid agencies and consumers find hard to reconcile.

Where do frozen peas come from?

Birds Eye, which has been freezing peas since 1946, sells 50 per cent of frozen peas in our shops. Virtually all of them are grown in the UK (only a shortage will see the company import from New Zealand) and the business supports 380 individual farmers. Turning over £50 million a year, Birds Eye – now part of Unilever – is essential to our farming economy. It does not pack 'own brand' peas for supermarkets or other names, and its corporate transparency makes the brand a safe choice if you want to buy peas with British provenance.

What's the process from farm to freezer counter?

While the peas are processed by state-of-the-art technology, artificial additives are not used. Birds Eye peas are harvested from June to August and, at the moment of ripeness, are picked using specially designed machines that shell and clean them before taking them to the factory. Here each batch is tested with a 'tenderometer', a machine that slices a sample and then puts it before a taste panel to check for sweetness. The peas are then blanched in water at 90°C for

60 seconds, cooled, and blast frozen in a special freezing tunnel at −25°C. The freezing conveyor belt has a bouncing motion, keeping the peas apart. They are held in stores, then packed throughout the year as and when they are required.

Are peas sprayed with pesticides?

Frozen peas were last tested for residues in 2003. Seventy-six samples were tested and residues of the fungicide Vinclozolin were found on one sample imported from Belgium. No residues were found on the British samples.

Podded, air freighted fresh peas (from Kenya, Guatemala and Peru) were tested for residues in 2004. Of the 72 samples tested, 27 contained residues and one (from Guatemala) was found to have exceeded safe levels of the fungicide Dithiocarbamate. The Pesticides Residue Committee says that there is no cause for concern and the authorities in Guatemala were notified. But do be concerned, some of the residues on the other samples were found to have traces of more than one chemical and, with limited knowledge of the cocktail effect of pesticide residues, this is unacceptable.

Can peas be grown without chemicals?

Farmers are being encouraged to reduce artificial treatments and introduce environmentally friendly pest control, using predators, companion planting and pheromone traps, but these measures are voluntary. Birds Eye has worked with the Wildlife Trusts Partnership and birdlife ecologists on the issue, but so far this remains at the research stage. British organic farmers are permitted to use certain treatments deemed 'natural' but admit that peas are a problematic organic crop. Waitrose sells organic British frozen peas, but can only source organic petits pois (a smaller variety of pea, not a small pea) from Europe. There are no GM peas on sale in Europe.

Why do frozen peas often taste better than fresh?

Peas lose their sweetness quickly after picking, even when left in the pod. While there is no better pea to eat than one picked and eaten within hours, the shell-on peas in shops may be several days old and the sugars turned to starch. Most frozen peas are picked, processed and frozen within about two and a half hours, and so retain their sugary taste. Waitrose claims the quickest field to freezer time.

Should I buy fresh imports during the winter months?

The peas, including mangetout and sugar snap peas, typically sent to the UK from African countries during winter are a cash crop. The downside is serious. Large tracts of land that should be used to grow food for countries with a food shortage are instead being used to supply a Western need for an out-of-season pea. Food miles are an issue. Sustain reports that South African peas are air freighted 5,979 miles to our supermarkets and require approximately two and half times the energy to produce, package and distribute as those sourced locally.

Should we avoid imports altogether?

No, but buy from retailers who purchase direct from responsibly run farms where the welfare of the workers is openly paraded. Peas from Africa are exported to the UK by the same companies who export French beans and other salad vegetables (see French Beans, page 188). Waitrose's Kenyan growers receive 50 per cent more than the government minimum wage, plus health checks, maternity leave, subsidised meals and free transport to work.

What's in mushy peas?

The great northern English fish and chip companion – if not served fresh – is basically large marrowfat peas, cooked until they collapse, then canned. Bicarbonate of soda is sometimes added to help soften the mush, and colourings may be added too. The irksome tartrazine (E102) is one of these (in Batchelor's brand), an additive that hyperactive children react badly to, also Brilliant Blue (E133). Together they make a startling green but some manufacturers use the colouring Green S (E142), which is preferable.

Where to buy fresh British peas

The British season runs from May to August, when farmers' markets will often feature fresh peas, especially in the east of England, which is the main pea-growing area. To find the markets nearest to you, check **www.farmersmarkets.net** (tel: 0845 458 8420), or **www.lfm.org.uk** (tel: 020 7833 0338) for London. Don't forget to use the pea pods to make stock for soup.

Organic Connections International Ltd, Riverdale, Town Street, Upwell, Wisbech, Cambridgeshire PE14 9AF
Tel: 01945 773374
www.organic-connections.co.uk
East Anglian-based box scheme that can deliver nationwide. It always has organic peas in season.

Solstice Ltd, New Covent Garden Market, Units A51–2, London SW8 5EE
Tel: 0800 328 7701
www.solstice.co.uk
A new service that supplies the freshest vegetables to London restaurants but now delivers nationwide, too. It sells British peas in May and June and pea shoots all year round.

Sunnyfields Organic, Jacobs Gutter Lane, Totton, Southampton SO40 9FX
Tel: 023 8087 1408
Home-delivery service that sells peas from the southwest during the British season.

Where to buy organic pea sprouts

Aconbury Sprouts, Unit 4 Westwood Industrial Estate, Pontrilas, Hereford HR2 0EL;
Tel: 01981 241155
www.aconbury.co.uk
Delicious, extra healthy sprouting peas and other seeds and pulses.

PHEASANT (AND OTHER GAME)

Game bird shooting may seem like an Edwardian tradition, and pheasant a niche meat enjoyed in gentlemen's clubs, but it comes as a surprise to find that there is in fact a pheasant mountain. We no longer export much pheasant and, as a result, prices at peak season are ridiculously low – not that you would notice this in shops, where an oven-ready pheasant is marked up handsomely. But the shooting culture varies. Anecdotal accounts telling of shoots burying thousands of unwanted shot birds may not be myths. This and the staggered slow release of hand-reared birds into the wild throughout the game bird season has much to do with the commercialisation of shooting – the pursuit of bigger 'bags' to please the paying punter. Responsibly run shoots, producing quality birds that have been carefully handled and processed, are another matter. This is meat to welcome into shops – including supermarkets.

When is the season for pheasant?

The pheasant shooting season begins on 1st October and finishes on 31st January. Fresh pheasant is available for about two weeks after that date. An old, loosely adhered-to law says that pheasant shouldn't be sold after 31st January but it's still possible to buy frozen pheasant meat, game pies and terrines throughout the year.

In the countryside, people give away pheasants – how much should I pay for them in shops?

Bear in mind that a pheasant must be plucked and dressed to be oven ready – a matter of about £2 of the retail price. At the peak of the season in December, when pheasants are very plump, pay about £3.50 – £4 maximum, or you are being ripped off (the pheasant market, after all, is heavily subsidised by shoots). This will serve three people generously and the bones make a gently gamy stock.

Is a game bird a wild bird?

Yes and no. About 10 per cent of the pheasants shot each year derive from the wild population, the rest are birds that have been reared on farms and then released into the wild. The same goes for partridge and, to an extent, mallard. Woodcock, snipe, teal, grouse and wigeon are all wild birds.

Is pheasant rearing and shooting cruel?

Compared to the rearing of broiler-house chicken, no. An intensively reared chicken may live for 40 days, confined in a densely stocked shed – a pheasant gets a minimum of five months, and should spend some of that time in the wild. (Releasing late in the season to ensure a steady supply of birds for the guns is frowned upon by conservation-ists, who nonetheless support shooting.) Two-thirds of reared and released pheasants escape being shot.

How are pheasants reared?

Pheasant chicks, or poults, are confined indoors until they are about ten days' old and then gradually given an increasing amount of outdoor access before being released into pens. For 500 birds a pen is typically 9 × 12 metres. Mature birds naturally escape from these pens later, before they are released, naturalising on farmland and in woodland.

But why are beak clips and other constraints used?

Pheasants are territorially aggressive and gamekeepers may put a soft plastic clip on beaks to prevent them damaging one another. Soft elastic is sometimes employed to stop young pheasants using their wings aggressively. The aim, say the keepers, is to rear a healthy, un-injured wild bird capable of fending for itself, and any constraint is temporary.

Why does commercial shooting have a bad reputation?

Problems arise when shoots rear too many birds, holding them intensively in pens, and releasing them throughout rather than before the season to keep the bag sizes large. This is wrong, say game associations such as the Game Conservancy Trust, the British Association for Shooting and Conservation, the Country Land and Business Association and the Gamekeepers Association. The secretive practice of large-scale 'big bag' shoots burying unwanted dead birds is a threat to the industry, and respect for the quarry is paramount for shooting's survival. Many argue that shooting, when accurate, beats the stress of road transport and the abattoir.

Is game shooting good for the environment?

Yes, farmers, themselves often involved in shooting, will plant a wider diversity of crops to attract birds, spray less and leave stubble in fields for longer – thus attracting all sorts of wildlife and protecting endangered birds such as the song thrush. Shooting generates an estimated £3.2 billion for the rural economy, and extra income for farmers. The Rural Stress Network says the social side of shooting is beneficial to the mental wellbeing of country people.

Is pheasant drug free?

Game farmers and keepers administer the drug, Avatec, to pheasants and partridges to guard against coccidiosis, a disease caused by a parasite. This is an antibiotic 'salt' that is also given to chickens during the fattening stage. The European Food Safety Authority says tests showed no residue of its main compound, lasalocid sodium, in meat or tissue, nor signs of it being either genotoxic or a carcinogen. More information about the effect of this drug is needed, however. It should be used by gamekeeping staff with care, as it is toxic in high doses. The sale of the controversial drug, Emtryl, is banned, but some game farmers stockpiled it before the ban and may still be using it. Good husbandry and low stocking densities are the best guard against disease.

What does a pheasant eat?

Before they are released they are fed a cereal-based diet, which can contain some fishmeal. After release, they live mainly on corn, grass and other plants, and grubs – they are not carnivorous.

Should I worry about shot?

It will not harm you – but, in an effort to widen the market for pheasant, larger processors are screening game birds for shot using metal detectors. They argue that better-quality birds are the solution to the pheasant meat mountain.

How long should pheasant be hung?

About a week, but with climate change it is becoming more advisable for this to be done in the fridge. If you are given birds 'on the feather', take them to the butcher, who can keep them in a large fridge. Oven-ready game keeps for about five days after plucking, and freezes well.

Are other game birds reared and released like pheasants?

Only partridges, and just the red-leg variety. The indigenous grey-leg partridge is a fully wild bird but quite rare. Mallard (wild duck) are usually fully wild, although shoots create an artificial environment to attract large numbers to lakes and ponds. Teal are rarer wild duck. Other fully wild game birds include grouse, black game and ptarmigan, which are found only in the north of Britain and have a short season in high summer. Woodcock and snipe are fully wild game birds that are found in small numbers throughout the country.

But 'game' seems to cover a number of types of meat in shops?

Because they often share a similar habitat and are 'managed' by game-keepers, hare, rabbit and venison come under the title. Not all venison is wild – deer parks and venison farms have sprung up all over the country. One meat that is sold as 'wild' but which is farmed is wild boar (although there are reported escapees in Britain). But try it anyway – they are slow-growing animals that must be reared naturally, and their full-flavoured meat makes an interesting alternative to pork.

Can game birds and wildfowl catch bird flu?

Yes. Game farmers and keepers who have registered their business in 2006 will buy poults as usual, but after a flu outbreak some estates and farms may choose not to buy them, because it is thought that hand-reared birds may have to be kept indoors. In March 2006 the authorities, DEFRA, said they would not advise shoots not to buy poults. A fairly relaxed attitude.

Can I buy game in supermarkets?

Waitrose has a much more imaginative approach to selling game than the other supermarkets. It stocks pheasant, partridge and wild duck in season, either whole or sometimes boned or jointed. It even sells filleted meat, which makes wonderful stir fry, casserole and curry meat. The versatility of their range is admirable.

Where to buy pheasant and other game

Butchers with game licences sell game birds in season. The following retailers offer a home-delivery service unless otherwise stated:

Blackface.co.uk, Weatherall Foods Ltd, Crochmore House, Irongray, Dumfries DG2 9SF
Tel: 01387 730326
www.blackface.co.uk
Blackface is an efficient home delivery service sending game birds, hare and rabbit sourced from local Scottish shoots, plucked or dressed (oven ready) and delivered in a cool box. Well-hung wild venison from the West Highlands is also available.

Cranborne Stores, 1 The Square, Cranborne, Dorset BH21 5PR
Tel: 01725 517210
www.cranbornestores.co.uk
Game birds direct from one estate – and the unusual offer of pheasant eggs in season (early summer).

Everleigh Farm Shop, Everleigh, Marlborough, Wiltshire SN8 3EY
Tel: 01264 850344
David Hammerson runs a superb service with the competence of a field marshal. All types of game in season and sometimes a frozen supply out of season.

E. J. and A. I. Fenton, Dundale Farm, Dundale Road,
Tunbridge Wells, Kent TN3 9AQ
Tel: 01892 822175
Dundale Farm is a traditional Wealden farm. The game comes from its own shoot. Products include pheasants, partridge, wild duck, venison, rabbit and wood pigeon. No home delivery and there is no farm shop but you can phone an order and pick it up from the farm, which is only a mile from the A21.

Furness Fish, Poultry and Game Supplies, Stockbridge Lane,
Off Daltongate, Ulverston, Cumbria LA12 7GB
Tel: 01229 585037
www.morecambebayshrimps.co.uk
Les Salisbury sources game from northern England.

Teesdale Game and Poultry, 82E Barnard Castle,
County Durham DL12 8BJ
Tel: 01833 637153
www.teesdalegame.co.uk
Fresh local game, including grouse, pheasant, mallard, partridge, hare, rabbit and wood pigeon. All cuts of venison, including sausages and mince. Home-made game pies and smoked products.

PORK PIES

Since 1999 a row has rumbled over pork pies, a dispute between the Melton Mowbray Pie Association, which wants to protect the use of the name within a certain radius of the namesake town, and large-scale raised-pie manufacturers, who trade on the name but make their pies nowhere near the town's location in Leicestershire. In December 2005 the makers of the real Melton Mowbray pies triumphed, and manufacturers such as Pork Farms, owned by food giant Northern Foods, will have to remove the words Melton Mowbray from their packaging or move their factory to within the 1,800 square mile 'Melton Pork Pie' zone.

But while the 'real' Melton Mowbray bakers' irritation over the geographical argument is understandable, it's what is in the pie that should matter most. And many of the best artisan-made pies are produced nowhere near Melton Mowbray. In a perfect world, a pork pie would be made with a high percentage of fresh, welfare-friendly pork, wrapped in a casing of pastry made with lard rendered from the same pigs so as not to waste a thing. Sad to say, this is not often the case. The origin of the pork and the naturalness of the other ingredients used in the pie are greater issues for consumers than whether the pie bulges at the sides in true Melton Mowbray style.

What kind of pork is in mass-market pork pies?
Ideally the meat should be British, and preferably from pigs that have been reared to a high standard of animal welfare. Unfortunately there are a lot of pies on the market made with meat from intensively reared pork that may or may not be British. Labelling laws permit a manufacturer to call a pork pie British as long as it is processed in this country – a loophole for manufacturers that ridicules growing demand for traceable meat.

How are most pigs reared?

Compassion in World Farming (CIWF) says that 70 per cent of pigs in the UK are reared intensively indoors, in groups. The government-approved space allowance for pigs (breeding sows and weaners) ranges according to their size. For example 0.40 square metres is the allowance for pigs weighing between 30 and 50 kilos – a tight squeeze. The bedding should be straw, though farmers can use other material, such as wood shavings or sawdust, hay, mushroom compost and peat, essentially giving the pig foraging material. The law, however, allows farmers to give pigs footballs or chains to 'play with' instead, an alternative condemned by CIWF. Sows about to give birth are put in farrowing crates to restrict movement and prevent piglets being crushed. Piglets and sow will remain in the crate for four weeks before being moved into a group. The average lifespan of a breeding sow is three years, during which time she will have approximately five litters of piglets. For more on pig welfare, see Bacon (and Pork), page 48.

How does pig welfare differ abroad?

The RSPCA says that intensive pig rearing in the UK is less cruel than that permitted in EU countries. Tethering the sows in the crates throughout their pregnancies – and therefore most of their lives – is still allowed in the EU. Pigs living in such conditions have no quality of life; they are used until exhausted, then disposed of. Manufacturers can easily 'slip' this meat (or pork lard) sourced abroad into pies, without having to reveal its origins.

Will I have to pay more for naturally reared pork?

Yes, up to twice as much, but even organically reared pork is good value, especially when used in pies because the cheaper cuts lend themselves well to these recipes.

Which cuts of meat are used to make pork pie filling?

The best meat to use is a mixture of shoulder and belly, but the ratio changes depending on the value of the pie. The more shoulder meat used, the more expensive the pie.

Should the meat in a pork pie be pink?

Authentic pies are made with fresh, not cured, pork and should be a grey-white colour inside. A pink interior is a sign that the pie is either made with cured pork (see below) or possibly includes food colouring.

Do pork pies contain anything other than natural ingredients?

Some of the cheaper ranges do. Pink meat can be a sign of potassium nitrate (saltpetre), or similar preservative. There may be potato starch to bulk out the filling (big profits for the manufacturer), gelling agents to hold it together, wheat rusk and various flavourings or even artificial colourings.

What type of pastry is used to make pork pies?

The crisp, often heavy, pastry is hot water crust and should be made using lard, but labels often show that bakers have used hydrogenated or partly hydrogenated fat. Do not be fooled into thinking that hydro genated fat is better for you. Too much lard may be bad for the heart but transfats in hydrogenated fat are linked to a far greater number of serious health problems (see Butter and Spreads, page 99).

What's in the jelly?

The jelly is a stock brewed from pork bones. Poured into the opening of the pastry after the pie has cooked and cooled, it protects it from drying out.

Should a pie have straight sides?

Genuine Melton Mowbray bakers say not. Pies with straight sides are cooked in a hinged metal cylinder, which is removed when the pie is nearly cooked so the sides can brown.

What should I look for when buying pork pies?

Read the label, if there is one, looking for natural ingredients – there should be no hydrogenated fat and no monosodium glutamate. On the other hand, there should be a high proportion of meat – above

40 per cent. Buy pies that contain guaranteed British meat and don't be fooled by the use of the 'Melton Mowbray' tag. For example, Morrisons sells a 'Vale of Mowbray' pie made from pork 'sourced in the EU', and their Melton Mowbray pie is made with EU pork fat!

What the supermarkets say

Marks & Spencer says it uses Danish fat in all but its 'Hand Finished Pork Pie' and 'Uncured Pork Pie', but it does use British pork (from pigs kept loose indoors) for all pies.

Waitrose uses 100 per cent British pork.

Sainsbury stocks a good range of pork pies called Melton Mowbray Pork Pies, which originate from the UK. Its conventional range is made with hydrogenated fat.

The Co-op pork pies are made using UK-sourced, indoor-reared pork, plus lard sourced from Italy and shortening containing hydrogenated vegetable oil.

Budgens sells pork pies made in Melton Mowbray. The pork is sourced from the UK and Belgium, the lard derived from an 'unknown' source. The pies also contain hydrogenated fat.

Tesco sells Melton Mowbray pork pies, plus Finest (expensive) and Value Pack (cheap) pies. None of the pies is made with outdoor-reared pork (although it is all British sourced) and Tesco's Finest pork pies contain hydrogenated fat, and lard sourced from Italy.

Where to buy 100 per cent British pork pies:

Cranborne Stores, 1 The Square, Cranborne, Dorset BH21 5PR
Tel: 01725 517210
www.cranbornestores.co.uk
Very good pies that top the list on flavour. Dark meat (from pigs reared on Dorset fields and woodland), good jelly and crisp, lardy pastry. Mail order available.

Dickinson & Morris, 10 Nottingham Street, Melton Mowbray,
Leicestershire LE13 1NW
Tel: 01664 482068
www.porkpie.co.uk
The brave company that headed the campaign against big business
and earned the original Melton Mowbray pie recipe a PDI uses
100 per cent British pork, despite being a larger manufacturer. Mail
order available.

Emmett's of Peasenhall, Peasenhall, Saxmundham,
Suffolk IP17 2HJ
Tel: 01728 660250
www.emmettsham.co.uk
For pies with a thin, crisp crust, stuffed with rare-breed free-range
pork, made by the Handmade Food Company. Emmett's also sells
excellent pork and bacon that they cure themselves. Handmade Pies
are also available at Partridges, 2–5 Duke of York Square, Sloane
Square, London SW3 4LY (tel: 020 7730 0651) and Fortnum and
Mason, 181 Piccadilly, London W1A 1ER (tel: 020 7734 8040).

The Ginger Pig, 8–10 Moxon Street, London W1U 4EW
Tel: 020 7935 7788
Truly delicious pies made by hand (in full view of customers) in a
wonderful butcher's shop using meat from specialist breeds.

F. C. Phipps, Osborne House, Mareham le Fen, Boston,
Lincolnshire P22 7RW
Tel: 01507 568235
www.britainsbestbutcher.co.uk
Exceptional pies made from Berkshire and Gloucester Old Spot pork.
Mail order available.

POTATO CRISPS

The nation's love affair with potato crisps is going through uncertain times. She loves me, she loves me not, wonder the makers of the golden discs that captured our hearts in the 1960s. Well Golden Wonder no longer feels loved, as the company hit the crash barrier in January 2006, the pain all the more excruciating as Walkers took the grand prix as market leader. The failure of Golden Wonder is down to the millions their main competitor spent on advertising, using ex-England football hero Gary Lineker to lure in the punters. But that is not the reason why commercial crisp fryers are feeling some pain.

Among the foods swept off the shelf in the Sudan 1 scare in February 2005 were packets of Walkers Worcester Sauce crisps containing traces of the illegal dye. Time will tell if the additive was more harmful than the colossal amount of salt in commercial brands, but there is no doubt that crisps, unhelpfully promoted by celebrities in adverts that aggressively target children, are becoming the bane of health-conscious parents' lives. There is a definite move towards snacking on wholesome nuts, seeds and fruit and a new band of crisp fryers has emerged, proving that while crisps will never be slimmers' food, they need not be the bogeyman of the lunchbox.

Why do all big-brand crisps taste, feel and look the same?
The big brands, including Walkers, blanch (wash) their peeled sliced potatoes before cooking them, removing starches and sugars to provide uniform colour, taste and crispness. This process also removes flavour, which is then 'put back' with the help of salt and other artificial flavourings. Supporters of blanching say that crisps made this way melt in the mouth, whereas crisps cooked from raw cut the gums.

How do the big brands differ from traditionally made crisps?
With few exceptions, traditionally made – often called hand-fried or 'kettle-cooked' – crisps are not blanched, just sliced and put straight in the oil. They vary in crispness and colour and have more flavour.

What's in the flavourings?

Labelling law differentiates between 'flavouring' and 'natural flavouring'. There are four types of flavouring used in food:

* **Artificial flavouring** – chemical flavours that imitate natural ones. These are very rarely used by crisp manufacturers.
* **Flavour enhancers** – love the terminology – are a problem. They include monosodium glutamate (MSG) and the related additives, guanylate and inosinate (E621–635). These are linked to hyperactivity, heart palpitations, migraine and depression, among many other health problems. Hydrolised vegetable protein (HVP), another flavour enhancer, is processed unspecified vegetable protein, which can be contaminated in small quantities by a cancer-causing chemical, 3MCPD.
* **Flavouring** – which the industry calls nature-identical flavouring; in spite of its clever name, it's certainly not natural. The chemical element of food with flavour is identified and isolated, then extracted and copied artificially. It is used to capture the flavour of ingredients such as herbs, where the smell dominates and the flavour is hard to define. It does not always work; these flavourings usually have a tinny ring to them.
* **Natural flavouring** – the most acceptable. Because vinegar would make a crisp soggy, or cheese would 'fall off', the flavouring is forced through special equipment and spray dried, ionising it into a powder.

Is there too much salt in crisps?

Crisps made from blanched potato slices are often saltier than crisps made from unblanched potatoes because much of the starch and therefore the flavour has been rinsed away. Check the pack for the salt content. Remember that if the nutritional information on the pack says sodium instead of salt, you must multiply this by 2.5 to get the salt content. So 1.2g sodium equals about 3g salt. A 34.5g single portion pack of Walkers contains 0.5g of salt (0.2g of sodium). With the recommended daily allowance of salt for an adult being 6g, that's one-sixth of the allowance gone in a snack – before you have eaten meals. Children should eat no more than half that amount.

Are there any other unnatural additives in crisps and other snacks?
Starch is sometimes used as a carrier for the artificial flavourings. This is especially common with 'snacks' made from re-formed dehydrated potato. The starch used can be wheat flour, rice flour or cornstarch. Sugars are sometimes added (in the form of maltodextrin), plus emulsifiers and plenty of colours.

Does it matter which oil potato crisps are cooked in?
Crisps can be cooked in any oil, but some of the oils used contain high levels of saturated fat. They might be palm oil, rapeseed or canola but need only be labelled as vegetable oil. Ideally, crisps should be cooked in sunflower oil but the big brands are wary of this because the oil must be changed often between frying batches to stop the formation of free fatty acids (FFAs). When FFAs are activated in the oil, the crisps that are cooked in it will not have a long shelf life. Changing the oil is costly, hence the higher price of crisps cooked in sunflower oil. FFAs are not activated as quickly in the 'vegetable' cooking oils favoured by the big brands, lowering the price.

What does 'hand cooked' mean?
The welcome revival of hand-cooked crisps, started by the Kettle brand in 1982, brought back the human element to crisp frying. Because these crisps are not blanched, and the skin is left on, they cannot be fried by automated machinery. Instead each batch is visually checked to make sure it's the right colour and crispness before being removed from the fryer.

Skin on or off?
Skin adds yet more flavour, so less salt is needed. It is virtually un-detectable to children.

Is the game up for big-brand crisps?

In fairness, they are beginning to change their ways. Walkers now fries in a type of sunflower oil and is beginning to imitate some traditional ways with flavour, but the MSG, HVP and higher salt levels in the big brands still make traditionally cooked crisps a better choice.

What impact do crisps have on the environment?

It is not so much the potato crops that cause problems as the oil in which crisps are cooked. Palm oil, or olein (its name when refined), forms part of the oil that mass-market crisps are cooked in. It is a problematic crop in Southeast Asia, where huge amounts of land have been cleared of jungle to make way for plantations. The World Wildlife Fund For Nature, which is currently assessing the situation, reports damage to wildlife, increased vulnerability to wave damage in coastal areas, and unfair treatment of indigenous tribes, who are forced off land where they have only traditional rights.

Are vegetable crisps healthier?

No – at least not the ones that are cooked in oil. There are, however, oven-dried apple crisps available. They do contain a lot of natural sugar, though, and are not a diet food.

What's in the supermarkets?

Sainsbury's own-brand crisps are cooked in sunflower oil and made using three potato types: Anya, Pentland Dell and Charlotte. The standard range is blanched but its Taste The Difference crisps are not blanched and the skins are left on.

Marks & Spencer sells 'full-on flavour' crisps that are cooked in palmolein (refined palm oil). Its range of hand-cooked crisps is cooked in sunflower or olive oil and the potato slices are not blanched.

Budgens' potato crisps are fried in refined 'vegetable' oil – it did not offer details of the type of vegetable used. The potatoes are blanched before frying.

Tesco sells Kettle crisps and **Waitrose** sells Burt's, Kettle and Tyrell's.

Where to buy naturally flavoured crisps hand cooked in sunflower oil

Organic crisps tend to be imported, with the exception of good organic hand-fried crisps from Kettle. The following traditionally made crisps are highly recommended:

Burt's Potato Chips, The Parcel Shed, Station Yard, Kingsbridge, Devon TQ7 1ES
Tel: 01548 852220
www.burtschips.com
Especially good rustic crisps made in Devon. They have a deep flavour and are cooked unblanched in sunflower oil, with natural flavourings and a low salt content. Even the no-salt crisps taste powerful. Mail order available.

Jonathan Crisp, Roysse Court, Bridge Street, Abingdon, Oxfordshire OX14 3HU
Tel: 0871 244 8510
www.jonathancrisp.co.uk
Unblanched Lincolnshire potatoes, hand fried in sunflower oil. Mail order available.

Pipers Crisps, Wellington House, Wellington Way, Elsham, Brigg, Lincolnshire DN20 0SP
Tel: 01652 686960
www.piperscrisps.com
Again, slices of potato hand fried in the traditional way.

Pret a Manger, 1 Hudson's Place, London SW1V 1PZ
Tel: 020 7827 8888
www.pretamanger.com
Unblanched crisps, hand fried in sunflower oil.

Seabrook Potato Crisps, Seabrook House, Duncombe Street,
Bradford BD8 9AJ
Tel: 01274 546405
A good choice if you prefer the soft texture of blanched crisps, these
are cooked in sunflower oil. Mail order available.

Tyrrells, Tyrrells Court, Stretford Bridge, Leominster,
Herefordshire HR6 9DQ
Tel: 01568 720244
www.tyrrellspotatochips.co.uk
Hand made on a Herefordshire farm, these are very crunchy crisps
made of unblanched potatoes fried in sunflower oil. They come in
several well-balanced natural flavours. Sweet apple crisps also available.

POTATOES AND OVEN CHIPS

Is it potatoes we love or the fat they are inevitably cooked with? The melting lump of butter, the dripping with the roast, or best of all the fat in the fryer. Fat carries flavour, and dosing a jacket potato with butter intensifies all that is nice about the taste of both the skin and the wadding inside. Trade organisations have a habit of coming up with jolly statistics, and apparently every year we eat 500 potatoes each. But lovely as they are, those 500 potatoes could taste even better. Loath as I am to say without scientific foundation that organic potatoes taste better than conventional ones, organic farmers tend to grow many more varieties and among them are potatoes with incredible flavour. Buy them and you will encourage farmers, currently struggling to profit from growing unsubsidised crops of endless, dull old Maris Piper, to diversify.

When are potatoes in season?
There are three British growing seasons for potatoes:

* **New potatoes or earlies** – these are planted from January to March and arrive in shops from May to July. There are even earlier potatoes, from the sunnier climes of Jersey and Cornwall, which arrive in shops as early as January and are utterly, unmissably delicious.
* **Second earlies** – planted between February and May, these are in shops from July to October.
* **Maincrop** – planted in April and harvested through September and October, these are varieties with good keeping qualities and will be in shops throughout the year.

How do the varieties differ?
Potatoes are divided into two groups, 'waxy' and 'floury'. New potatoes have a waxy texture, and indeed most potatoes do if eaten

when relatively small, soon after picking. Famous waxy varieties include the early Jersey Royals and Cornish potatoes. All waxy potatoes are good in salads or gratins, where they need to hold their shape. Floury potatoes have a more granular texture and are the ones that 'chip', mash or roast the best.

Why do there seem to be only a few varieties of potatoes in shops?

This is an area of horticulture where the lack of diversity is virtually criminal. Maris Piper, King Edward, Estima and Cara are the names you will almost always see on potato bags (if you see a name at all). Which variety of potato is grown is now a matter for the retailers and processors (makers of oven chips and so on), when it was once the domain of growers. Potatoes with long keeping qualities are particular favourites with the supermarkets. About 80–100 varieties of potato can be grown in the UK but just 5 per cent of these are grown commercially. As a result we have dull uniformity when we could be excitedly anticipating the approaching season of scores of types throughout most of the year. I should add that organic growers have found that growing a greater variety helps prevent the spread of disease.

How many of the potatoes on sale are British?

About 80 per cent, but it may be less when there is a particularly wet autumn and farmers are unable to 'lift' the crop. Country of origin will be shown on the pack, or sack, or near the box if they are sold loose. Keep in mind that imported potatoes use more fuel to get to the UK – although the Scottish crop is no nearer to the south of England than France, so buying the odd French potato is a loyalty rather than a food-mile issue. Jersey Royal potatoes travel to the UK via boat, the least fuel-greedy transport.

Should I worry about pesticides in potatoes?

Residues on potatoes are always a cause for concern. While the government's set maximum residue levels are rarely exceeded, some of the chemicals used in potato cultivation are known to be toxic. Aldicarb is a nerve poison used to kill insects and worms on potatoes but environmental campaigners say it is also taken up by the roots and circulated around the whole plant. The World Health Organisation classifies it as 'extremely hazardous'. In 2003 the government tested 144 potato samples, finding detectable levels of aldicarb on 2 per cent. In 2004 73 'maincrop' potatoes were tested for 23 residues; 18 contained residues of aldicarb.

Are pesticides the only chemicals used?
No. Residues in the 2003 report included chlorpropham, which is used during the storage stage as a plant growth regulator that prevents potatoes sprouting. Chlorpropham is a powerful 'pre-emergence' weed killer that prevents weeds even from germinating. It allows the industry to store potatoes for up to ten months. The potatoes are sprayed with the chemical soon after arrival in long low sheds that have large electric fans to keep the air moving.

How are organic potatoes stored?
Organic farmers are not permitted to use synthetic growth inhibitors. At present they must store potatoes in cool, dark conditions, but the search is on for a natural sprout inhibitor.

Are oven chips good for you?
They are much lower in fat than deep-fried chips but the fat used can be hydrogenated and contain unhealthy transfats (see page 99). McCains oven chips are made without hydrogenated fat. McCains oven chips are produced using the following process (the company uses just one type of potato, by the way – 600,000 tonnes of them per year, 90 per cent of which are British):

The potatoes are washed.
Their skins are loosened with high-pressure steam.
The peel is brushed off, then collected to be used as cattle
    feed.

Black spots, bruises and rotten parts are removed.
The potatoes are put through a high-speed strip cutter.
They are then blanched at 82°C for several minutes to destroy
  enzyme activity and remove reducing sugars.
The chips are fried at 200°C for 30 seconds to five minutes.
Finally they are blast frozen before packaging.

Well, no additives to speak of, so innocent enough – but when one realises that all this (apart from inspection) is done by machine, that is a lot of fuel consumption for a job that could easily be done in the home kitchen using only our hands. Note for those who are time poor: it takes approximately 60 seconds to peel and cut a potato.

Are any UK-sold potatoes genetically modified?
No, they are not permitted for sale.

Which are better, muddy or clean potatoes?
Muddy ones are better because the mud helps them keep, so don't be lazy – a nail brush speeds up the job of cleaning them no end. Some potatoes need mud – Jersey Royals, for example, need it to keep their skins nice and soft so they can be scraped away. Some supermarkets insist that the Jersey potato co-operative scrub the potatoes and pack them into plastic trays. Boycott these at all costs.

Do organic potatoes taste better?
Some of the most delicious potatoes I have eaten are organic, but this may be because organic farmers grow some interesting older varieties. Natural fertilisers do affect taste, however. The Jersey growers use seaweed from local beaches and attribute the lemony flavour of their potatoes to this.

How should I store potatoes?
Potatoes keep best in the dark at 16°C, taken out of their plastic bags, but most homes are warmer than this. They will blacken, however, if kept too long below 11°C, so the fridge is not really the place for

storage either. Best of all, store them in a metal bin outside, preferably in a paper sack.

Should I buy only potatoes that look perfect?

Do not buy green potatoes, or ones that are soft or have wrinkly skins or nasty black spots. You can knock off the odd sprout. Knobbly is fine, and sometimes a characteristic of an interesting breed.

How should the different types be cooked?

The following commercial types suit these basic uses, but Maris Piper, King Edward and Desiree will do most things, in a dull way:

* **Boiling and mashing** – Saxon, Nadine, Estima
* **Roasting** – Wilja, Romano, King Edward
* **Baking** – Cara, Marfona, Estima
* **Chipping** – Maris Piper, King Edward, Sante
* **Salads** – Nicola, Maris Peer, Charlotte

What the supermarkets say

Sainsbury sources its main crop of potatoes from the UK, stating a preference for buying British when in season. When British ones are not available, the potatoes can be imported by road or sea freight from France, Israel, Egypt, Spain, Italy and Portugal. Sainsbury sells organic potatoes.

Marks & Spencer states that although British produce is always its first choice, the British potato crop can become unavailable as M&S does not use persistent sprout-suppressant pesticides. When the crops cannot be obtained in the UK, it sources abroad in Israel or Spain. There is an organic alternative.

The Co-op main crop of potatoes is 100 per cent British. Its new potatoes are sourced from Israel, Egypt and Majorca and delivered by road and sea freight. There is a range of organic new potatoes. All potatoes from the Co-op are sold in biodegradable packaging.

Budgens sells exclusively British potatoes, including an organic equivalent.

Tesco sources its potatoes from Europe, the UK, Israel and Egypt. It offers organic potatoes too.

All supermarkets sell Jersey Royal potatoes when in season and some sell the Cornish equivalent.

Both Sainsbury and Waitrose are involved in admirable programmes that encourage the farmers that supply them to grow unusual varieties – these are on sale during the second early and maincrop season and are well worth seeking out. **Waitrose** also sells own-label organic oven chips.

Where to buy British potatoes

When out driving, look for potato sales at the farm gate or smallholders' honesty-box sales. I have bought excellent potatoes this way, at bargain prices in easy-to-store paper sacks.

Farmers' markets are also a good source of potatoes. To locate the one nearest to you, check **www.farmersmarkets.net** (tel: 0845 458 8420), or **www.lfm.org.uk** (tel: 020 7833 0338) for London. Check for your nearest farm-gate sale at **www.bigbarn.co.uk**.

Carroll's Heritage Potatoes Ltd, Tiptoe, Cornhill-on-Tweed, Northumberland TD12 4XD
Tel: 01890 883060
www.heritage-potatoes.co.uk
Their mission is to reintroduce to the consumer a range of potatoes that have disappeared from the market over recent decades. Twelve varieties of Heritage potatoes (pre 1950) are on sale from July to March. Mail order available.

The Jersey Royal Potato Post, Woodlands Farm,
La rue de Maupertuis, St Helier, Jersey JE2 3HG
Tel: 07797 746464
www.jerseyroyalpotatopost.com
Very fresh, lemony-flavoured Jerseys, delivered to your door in protective packaging.

Ryton Organic Gardens, Coventry, Warwickshire CV8 3LG
Tel: 024 7630 8201
www.gardenorganic.org.uk
The Henry Doubleday Research Association, now re-branded Garden Organic, is a trust that protects old food plant varieties. There is a shop at its gardens near Coventry where organic rare varieties are sold in season.

Good box schemes around the UK that will deliver potatoes

Nationwide
Abel & Cole, 8–15 MGI Estate, Milkwood Road,
London SE24 0JF
Tel: 0845 262 6262
www.abel-cole.co.uk

East Midlands
Manor Farm, 77 Main Street, Long Whatton,
Loughborough LE12 5DF
Tel: 01509 646413
www.manororganicfarm.co.uk

West Midlands
Boxfresh Organics, Unit 5C, Rodenhurst Business Park,
Rodington, Shropshire SY4 4QU
Tel: 01952 770006
www.boxfreshorganics.co.uk

Northeast
North East Organic Growers, Earth Balance, West Sleekburn
Farm, Bedlington, Northumberland NE22 7AD
Tel: 01670 821070
www.neog.co.uk

Northwest
Mossley Organic And Fine Foods, 11–13 Arundel Street, Mossley,
Manchester OL5 0NY
Tel: 01457 837743
www.mossleyorganicandfinefoods.co.uk

London, Midlands and Southwest
Riverford Organic Vegetables Ltd, Wash Barn, Buckfastleigh,
Devon TQ11 0LD
Tel: 0845 600 2311
www.riverford.co.uk

Northern Ireland
Burrenwood Produce, 38 Burrenbridge Road, Castlewellan,
County Down BT31 9HT
Tel: 028 4377 1844

Wales
Graig Farm Organics, Dolau, Llandrindod Wells, Powys LD1 5TL
Tel: 01597 851655
www.graigfarm.co.uk

Scotland
Damhead Organic Foods, 32A Damhead, Old Pentland Road,
Lothianburn, Edinburgh EH10 7EA
Tel: 0131 448 2091
www.damhead.co.uk

PRAWNS

If a generation can identify itself by the most popular food in the pub, right now we are smack in the midst of the tiger prawn era. There is so much to love about the springy-fleshed, chicly oriental warm-water prawn. Its pinkness, its gentle taste, the way that you can buy them raw and they don't fall to bits when you sling them into the curry pot. Coated in breadcrumbs, they are the goujon of goujons – the pert little things 'dip' neatly, their firm tails a perfect natural handle to grip between index finger and thumb. Surely there's nothing wrong with a plate of butterflied prawns . . .?

Oh, believe me, I really hate to do this, but most tiger (and king) prawns are seriously problematic. Once it was predicted that they would help boost the economies of developing countries; now the prawn trade is being held responsible for causing severe environmental damage, adversely affecting the communities who should have thrived on their success.

But what of those other prawns? Sweet, succulent North Atlantic prawns, spiky langoustines (Dublin Bay prawns or scampi to some), tiny brown shrimps from Morecambe Bay and those bright red prawns from the African coast; some we can eat in abundance, some we shouldn't – it is a different story for each.

Where do tiger and king prawns come from?
They are cultivated mainly in developing countries – among them Indonesia, Vietnam, China, Bangladesh, Thailand, Honduras and Guatemala – and a proportion are fished from the wild for sale. Significantly, fishing from the wild stock serves to harvest fry for the fish farms. Both methods are giving international environment agencies the heebie-jeebies, and understandably so.

What's wrong with prawn farming?
Prawn farming, they claim, has been responsible for destroying 25 per cent of the world's mangrove forests – vegetation so vital to oxygen

production that you could dub it Rainforest-on-Sea. But clearing mangroves to make way for the farms is only one of the problems. Stocking prawns at high densities in an effort to make prawn farming more profitable necessitates the use of pesticides, growth-promoting hormones and antibiotics. Along with a mass of effluent emanating from farms, toxicity spreads into the local marine environment, water supply and agricultural land.

What's wrong with warm-water prawn trawling?
News of the southern hemisphere wild prawn harvest provides little comfort. Trawling for fry (to supply farms) damages marine stocks and consequently the income of local fishermen. Warm-water prawn trawling damages the seabed and with it spawning areas for wild species. Many of these are anyway brought up as by-catch (essentially wasted fish). Scientists have recorded ratios of 20 kilos of by-catch brought up in nets yielding just 1 kilo of prawns.

But surely some sacrifice must be made to provide trade opportunity for developing countries?
This is very debatable. With prawns costing around £20 per kilo in UK supermarkets, the far-away farmers leapt at the chance to cash in. However, they found intensive aquaculture is no sure-fire hit. Frequent problems with disease and contamination have seen entrepreneurial farmers disappointed. In *Not On The Label* (Penguin, 2004), Felicity Lawrence records in riveting detail how 70 per cent of World Bank-funded farms in Indonesian countries have now been abandoned.

Are there sustainable methods of farming or fishing prawns in the southern hemisphere?
A small niche of suppliers is making sustainability a selling point. These include organic farmers and those who loosely stock and slowly grow prawns without the help of antibiotic growth promoters. Some have joined the ETI (Ethical Trade Initiative), which strives to improve working conditions, wage levels and child labour. On the

fishing front, a small number of fisheries is using special nets that provide escape hatches for the by-catch.

Why do we not see more sustainably farmed warm-water prawns in the UK?

Most sustainable farms and sources are small scale, and importers struggle to meet the cost of EU import regulations. They blame these 'indirect import tariffs' for their inability to get prawns to the UK, saying that only the big firms sending large container loads of standard, conventional warm-water prawns can afford the cost.

Are prawns safe to eat?

Almost all warm-water prawns on sale in the UK have been previously frozen, although live prawns can be air freighted packed in frozen sawdust. Check prawns for black spots (melanosis) on their shell, a sign of poor quality. Bear in mind that growth promoters, hormones and antibiotics can be used to rear warm-water prawns; there is no way of knowing unless you buy organic and even then the growing techniques are hazy.

In 2002 a serious safety scare was triggered when 16 out of 77 samples of warm-water king and tiger prawns from Southeast Asia tested positive for illegal and unacceptable residues of nitrofuran drugs. These drugs are no longer permitted in the European Union for use in food-producing animals due to concerns about increased risk of cancer in humans through long-term consumption. The problem prawns were from all over Southeast Asia and batches were being sold all over the UK. The Food Standards Agency insists that all were withdrawn.

Are pink North Atlantic prawns a good alternative?

Yes, the pink prawns that you find frozen (either with shells on or off) or used in sandwiches in many UK shops and supermarkets are a better choice because:

- They are wild, though not overfished (being the main food for the endangered cod, they are in fact very abundant).
- No chemicals are used in their production (but they will be glazed with a mixture of water and salt to protect them during freezing.
- They are local and do not share the food-mile issues of warm-water prawns.

Why are North Atlantic prawns always sold cooked and frozen?

They deteriorate quickly after they are caught, so are always boiled on board fishing vessels and blast frozen. It would be nice to have a (luxurious) supply of live prawns but this is unlikely to happen unless inshore fishermen rise to the challenge and sell them direct when landed. Cooked pink prawns will, however, withstand gentle reheating.

Are there other cold-water prawns?

Yes, there are two other types from the North Atlantic:

- **Langoustines** – scampi to some, prawns to the Scottish, and Dublin Bay prawns to the Irish and Americans, these are available raw and cooked or occasionally live from near the point of capture. Most langoustines are trawled but traditional creel-caught langoustines are available at a higher price. Creels are stationary pots (like baskets), lowered on to the seabed, and creel-caught langoustines will be the least damaged or stressed. The Spanish, who are mad for langoustines, buy road-freighted live langoustines that travel in seawater tanks.
- **Brown shrimps** – these are sold cooked and are the tasty Morecambe Bay 'potted' shrimp crustacean. The fisheries are small scale and catch the shrimps by dragging rigid mesh nets behind tractors over beaches at high tide, a job once done by horses.

Should I eat those red wild prawns in Spanish tapas bars?

Avoid them – they are often sold as Spanish but are from Africa. They are fished from African waters by well-subsidised European (mainly Spanish) fishermen, who have few fish left in their own fishing zones. The practice takes the prawns from African fishermen who rely heavily on them for food.

Why do prawns sometimes have that slimy feel once defrosted?

Peeled prawns of all types are 'glazed' with salt and water before freezing to protect them from freezer burn and drying out. The drained net weight of the prawns should be shown on the pack along with the net weight but some canny manufacturers try to get as much glaze as possible on to the prawns. There should be no more than 8–12 per cent glaze (look for 'low glaze' on labels) but some packs have been found to contain up to 45 per cent. If the prawns look very iced up, avoid them.

What the supermarkets say

All supermarkets sell frozen North Atlantic prawns, many sell potted shrimps but few sell langoustines, except breaded, as 'scampi'.

Waitrose does not sell trawled wild prawns and all its farmed warm-water prawns are reared in Madagascar, Honduras and Ecuador on farms committed to maintaining high standards of environmental stewardship, animal welfare, improved labour practices and contribution to local communities.

Sainsbury sells conventional tiger prawns but also a small quantity of organically farmed warm-water prawns.

Marks & Spencer's North Atlantic prawns are wild-trawled from Greenland and sold cooked and frozen. They are some of the best North Atlantic prawns available. However, its tiger prawns, farmed in Madagascar, are produced sustainably. It also sells farmed Australian Crystal Bay prawns.

Where to buy prawns

Andy Race Fish Merchants Ltd, Mallaig, Inverness-shire, Scottish Highlands PH41 4PX
Tel: 01687 462626
www.andyrace.co.uk

Once a herring port, Mallaig is now the main landing place for Britain's langoustine catch. Race, whose premises are right on the port, has the freshest langoustines in town and will send them nationwide via courier.

Brendan Sellick, Stolford Fisherman's Shop, Bridgewater Bay, Somerset TA5 1TW
Tel: 01278 652297

Brendan Sellick catches brown shrimps and prawns in summer using a Stone Age-designed sledge (called a mud horse), braving the mud flats of Bridgewater Bay where conger eels can nip your ankles. Seasonal availability, so call before you visit.

Club Chef Direct, Lakeside, Bridgewater Road, Barrow Gurney, Bristol BS48 3SJ
Tel: 01275 475252
www.chefclubdirect.co.uk

Raw langoustine tails (peeled) are available. The company can deliver live langoustines to restaurants and may do so to private individuals, depending on quantity and availability.

Furness Fish, Stockbridge Lane, Off Daltongate, Ulverston, Cumbria LA12 7GB
Tel: 01229 585037
www.morecambebayshrimps.co.uk

Morecambe Bay potted shrimps and peeled cooked brown shrimps to use how you want. Les Salisbury peels the shrimps by machine, but also has a limited supply of hand-peeled ones. Home delivery available.

Holker Food Hall, Cark-in-Cartmel, Nr Grange-over-Sands, Cumbria LA11 7PL

Tel: 015395 58328

www.holker-hall.co.uk

Potted shrimps from the doorstep – the Cavendish family are landowners at Morecambe Bay, home to the famous shrimp fishery.

Loch Fyne Seafood, Clachan, Cairndow, Argyll PA26 9BL

Tel: 01499 600264

www.lochfyne.com

A company that takes sustainability seriously – creel-caught langoustines from Scottish waters. Home delivery available.

PULSES

Here we are in a country that goes to huge lengths to import air-freighted fresh holy basil from Thailand each week, that insists on strawberries in supermarkets all year round, but which can barely import a decent dried pulse. Of all foods, pulses are among the most sustainable, least sprayed and most economical to transport. They are also one of the healthiest foods. Yet most of the ones the UK deigns to import are poor quality or end up in cans covered with sweet, salty tomato sauce. Yes – baked beans!

While it's true that green Puy lentils, a French pulse, have found their way into many starred restaurant kitchens and dal is an Indian takeaway essential, food snobbery still marks out most types of pulse as part of an (unreconstructed) hippy diet. It is a pity. Including these foods regularly in your diet dramatically brings down the cost of nourishment, meaning that more can be spent on other sustainable foods, such as naturally reared meat and organic vegetables.

What are pulses?

'Pulse' is a cover-all term for the edible seeds of legumes, such as beans, lentils and peas. The word comes from *puls*, the Latin for pottage, the staple garden soup and vital food for the rural poor before the Industrial Revolution. Pulses are usually sold dried, ready to be reconstituted by soaking in water and cooking. There are over 1,000 species but the types best known in the UK are lentils (green, brown, red and black), chickpeas, black-eyed peas and yellow split peas, and beans. There is a long list of the latter, from haricot (the base for baked beans) to cannellini, borlotti, kidney, flageolet, adzuki, lima, mung and butter beans. Some pulses are sold hulled, which means they will not keep their shape when cooked. In India, split, hulled whole pulses are called dal.

What's so good about pulses?

Everything. They provide a valuable source of protein and are also full of vitamins and minerals, low in fat and high in fibre. They fix the atmospheric nitrogen in the soil, which makes them important for the environment. They need comparatively little water for growth and are fairly hardy crops, so shouldn't require much chemical assistance.

But are pulses a sprayed crop?

They are a fairly hardy crop but, put it this way, they are sprayed with chemicals in countries that can afford it. Farmers in poorer countries have little choice other than to grow pulses using traditional means.

Are there pesticide residues on beans?

In 2004 the Pesticide Residues Committee (PRC) tested 81 samples of pulses. Four samples were organic and no residues were found on these. Residues were found on 11 conventional samples – a relatively low number but two did exceed the maximum residue levels. The PRC concluded that there had been no risk to human health but one of the residues found was inorganic bromide, an ozone-depleting chemical. Worse, many of the samples with residues were of 'unknown origin', so if the PRC had thought them dangerous it would have been difficult tracing the culprit.

Are pulses fairly traded?

Not usually. Most are a commodity crop and therefore pulse farmers are vulnerable to fluctuations in world trading prices and dependent on supply and demand. For the time being, a shortage or over supply is reported to be unlikely, so the price is pretty stable. A few fairly traded beans are coming into shops, however.

What's in a can of baked beans?

You guessed it – the beans are the best part, and the reason for their successful 'healthy' image. But a 210g can of beans contain nearly 2g of salt – almost 1g per helping, which is a third of the daily allowance recommended for a three-year-old. Heinz has reduced the salt content in its beans but when buying beans check the salt content and compare with other brands.

Why do some pulses take forever to cook?

Either because they are old or because they have been grown in a country where they are not native and which has the wrong soil type. As for old beans, note that if you travel to southern Europe, where beans are regularly eaten, you will find fresh beans in season and dry beans from the new harvest that seem to cook in no time. The age of pulses will not affect their goodness or flavour, but you can use a lot of fuel cooking them. A pressure cooker will cut the cooking time dramatically.

Do all pulses need soaking?

No. Lentils can be cooked straight away but most beans and peas should be soaked in cold water overnight. It is possible to cook them from dry but it takes hours and their skins are likely to split.

Are canned pulses inferior to dried?

Not at all. Despite being more expensive and a bit of a strain to carry back from the shop, canned pulses are often the best ones to buy. Having said that, there is nothing quite like making a braised bean dish from scratch with dried beans, where all the seasoning, garlic, vegetables, bacon etc cook together slowly, because the flavours will penetrate the beans. The slimy liquid inside a can of beans is water and salt whizzed with a few of the beans to make a thick juice.

Where to buy good pulses

When you buy pulses, check the country of origin. The traditional producing countries are India and Pakistan, Bangladesh, Africa, Turkey and the Middle East. Some delicious varieties of lentils and beans are grown in southern Europe and many favourite beans hail from Latin America.

Brindisa, 32 Exmouth Market, Clerkenwell, London EC1R 4QE
Tel: 020 7713 1666 (or call 020 8772 1600 for stockists)
www.brindisa.com
Beans from various small artisan producers, available dried or bottled in brine.

Machiavelli, Unit F, Hewlett House, Havelock Terrace,
London SW8 4AS
Tel: 020 7498 0880
www.machiavellifood.com
Lentils 'di Monte Catello' – small brown lentils with plenty of body and flavour, for braising with pork or lamb dishes, plus good yellow and white polenta. Mail order available.

Merchant Gourmet, 2 Rollins Street, London SE15 1EW
Tel: 0800 731 3549
www.merchant-gourmet.com
Black Beluga lentils, Puy lentils, golden pearl lentils – excellent-quality pulses in easy-to-store boxes. Home delivery available.

Suma Wholefoods, Lacy Way, Lowfields Industrial Park, Elland,
West Yorkshire HX5 9DB
Tel: 0845 458 2290
www.suma.co.uk
Canned and dried beans and pulses (organic) available by mail order.

Whole Earth, Combe Lane, Wormley, Godalming,
Surrey GU8 5SZ
Tel: 01428 685100
www.wholeearthfoods.com
Low-sugar, low-salt baked beans made with organic ingredients.

Where to buy sprouted pulses

Aconbury Sprouts, Unit 4 Westwood Industrial Estate, Pontrilas,
Hereford HR2 0EL
Tel: 01981 241155
www.aconbury.co.uk
Delicious, extra healthy sprouting lentils, pulses and peas and other
seeds.

READY MEALS

We are the time-poor. Too busy to peel, chop, slice and cook. Too late back from work to witness a stew simmer in its pot, or perhaps – understandably – just a little disorganised. Ready meals are widely accepted as the answer and supermarkets are literally stuffed with shelf upon shelf of 'solutions' to every meal problem. Fashion is never more present than in the ready-meal section. From Thai green curry to Middle Eastern meze, from Fusion cuisine to canapés, the new popularity of a dish is celebrated with its usually inauthentic reproduction in the ready-meal factory. Most hilarious are the ready-meal takeaways; the repro curry-house take-out to take away two days before the takeaway. Does this mean we are officially too busy to call for a takeaway?

But while the busy person is well justified in finding someone else to clean the house, iron, tend the garden or wash the car, outsourcing the cooking is more irksome. With such a wide variety of raw materials out there, each with its own set of problems, what lies beneath that transparent film that must always be pierced before cooking? And how much are we paying for those six tiny pieces of chicken floating in a starchy sauce. Put another way – who is having the last mocking laugh?

What can the label on a ready meal tell me?
There may be plenty of text on the label but it does not reveal much. By law there is an ingredients list but there is also voluntary nutritional information, which includes levels of salt, fat and sugar per serving, pack or measured quantity (e.g. per 100g). Labelling the source of the raw materials used in the meal is not a statutory requirement but the label must say where the meal was made. The net weight of the meal will also be on the label.

If the meal was made in the UK, does that mean it is 100 per cent British?

No. The ingredients in a ready meal can be sourced from another country, then processed, packed and labelled British. This is especially worrying with meat, which may have been exported from a country using production methods banned in the UK. This lack of traceability is the worst aspect of ready-made foods. The Food Standards Agency admits there is a problem and is currently considering country of origin labelling on all processed food. It makes no sense to have the most stringent labelling scheme in the world for beef (see Beef, page 58, and Burgers, page 91) and yet be so relaxed about the origins of the beef in a cottage pie.

How do I know what quantity of each ingredient is in a ready meal?

By law, the ingredients list shows the raw material used in the greatest quantity first and the one used in the smallest amount last. You will be amazed how low down the list certain items can be. In a braised meat ready meal, meat may come after modified maize starch, a cheap filler beloved of manufacturers. Water can be high on the list and, in conjunction with gelling agents and salt, can bulk up a meal handsomely.

How does a ready meal last for such a long time?

Preservatives, stabilisers, emulsifiers and a whole palette of additives offering hundreds of artificial ingredients help keep the meal looking and smelling good and – crucially – on the shelf for the longest possible time. It is very much in the manufacturers' or retailers' interests to preserve ready-made food for longer than the normal time. All these additives are permitted for use in the UK but there are concerns about certain colours and, frankly, you wouldn't add any of this stuff if you were cooking yourself, so do you want it in your food?

How can I tell if a ready meal is made with high-quality ingredients?

You can't, but a good tip is to read the ingredients list and check the salt content. The ingredients list should show no preservatives or flavour enhancers, no starch fillers (modified maize starch) or 'gum' fillers at all, bar a small amount of salt (any more than 0.5g per 100g is too much). There should be no hydrogenated fat (see Butter and Spreads, page 99) and no MSG flavour enhancer. The absence of these additives and unpleasant ingredients indicates flavoursome, good-quality raw materials such as well-hung meat and fresh vegetables, the use of natural meat stock, real butter, herbs and natural seasonings. Asian ready meals are refreshingly free of additives and salt, as spices act as a natural preservative and give loads of flavour, but the origin of the meat is questionable. You can assume it is not naturally reared, free-range or organic unless it specifies this on the label.

Who makes my ready meals?

Mass-market meals, pies and processed foods are served up by some of the UK's largest food giants, who manufacture millions of 'convenience' meals, snacks, prepared salads, pies, puddings, soups etc. The evangelical attitude of the major manufacturers centres on their mission to solve the problems brought about by busy modern lifestyles, and they see convenience food as the future. They pride themselves on their technology and their ability to make full use of artificial additives.

One big manufacturer is Kerry Foods, which processes ready meals and other foods for all the major and small supermarket chains plus other brands including Bowyers and Mattesons. The company recently acquired Noon, a West London Asian ready-meal manufacturer. It also has 'leading global positions in bio- and pharma-ingredients'. These include hydrolysates, emulsifiers, yeast, enzymes and hydrocolloids – food ingredients or 'platforms' through which, says Kerry on its website, 'the nutrition, flavour, texture and shelf life of food and beverages are enhanced'. For lovers of good old-fashioned natural ingredients and home cooking, it is depressing stuff. Kerry

Foods also owns Mastertaste, a flavourings manufacturer in Illinois, a company they are proud to have expanded and broadened.

Which is the best way to preserve ready-made food?

Freezing – frozen ready meals can be made without any preservatives and last for at least three months. Always check the ingredients list on the label for artificial additives, however, even on frozen foods.

Are ready meals good value for money?

They are rather expensive if you calculate the cost of each ingredient. A little goes a long way. Vegetable ready meals based on a couple of potatoes and a teaspoon of onion, or similar, contain ingredients worth just a few pence. The small amount of meat in ready meals is likely to be the cheapest on the market – often imported – and cheap bulk is often used as a filler. Some of the biggest rip-offs come with the Christmas 'solutions'. Why, for example, does a pot of double cream need to double in price just because a spoonful of three-star brandy is stirred into it? There is plenty of profit in ready-made foods – one of the reasons so many exist and innovation knows no bounds. I am persistently told that the emergence of the latest creation was brought about by customer demand but temptation via the seduction of innovation is closer to the truth.

What is the difference between an organic and a non-organic ready meal?

Under EU law, to be labelled 'organic' 95 per cent of the ingredients in a processed food must be organically produced. The organic ingredients should be listed along with any non-organic ingredients. The policy of most British organic manufacturers is not to use artificial additives or processed ingredients, most of which are banned under accreditation rules. The only non-organic ingredients should be obvious items such as water and salt. However, 29 additives are permitted for use in organic foods in Europe. They include fillers such as guar and xanthan gum, which bulk out food and emulsify sauces, and sulphur dioxide (E220), a controversial additive used to preserve wine and fruit. Annato colouring is permitted – even though it is deemed 'safe', surely colouring goes against the principles of organic food? Some preservatives are permitted, including metabisulphates, which are used to preserve meat. The list, which is under review, is, however, one hell of a lot shorter than the additives menu on offer to conventional manufacturers.

Are ready meals safe?

Nearly 100 per cent. First, they are made in factories where hygiene is the number one consideration. Touring these factories requires wearing extreme amounts of protective clothing, and endless controls and technology are employed to monitor for contamination. Secondly, the preservative content is designed specifically to prevent any part of the meal going 'off'. Look at a meal when it is well past its sell-by date and it still looks and smells edible, though I would not advise disobeying the manufacturer's instructions on 'best before' dates. Problems arise with individual ingredients, however. Many ready-made products were withdrawn in 2005 when they were found to contain Sudan 1, a carcinogen. Chicken injected with water or non-chicken proteins (usually derived from pork) has also been found in ready-made food but is now banned for sale in the UK. In rare cases, condemned meat has been found in ready meals. In December 2000 five men were jailed for cleaning up pet-food-grade poultry that eventually ended up in products sold in supermarkets and butcher's shops.

Are there pesticide residues in ready meals?

The Pesticide Residue Committee has not tested ready meals such as braised meat dishes, pies and curries in the last five years. Considering the quantities of imported produce they could contain, this is a cause for concern.

Are ready meals bad for the environment?

Ready meals are always over packaged, often with two or three layers that include printed cardboard and plastic. Both are difficult to recycle. Plastic containers are bulky and lightweight and therefore uneconomical for local authorities to transport. Added to this, when used for food they are usually too contaminated for treatment. Cardboard containers are sometimes lined with plastic (e.g. Tetra Pak) and some local authorities do not have facilities for recycling them and separating out the materials. Waste Watch, a government-funded watchdog, has reported that over 28 million tonnes of waste are generated by UK households, and that only a very small proportion of this (11 per cent) can be recycled. The rest is chucked into landfill. The government says that 10 per cent of all industrial and commercial waste is generated by our food industry, with the worst offender being packaging. The retailers have all signed pledges promising a reduction.

What's in the supermarkets?

Beware the allure of the up-market 'better than the rest' ranges. These include Tesco's Finest, Sainsbury's Taste the Difference and Asda's Extra Special. They look good in the box and sell at a higher price but, as Joanna Blythman points out in her book, *Shopped* (Fourth Estate, 2004), 'on some products the ingredients list is illuminating evidence of the gastronomic gulf between these aspiring home-entertaining specials and the home-cooked article'. She cites boeuf bourguignon as an example. The authentic recipe contains just 13 ingredients but one 'better than the rest' boeuf bourguignon she found contained over 40 ingredients, many of them artificial additives. This taste compromise, and the hiked-up price, can make these so-called upmarket ranges actually less appealing than their often-simpler budget counterparts.

Most non-organic supermarket ready meals are still made using preservatives, flavourings and unpleasant ingredients such as hydrogenated fat (see page 68) but this year two chains have said they are committed to the progressive removal of certain ingredients and additives.

Tesco announced that it will take hydrogenated fats out of its entire range of 450 ready meals, as well as any other ingredient not found in the domestic kitchen. At the time of writing, Tesco foods still contain additives and hydrogenated fat, so keep reading labels. Campaigners for the removal of food additives and hydrogenated fat are delighted by this move, as it is likely to be copied by the other chains.

Marks & Spencer uses no hydrogenated fat in ready meals or other ready-to-eat products. It also uses no MSG or tartrazine colour, both of which can adversely affect hyperactive children. However, it still uses other colourings and flavourings, which it has pledged to remove by mid 2006, and it uses preservatives in some meals. It is to be applauded for using only free-range eggs.

The Co-op uses artificial additives but has an 'open' labelling system that flags up those that may cause concern. It also flags up the use of eggs from caged hens in certain foods.

Waitrose uses only free-range eggs in its ready meals, but at the time of writing has no plans to remove hydrogenated fat and artificial additives from its range.

At the time of writing, **Sainsbury** continues to add hydrogenated fat and artificial additives to its ready-meal range.

Incidentally, in 2004 Birds Eye, one of the UK's leading manufacturers of ready-made foods, announced the removal of all additives in its products.

Which ready meals should I buy?

Cartmel Village Shop Sticky Toffee Pudding, The Square, Cartmel, Cumbria LA11 6QB
Tel: 01539 558300
www.stickytoffeepudding.co.uk
A great standby additive-free pudding, made with fresh cream, free-range eggs and cane sugar, that just needs heating. Home delivery available; also stocked in some supermarkets.

Daylesford Organic Farm Shop, Daylesford, Nr Kingham, Gloucestershire GL56 0YG
Tel: 01608 731700
www.daylesfordorganic.com
Soups made entirely from organic produce: smoky beetroot and bacon, butternut squash, honey and sage, celeriac and apple. Home delivery available.

Down From The Hills, Hinton Barns, Peterchurch, Herefordshire HR2 0SQ
Tel: 01981 550500
www.downfromthehills.co.uk
Excellent ingredients in preservative-free frozen meals. Down from the Hills uses rare breeds in its meat dishes (Oxford Down lamb goulash, Longhorn beef in red wine and Gloucester Old Spot pork in a delicious cassoulet) and all the vegetables are locally sourced when possible. Its fish pie is made with organic Irish salmon and fish from a Cornish supplier. Puddings include apple and quince crumble and lemon posset. Home delivery available.

Duchy Originals, The Old Ryde House, 393 Richmond Road, East Twickenham TW1 2EF
Tel: 020 8831 6800
www.duchyoriginals.com
Wholesome soups made with organic ingredients: chestnut mushroom, celeriac, leek and bacon, pea and ham, roasted vegetable. Available from main supermarkets or contact for other stockists.

Eazy Cuizine, Unit 5, Prestwood Court, Leacroft Road, Risley,
Warrington WA3 6SB
Tel: 01565 653244
www.eazycuizine.com
Frozen, additive-free meals including pies, children's meals and
dinner-party foods, made with local meat and fish harvested from a
sustainable source. Dishes include haddock succotash with butter
beans, bacon and chives, coq au vin, Welsh lamb rogon josh, tagine
and hot pot. Home delivery available.

Fresh Element, Unit 3, John Buddle Work Village, Buddle Road,
Newcastle upon Tyne NE4 8AW
Tel: 0191 226 7323
www.freshelement.co.uk
'Meal kits' containing local raw ingredients, ready to be put in the pan
for restaurant-style food. Starters include hand-dived scallops with
hazelnut and coriander butter; main courses roast fillet of organic beef
with parsnip mash and port wine sauce. There are nice puddings such
as hot marmalade pudding with Drambuie custard. Home delivery
available.

Gastronaut, Sherbourne Priors, Watery Lane, Sherbourne,
Warwickshire CV35 8AL
Tel: 01926 620230
www.gastronaut.org.uk
Warwickshire chef Damon Corey makes frozen, additive-free meals
with locally sourced meat or vegetables where possible. Main courses
include braised Packington pork with haricot beans, Cumberland
sausage and sage, or aubergine, ricotta and lentil moussaka. Puddings
include an apple 'cobbler' (apples braised with Calvados, then topped
with cinnamon buns). Home delivery available.

The Grocer on Elgin, 6 Elgin Crescent, London WII 2HX
Tel: 020 7221 3844
www.thegroceron.com

Imaginative provincial European-style meals, made with ingredients from small producers and sold packed in bags ready to heat or use. Starters include wild mushroom broth, roast garlic and tomato soup and grilled vegetables; mains include lemon and thyme risotto and duck confit; puddings saffron poached pears, vanilla custard or rhubarb and raspberry compote. Side dishes include black truffle mash, a good ratatouille and spiced Puy lentils. Home delivery available.

Jeremy's Soups, Unit 4, Appleby Business Park, Drawbriggs Lane,
Appleby-in-Westmoreland, Cumbria CA16 6HT
Tel: 01768 353311

Jeremy and Helen Kent make fresh, additive-free soups using local produce, including traditional recipes such as leek and potato, pea and ham, cream of chicken, plus the more contemporary: butternut squash and sweet potato, lentil and bacon, red pepper, tomato and black olive and a sweet cream of garden pea. Home delivery available.

Look What We Found!, Stanelaw Way, Tanfield Lea, Stanley,
County Durham DH9 9XG
Tel: 01207 288769
www.lookwhatwefound.co.uk

Innovative, additive-free braised dishes made with produce from local farms and preserved in ambient packaging ready to be heated (handy for camping trips or storing in bulk, as they do not need to go in the fridge). Every dish is named after the farmer who supplies the main ingredient. There is Shaun Richardson's citrus-braised Herdwick mutton, Mark Robertson's Northumberland cheese soup and Colin Kerr's Alnwick Castle Estate venison meatballs in damson jus.

Madhuban Curry Sauces, Main Line Business Centre, 74 Station Road, Liss, Hampshire GU33 7AD
Tel: 01730 891177
www.madhuban.co.uk
Natural curry sauces made with fresh spices from recipes developed at the Madhuban restaurant in Liss. Stir meat or vegetables into the sauce and simmer until cooked. Sauces include a good korma, bhoona and jalfrezi. Home delivery available.

Manna Organic, Unit 11F Hybris Business Park, Warmwell Road, Crossways, Dorset DT2 8BF
Tel: 01258 863716
www.mannaorganic.co.uk
Simple, practical dishes made with meat, fish, dairy and vegetables from local suppliers. Dorset beef with red wine, pork meatballs, chicken, ham and mushroom pie, stuffed Portobello mushrooms and roasted red peppers. Puddings include chocolate torte and lime cheesecake. Additive free, and delivered frozen. Home delivery available.

Parkers Menu, 2 Swan Yard, Sherborne, Dorset DT9 3AX
Tel: 01935 814527 (also at 1 Napper's Court, Charles Street, Dorchester DT1 1BS; tel: 01305 751223)
www.parkersmenu.co.uk
Dorset company making a wide range of frozen dishes using local ingredients. Everyday dishes include pork meatballs, cottage pie, stew and dumplings plus several vegetarian meals. Grander, dinner-party-style food includes goat's cheese tartlets, pork in Blue Vinney sauce, beef Wellington, chocolate roulade and an impressive pavlova. Phone 01963 250570 for home delivery.

Pipers Farm, Cullompton, Devon EX15 1SD
Tel: 01392 881380
www.pipersfarm.com

Peter and Henrietta Greig's seasonally changing menu makes the best use of their Devon Ruby beef, home-reared chicken, local lamb and pork. Frozen, additive-free dishes are practical, home-cooking style and include big casseroles sold either ready cooked or as marinated meat to cook at home. Home delivery available.

Romy Cuisine, PO Box 106, Hay-on-Wye, Powys HR3 5YH
Tel: 07855 531550
www.romycuisine.co.uk

French chef Guy Simon makes classic pâtés and terrines in Wales using locally reared duck, pork and wild game. Home delivery available.

Two Fishwives, A12, Alpha Business Centre, 7–11 Minerva Road, London NW10 6HJ
Tel: 020 8537 1168
www.twofishwives.com

Fishy things made using fish from a sustainable source: mackerel, sweet potato and horseradish fishcakes; smoked haddock, snipped chives and red chilli fishcakes. The house fish pie is made with haddock and cod (in season) and there are special fish cakes for small children.

Worth Eating, Worth Cottage, Worth, Wookey, Wells, Somerset BA5 1LW
Tel: 07779 143440

Julian Langdon makes flans using thinly rolled pure butter pastry that is baked to a crisp. Many of the ingredients for the pastry and fillings are local and natural: eggs from Farmhouse Freedom Eggs (see Mayonnaise, page 243), flour from Shipton Mill (see Flour, page 181) in the Cotswolds, plus Cheddar, bacon and butter from Somerset. Fillings include leek and bacon, Stilton, leek and walnut and a sweet tart filled with mincemeat, cream cheese and apple.

The Yorkshire Soup Company, Unit 5E Barker Business Park, Melmerby, Ripon, North Yorkshire HG4 5NB
Tel: 01765 641920
www.yorkshiresoup.com

Belinda Williams has based her soup recipes on traditional British pottages and broths. She makes them by hand, using locally sourced meat, potatoes and other vegetables. The highly imaginative range includes beetroot, parsnip, ginger and horseradish; minted new potato and spring onion; tomato and red pepper with Wensleydale cheese; cucumber, lettuce, asparagus and fresh herbs; onion with Theakston ale and mustard.

RISOTTO RICE

Fifteen years ago pudding rice was the only short grain rice used in British homes and a real risotto was a rare treat, served only in restaurants. Now we can buy authentic risotto rice in almost any supermarket. Why the phenomenon? In the north of Italy, where risotto rice is grown, rice has always been preferred to wheat – so much so that campaigns against pasta were famously waged by Futurist intellectuals. But in the UK such high-brow arguments were unnecessary. Ruth and Rose, Antonio or Jamie, had only to give a recipe and everyone went hunting for Arborio. All trends attract snobbery, however, and cooks now debate the merits of other short grain types that can do the job. Meanwhile, the shimmering, watery landscape of Italy's Po Valley copes with EU agricultural policy change...

Where is short grain rice grown?
The majority of short grain rice exported to the UK is grown in the north of Italy but a small amount, suitable for making paella, comes from Spain. It is worth noting that sushi rice is also short grain and imported from Asia.

How is it grown?
The paddy fields lie in river deltas, which are artificially flooded in order to protect the plants from low night-time temperatures. The soil is nourished with fertiliser – ideally manure but artificial fertilisers can also be used. Springtime weeding is important, as weeds can sap the nutrient quality of the rice. In Europe, planting and harvesting are carried out by machine.

How is short grain rice processed?
The milling process alters according to the type of rice but essentially the purpose is to hull, then mill the rice to remove the outer, transparent layers of the grain, leaving mainly the white, starchy centre.

What impact do the paddy fields have on the environment?

The ecosystem in northern Italy, where risotto rice has been culti-vated since the year 1600, is directly connected to rice growing, and any changes to the scale of the industry affect this. Recent changes to the agricultural subsidy system threatened to reduce the amount of rice grown in Italy, which would in turn affect the waterfowl and other wildlife around the paddy fields. But the growers appear to have responded by growing a wider variety of rice, including long grain, for the European market.

Does rice contain pesticide residues?

No pesticide residues were detected in short grain and risotto rice when the Pesticide Residues Committee took random samples in 2000, but more recent data is needed.

How do risotto rice types differ?

The three main risotto types are Arborio, Carnaroli and Vialone Nano. Carnaroli has a high starch content and makes the creamiest risotto; it is often preferred by chefs, as the starchy centre stays chewily firm in spite of absorbing plenty of liquid. Arborio makes a humbler, lighter risotto, while the shorter, rounder grains of Vialone Nano are reputed to have the highest absorption ability, making it suitable for wet, soupy risottos and the traditional choice for *risi e bisi* (rice and peas).

How much should I pay for risotto rice?

You can pay up to £8 a kilo but good-quality Arborio and Carnaroli can be bought for £3–3.50 per kilo. Based on using 75g per helping, the cheapest plate of risotto comes in at an economical 24 pence.

How should I store rice?

A cotton cloth sack is ideal, as the rice can breathe without mites getting at it, but a plastic bag sealed with a clothes peg should protect it well, too.

Where to buy risotto rice

Italian delis, plus many supermarkets, stock the well-known Gallo brand of Arborio and Carnaroli rice, grown in the Po Valley north of Milan. Expertly milled, it is very reliable and economical to buy. Gallo also produces 'easy cook' rice for quick risotto, which has been par-steamed, then dried. Organic versions are available.

Riso Scotti is another good northern Italian, larger-scale rice producer, available from supermarkets and independent food shops.

Brindisa, 32 Exmouth Market, Clerkenwell, London EC1R 4QE
Tel: 020 7713 1666 (or call 020 8772 1600 for stockists)
www.brindisa.com
Sells Calasparra, a short grain white rice grown in Murcia, near Valencia, the home of paella. Makes creamy paella but the rice has plenty of bite.

Carluccio's, 12 Great Portland Street, London W1W 8QN
Tel: 020 7580 3050
www.carluccios.com
Riso Carnaroli from Vercelli in the Po Delta. Makes a good, creamy risotto. Mail order available.

Gallo, 5 Park Court, Riccall Road, Escrick, York YO19 6ED
Tel: 01904 728911
www.risogallo.co.uk
Arborio, Carnaroli, Vialone Nano from one of the Po Valley's oldest and best suppliers. Also available in supermarkets.

Savoria, 229 Linen Hall – CKp, 162–168 Regent Street, London W1B 5TB
Tel: 0870 242 1823
www.savoria.co.uk
Online shop selling good-quality rice from small-scale Italian producers. Choose from Gli Aironi and Principato di Lucidio.

Suma Wholefoods, Lacy Way, Lowfields Industrial Park, Elland,
West Yorkshire HX5 9DB
Tel: 0845 458 2290
www.suma.co.uk
'Bird friendly' short grain rice (ideal for paella), grown by a bird
conservation charity in Spain in partnership with the RSPB. White
and brown rice available.

SALMON

Chief among the controversies surrounding farmed salmon is the danger of ingesting cancer-causing chemicals. The debate has raged hotly since a report in *Science* in January 2004. The article revealed that carcinogenic chemicals in Scottish salmon were so high that consumers should eat no more than one portion a week. In 2005 it was reported that malachite green, a banned chemical toxic to humans, was found in fresh salmon from a Morrisons supermarket.

Other salmon troubles are numerous: the wild population is down in number, fish farms are polluting the waters along the west coast of Scotland and many species of wild fish are exploited in order to feed the farmed ones. Then there is the super-sized GM salmon, looking to be licensed for sale in EU countries. Sales of conventionally farmed salmon are down, but organically farmed up – the popularity of this premium-priced fish begging the question whether the whole cheap salmon project was a good idea after all.

How are salmon contaminated?

The fish are fed meal made from fish harvested from the wild stock. The Marine Conservation Society (MCS) estimates with concern that it takes as much as 5 kilos of wild fish to rear 1 kilo of farmed. Fish oils are added to promote growth, but here's the nub: these oils can be derived from wild marine species, harvested from deep waters contaminated with dumped toxic waste. Farmed fish fed on these oils can take on the same toxins. Ironically it is the oil in fish that is nutritionally highly regarded, and food safety and nutritional health authorities do not know where to turn on the issue.

Immediately after the 2004 *Science* report, the Food Standards Agency declared that 'the known benefits of eating one portion of oily fish [meaning salmon] outweigh any possible risks'. Six months later, however, it tightened this advice, recommending one to two portions a week for women who might bear children (similar advice to that in *Science*) and between one and four helpings for others. The odd part of the report was the barest mention of salmon, spreading the advice across the oily fish range, from swordfish and shark to mackerel and tuna – blurry guidance for consumers desperately in need of clarity. Oily fish such as mackerel and tuna have been found to contain mercury, though in small quantities. The problem that needed to be addressed at the time, however, was salmon.

What else is in the feed?

Antibiotics, anti-parasitical medicines and colorants are permitted in the feed for farmed fish under government Feeding Stuff regulations. But how did the Morrisons' salmon become contaminated with a chemical banned in the UK? DEFRA describes the findings as 'puzzling' but the industry admits that policing the often-remote farms on the west coast of Scotland, sometimes cut off by bad weather, is a problem. Farms bearing the Scottish Quality Salmon logo (SQS) receive two inspections a year, plus separate inspections by retailers. They have been praised for raising standards, but note that they still allow the use of wild stocks to feed farmed. SQS represents about 60 per cent of the salmon produced in Scotland. Its logo sometimes appears on packs.

Could GM salmon be sold in the UK?

No GM salmon are on sale in the UK yet but the EU will allow sales subject to the fish passing nutritional safety and environmental standards tests. Supermarkets are, however, unlikely to stock it. The GM fish in question can grow eight times faster than normal fish and contain anti-freeze proteins to protect them from cold winters. The MCS says 30 per cent of salmon in Norwegian rivers are runaway transgenic fish, and it disputes claims from GM technologists that these are too large and inactive to attack the wild species.

Are there sustainable salmon farms?

Organic salmon farms win on the fish-feed issue: Soil Association-certified farms use 50 per cent responsibly caught fish and the rest is derived from fish processors' waste – heads, skin and bones. The feed is free from antibiotics, hormones, colourings and other chemicals. Welfare standards for the fish are also high. Before you dash out and buy, however, note that the environmentalist sector is split as to whether the Soil Association, which has such high standards for agriculture, ever should have certified aquaculture at all. Those against argue that it is not possible for a fish farm to remain clean and uncontaminated by others, given the movement of the sea. The Soil Association responds by saying that until a better solution is found, or the unlikely happens and salmon farming is banned, it is better that there is a standard that shows up the rest.

Organic farms do not exist on the Scottish mainland coast but in Orkney, Shetland, Northern Ireland and the Irish Republic.

Given the issues about farmed salmon, is it best to buy wild salmon?

Yes, but only as a rare treat. Numbers of wild Atlantic salmon around the coast of Britain are severely depleted. The Marine Conservation Society says that overfishing, pollution, environmental changes and availability of food are responsible for this. But, along with many other environmental campaigners, it makes the point that salmon farms are responsible for the loss of stocks around Scotland. There is an impact, it says, on wild salmon with transmission of sea lice (to wild fish) and genetic impairment caused by interbreeding after escape. Fish ranching (the release of hand-reared fish into rivers and lochs) is viewed as a tentatively promising resolution, but at present schemes are in their infancy.

Wild salmon stocks around the coast of Ireland are well managed, however. A commercial fishery exists on the west coast, where a strict, low quota of salmon may be netted in estuaries only in June and July, with four days a week on which fishermen are permitted to fish for them for only a few hours a day. Wild Irish salmon has a pleasing dense, muscular texture, little fat, and a rich, pure flavour. Wild salmon's scarcity, however, means the price will be much higher than that of conventionally farmed fish.

Does the quality of smoked salmon vary?

Yes, not only because the quality of farmed salmon is so variable (wild fish, however, is out there on its own as the best) but because smokehouses use different methods. The various mediums used to aromatise and flavour the smoke will dramatically affect the flavour. In the UK, smokehouses commonly use oak or beech shavings but peat is used in Scotland and Ireland, giving the salmon a deep earthiness. Hickory is typically used in the US. It is a matter of personal choice. All salmon is cured in salt before smoking. Using dry salt yields a dry-textured salmon, while a wet cure in brine delivers firmer, translucent flesh.

I would argue that nothing beats the subtlety of smoked wild salmon and that smoked conventional salmon is frequently flabby with fat and can have a revolting aftertaste. Smoking is a skill, and the variability in fish means they virtually need individual attention during the process. Consequently artisan smokehouses deliver fish that are consistently delicious. Organically farmed smoked salmon is often lacking in flavour. Obviously there is a huge price difference between wild and farmed smoked salmon, with wild being at least three times more expensive.

What the supermarkets say

All the supermarkets revealed that most of the fresh and smoked salmon they sell is conventional farmed fish, from either Scotland or Norway. This salmon – even with varying production standards – has issues relating to marine pollution, impact on wild fish and contamination. It is best to choose an organically farmed alternative, or responsibly harvested wild salmon.

Sainsbury stocks canned and fresh Scottish and Alaskan salmon certified by the Marine Stewardship Council (MSC), plus organically farmed salmon. Its conventionally farmed salmon is imported from Norway.

Marks & Spencer sells smoked wild Alaskan salmon (MSC approved). Its conventional farmed salmon is Scottish.

Waitrose sells Soil Association-certified organic salmon from the Orkneys and wild Alaskan salmon (MSC approved), both fresh and smoked. Its conventional farmed salmon is Scottish.

Tesco sells MSC-approved wild Alaskan fresh and smoked salmon under its Finest range, plus organic Irish salmon.

The Co-op sells MSC-approved wild Alaskan salmon marinated and 'ready to cook'.

Where to buy wild Irish salmon

During its short season in June and July, wild Irish salmon is available in the UK from:

Matthew Stevens & Son Ltd, Back Road West, St Ives, Cornwall TR26 3AR
Tel: 01736 799392
www.mstevensandson.co.uk

Where to buy organic salmon

Andy Race Fish Merchants Ltd, Mallaig, Inverness-shire, Scottish Highlands PH41 4PX
Tel: 01687 462626
www.andyrace.co.uk
For salmon from Orkney. Mail order available.

Club Chef Direct, Lakeside, Bridgewater Road, Barrow Gurney, Bristol BS48 3SJ
Tel: 01275 475252
www.chefclubdirect.co.uk
Smoked or fresh organic Glenarm salmon, reared in large cages far out to sea in tidal waters off the coast of Northern Ireland. This salmon has a wonderful colour and plenty of flavour and is widely accepted as the best organic salmon available. Home delivery.

The Fish Society, Freepost, Haslemere, Surrey GU27 2BR
Tel: 0800 279 3474
www.thefishsociety.co.uk
Salmon from Orkney and Shetland. Home delivery available.

Inverawe Smokehouses, Taynuilt, Argyll PA35 1HU
Tel: 01866 822446
www.smokedsalmon.co.uk
Award-winning, pale-coloured, smoked organic salmon cut beautifully into very thin slices.

Where to buy good, non-organic conventionally farmed salmon

Loch Fyne Seafood, Clachan, Cairndow, Argyll PA26 9BL
Tel: 01499 600264
www.lochfyne.com
Fresh and smoked salmon using fish from The Sustainable Salmon Company, Loch Duart (see **www.lochduart.com**). This is hailed by marine conservationists as the way forward for non-organic salmon. Fish are reared on a natural diet using a rotational fallow system, minimising loch bed pollution. Welfare standards are high and it is an RSPCA-approved Freedom Food. Available online fresh, smoked and marinated.

Where to buy responsibly harvested smoked salmon

Bleiker's Smoke House Ltd, Glasshouses Mill, Glasshouses, Harrogate, North Yorkshire HG3 5QH
Tel: 01423 711411
www.bleikers.co.uk
Organic smoked salmon from this expert smokehouse near Harrogate. The Bleikers also cure fish in gin, Seville orange juice and beetroot. Mail order available.

Frank Hederman, Belvelly Smokehouse, Cobh,
County Cork, Ireland
Tel: 00353 21 481 1089
www.frankhederman.com
Wild salmon caught in the Cork river estuaries, cured in dry salt, then smoked over beech chips. Frank Hederman is a member of the Slow Food Wild Irish Smoked Atlantic Salmon 'Presidium' (posh for 'association'!). Mail order available.

Hebridean Smokehouse Ltd, Clachan, Locheport,
Isle of North Uist HS6 5HD
Tel: 01876 580209
www.hebrideansmokehouse.com
Specialises in peat-smoked salmon. Mail order available.

Ummera Smoked Products, Inchybridge, Timoleague,
County Cork, Ireland
Tel: 00353 23 46644
www.ummera.com
Ummera smoked wild salmon has been netted as it enters the estuaries on the west coast of County Cork during the salmon fishing season. The company is committed to sustainability and works with the Slow Food movement and the Irish government to give smoked wild Irish salmon a special status. The fish is brined, with the addition of a little sugar, before smoking. Mail order available.

SALT

Living without it would be impossible but salt still gets more bad press than good. Food manufacturers are currently falling over themselves to reduce the amount they use and school caterers will soon face the cane from the education authorities if they do not follow suit. The root of all this comes from salt's obvious ability to enhance flavour. For example, a product containing low-grade, flavourless poultry, with a sauce bulked out with bland starch, does well to include a lot of salt. But bear in mind that only 5 per cent of the world's salt is used for food, and therefore the salt you choose has little impact on the industry. Having said that, some salts are healthier than others, so your choice will affect you and those you feed.

Where does salt come from?

The majority of salt sold in the UK is mined in Cheshire, then processed and sold to other brands and supermarkets, who mark it up with their own label. Worldwide, the largest producers are the US and China. Salt has a fascinating past, well documented in Mark Kurlansky's book, *Salt: A World History* (Jonathan Cape, 2002).

What is the difference between rock, sea and table salt?

* **Rock salt** – is mined from natural underground deposits of the mineral, halite, which derives from ancient seawater.
* **Sea salt** – is produced from the evaporation of seawater or natural brine. Once the H_2O has evaporated, crystals are left in the pan. This salt is known as panned, or hand harvested.
* **Table salt** – is taken from the same source as rock salt, comprises virtually all food-grade salt. It is cheaper to produce than the other two, and the most highly processed. Fresh water is forced down a shaft to salt deposits up to 850 metres underground. Brine (heavily salted water) is created by dissolving the deposit and is then pumped back to the surface. The water is then removed using

heat in a vacuum evaporator. This process yields evaporated salt, the purest of all salts: almost 100 per cent pure sodium chloride. The brine may be treated with chemicals prior to evaporation, including a sulphuric acid treatment to reduce hydrogen sulphide.

What is the anti-caking agent added to table salt?

This is hexacyano ferrate, which is used to make salt flow freely. Its detractors say the additive makes it harder for the body to absorb the salt but the salt industry claims the chemical poses no risk to human health.

Why is iodine added to some salt?

The body contains little iodine, and needs little, but a total absence of iodine causes health problems. In some parts of the world there is no iodine in the environment at all so governments have legislated to add iodine to salt as a preventative health measure. It is not routinely added to salt in the UK, but salt with added iodine is available.

How much salt should I eat?

Always taste food before adding salt; it may not need it. Also, be aware that salt is 'hidden' in many everyday foods, including break-fast cereals, bread, biscuits, stock cubes, soup, ready-cooked meals (especially those containing meat) and food aimed specifically at kids such as lunchbox items, crisps and other snacks. The health author-ities advise eating no more than 6g salt per day for adults, including that in processed foods, so check ingredients lists on labels. The Food Standard Agency guidelines for children are as follows:

1–3 years: 2g salt a day (0.8g sodium)
4–6 years: 3g salt a day (1.2g sodium)
7–10 years: 5g salt a day (2g sodium)
11 and over: 6g salt a day (2.5g sodium)

Note that sodium (often noted on labels instead of salt) is more than twice its strength: 1g sodium = 2.5g salt. It is a ruse by the industry to make you think you are eating less salt.

Which salt is better for you?

The widely held opinion is that while we all need some salt of any kind, rock and sea salt are better for you because they contain other healthy trace elements found in seawater. These give the salt a stronger taste and a slightly lower sodium content. In 2001 the writer, Jeffrey Steingarten, sent 13 types of salt for analysis, including many 'chic' gourmet salts. Fleur de sel from Guérande in France was found to contain the highest levels of magnesium; Oshima Island salt from Japan was high in calcium and sulphates.

Do 'gourmet' salts taste better?

The flavour is not necessarily better but the texture of salt is known to have an impact on the flavour. The effect of a few soft crystals of salt (such as Maldon or fleur de sel) dissolving on the tongue is more pleasant with some foods than fine or hard crystals, hence their popularity. Jeffrey Steingarten carried out a second study, this time examining whether gourmet sea salt can be distinguished, tastewise, from ordinary table (rock) salt. Fleur de sel de Guérande (not salt from the other fleur de sel production region, Isle de Rey) was found to be just distinguishable, along with the Oshima salt. Okinawa salt from Japan proved to be the most distinguishable.

What is the environmental impact of salt production?

The bigger the mine or manufacturer is, the bigger the impact that plant will have on its surroundings and the bigger the monopoly that company will hold over smaller producers. There are shocking reports about how intensive sea salt production has damaged the ecology of marine and wetland areas in Venezuela and Mexico.

Which salt should I buy?

Go for rock salt as everyday salt to use in cooking etc, and use panned sea salt for sprinkling on food.

Where to buy salt

**Halen Môn Welsh Sea Salt, The Anglesey Sea Salt Company/
Cwmni Halen Môn, Brynsiencyn, Llanfair PG, Isle of Anglesey/
Ynys Môn LL61 6TQ
Tel: 01248 430871
www.seasalt.co.uk**

Hand-panned, delicately flavoured sea salt from Llanfairpwllgwyn-gyllgogerychwyrndrobwllllantysyliogogogoch in Anglesey. Smoked salt also available.

**Here Organic Supermarket, Chelsea Farmers' Market,
125 Sydney Street, London SW3 6NR
Tel: 020 7351 4321**

L'Himal pink salt, harvested from the salt basins of the Himalayas.

**Maldon Crystal Salt Company, Wycke Hill Business Park, Maldon,
Essex CM9 6UZ
Tel: 01621 853315
www.maldonsalt.co.uk**

Famous salt from Essex with a usable, crumbly texture, endorsed by almost every chef.

**Oceans of Goodness, 1 The Warren, Handcross,
West Sussex RH17 6DX
Tel: 0845 064 0040
www.oceansofgoodness.com**

'Natural' salt extracted from wild wrack seaweed, this has a good mineral flavour that is delicious with lamb, fish and shellfish especially. Comes in a useful grinder.

Saltpepper, 13 Zion Terrace, Hebden Bridge,
West Yorkshire HX7 8BD
Tel: 0845 345 7488
www.saltpepper.co.uk
West Yorkshire-based specialists making interesting salt blends, such as cumin and ginger or celery and chilli (good with hard-boiled eggs), and a coarse Spanish sea salt. Mail order available.

Steenbergs Ltd, PO Box 48, Boroughbridge, York YO51 9ZW
Tel: 01765 640088
Three interesting salts – two hand panned from the Algarve, including one with a mix of peppers and herbs, and a beautiful Lava Red Salt from Kauai in Hawaii that is coloured by volcanic clay and has a gentle salinity. Mail order available.

SAUSAGES

Dare to suggest who should win prizes for the best sausage and witness a deluge of disagreement. The savouring of this favourite food is certainly subjective but the big question is, 'What makes a bad sausage?' Each day five million people in the UK eat sausages, but most are in the dark about their content. Pork, herbs and bread, hand linked in a natural skin? We wish. Meet the sausage that is just one third pork ...

What's in a sausage?

British-style sausages – or bangers – can be made with any meat but 83 per cent of those eaten in the UK are made with pork. The traditional recipe includes pork cuts (shoulder and belly) and pork fat, seasoning and bread. It would be nice to say that little else goes in but this is not the case. Cheap sausages can be made with only 30 per cent pork, 20 per cent mechanically recovered meat (MRM), a process that literally sucks it from the bones and mashes it to a slimy paste, plus 15 per cent water, 30 per cent cereal rusk and 5 per cent assorted additives, including flavourings, colour, sugar, flavour enhancer and preservatives. Sausages like these are often served in schools and hospitals.

Shouldn't a sausage be mostly meat?

Not always. By law, sausages need only contain a minimum of 40 per cent meat, but pork meat can consist of up to 30 per cent fat and 25 per cent connective tissue and still be described as meat. Connective tissue can be fat, skin and gristle. It may also contain pork cheek and jowl, home to the pituitary glands where drug residues and disease are concentrated. Beef and lamb meat can contain up to 25 per cent fat and 25 per cent connective tissue. MRM cannot be labelled as part of the meat content but is shown on the label.

What are the skins made of?

Artificial collagen (derived from cow's feet) and plastic skins are used on cheap sausages. Real sausages use pork intestine for bangers and lamb intestine for chipolatas. Never prick natural skins before cooking, or the sausages will split and all the juices and fat will run out.

What should good sausages contain?

Ideally 80 per cent pork belly and shoulder, 10 per cent breadcrumbs, 5 per cent water and 5 per cent herbs and spices, plus salt.

Can I be sure my British sausages are really British?

No, loopholes in the law allow sausages filled with imported meat to be labelled British as long as they are made or packed in the UK. Real UK sausages sold in packs tend to add logos such as the Quality Standard Mark, which can only be awarded to UK pork, so beware packaged sausages with no logo. If buying sausages loose, ask the butcher about the country of origin.

Should I be concerned about animal welfare when it comes to sausages?

Yes, unless they are filled with meat from naturally reared pigs or Soil Association-certified organic pork. Imported pork can come from pigs who live short lives in overcrowded conditions on concrete floors, unable to behave naturally. The majority of British pork is produced under the Assured British Pigs scheme (and the equivalent in Scotland). This is indoor reared and does not guarantee good welfare but standards in the UK are considered to be far higher than in the rest of the EU. The Freedom Food scheme is operated by the RSPCA and tolerates a number of factory-farming methods, although the pigs do have to be kept on straw bedding. For more details about pig welfare, see Bacon (and Pork) page 48.

Is all outdoor-reared pork welfare friendly?

There is no recognised scheme for outdoor-reared pork and farmers argue about the benefits of 'free range'. Modern (bald, thinner) commercial breeds have problems with the extreme temperatures, while traditional fat, hairy breeds are happy to roam and forage like wild pigs. The ideal system is housing in a light airy, straw-filled barn with access to outdoors, plus plenty of water and a wholesome, varied diet. Pigs should not be fed growth promoters such as antibiotics, traces of which can end up in the meat (these are sometimes fed to pigs under veterinary supervision), or too much high-protein feed like soya – which, by the way, is often GM derived in non-organic systems. Lastly, pigs suffer on long journeys, so slaughter at a local abattoir is kinder.

What additives can sausages contain?

Polyphosphates to retain and bind added water, soya for bulk and to retain fat, artificial colourings and preservatives (these can cause hyperactivity in children, so parents beware). Other additives include nitrates, nitrites and the flavour enhancer, monosodium glutamate (E621), or other glutamates (E622–5).

Is too much salt added to sausages?

Yes, especially if the meat content is low. A 2003 Food Standards Agency report found the saltiest sausages to be Richmond Irish, Walls Thick, Sainsbury's Pork, Tesco Pork & Beef, Iceland Pork & Beef, Tesco Vegetarian Lincolnshire and Linda McCartney vegetarian.

What should I look for when buying sausages?

Choose sausages that look plump and shiny with no visible air bubbles and, for interesting differences in flavour, buy sausages made from traditional breeds. These include British Lop, Tamworth, Gloucestershire Old Spot, Berkshire, Saddleback and Middle White.

Premium sausages usually have plenty of good news on labels regarding lean British meat and no additives but animal welfare remains a grey area.

What the supermarkets say

Sainsbury's own-brand sausages are made with British (Landrace or Large White) pigs. The sausages contain no MRM and are made only from shoulder, belly and other meat trims and natural casings. There is a standard sausage and a very good organic version using pork from farms with a good standard of welfare.

Marks & Spencer cannot specify the breed of pig it uses but says the pork hails from either the UK or Denmark. The pigs are reared indoors on straw and slatted floors and are not fed animal proteins or growth promoters.

Tesco sausages use pork from a variety of breeds sourced from the UK or the EU. The skins are usually synthetic but the Finest range is made using natural skins from the UK.

The Co-op sources pork for its sausages from the UK and the EU. The pigs are fed a vegetarian cereal-based diet containing non-GM soya.

Budgens uses shoulder and belly trimmings from Large White or Landrace boars to make their sausages.

Waitrose pigs are fed a cereal-based diet. They are all born and reared outdoors with access to shelter. At most, the pigs are slaughtered after 26 weeks. Excluding one preservative and one antioxidant, Waitrose sausages are made with natural flavours and ingredients.

My favourite sausages

For what it's worth – I have been buying these for 15 years and would drive a long way for them.

John Robinson and Sons, High Street, Stockbridge, Hampshire SO20 6HE
Tel: 01264 810609

Perhaps the best sausages in Britain, made on the premises with pork shoulder meat and a perfect balance of seasoning and stuffed into natural casings. There is no mail order but anyone passing through the town on the A30 would be crazy not to stop.

Great sausages that can be delivered to your door

Cranborne Stores, 1 The Square, Cranborne, Dorset BH21 5PR
Tel: 01725 517210
www.cranbornestores.co.uk
Very full-flavoured sausages made with pork from pigs that graze in woodland on the Cranborne Estate.

Crombies of Edinburgh, 97 Broughton Street,
Edinburgh EH1 3RZ
Tel: 0131 557 0111
www.sausages.co.uk
A hundred types, from the traditional to the weird and the wonderful – e.g. 'basil, beef and blackberries'.

The Masham Sausage Shop, 11 Silver Street, Masham, Ripon,
North Yorkshire HG4 4DX
Tel: 01765 650200
www.mashamsausages.co.uk
Twenty-five varieties of traditionally made sausages, mainly pork but also duck, venison and wild boar.

Michael Kirk, 56 Woolpack Street, Wolverhampton, West
Midlands WV1 3NA
Tel: 01902 425064
www.porkiepies.com
A huge variety of prize-winning sausages, made with pork from Shropshire farms.

**Musks Ltd, 4 Goodwin Business Park, Newmarket,
Suffolk CB8 7SQ
Tel: 01638 662626
www.musks.com**
Very popular 'Newmarket' sausage, reportedly the late Queen
Mother's favourite, made with shoulder meat from British free-range
pigs and a nice peppery seasoning, in natural casings.

**Procter's Speciality Sausages, Red Lion Yard, High Street,
Colchester CO1 1DZ
Tel: 01206 579100
www.procters-sausages.co.uk**
A range of traditional hand-linked sausages and Continental recipes.
All pork is sourced locally from Freedom Foods-registered free-range
farms and casings are natural. Mail order available.

**Real Meat Company, Warminster BA12 0HR
Tel: 01985 840562
www.realmeatco.sageweb.co.uk**
Sausages made with 80 per cent meat and no additives. Home delivery available.

**Well Hung Meat, Tordean Farm, Dean Prior, Buckfastleigh,
Devon TQ11 0LY
Tel: 0845 230 3131
www.wellhungmeat.com**
Soil Association-certified sausages with 100 per cent meat content.
A mild type for breakfast and a robust 'well hung' sausage for supper.

SOFT DRINKS

Soft drinks – specifically mass-market fizzy drinks – come more loaded with trouble of every kind than any other food. Some have absolutely no point. There is no nourishment in sugar, it just provides a brief spurt of energy. No one wants to deprive kids of the odd treat; we all loved our childhood lemonade, but the horrifying aspect of fizzy drinks is how *everyday* they have become. They represent 20 per cent of children's daily liquid intake and may well have contributed to the childhood obesity 'epidemic' – denied, of course, by the industry. Such sugary drinks are also terrible for children's teeth and it is worrying, given kids' love of cola, how much caffeine they must be taking in. Worldwide, there is anger about the manufacture of soft drinks in developing countries. The best advice is to buy less; even that will pass a big message on to the industry.

What are the basic ingredients in soft drinks?

Water, a sweetener, an acid and a flavour. Optional ingredients include fruit and/or fruit juice, carbon dioxide, preservative and colour. Water makes up approximately 86 per cent of a carbonated drink.

Why do soft drinks contain acid?

For two reasons: first, it creates what the industry calls the taste profile, balancing the sweetness (no one wants a purely sugary drink), and secondly it inhibits the growth of micro-organisms such as yeasts, moulds and bacteria. The acids used are citric acid, malic acid and phosphoric acid. Citric and malic acid are found naturally in citrus fruit, blackcurrants, strawberries and raspberries, while phosphoric acid is a powerful mineral acid with the chemical formula H_3PO_4. An agro-industrial chemical (it is used in the manufacture of fertilisers), it has a tangy taste that can replace ginger, lemon and orange. It is very strong and is used in the manufacture of Coca-Cola and Pepsi. In terms of health effects, large quantities of phosphoric acid may reduce the absorption of calcium, increasing the incidence of osteoporosis especially in young women.

How do drinks get to be fizzy?

With the addition of carbon dioxide (CO_2). The CO_2 used in fizzy drinks is a by-product of various industries, including the petroleum, fertiliser and gas industries, and is made during alcoholic fermentation, too. CO_2 can be contaminated with benzene, a cancer-causing poison. In March 2006 batches of soft drinks, including Coca Cola, Sprite and Dr Pepper, were withdrawn after twice the safe level of benzene was found in the CO_2 supplies used to make them.

Is ordinary water used in the manufacture of soft drinks?

No, a variety of treatments is used to remove impurities, including colour, organic matter, alkalinity and bacteria.

Do labels carry information about the contents of the drink?

They will show the ingredients in order of highest quantity but do not have to show nutritional information unless a specific claim is being made, such as 'low sugar'. Labels do show the country of origin and the name and address of the supplier – handy if you want to contact them and ask some awkward questions. Interestingly, Pepsi does not reveal the quantity of phosphoric acid in its cola. It says this information is commercially sensitive. Soft drinks typically contain 10 per cent sugar.

What types of sweeteners are added to soft drinks?

Unless cane sugar is specified on the label, it will be beet sugar (see Sugar, page 388), which is 99 per cent sucrose. This gives energy but almost no other nutritional benefit. Cane sugar contains a trace amount of minerals but is otherwise just as pointless nutritionally. 'Reduced-sugar' drinks contain 25 per cent less sugar but are not sugar free; 'no added sugar' means sugar is in the drink in a natural form, such as fruit concentrate; this can still cause tooth decay and be high in calories. Artificial sweeteners are added to 'sugar-free' drinks and very often to reduced-sugar ones. They include aspartame (Nutrasweet), cyclamate, saccharin and acesulfame-K. Aspartame is an extremely controversial additive linked to headache, memory loss, mood swings and seizures; new evidence has linked it to leukaemia and lymphoma, too. Its use, however, is permitted in 90 countries. Cyclamate is also problematic and the Food Standards Agency recommends parents allow their children no more than three glasses of diluted soft drinks containing cyclamate a day. The FSA continues to approve all these additives for use in the UK, although an urgent review of aspartame is to take place because researchers in Bologna found that rats given the acceptable daily intake of aspartame developed tumours.

Which additives should I worry about?

* **Colours** – soft drinks manufacturers like to use artificial colours because they are cheaper to manufacture. Some colourings are known to cause hyperactive behaviour in children. The main ones to avoid are sunset yellow (E110), tartrazine (E102), ponceau 4R (E124) and carmoisine (E122), but parent watchdogs are concerned about many others. Annatto (E160b), now used in place of tartrazine, is believed by the Hyperactive Children's Support Group (HACSG) also to be an allergen. Natural colours can be used, derived from fruits and vegetables, but they are not always suitable.
* **Preservatives** – sodium benzoate (E211) has also been identified as a possible allergen for children.

If certain additives are allergens, why are they permitted?

Firstly additives are tested for toxicity, not as potential allergens. Secondly the last government-backed study on children and additives was ruled inconclusive, although it is clear that the report found that those mentioned above could cause allergic reactions. This has prompted a further study, with results due in 2007. Parent groups are increasingly frustrated by the lack of attention paid to their own anecdotal evidence.

What types of flavourings are used in soft drinks?

They can be 'artificial', 'natural' or 'nature identical' although few actual artificial flavours are used by the drinks industry. Even so:

* **Artificial flavouring** is a chemical flavour that imitates a natural one.
* **Nature-identical flavourings** are often labelled 'flavouring' but are not natural. The chemical in a natural flavour is identified, then synthetically manufactured to recreate the flavour in the soft drink.
* **Natural flavourings** are extracts of genuine fruits.

So should I give fizzy drinks to a child?

They'll do no harm on occasion. It can be hard to avoid them at parties and so on. If your child suffers from hyperactivity, try to explain why fizzy drinks should be avoided. Good alternatives include over-diluting squash and mixing carbonated or naturally fizzy water with fruit juice. The Food Standards Agency admits that children who have lots of sugary drinks, such as fizzy drinks and squashes, are more likely to be overweight. They recommend water or milk for children.

Why, when a link exists between soft drinks and obesity, is little action taken?

There is a suspected correlation between the power of big business and the lack of, or painfully slow, action against fizzy drinks manufacturers by the authorities. One welcome change would be to curb television advertising aimed at children. Frankly, adult adverts are just as influential. But it would be helpful if celebrities gave the better-known brands a wide berth instead of endorsing them. Greed in soft-drinks culture is not just for the stuff in the can.

Is drinks manufacture environmentally friendly?

As with all mass production, manufacturing drinks needs energy. Added to that are transportation and litter issues. Annually 6 billion aluminium cans, 225 million plastic containers – mostly plastic bottles – and 6 billion glass containers must be disposed of. Cans and glass are fine, if recycled, but it is reported that less than a third of steel and aluminium cans are recycled in the UK, the remainder being land-filled or incinerated. Serious allegations have been made about the production of Coca-Cola in India. In two communities, Plachimada and Mehdiganj, Coca-Cola had been distributing solid waste to farmers, calling it 'fertiliser'. Tests carried out by the BBC found the waste to be effectively toxic. Coca-Cola stopped this practice when ordered to do so by the state government. There are also allegations regarding water pollution and shortage.

Where to buy natural soft drinks

Choose drinks based on natural fruit juices. If they contain added sugar, cane sugar is preferable. Keep in mind that any sugary drinks should really be only for treats. Watch out for the fruit-flavoured mineral waters; they are often sweetened or contain sweeteners. There are some good organic fruit cordials, which can be quite heavily diluted for young children.

Belvoir Fruit Farms, Belvoir, Grantham, Lincolnshire NG32 1PB
Tel: 01476 870286
www.belvoircordials.co.uk
Cordials and sparkling drinks made from fresh juice, 100 per cent natural ingredients and sparkling Belvoir spring water. Organic range available.

Bottlegreen Drinks Company, Frogmarsh Mills,
South Woodchester, Gloucestershire GL5 5ET
Tel: 01453 874000
www.bottlegreen.co.uk
Flavours include elderflower, cranberry, ginger and lemongrass, blueberry, elderflower light, blackcurrant, and citrus.

Fentimans, 6 Rear Battle Hill, Hexham,
Northumberland NE46 1BB
Tel: 0118 946 4706
Well-balanced flavours and natural ingredients. The range includes
Seville Orange Jigger, Victorian Lemonade, Curiosity Cola, shandy,
dandelion and burdock and ginger beer.

Luscombe Organic Drinks, Colston Road, Buckfastleigh,
Devon TQ11 0LP
Tel: 01364 643036
www.luscombe.co.uk
Luscombe is a small-scale, very principled juice and fruit drink
producer. Its natural organic drinks are free from concentrates,
preservatives, additives and colourings. Mild and hot ginger beer,
Sicilian lemonade and elderflower 'bubbly'. Home delivery available.

Rocks Organic Cordial, Loddon Park Farm, New Bath Road (A4),
Twyford, Berkshire RG10 9RY
Tel: 01189 342344
www.rocksorganic.com
Very natural, with strong 'real' pulpy fruit and cane sugar. No preservatives, colours or sweeteners. Flavours include ginger, tangerine,
cranberry, elderflower, lime and summer fruit.

Thorncroft Healthy Thirst, Thorncroft Ltd, Durham Lane
Industrial Park, Eaglescliffe, Stockton TS16 0RB
Tel: 01642 791792
Drinks with a healthy slant. Flavours include gingko, detox, nettle,
cranberry, elderflower, pink ginger and rosehip.

Whole Earth, Combe Lane, Wormley, Godalming,
Surrey GU8 5SZ
Tel: 01428 685100
www.wholeearthfoods.com
Organic cola, sold in cans, with a good lemony taste. Also cans of
organic cranberry juice and carbonated spring water.

SOY SAUCE

The lengthy, resonating flavour that characterises soy sauce is described as 'umami' but it comes in two guises, natural and chemical. The former is the result of amino acids developing as the soy sauce brews naturally; the latter comes through the simple addition of monosodium glutamate, the chemical equivalent of natural umami. Either way, we are hooked on soy sauce, using it in stir-fries, noodle soups and marinades. But should we worry about the salt, and how can we tell the difference between the slow-brewed type with 500 years of tradition behind it and the ones that are made in just a few days?

What is the difference between the various types of soy sauce?

There are three types:

* **Japanese naturally brewed soy sauce** – made using the koji process, a technique similar to wine making. *Aspigillis* bacteria are added to soya, wheat and water and the mash exposed to humid heat to grow a mould. The sauce is then brewed for up to six months. Amino acids develop as the soya bean breaks down and the slow-brewed wheat gives the sauce its earthy aroma. Japanese soy sauce is naturally acidic, about 4.8 PH. Naturally brewed soy sauce contains no added sugar, colour or flavour, though it does contain salt.

* **Chinese fermented soy sauce** – made with soya and no wheat, Chinese soy sauce is less acidic. Sodium benzoate or potassium sorbate is usually added to preserve it. Japanese soy sauce is extracted by pressing the mash, while Chinese sauce is water that is flushed through the mash, taking on only its flavour. The liquid must then be coloured with caramel, and salt, sugar and sometimes artificial flavourings are added.

* **Hydrolysed vegetable protein (HVP) soy sauce** – a highly processed and disgusting product. Hydrochloric acid is added to the soya beans, creating flavour-producing amino acids. HVP has been found to contain the carcinogen, chloropropanol, sometimes called 3MCPD. Fortunately HVP soy sauce represents a small percentage of soy sauce sold in the UK, and labels will reveal any HVP. However, there is a risk that it is used by the catering sector for low-grade oriental and Southeast Asian food. Watch out, too, for Chinese fermented soy sauce that has added HVP. Always check labels.

What is the difference between light and dark soy sauce?

These are Chinese-style sauces and the only difference is extra caramel and sugar. Dark soy has 15 per cent caramel and light 1 per cent.

What is the salt content of soy sauce?

All soy sauces contain salt and the level will be marked on the label – there is usually about 0.7g per 5g serving. Bear in mind that 6g of salt is the recommended daily allowance for adults. Watch out for the manufacturers' trick of giving only the sodium content. It is a labelling smokescreen – 1g of sodium is 2.5g of salt.

Does soy sauce contain monosodium glutamate?

Many do, but the Japanese naturally brewed sauces do not unless stated on the label. MSG poses a risk as an allergen and, controversially, a trigger for hyperactivity. It may be labelled E621, or 'flavour enhancer'.

Does soy sauce have any health benefits?

The soya bean in the sauce is completely broken down, so there is little nutritional value. Preservative-free soy sauce has antibacterial qualities.

Could soy sauce contain GM soya?

Yes, but many brands avoid its use because UK retailers and shoppers have rejected the GM concept. GM ingredients are permitted in foods sold in the UK, but not their manufacture. Organic soy sauce is guaranteed GM free.

If soy sauce is naturally brewed, is it alcoholic?

Yes, but it is only 2.7 per cent alcohol, so you would have to put back a few bottles.

Does soy sauce manufacture create a lot of waste?

The mash from naturally brewed soy sauce usually goes into livestock feed. If you use a lot of soy sauce, buy large bottles from oriental stores to avoid creating a bottle mountain and decant them.

Where to buy naturally brewed soy sauce

Goodness Direct, South March, Daventry, Northamptonshire NN11 4PH
Tel: 0871 871 6611
www.goodnessdirect.co.uk
This online store sells organic soy sauces including Clearspring Kigisa Shoyu and Clearspring Johsen Shoyu sauce (both matured for two years in cedar casks); also Clearspring wheat-free tamari soy sauce and sauces made by Meridian and Sanchi.

Kikkoman Trading, Unit 3, 1000 North Circular Road, Staples Corner, London NW2 7JP
Tel: 020 8452 8757
www.kikkoman.com
GM-free, naturally brewed, slowly made Japanese sauce using natural ingredients. Chefs hail its multilayered umami taste as the best. Supermarkets stock only small bottles but oriental supermarkets sell it in economical 1 litre or 2.5 litre containers. All Kikkoman for UK shops is brewed in Holland, so it is low in food miles.

Wally's Delicatessen, 42–44 Royal Arcade, Cardiff,
South Glamorgan CF10 2AE
Tel: 029 2022 9265
www.wallysdeli.co.uk
Specialists in oriental ingredients selling several soy sauces, including
Pearl River naturally brewed soy sauce.

SPICES

They load food with flavour, then blast their aromas into our sensory memories but the third purpose of spices is often forgotten. Spices are known to have preservative properties and for that reason they have been an important food to exporting and importing countries for centuries. All should be well: surely when it comes to spices you have a natural, salt-free flavour agent that helps food keep without artificial additives? No. The Sudan 1 scandal of 2005 has resonated. The modern world of spices has its problems with food hygiene and traceability, and spices should be bought with care.

Surely there's no danger in something as pure as spices?

Ground chilli can contain added colour but the Food Standards Agency reports that regular sampling shows none has been imported since 2003 aside from that used in the Premier Foods Worcestershire sauce that triggered the 2005 food scare.

Spices in general can contain residues of chemicals used to decontaminate them. Spices contain oils and are susceptible to contamination from pests, bacteria and moulds. These hazards arise in all stages of production: impure soil, unhygienic handling, dirty storage premises, incorrect packaging. Consumers can put themselves at risk if they do not store spices properly (see below). Not only could contaminated spices cause a serious food poisoning outbreak but their flavour and aroma may be spoiled.

What is at the root of the problem?

The spice business is like a large river fed by thousands of small tributaries. A spice could be harvested in a remote Asian village, then handled and treated by a series of agents before being finally packaged and put on shop shelves. Tracing a packet of spice back to its source is a difficult job for the major producers.

What can be done to make spices safe?

The major importing nations (which include the EU, the US, Japan and West Asia) insist on a low count of bacteria and micro-organisms, and various methods have been developed to control contaminants:

* **Temperature treatment** – the most natural method, whereby spices are heated (steam pasteurisation) or deep frozen. The downside is that flavour can be lost, especially with steam pasteurisation.
* **Fumigation** – chemical gases are pumped into a closed container. Some of the gases used have been found to be carcinogens and environmentalists have called for them to be phased out globally. They include ethylene oxide and methyl bromide.
* **Irradiation** – beams of radiation are passed over the spices at low temperatures, the transfer of energy killing bacteria. It is very effective, and the low temperature has the least effect on flavour, but irradiation encourages the formation of free radicals. A free radical is an unstable molecule that can inflict damage on body tissue. Irradiation also halts vitality in food – an irradiated apple, for example, will not continue to ripen. In the UK irradiated foods must be labelled 'treated with ionising irradiation' or 'irradiated'. Irradiation is routine in Chinese-produced spices.

Which method is preferable?

Both fumigation and irradiation are banned by the organic sector, and the major retailers dislike selling spices that are labelled irradiated. Spices that have been steam pasteurised or frozen are preferable.

How should I store spices?

Buy them in small amounts, keep them dry and cool, in a dark place, and use quickly; if incorrectly stored they can grow moulds or become infested with mites. Reputable brands carry much less risk but the safest choice is to buy whole spices, toast them in a hot, dry pan and grind them yourself in a pestle and mortar or spare electric coffee grinder, as and when you need them.

What about those brightly coloured dyes?

The addition of red Sudan dyes to chilli powder is illegal – they are known carcinogens. Batches are random tested for Sudan dyes at ports by the authorities and any contaminated ones are withdrawn from sale. Contact the Food Standards Agency for a list of companies that have been caught using Sudan dyes (**www.food.gov.uk**).

What the supermarkets say

Sainsbury, **Tesco** and **Waitrose** do not fumigate or irradiate their own-brand spices; all use steam treatment and sift ground spices when appropriate.

Marks & Spencer claims that, although it currently sells only black peppercorns, it can trace the spices used as ingredients in its other products back to their original country and, 'in many cases, back to the grower'. Its suppliers control contaminants by way of a heat treatment.

The Co-op states that documented traceability systems enable suppliers to trace spices back to the distributor. No artificial dyes are used, and a heat treatment is used to control contaminants.

Where to buy spices

Always check the packaging for mention of irradiation and ask about fumigation. Be curious when buying from markets or ethnic shops – ask the vendor questions. They should be happy to answer your informed queries but if not, do not buy from them. Ideally spices should be fresh – a very pungent aroma and good natural colour is an encouraging sign. Organic – certified by the Soil Association – is a safe choice.

Armadeli, 9 Bramley Road, London W10 6SZ
Tel: 020 7727 8866
www.armadillocafe.co.uk
Three good organically sourced spice mixes: Malay Masala, Ras al-Hanout and Cajun. Also red salt from Kauai in Hawaii.

Hambleden Herbs, Rushall Organic Farm, Devizes Road, Rushall, Wiltshire SN9 6ET
Tel: 01980 630721
www.hambledenherbs.com
Soil Association-certified organic spices.

The Organic Herb Trading Company, Milverton, Somerset TA4 1NF
Tel: 01823 401205
www.organicherbtrading.com
Imports and distributes dried organic herbs and spices. Mail order available.

Sambava Spices, Unit 2, Roseberry Place, Bath BA2 3DU
Tel: 01225 426309
www.sambavaspices.com
A small company that pays special attention to sourcing spices from a traceable, safe supply. Sambava imports only whole spices, and grinds them in small batches so the aromas are extra fresh.

Seasoned Pioneers, 101 Summers Road, Brunswick Business Park, Liverpool L3 4BJ
Tel: 0800 068 2348 or 0151 709 9330
www.seasonedpioneers.co.uk
Excellent and original spices and blends packed in airtight foil pouches to protect them. None are irradiated or fumigated. Mail order available.

The Spice Bazaar, The Rectory, Bishops Nympton, South Molton, Devon EX36 4NY
Tel: 01769 550158
www.thespicebazaar.com
Non-irradiated or fumigated spices from a small family business in North Devon. Excellent website. Mail order available.

The Spice Shop, 1 Blenheim Crescent, London W11 2EE
Tel: 020 7221 4448
www.thespiceshop.co.uk
None of the spices in this shop is treated with fumigation or irradiation. Mail order available.

Steenbergs Organic Pepper and Spice, Steenbergs Ltd, PO Box 48, Boroughbridge, York YO51 9ZW
Tel: 01765 640088
www.steenbergs.co.uk
An impressive range of 95 per cent organic fairly traded spices from India, Sri Lanka and Turkey, beautifully packed in small amounts. Spice blends are made in Yorkshire. Fairtrade Madagascan vanilla pods shortly to become available. Mail order.

STOCK

Risottos, soups and winter braises are at their best made with home-made stock but what if you are in a hurry or cannot face that pot of simmering bones? Stock cubes were the saviour of cooks for decades while those precious bones from the roast went in the bin. But the ingredients they contain that give them flavour have become controversial and many cooks are looking for an alternative. Natural stock can be bought but be prepared to pay top dollar. Suddenly it seems a sin to throw away those bones after the roast ...

What is stock made from?

Ideally it is a broth extracted by slowly simmering bones with a few vegetables and herbs. Sometimes the bones are lightly roasted first to flavour and colour the stock but salt should be added only in the barest amount.

What's in a stock cube?

A typical stock cube will contain extracts of meat, meat fat, starch, colouring, dried vegetables and herbs but they take much of their strong flavour from the addition of salt or monosodium glutamate and a lesser-known 'flavour enhancer' called acid hydrolised vegetable protein (HVP). There are several health risks connected with these ingredients:

* Salt raises blood pressure, increasing the risk of heart disease and strokes. A Knorr beef stock cube contains 1.66g sodium, which is 4g salt; the Food Standards Agency recommends eating no more than 6g of salt a day.
* Monosodium glutamate can be identified on labels as E621–625. It can also be hidden under other names, including guanylate and inosinate (E-number code E626–635) Some stock cubes contain a highly potent combination of three types of glutamate. Intolerance varies, but some people show consistent symptoms. Hyperactive

children are vulnerable to its effects, which range from rages, anxiety attacks, mood swings to heart palpitations, migraine, sweats, depression and dizziness. Some manufacturers no longer list the identifying E number or the chemical name but simply write 'flavour enhancer' on the label. Be wary.

✽ HVP is vegetable protein processed using hydrochloric acid. This process has the peculiar effect of transforming the flavour from vegetable to meat. Bizarrely it is used in the manufacture of vegetarian food – and vegetable stock. Found in HVP is the chemical contaminant, 3MCPD – a chloropropanol that has been found to be carcinogenic when given to rats. It is not permitted in organic stock cubes.

Why do the manufacturers use these additives?

It seems crazy when there is a mountain of bones from good-quality, traceable livestock, most of which are sent for rendering at huge cost to the meat industry. The simple answer is economics. Using artificially developed flavourings, colours and other food 'enhancers' is a yet cheaper option for food manufacturers keener on boosting profit than giving customers wholesome food made from fresh ingredients.

Is stock powder better?

Stock powders often contain the same nasties. Don't be fooled by the 'natural' style packaging of the often-recommended Marigold Swiss Vegetable Bouillon Powder. It contains the dreaded HVP, in spite of a claim on the label that it does not contain artificial flavourings. Marigold does, however, make an organic version without it.

What is the origin of the bones used in meat stock cubes, fresh meat stock or concentrate?

Only the manufacturers know. Unless specified on the label, or the stock is organic, the meat content could have been intensively reared, on any feed, anywhere. Labelling laws allow imported meat to be used in stock labelled 'made in the UK'. Conversely, British beef bones are not permitted for use in the manufacture of beef stock in the UK – a 1997 law designed to protect customers from 'hidden' ingredients that pose a vCJD risk. This is now somewhat outdated, since the ban on beef on the bone has been lifted, and news is emerging of BSE in exporting countries. Manufacturers who sell direct to the public – farm shops, for example – are permitted to use British beef bones.

What's in the fresh stocks in supermarket chiller cabinets?

So far the fresh ones are good, although watch the salt levels, which are marked on the nutritional information. The ingredients are natural, but if you are a committed buyer of organic or naturally reared meat, it is impossible to guarantee the provenance of the meat in any but the organic fresh stocks.

Fresh stocks are good news for anyone who wants to make a quick gravy, but if you need a large quantity – for a risotto, say – the cost of the stock will probably be higher than that of any other ingredient. Remember the whole point of stock is that it is a gift – easy to make using the bones after cooking a roast.

Where to buy meat stock made with natural ingredients

Daylesford Organic Farmshop, Daylesford, Near Kingham, Gloucestershire GL56 0YG
Tel: 01608 731700
www.daylesfordorganic.com
Organic chicken or vegetable stock, simmered with a huge variety of vegetables.

Joubère, Pasta Reale House, Fleming Way, Crawley,
West Sussex RH10 9JW
Tel: 01293 649700
www.joubere.co.uk
This innovative company made the first fresh stocks for supermarkets, using only natural ingredients. Its stock is available from
many major supermarkets and independent shops and it offers
organic versions, too.

Pipers Farm, Cullompton, Devon EX15 1SD
Tel: 01392 881380
www.pipersfarm.com
Frozen chicken stock made with wings and bones from their own
naturally reared chickens. They use absolutely no seasoning, so
customers can add their own.

STRAWBERRIES

Sinking your teeth into a strawberry's reservoir of juice is by rights a privilege available for only six weeks of the year. But strawberries have preceded even the French bean as a year-round staple, and the perpetual strawberry harvest often comes at the expense of taste, texture – and food miles. Now British growers have fought back to extend our strawberry season using polytunnel cultivation, and detractors claim the countryside will soon be wrapped in a fetish of polythene. The debate rages, it has even been a theme in 'The Archers', but another tragedy looms. Meet Elsanta, the most successful strawberry on the block. Big, with a long shelf life, it's the supermarkets' favourite and the reason for the demise of the old varieties that gave British strawberries their great reputation. Hmm. Is this fighting back? Or a case of can't beat 'em, join 'em?

When does the British strawberry season begin?
Once strawberries cropped in June, followed by a smaller crop in late August. New varieties and the polytunnel culture mean farmers can crop strawberries from mid May until November. Strawberries now account for 80 per cent of the soft fruit grown in the UK. The change in the market has been driven by supermarket and consumer demand for more UK-grown, cheap, long-lasting strawberries. And there is, for the first time, now a tempting subsidy to strawberry growers under the new Single Payment Scheme, a move that could potentially flood the market.

Are polytunnels good or bad for cultivation?
Polytunnels would be great if they were not so hideous. Their controlled environment means that pesticide, fungicide and herbicide use is 30 per cent lower than that in open fields. Keeping fruit dry keeps botrytis (grey mould) at bay, and tunnels provide perfect conditions for pest control using natural predators. Tunnel cultivation reduces costs and boosts production, giving consumers cheap, home-grown

strawberries for six months, not six weeks, of the year. Despite being good news for our farmers, this last point has totally robbed the British strawberry of its romance.

What's the answer to the polytunnel problem?

Friends of the Earth says that planning law should govern polytunnel use; at the moment the National Farmers Union (NFU) suggests only a voluntary code to regulate the number, size and colour of the tunnels. Britain's architects – respond!

Who picks my strawberries?

A booming fruit industry relies on an immigrant workforce, simply because the British are not prepared to do this work on the pay offered by farmers trying to keep costs low. While this situation can certainly be mutually beneficial to both flexible workforce and employer if handled within the law, there are serious concerns about the ethicality of much of this practice. There are reports that illegal working practice continues. As usual, the answer lies in economics. To have a clear conscience, we must pay more for strawberries and, perhaps idealistically, encourage employers to raise wages.

Are there pesticide residues on strawberries?

Yes, on the majority. Strawberries were last tested for residues by the Pesticide Residues Committee in 2004. Residues were found on 38 out of 48 samples. The samples, which were on sale in UK shops, were from various producing countries. Ten originated in the UK. Two of the samples (one from the UK) contained residues of six different chemicals. This is a cause for special concern, as it is the effects of the multiple residues that we know least about. Two of the samples were organic and contained no residues at all. This is not a comprehensive survey of organic but it is consistent with tests on other organic produce by the PRC, so it would seem that organic strawberries are a good choice if you want to avoid residues of agricultural chemicals.

Is strawberry growing environmentally friendly?

Ideally strawberries should be farmed in rotation, either in fields or in tunnels. But some farms sterilise the soil with chemicals in order to remove the pathogens that can cause disease in the crop. This way they do not need to rotate. Environmentalists say this destroys the nutrient quality of the soil. Traditional farmers say packing too many plants into a tunnel reduces airflow and encourages disease, but polytunnel enthusiasts claim they can control pests and disease with much more ease, reducing the need for pesticides.

What's so bad about Elsanta?

Strawberry farming is turning into a monoculture with this farmers' favourite breed. Firm but admittedly sweet, it has a good shelf life and can survive the journey from farm to holding depot to supermarket – a matter of at least four days. Strawberries used to be picked and eaten locally, and only ever survived a day before being suitable for jam. This was the tender, juicy fruit whose stalk and hull would come out entirely when pulled. Traditional farmers dislike Elsanta, saying it does not ripen evenly. Growers currently doing reasonably nicely supplying supermarkets claim Elsanta matches the old varieties on taste. This is rubbish. The firm texture ruins the eating quality, sweet or not. Some of them are so crisp that it is more like biting into an apple than a strawberry.

Are strawberries good for me?

Eight strawberries yield as much vitamin C as an orange and are high in fibre and folates. They also make good emergency toothpaste. Half a strawberry rubbed on the teeth cleans them up to a squeak – but brush properly later.

What the supermarkets say

Marks & Spencer imports its strawberries via air freight from Europe, Australasia, the Americas and Africa. However, it claims its first preference is to buy British when available. It sells 100 per cent British fruit from June to September.

Sainsbury imports its strawberries by air, road and sea freight from Israel, Egypt, Morocco, Spain and Holland. However, it states that it always prioritises the British product 'if the quality is acceptable', which is a bit of a get-out clause.

Waitrose sells only British strawberries when the season is on.

The Co-op sources its fruit from all over Europe and Africa, but is 'working with' British farms to sell their produce whenever available.

Budgens sources its strawberries from the UK, Israel, Egypt, Jordan, Holland, Belgium and the US. All except UK strawberries are transported by air freight.

Where to buy traditional varieties

Shoppers searching for treasured traditional varieties must head for a nearby pick-your-own. Call in advance to check, but the season should start in the first week of June. Look out for strawberries at farmers' markets and farm shops. To find your nearest farmers' market, check **www.farmersmarkets.net** (tel: 0845 458 8420), or **www.lfm.org.uk** (tel: 020 7833 0338) for London. For details of farm shops, look at **www.farma.org.uk** or **www.bigbarn.co.uk**.

Boddington's Berries, The Ashes, Tregoney Hill, Mevagissey, Cornwall PL26 6RQ
Tel: 01726 842346
www.boddingtonsberries.co.uk
A 25-year-old fruit farm growing strawberries inside polytunnels and out. Louise Boddington is now trialling older varieties, Royal Sovereign and Cambridge Favourite, on the farm (not yet ready for commercial sale).

Chettle Stores, Chettle, Blandford Forum, Dorset DT11 8DB
Tel: 01258 830223
Strawberries from a small farm in the village – picked only when perfectly ripe.

Essington Fruit Farm, Bognop Rd, Essington, Wolverhampton WV11 2AZ
Tel: 01902 735724
www.essingtonfarm.co.uk
The Simpkin family are strawberry fanatics, with a special interest in breeds, all of which are labelled in their open strawberry fields so you can pick by variety. Grower Mr Simkin does not rate Elsanta's flavour, but 27 new and old varieties are available.

The Fruit Garden, Groes Faen Road, Peterston-super-Ely, Vale of Glamorgan CF5 6NE
Tel: 01446 760358
Lucy George grows 25 varieties of strawberries, including the delicious woodland-strawberry-flavoured Mara de Bois, Ciflorette and Rosie. They are grown in polytunnels at tabletop height, a pest avoidance measure that also makes picking a comfortable job.

Holly Farm, Stutton, Ipswich, Suffolk IP9 2SU
Tel: 01473 328294
Five varieties of strawberry, grown at tabletop height in tunnels.

Kenyon Hall Farm, Winwick Lane Croft, Warrington WA3 7ED
Tel: 01925 763646
www.kenyonhall.co.uk
Honeoye, Elsanta, Florence and Pandora varieties, grown outside.

Manor Farm Fruits, Hints, Tamworth, Staffordshire B78 3DW
Tel: 01543 481214
www.manorfarmfruits.co.uk
Elaine Clarke grows five varieties of strawberries outdoors for PYO.

Milbourne Farm Fruit, East Town Farm, Milbourne, Ponteland, Northumberland NE20 0EE
Tel: 01661 881278
All the Scottish-bred strawberries (it's an Elsanta-free zone) are grown outdoors on this small, family-run farm.

SUGAR

Every human, animal and plant needs sugar to survive, but the sugar we get is the one that is the least beneficial. We could happily exist on the sugars that occur naturally in fruit and vegetables or dairy foods, but the sugar that too many have a taste for is refined white. It makes superb cakes and pâtisserie, it gives that cup of tea or coffee an extra kick – and it turns up in an awful lot of junk food. But if eating less sugar is a good policy, at least buy the right one – shopping for sugar is a moral as well as a health choice.

What is the difference between 'sugar' and 'cane sugar'?

The contents of bags of white sugar marked 'sugar' are refined from sugar beet, a crop that grows in Europe. Bags labelled 'cane sugar' (both brown and white) are derived or refined from sugar cane, which is grown in tropical climates. The Sugar Bureau, a trade association, says the two are identical. Marmalade makers retort that cane is superior for their art, but the devil is in the detail:

* **Beet sugar** – can only be white – once refined, beet sugar is 99 per cent pure sucrose. The by-products of beet refining are not fit for human consumption, just a foul-smelling mass suitable for live-stock feed. Beet sugar is refined by washing, slicing and boiling the beets to produce a sugary liquid. This is treated with lime and carbon dioxide gas to remove the impurities. In the final stages the crystals are separated from the liquid using centrifugal force.
* **Cane sugar** – can be white or brown. Brown sugar contains small traces of protein and minerals but it is only marginally more nutritious than beet sugar. The by-products of white cane sugar production are edible and include black treacle, golden syrup, molasses and various brown sugars.

What effect does sugar farming have on the environment?

Environmentalists deplore beet farming for its corrosive effect on the soil and its use of pesticides – it is staggering to notice that British Sugar, producer of beet sugar and parent of the Silver Spoon brand, offers a supply of 'topsoil' from its website, 'derived from the country's prime arable soils'! This topsoil is separated from the sugar beet delivered to the beet factories. How nice it would be if it could be taken back to the fields where it belongs.

Chemical use on conventional sugar cane is routine. As regards pesticide residues, sugar appears to be exempt from testing by the government-backed Pesticide Residues Committee. According to a spokesman, sugar is too refined a product for pesticide residue testing to be an issue.

Is sugar fairly traded?

That depends on the type of sugar. Put it this way, in its report on European sugar production, Oxfam states that beet farmers in Europe have been receiving generous subsidies for decades to grow sugar beet, while the average pay to an Ethiopian sugar cane farmer is about a US dollar a day. Quite apart from the scandalous amounts the subsidies have cost taxpayers, the unfairness of the trade policy has worked against cane sugar producers. Added to this, the big players who monopolise the beet sugar business make handsome profits. In 2004 British Sugar made £175 million profit and their business is subsidised by us! And this situation has existed for decades with no changes in agricultural policy until now. Fairly traded sugar is available, however (see below).

Will the reforms to the Common Agricultural Policy help?

Hard to say, but the current plan, simply put, is to reduce the beet farmers' subsidy by 50 per cent and continue only to support the most efficient EU producers. No doubt compensation will be offered to the redundant farmers, paid for by – er – us? A plan to reduce the amount of sugar grown, both in the EU and through imports, suggests that there is over capacity already in the sugar industry and the most 'efficient' farmers will supply all that is needed, while the farmers in developing countries still won't get a piece of the action.

Is sugar nutritious or dangerous?

Sucrose gives us energy, but little else. The sugar industry argues that the current obesity epidemic, which has seen a whole new young generation succumb to type-2 diabetes, is a direct result of lack of exercise. There may be some truth in this but the temptations of sweet things marketed in so many imaginative ways is very strong, especially for the young. What is not in any doubt is that too much sugar is bad for you and many processed foods contain large amounts of it. Some products, however, make a virtue of using only cane sugar, which at least contains a few more beneficial minerals.

How do granulated and caster sugar differ?

The difference is in the size of the crystals. Caster sugar has the smallest grains and blends easily into mixtures, ensuring an even texture. Granulated crystals are larger and slower to dissolve, so more suitable for tea and coffee.

How do the various brown sugars differ?

Brown sugar begins as shredded cane, which is then crushed between heavy rollers. The pulp is sprayed with hot water and lime added to clean (absorb) impurities from the resulting juice. The liquid is filtered, then boiled in a vacuum to form a thick syrup. The crystals that form in the syrup are separated using a centrifuge – they are the raw sugar, the liquid is molasses. Much of the raw sugar is sent to the UK to be refined into white sugar (think Tate & Lyle) – where, incidentally, delicious black treacle is a by-product of the refining process; raw sugar is sold as two main types:

* ❈ **Demerara** – originally from British Guyana, the crystals are hard and yellow and the sugar has a light fragrance. Molasses is sometimes added to white beet sugar to make it 'brown'; this is called London Demerara.

* **Muscovado** – made by leaving the molasses to drain from the sugar naturally, with no centrifuge. The result is a soft, moist sugar, sold either as dark or light. Muscovado sugars, light and brown, are more of a whole food than plain 'soft brown' sugar.

Can sweet things be contaminated with GM sugar?

A type of herbicide-resistant sugar beet has been developed but currently, due to consumer resistance, neither the British sugar business nor the supermarkets will consider selling it. A further blow was dealt to its future in 2005 when it was found that the plant was no good for biodiversity because, despite it not dying when sprayed with herbicide, the wildlife around it perished. So much for the environmental merits of GM.

What the supermarkets say

Marks & Spencer does not sell own-brand cane sugar but has own-brand beet sugar (granulated) sourced from the UK. It does not specify on the ingredients list whether the product contains cane or beet sugar.

Sainsbury's own-brand sugars are sourced from Mauritius, apart from the Demerara variety, which comes from Barbados.

Tesco buys its sugar from Malawi, Mauritius and various other unspecified sources. Its own-brand granulated variety is a beet sugar sourced from the UK. It does not differentiate between beet and cane sugar on the labels. It does not sell an organic or Fairtrade alternative.

Waitrose does not sell an own-label organic sugar but it does stock light brown Muscovado and the other less refined sugars from Mauritius.

The Co-op sells own-brand dark brown soft sugar, dark Muscovado sugar and Demerara sugar, all sourced from Mauritius. It also sells a Fairtrade range (golden and white granulated sugar) that is sourced from the Kasinthula cane growers in Malawi, a co-operative of small-scale plantation holders who receive a fair deal for their sugar cane. The Co-op will not sell own-brand beet sugar.

Which sugars to buy

Belle de Sucre, Atelier, Château de Cornou, 20 Aisance de Cornou, F-45210 Nargis, France
E-mail: belledesucre@wanadoo.fr

Decorative sugar lumps made in France in every shape and size – from little coat buttons, to tea leaf or coffee bean shapes, to croissant shapes and small men whose arms hook over the side of the tea cups. Also bars of coloured sugar. The sugar is a mixture of cane and beet. Available from Harrods (tel: 020 7730 1234).

Billingtons, PO Box 26, Oundle Road, Peterborough PE2 9QU
Tel: 01733 422368
www.billingtons.co.uk

Billingtons deals with over 2,000 growers in Mauritius, buying a variety of sugars, including golden caster sugar and icing sugar. It also sells fairly traded granulated and Demerara sugar and an organic golden caster sugar.

Steenbergs Ltd, PO Box 48, Boroughbridge, York YO51 9ZW
Tel: 01765 640088
www.steenbergs.co.uk

Five organic, fairly traded sugars from Cuba, each flavoured with different aromatics: vanilla, lemon, lavender, rose and cinnamon. Use the rose or lemon sugar in tea, the vanilla as a dusting for cakes, the lavender on berries and the cinnamon on buttered toast. Mail order available.

Traidcraft, Kingsway, Gateshead, Tyne and Wear NE11 0NE
Tel: 0870 443 1018
www.traidcraftshop.co.uk

Fairtrade sugar including various brown sugars from Mauritius and raw cane sugar from Paraguay. Available online or from Oxfam shops.

SUSHI

When a specialist food loses its deluxe status and becomes available to everyone, it should be time to celebrate. In the case of sushi the transformation has been truly remarkable. Ten years ago, regular sushi hunters in the UK would have had to travel far to track down their exotic prey. Now the Western world is a sushi democracy and any city dweller can pop out to the supermarket for a good helping of *maki* rolls, and pay under a fiver for it. No one knocks sushi. We are mesmerised by its artfulness (we'd just as happily wear it as eat it), cheered by the low calorie count and ecstatic about the nutritional goodness in the slivers of fish that rest on those compact rice lozenges ... But it's not all good news. The British Heart Foundation may well wish a 'sushi all round' scenario upon us, but this ongoing fest has serious sustainability issues. Sushi boxes rarely carry much information, a situation that must change.

What shouldn't we love about sushi?
The body count of the fish used in its manufacture is the big problem. Blue fin tuna is listed as critically endangered, while stocks of yellow fin – the one used in supermarket sushi – are dropping due to irresponsible harvesting. While the species number suffers, more and more tuna is coming on to the market and, most worryingly, the price of tuna is low, hence the arrival of sushi in supermarket chillers next to the sandwiches.

How do I know the tuna in sushi is dolphin friendly?
Line-caught tuna is generally dolphin friendly, but be aware that some is tuna caught on long lines – ones with hooks that trail from boats for up to 100 kilometres. This fishing technique is a danger to other marine species, including albatross and turtles. There is a 'dolphin safe' logo (see Tuna, page 423), but it is unlikely to be shown on bento boxes, in sushi takeaways or in fish shops. Ask about the retailer's dolphin policy when buying fish or sushi.

Where does all that fish come from?

The salmon used in supermarket sushi is without exception farmed and, depending on the husbandry, this can be problematic in terms of marine pollution and the decimation of wild stocks used for feed (see Salmon, page 345). Another favourite sushi ingredient, warm-water prawns, is fraught with marine pollution issues (see Prawns, page 316). Worse, environment agencies report that the massive deforestation of mangrove forests in Southeast Asia to make way for prawn farms leaves the coastline dangerously unprotected, and contributed to the tragedy of the 2004 tsunami.

What about the other sushi ingredients?

The majority of sushi is made with fish, raw and cured, and almost all types include rice, too. The rice is a sweet, short grain variety and is mixed with vinegar and sugar, which lowers the PH, naturally preserving it even at room temperature. Wasabi, the hot green radish paste eaten as a condiment, is also antibacterial but be aware that it contains artificial blue and yellow – or green – dyes (see Mustard, page 254, for a source of natural wasabi). Production of nori, the 'seaweed' sheets made from sea algae, is environmentally sound but threatened by marine pollution.

Is sushi safe?

Against all odds – yes. You would imagine that a combination of cooled cooked rice and raw fish should carry a cigarette-pack-style health warning but the Health Protection Agency reports no trouble with sushi. It is, however, illegal for restaurants, takeaways and shops to sell sushi or sashimi that has been bought in that has not been previously frozen at –20°C for 24 hours. Restaurants, takeaways and shops that make the sushi on the premises are not subject to the 'freezing' law. Some fish can contain worms, which the Food Standards Agency (FSA) says can cause illness. These worms die at low temperatures.

The FSA advises pregnant women not to eat raw fish unless it has been previously frozen, recommending buying fish from shops or takeaways that are subject to the 'freezing' law. It says that concerned expectant mothers should be cautious in restaurants where the sushi is freshly made. It is a matter of reputation – a top-ranking sushi restaurant is unlikely to put itself in a situation where live worms are crawling out of the food.

How fresh is the fish?

Ideally the fish arriving in the UK is not more than four days old from the catch time, stored at 0.4°C. In the case of frozen fish, it is often blast frozen on board the boat. Once defrosted, it retains its fresh flavour.

Is sushi 100 per cent good for you?

The Japanese have the lowest heart disease rate in the world, but it is not known whether this is down to their fish eating or the general diversity of their diet. The oils in some fish, such as mackerel, salmon and tuna, are very beneficial to heart health. There have been concerns about mercury levels in oily fish and dioxins in some farmed salmon. Weighing good up against bad, the benefits of the essential fatty acids in the fish oils win, and mercury levels are tiny in wild fish. If you are concerned about contaminants in farmed salmon, choose organic or wild Irish salmon (see Salmon, page 345). When eating sushi, do choose a naturally brewed soy sauce, such as Kikkoman (see page 371), that does not contain monosodium glutamate (E621–635).

Where to buy sushi

The following delivery services use some responsibly harvested fish:

Feng Sushi, 13 Stoney Street, London SE1 9AD
Tel: 0207 407 8744
www.fengsushi.co.uk
The yellow fin tuna in this London chain is line caught, the salmon is sustainable (from Loch Duart) and the mackerel line caught from the south coast. A company with a big conscience, they will not serve the endangered blue fin tuna. Check the website for branches.

Moshi Moshi Sushi, 102 Fruit and Wool Exchange,
Brushfield Street, London E1 6EX
Tel: 020 7248 1808
www.moshimoshi.co.uk
Moshi Moshi removed all blue fin tuna from the menu once it realised
there was a shortage. Branches in Brighton and London (check the
website for details).

Pret a Manger, 1 Hudson's Place, London SW1V 1PZ
Tel: 020 7827 8888
www.pret.com
For a large company (which is part owned by McDonalds), Pret is
careful where it sources the tuna used in its sushi, choosing only line-
caught, dolphin-safe yellow fin. It also takes the artificial colouring
out of its wasabi. Delivery to some areas only.

Yo! Sushi – and Yo! To Go home delivery, 95 Farringdon Road,
London EC1R 3BT
Tel: 020 7841 0700
www.yosushi.com
Uses only line-caught yellow fin tuna from a sustainable source in
the Maldives. Branches in London, Birmingham, Brighton and
Manchester (check the website for details).

Where to buy sushi ingredients
If you care about the marine environment, make your own sushi and
choose yellow fin tuna caught by pole and line (from the Indian
Ocean). Organically farmed salmon is a safe choice; wild salmon from
the Pacific is responsibly harvested, as is mackerel sourced from the
south coast. Contact the Marine Stewardship Council for stockists
(www.msc.org).

For organic sushi ingredients (not fish), try www.goodness
direct.co.uk or www.clearspring.co.uk.

Japanese Kitchen, 9 Lower Richmond Road, London SW15 1EJ
Tel: 020 8788 9014
www.japanesekitchen.co.uk
Sushi sets and individual Japanese ingredients available by mail order.

The Japanese Shop, 1 Westminster Arcade, Parliament Street,
Harrogate, North Yorkshire HG1 2RN
Tel: 01423 529850
Sushi rice and other good Japanese ingredients, but no fish. Branches
in York and Chester

For very fresh fish, via home delivery

Matthew Stevens & Son Ltd, Back Road West, St Ives,
Cornwall TR26 3AR
Tel: 01736 799392
www.mstevensandson.co.uk
Wonderfully fresh fish from this environmentally responsible fishmonger who specialises in fish caught by local boats, and is careful to
buy tuna from a sustainable source. Be prepared to buy an alternative,
as Matthew sources fish seasonally and only when he can buy a good
size. (See also Tuna, page 423.)

TEA

The elegance of porcelain cups, the exotic provenance, the crystalline beauty of the brew and the obsessive rituals of making it elevate tea above junkie attitudes to coffee. You are, perhaps, the cup of tea you drink. Green tea enthusiasts are healthy people who do pilates and feng shui their offices; Lapsang sippers have bags of time to hand and an irresistible urge to show off the Limoges. But drinkers of builder's tea are the exception: most of us need a mega-dose of tannin to kickstart the morning, and we in the UK (along with Russia) are the biggest tea drinkers in the world. Putting aside the taste and any benefits to be had from drinking tea, read between the tea leaves and you may change the way you buy it for ever.

Where does tea come from?
Tea is grown in 36 countries but the big five are India, China, Sri Lanka, Kenya and Indonesia, who produce 80 per cent of the world's tea.

How do teas differ?
Oddly enough, all the tea we buy is from the same leaf, *Camellia sinensis*, handled differently after picking. Teas from different tea gardens and tea nations differ in flavour, however, and are often blended, unless labelled single estate.

* **Black tea** is also black to look at and is used for the full-flavoured tea beloved of the British since its arrival here approximately 350 years ago. The leaves are withered, rolled to release their oils, allowed to ferment, then heat-dried. High-grade teas are rolled into wiry twists but commercial granular tea for teabags and the mass market is crushed, a cheaper process.
* **Green tea** is not fermented. The fresh leaves are steamed or fired to preserve their natural flavours and goodness (it has high levels of antioxidants), then rolled to release the oils. Green tea is

traditionally grown and made in China (where the leaves are fired in dry heat) and Japan (where the leaves are steamed).

* **Oolong tea** is sun or air dried and only partly fermented – it is sometimes sold as Formosa or Green Oolong.
* **White tea** is a delicate, partly fermented Chinese tea made from the unopened spring buds of the tea plant.

Are there chemicals in my tea?

Tea was lasted tested for pesticide residues in 2005 but the report is not due until March 2006. Previously, in 2001, 46 tea brands were tested and residues were found on five samples. The residues did not exceed government-approved maximum levels but this is still unsatisfactory in a drink that should be 100 per cent pure.

Is tea an environmentally friendly crop?

Tea is grown in a monoculture – in other words just one type is planted over vast areas. This reduces biodiversity, i.e. wildlife, and increases the need for agricultural chemicals. Not only is the use of chemicals a threat to the natural environment (water supply, wild animal, bird and insect life) but it can also be dangerous to estate workers and farmers who apply it. There are organic tea farms, which do much to lessen the impact of growing tea on the environment, and organic tea is now widely available.

Who picks the tea leaves?

Of all global crops, working conditions in tea gardens are the most worrisome. The workforce can be trapped within the plantations that produce most of our tea, dependent on the plantation 'owners' for medical aid, housing, fuel, food and in many cases the (often partial) education of their children, who themselves will be destined for life on the plantation. Tea production is very labour intensive and estate workers' conditions are a serious cause for concern. Wages are low: in India the rate varies from less than a US dollar a day to just over a dollar. Rates in the rest of the world's tea gardens are much the same but it is estimated that the living wage should be above two dollars a day. Problems on estates also include sexual discrimination, poor working conditions and abuse of migrant workforces who often have no rights or citizenship in the country where they work. Small tea farmers may fare better, and it is an area where Fairtrade initiatives can work well.

Why are tea garden workers so poorly paid?

There has been a long-term decline in tea prices due to over supply, but it is also the case that, unlike coffee, tea perishes quickly, forcing hasty, low-price sales. Tea 'blending' encourages competitiveness, as tea-packing companies do not have to return to the same estate each time. Developing countries also suffer from the tariff system imposed by Western importing countries. Tea exports are an important opportunity for countries to earn foreign exchange, but with so little to be gained their poverty continues.

So is all tea, apart from Fairtrade, unfairly traded?

Not necessarily. Some of the bigger conglomerates and all UK retailers have signed up to the Ethical Trading Initiative (ETI) and also the Ethical Tea Partnership (ETP). Both schemes promise an admirable code of conduct and there are examples of the good done by these companies in individual cases. However, auditing corporate behaviour is slow, can be infrequent and is not always possible.

Will buying Fairtrade help?

Yes. Fairtrade can work to boost incomes in various ways. The Fairtrade organisation either buys direct from an estate, if the social welfare and income of the workers is good (and continuously monitored and audited), or it buys from groups or co-operatives of smallholder farmers, or gives farmers and workers shares in processing plants.

Who puts my tea into the teabag?

The main players in the UK are Unilever, which owns Brooke Bond PG Tips, and Tata Tea, which owns Tetley. Both are signed up to the

ETI and ETP, along with Twining's, Jacksons of Piccadilly, and Betty's and Taylor's of Harrogate. The principles of these trading schemes are good but, as mentioned earlier, auditing and monitoring their implementation can be difficult.

Can I buy ethically traded tea in the supermarkets?

Most supermarkets stock at least one ethically traded tea. Asda, Morrison, Sainsbury, Somerfield, Tesco, the Co-op and Marks & Spencer (Café Revive) each have an own-brand Fairtrade tea. Look out also for other Fairtrade brands: Tea Direct, Dragonfly Tea, Percol (Asda and Booths only) and the Hampstead Tea and Coffee Company.

Where to buy tea

All the companies listed below can supply tea by post.

Clipper Tea, Beaminster Business Park, Broadwindsor Road, Beaminster, Dorset DT8 3PR
Tel: 01308 863344
www.clipper-teas.com

Fairtrade and organic teas of every type for the first company to earn a Fairtrade logo. Clipper has also conquered the problem of taste compromise that can accompany good corporate behaviour, and their teas are consistently delicious.

D. J. Miles, The Vale Yard, High Street, Porlock, Somerset TA24 8PU
Tel: 01643 703993
www.djmiles.co.uk

Family-run specialist tea blenders who are committed to the Ethical Tea Partnership. Their Original Blend Loose Tea makes the best strong cuppa on the market.

Rare Tea Company, 124 Marlborough Road, London N19 4NN
Tel: 07952 019982
www.rareteacompany.com

Henrietta Lovell travelled to China herself to find the most exclusive tea, bringing back white silver tip tea and jasmine silver tip tea whose rolled leaves unfurl like corkscrews when boiling water is added. Her company is newly set up, but aims to reinvest in the welfare of those who work in the tea gardens, with a strong emphasis on ethical trading.

Steenberg's Organic Tea, PO Box No 48, Boroughbridge,
York YO51 9ZW
Tel: 01765 640088
www.steenbergs-tea.com

Organic Fairtrade Darjeeling from this small supplier of equally excellent spices and salt.

Traidcraft, Kingsway, Gateshead, Tyne and Wear NE11 0NE
Tel: 0870 443 1018
www.traidcraftshop.co.uk

The majority of Traidcraft tea comes from estates with good wages and conditions for workers, or from factories buying from small-scale growers on fair terms.

Union Flowering Teas, The New Roastery, Unit 2,
7a South Crescent, London E16 4TL
Tel: 020 7474 8990
www.unionroasters.com

Unique, hand-sewn bouquets of ethically sourced tea leaves and flower petals from four difference provinces in China, which open into a 'flower' when in hot water. They make excellent presents and the associated programmes that bring aid to suppliers are interesting reading. There are nine varieties of flowering teas, including a delicious jasmine. 'Numi's Bouquet' contains all nine.

TOFU

Like people, some foods have a permanent halo even if they don't always deserve it. Tofu, the angelic-sounding bean curd eaten by a generation of vegetarians in place of meat, is one such food. It was first made in China over 2,000 years ago and was brought to Japan by Keno priests in 700AD. Hand-made tofu is still a matter of pride and artisan skill in Japan, but traditionalists say corners have been cut for the mass-market product. Commercial tofu manufacture has turned what should be a flavoursome, meaty curd into a bland, opaque gel, with some major environmental concerns.

What is in tofu?

Tofu is made from ground cooked soya beans, water and a coagulant that sets the bean paste into curds. The curds are then pressed to remove liquid, leaving a cake that can be cut, eaten fresh, cooked or diced into soups and stir-fried dishes. It is also known as bean curd.

How is tofu made?

As with bread, there is artisan made and the tofu equivalent to sliced and wrapped. Traditional tofu is still made in Japan, where there are thousands of tofu 'corner shops'. For connoisseurs, the crucial point is the coagulant. Nigari, the mineral magnesium chloride taken from evaporating seawater, is the traditional substance used to curdle the soya paste and gives tofu a multifaceted, earthy flavour. But modern manufacturers can use calcium sulphate, or gypsum, which is more commonly used to plaster walls. Gypsum retains a lot of water, boosting the manufacturers' profits handsomely, but it gives tofu a bland, chalky taste. The industry insists that gypsum's calcium content is a good thing. The most artificial coagulant used is glucono delta lactone, a highly refined chemical derived from maize. Anti-foam agents are sometimes added as the beans cook – another safe, yet artificial processing aid.

Where does the soya come from?

The big issue with soya is genetic modification. One type of GM soya has been licensed for use in the UK but any food product, including soya, must be clearly labelled if it is derived from a genetically modified organism (GMO), unless less than 0.9 per cent of EU-approved or 0.5 per cent of non-approved GM material has been unintentionally added. The regulations insist that labels should indicate either 'this product contains genetically modified organisms' or 'produced from genetically modified soya'. GM's detractors say crops are being gradually contaminated with GMOs.

How can I avoid GM soya?

Buy organic tofu, simply because the organic sector in both the US and the UK best polices the movement of GM-contaminated material. While there is no 'test' for organic integrity (it depends on traceability), organic foods in the UK are more closely monitored. Trading standards offices in the UK are particularly concerned at present, using their valuable resources to prosecute fraudsters passing off non-organic foods as organic.

If tofu is a good alternative to meat, is it eco-friendly?

Not always. Soya farming has grown hugely to meet demand. With not enough being grown and no more suitable agricultural land where it can be cultivated, huge rainforest areas in the Amazon delta are being cleared to make way for it.

Is tofu safe?

Recent testing of tofu found no pesticide residues above the maximum level permitted. There has been some worry, however, that with oceans increasingly polluted by metals (lead, mercury, aluminium) and dioxins, traditionally panned nigari might have associated health hazards. Modern methods of ionisation used to remove the minerals from seawater can get rid of these poisons, but very little information is available as to the real extent of the problem, if indeed there is one at present.

Is Quorn tofu?

Quorn is made not from soya but from a mycoprotein – a type of fungi. The organism was found occurring naturally in the soil in a field in Marlow, Buckinghamshire. Marlow Foods owns the brand and in the early 1980s mycoprotein was grown on a large enough scale to launch a range of products nationally. In 1985 mycoprotein was approved by the Ministry of Agriculture, Fisheries and Food as being suitable for food use, and the first Quorn product – a savoury pie – was launched.

How can I spot good-quality tofu?

Taste it. Good soya bean tofu has a tearable, cake-like quality and a rounded grain flavour. Poor tofu is bland and rubbery. There is a delicious sesame tofu, integral to the dairy/meat/fish-free diet of Japan's monastic Shojin cooking, that has a light, jelly-like texture and masses of flavour. When eating out in Asian restaurants, ask for details about the tofu you are served.

What's the difference between firm, soft and silken tofu?

Firm and extra-firm tofu are pressed for longer, and hold their shape well when cooked or stirred into salads.

Soft or silken tofu is a fresh, soft, jelly-textured tofu that is delicate when eaten raw but excellent stirred into sauces or seasoned and used to dress salad.

Sesame silken tofu is the traditional tofu made in the monasteries of Kyoto. Hard to obtain in the UK, it has a jelly texture but much more flavour than soya tofu.

How long will tofu keep?

Most fresh tofu is sold chilled and will keep for three to five days in the fridge, but it is also possible to buy store-cupboard tofu that can be reconstituted.

Where to buy tofu

Clean Bean Tofu, Taylors Yard, 170 Brick Lane, London E1 6RU
Tel: 020 7247 1639
Available at Borough Market, between Borough High Street and
Bedale Street, London SE1 9AH (every Saturday) and Spitalfields
Markets, 109 Commercial Street, E1 6BG (every Sunday).
Organic tofu, freshly made using traditional methods.

Dragonfly Foods, 2a Mardle Way, Buckfastleigh,
Devon TQ11 0NR
Tel: 01364 642700
www.beany.co.uk
Hand-made natural, smoked or deep-fried organic tofu made with
nigari.

Okinami Japanese Shop, 12 York Place, Brighton,
East Sussex BN1 4GU
Tel: 01273 677702
www.okinami.com
Mori-nu fresh, soft (creamy) silken tofu and firm silken tofu from
Japan. Also Mitoku Snow-dried macrobiotic tofu, hand-made in
the Japanese highlands for adding to braises and soups. Mail order
available.

The Organic Delivery Company, Unit A59,
New Covent Garden Market, Nine Elms Lane, London SW8 5EE
Tel: 020 7739 8181
www.organicdelivery.co.uk
Stocks Clearspot tofu and Taifun tofu in four flavours, including
silken natural and smoked almond and sesame. Home delivery
available in some areas.

Soyfoods Ltd, 66 Snow Hill, Melton Mowbray,
Leicestershire LE13 1PD
Tel: 01664 560572
www.soyfoods.co.uk
Tofu freshly made from organic soya beans and nigari, guaranteed free of gypsum and acidity regulators. Home delivery available in some areas.

TOMATO KETCHUP

That moment of anticipation as the tomato ketchup travels slowly down the neck of the bottle will be familiar to anyone who loves it on hot, chunky chips. Since its invention by Henry J. Heinz in 1876, ketchup has been the most popular sauce to eat with fried food. In the US 97 per cent of homes has a bottle in the kitchen, while in the UK over 50 per cent of the chips we eat are slathered with ketchup and we buy 60 million bottles of it a year. But as both nations began to make the connection between obesity and the fry-up, ketchup found itself in the firing line. No matter, said Heinz, this stuff is actually healthy – go eat more of it! But the fact remains that ketchup tends to be served with unhealthy foods such as chips and processed meats, and no matter how much of it you shake over the chips it will never make them good for you.

But is it as healthy as Heinz says?

In the US the company has just been given permission by the Food and Drug Administration to use a 'Qualified Health Claim' on their labelling and extol the virtue of the carotenoid lycopene, which is found in the skin of tomatoes and other red fruit. Lycopene is a known cancer-fighting antioxidant and, while it is present in raw tomatoes, cooking them makes the lycopene easier to absorb, hence Heinz's claim that ketchup is good for you. But while there is 2mg of lycopene in 10ml (2 teaspoons) of ketchup (as opposed to 85g of raw tomatoes), it is far better to eat 125ml of pasta sauce, which contains 28mg of lycopene – not least because it is served with a less fatty food. In the past, Heinz has been criticised by health authorities for promoting ketchup as a health food, but it must be said that ketchup is nothing like as bad for you as the food you eat it with.

What's in tomato ketchup?

In Heinz tomato ketchup, the so-called brand leader with 77 per cent of the market, there is sugar in the form of glucose syrup, plus vinegar, aromatics and salt. Heinz does not use artificial additives of any kind and claims that a secret process gives the sauce its gloopy thickness, negating the need for emulsifiers or thickeners, natural or not. It is not prepared to reveal its special method to anyone, so imitators may resort to additives; read the labels if you want to avoid these. Do bear in mind that as well as lycopene, your 10ml serving will contain salt (0.2g per 10g) – a high level when the other salt in the meal is taken into account. Each serving will also have 2.6g (about half a teaspoon) sugar, so don't encourage the children to eat too much.

Heinz also makes an organic ketchup, which contains organic tomatoes, sugar, spirit vinegar, salt, spices, onion powder and garlic powder. The salt and sugar content are the same as for conventional ketchup.

Where do the tomatoes in ketchup come from?

Tomatoes for ketchup sold in the UK are sourced from Europe, the world's largest producer, cultivating 8.5 million tonnes of tomatoes a year. European tomato growers receive £280 million each year in subsidies from the EU (funded by taxpayers). One and a half million tonnes of EU-grown tomatoes are sold fresh, the rest are processed for the ketchup-canning and sauce business. In 2004 the EU reported that of those 7 million tonnes of tomatoes, 40 per cent was wasted during processing. Even so Europe over-produces tomatoes. These are usually canned then 'dumped' on developing countries in exchange for opening up trade relationships (see Canned Vegetables and Fruit, page 106). Subsidy reform has taken place in other areas of agriculture with new systems of payment to farmers, but reform in the tomato sector has not been carried out along the same lines. So the European taxpayer bears the cost of overproduction, and it is mainly big business getting the benefit.

Is tomato ketchup good for the environment?

Much is made of the importance of colour and sweetness in the tomatoes that are specially bred for ketchup, but environment agencies report that pursuing this standard is not sustainable. Tomato crops need vast amounts of energy (especially if they are grown indoors) and water – it has been reported that up to 11 litres of water is used to produce 1 litre of ketchup. An Australian government report revealed that wastage of tomatoes that do not make the standard grade for processing can be disgraceful. Up to 49 per cent may not make the grade on the farm and will remain on the vine unpicked, while a further 10 per cent can be lost during processing. Added to this, hundreds of old tomato breeds are disappearing, as major seed manufacturers develop, control and sell only a few types of hybrid seed that grow into plants whose own seeds will be sterile, so that growers have to keep buying more seeds from them. Pesticide use in countries growing 'sauce tomatoes' is also a problem.

Is our passion for ketchup fair to British tomato growers?

It's a pity British farmers are not supplying the ketchup trade when they have been applauded for their low use of pesticides and have reduced wastage of energy and fossil fuels used to grow tomatoes in greenhouses. Note that they have done this without receiving any subsidy. Ketchup producers argue, justifiably, that their tomatoes need a longer growing season with more sun.

Where to buy environmentally friendly ketchup

Daylesford Organic Farmshop, Daylesford, Nr Kingham, Gloucestershire GL56 0YG
Tel: 01608 731700
www.daylesfordorganic.com
Daylesford makes an organic ketchup that is more like an Italian sauce, with a good thick texture. Mail order available.

Goodness Direct, South March, Daventry,
Northamptonshire NN11 4PH
Tel: 0871 871 6611
www.goodnessdirect.co.uk
This online shop sells the excellent Meridian tomato ketchup, which
is made with 65 per cent very ripe tomatoes and is starch free, and
Biona organic ketchup, made with good ingredients and sweetened
with agave syrup.

Whole Earth, Combe Lane, Wormley, Godalming,
Surrey GU8 5SZ
Tel: 01428 685100
www.wholeearthfoods.com
Whole Earth's organic ketchup is popular but has a low percentage of
tomato (17 per cent) and contains rice flour starch for bulk.

TOMATOES

It is a standard routine to hold up the British tomato as a cannonball-hard, colourless joke. The typical line goes that it will never be a patch on those that have enjoyed the skin-scorching rays of the Sicilian sun, or sapped their flavour from the volcanic soil of Campania. But both statements are shrouded in myth, and there are other issues, too – a whole box of them. GM tomatoes, pesticide use, state-of-the-art growing techniques – and whether to avoid those suspiciously shiny, deep red 'vine-ripened' Spanish fruits that have slipped into every shop.

When are tomatoes at their sweetest?

Tomatoes taste best when they are in season, which in the UK means between July and October for outdoor-grown tomatoes. Tomatoes grown under glass or in polytunnels ripen as early as February and the season for these can continue up to the first frosts in November. Without direct sunlight, however, no tomato will ever have a true sun-ripened flavour or look ripe all the way through when cut open. Southern European countries have a longer season and tomatoes begin to come into the UK in April and continue until November. Southern European tomatoes are at their best from June onwards, when the outdoor-ripened tomato season is in full swing.

The best way to tell if a tomato is going to have the maximum flavour and sweetness is to use your nose. Aroma only comes from proper sun ripening on the vine. Don't be fooled, however, by 'vine tomatoes', whose stalk will have the lovely hot-dust smell but which may well have been grown indoors.

How are tomatoes grown in the UK?

There are various techniques for growing tomatoes commercially, all of them approved by the British Tomato Growers Association (BTGA):

* **Small-scale tomato growing** – smallholders who grow tomatoes in soil with a muckheap in the corner of the garden are a dying breed. Over 90 per cent have packed in production in the last 30 years, and there are now no commercial outdoor tomato growers.

* **Hydroponic systems** – many larger farms in the UK (but also in Holland) use hydroponic technology. The tomatoes are grown under glass, cultivated not in soil but in water and fed inorganic nutrients. Supporters of this technique say it is more productive while saving water and there is little need to use chemicals to control weeds or pests. The disadvantages are that it is expensive, consumes a lot of energy and some believe there is a compromise on flavour.

* **Glasshouses and polytunnels** – growing tomato plants in soil in temperature-controlled greenhouses or polytunnels may yield less tasty tomatoes than those grown outdoors but they are shielded from pests and disease. BTGA members (who are aiming to be pesticide free) favour bio-control – the use of natural predators rather than chemicals to fight pests. They do, however, use some of the 100 pesticides permitted for tomatoes in the UK. In spite of the obvious advantage to organic growers, polytunnels are controversial. Environmentalists complain that large areas of rural Britain are now covered in plastic and that this is not only ugly but detrimental to wildlife.

Is it better to buy British or imported tomatoes?

In spite of the obvious taste advantage of imported sun-ripened tomatoes from southern European countries such as Italy and Spain, it is still often better to buy British when in season, not least because of the scandalous amount of EU subsidy paid to large-scale EU farms. British farms are minnows in comparison (see Canned Vegetables and Fruit, page 106), and do not receive subsidy. Imported tomatoes are bred for their resilience to long-distance travel and, though a good red colour, can be hard and unripe. They never quite compare to the sweet, juicy tomato of the holiday encounter. It seems clear that countries such as Italy grow the best tomatoes for themselves rather than exporting them.

The UK imports tomatoes mainly from the Canary Islands, Holland, Israel, Italy, Morocco, Poland and Spain. Dutch tomatoes are grown with minimal pesticides but tend to lack aroma and flavour. Spanish tomatoes are very controversial. They are cultivated mainly in tunnels, and Spanish growers have severe problems with pest resistance that environmentalists put down to pesticide overuse. All the export countries listed above are permitted to use a wider range of chemicals than British tomato growers.

Are there pesticide residues on tomatoes?

Yes, and it does not make comfortable reading. In 2004 the Pesticides Residue Committee (PRC) tested 160 samples of tomatoes for 105 chemicals. Of those, 70 contained residues, with 38 of them containing more than one chemical. Three of these samples were of UK origin. The residues on most were fungicides, sprayed on the crop to prevent moulds growing. One Spanish sample exceeded the maximum recommended residue level (MRL) and one UK sample contained levels of a chemical not approved for use. The British-grown tomatoes come out of this report rather better than the imports but the result is still disturbing. Although the PRC maintains that none of the levels found poses a risk to human health, environmental agencies argue that MRLs are set too high. Note that five samples were organic and none of these contained residues.

Are there any GM tomatoes in the shops?

Tomatoes do not belong to the short list of genetically modified foods registered for cultivation in the EU and there are no imported fresh GM tomatoes for sale in the UK. They have been found in processed food – famously in 1995 in a Sainsbury's tomato paste. It was withdrawn, and supermarkets have since been keen to avoid repetition of the incident. By law, ready-made pasta sauces, pizzas and indeed all manufactured foods should state the GM content in any ingredient if it makes up more than 0.9 per cent of that ingredient. Labelling is not required if the content falls below that level, a disquieting allowance made for contamination.

Who picks your tomato?

Can you buy a tomato that has been grown without cruelty to people? Knowing if the farm worker who picked or packed the fruit was well paid, well housed or even legal is impossible unless you buy from a member of the British Tomato Growers Association, which operates an open-door policy on all farms, inviting inspection from the public. The BTGA represents 90 per cent of British growers but supermarkets generally do not display its logo. There seems no reason for this other than a reluctance to see other produce shown up.

What the supermarkets say

Tesco stocks 100 per cent British tomatoes in its Finest (i.e. most expensive) range but otherwise imports tomatoes from all over Europe and Africa.

Waitrose stocks 15 types of British tomato during the UK tomato season, mainly grown in the Arreton Valley, Isle of Wight.

Sainsbury sells predominantly British tomatoes in June, July and August and also a range of organic tomatoes all year round. During the winter it sells British 'Billington' speciality tomatoes, grown mainly indoors. Its other tomatoes come from all over Europe, the Canary Islands and Israel.

The Co-op says it is 'working with' UK growers to 'utilise' the tomato crop when in season, indicating that it has not quite perfected the situation. It also sells organic tomatoes. Its other tomatoes come from Europe, Israel and Morocco.

Where to buy good tomatoes

Local street or 'chartered' markets are a good source of locally grown tomatoes or delicious British overripe supermarket rejects – cheap enough to buy by the box. Alternatively locate your nearest farmers' market on **www.farmersmarkets.net** (tel: 0845 458 8420), or **www.lfm.org.uk** (tel: 020 7833 0338) for London.

Many of the nation's dwindling but precious band of artisan growers grow organically – seek them out through box schemes and farmers' markets. If choosing imported organic tomatoes, note that fossil fuel will have been used to transport them.

Riverside Vineries, La Robergerie Farm, Robergerie Lane, St Sampson's, Guernsey GY2 4NJ
Tel: 01481 249293

The Higgs family are tomato specialists who have been farming on Guernsey for 100 years. They farm organically under glass, using traditional techniques and planting the vines in soil. Currently three organic types are available via **www.organicfarmfoods.co.uk**, or phone for other stockists. They also supply the Riverford organic box scheme (see below).

Nationwide and local vegetable box schemes

Abel & Cole, 8–15 MGI Estate, Milkwood Road, London SE24 0JF
Tel: 0845 262 6262
www.abel-cole.co.uk
Home delivery to London and parts of the Home Counties, the South and West.

Boxfresh Organics, Unit 5C, Rodenhurst Business Park, Rodington, Shropshire SY4 4QU
Tel: 01952 770006
www.boxfreshorganics.co.uk
Home delivery to Shropshire and parts of the West Midlands.

Graig Farm Organics, Dolau, Llandrindod Wells, Powys LD1 5TL
Tel: 01597 851655
www.graigfarm.co.uk
Home delivery nationwide.

Riverford Organic Vegetables Ltd, Wash Barn, Buckfastleigh,
Devon TQ11 0LD
Tel: 0845 600 2311
www.riverford.co.uk
Home delivery in London, the Midlands and the Southwest.

TROUT

Thanks to fish farms, trout is a cheap enough dish for every day. But could this inexpensive fish come at a heavy cost in other terms? While trout farming escapes much of the hoo-hah hurled at salmon aquaculture, it does share some of its troubles – but more of that later. Wild stock numbers of trout, and its migratory cousin the sea trout, are under close watch by environment agencies. The threat of river pollution, climate change and overfishing are ever present, and some strange measures are employed to ensure the angler has enough fish in his bag to spend the evening boasting in the pub.

Is the wild population safe?

Non-migratory trout species – including the indigenous brown trout and the rainbow trout, which originated in northwest America – are found in British rivers. The Environment Agency (in England) says numbers of juvenile fish are healthy but there is little reliable evidence about the adult population. It warns, however, that water pollution and water temperature changes remain a threat, and that the current decline in 'fly life' on British chalk streams could also damage the stock. Wild trout are not easy to buy; you may have to rely on the generosity of an angler friend.

Is sea trout overfished?

Numbers of sea trout – which migrate out to sea before returning to the rivers – are above average, although the RSPB has warned that numbers in Scotland collapsed in 37 rivers due to the rapid expansion of salmon farming in the region. The Scottish salmon farming industry disputes this, saying there's no evidence that salmon farming is responsible for the decline of wild stocks. The majority of sea trout we eat are netted in coastal waters, but netting is decreasing.

How is trout farmed?

In the UK, trout is farmed mainly in southern England, central and southern Scotland and North Yorkshire, where the clean rivers provide perfect conditions. Around 16,000 tonnes of trout are reared each year, with a (shop) till value of £22 million. The trout are reared in ponds or tanks, with a constant water supply provided by gravity. The fish get their exercise swimming against the flow and are harvested when they reach 300–400g. Screens prevent escape, and flow of waste, which must be monitored to prevent polluting the rivers.

What feeds farmed trout?

Farmed trout are fed on about 60–70 per cent fishmeal plus cereal and other nutrients. Fishmeal is derived from the wild population, begging the question whether aquaculture is sustainable in the long run. Residues of dioxins and PCBs – dangerous chemicals that are ingested by fish fed on meal sourced from polluted oceans – have been found in trout but the authorities are satisfied that the levels are too low to cause harm.

Is trout farming welfare friendly?

High stocking densities are a problem if the water levels are low, decreasing the oxygen, which can literally have the fish gasping for 'air' and harming each other as they fight to breathe. There are various methods of slaughter. The most humane is via electric shock but in the worst case fish are slowly suffocated while on ice, a method some farms prefer as it increases shelf life.

Is trout farming chemical and drug free?

No. Trout are routinely fed antibiotics and treated against parasites. They are also fed pigment to give a nice pink colour that resembles the flesh of wild fish.

Is trout good for you?

High levels of omega-3, which helps to prevent heart disease, are found in trout. Nutritionists recommend at least two helpings a week.

How does the flavour of the different species differ?

Sea trout has large flakes and a quiet salmon flavour; it is an elegant fish that needs little more than poaching in a court-bouillon then eating cold to make the most of its subtlety. Brown and rainbow trout have softer flakes with a sweetish, crustacean taste. They can stand up to cooking over dying embers, and serving with sour citrus sauces.

Is it true that farmed trout are genetically modified?

No, but the eggs of conventional farmed trout are often genetically manipulated, changing the sex of the trout from male and female to 'triploid', meaning they are neither. The industry says this is to protect the wild fish (brown trout) in rivers, because the triploid fish cannot mate, but critics say that the real reason for using this technique is because they grow quickly to a larger size. Triploid fish are also sometimes stocked in rivers and lakes to provide anglers with plenty of fish.

How do organic farmed trout differ?

Organic fish are normal male and female. Half the fishmeal given to Soil Association-certified organic fish must be a by-product of wild fish caught for human consumption and the remainder must come from a certified sustainable source. The cereal in the feed is 100 per cent organic and the trout cannot be treated with antibiotics. Stock densities are low and the fish are not fed pigments. The resulting white flesh does not affect the taste, and there is little difference in flavour between conventional and organic.

Can anyone catch their own trout?

Rod licences are available from post offices, or phone 0870 166 2662. Be aware, though, that to keep up with demand, 'triploid' trout, whose eggs have been treated so they cannot reproduce, are employed to restock. The Environment Agency is not yet certain of the effect of triploids on the wild population.

What's in the supermarkets?

All supermarkets with wet fish counters sell conventional farmed trout, from Britain, France, Ireland and Denmark. Sainsbury and Waitrose also sell organically farmed trout in some stores. Sea trout is not available in any supermarkets.

Where to buy farmed trout from a sustainable source

Buy direct from conventional trout farms – they often have farm shops or stalls at farmers' markets – and ask about feed, medicines and welfare. Contact the British Trout Association (**www.british trout.co.uk**) for a list of farm shops and farmers' market suppliers.

**Hawkshead Trout Farm, The Boat House, Hawkshead, Cumbria LA22 0QF
Tel: 01539 436541
www.organicfish.com**
Pioneers in organic trout farming, selling gutted trout, fillets and smoked trout. Mail order available.

**Purely Organic, Deverill Trout Farm, Longbridge Deverill, Warminster, Wiltshire BA12 7DZ
Tel: 01985 841093
www.purelyorganic.co.uk**
Trout reared in ponds fed by underground spring water. The water previously flows through organic watercress beds, picking up live food, including stickleback, shrimp and minnow, which makes a valuable supplement to the farmed trout's organic diet. Mail order available.

Where to buy fresh sea trout

The following fishmongers will deliver fresh sea trout to your door, subject to availability:

Club Chef Direct, Lakeside, Bridgewater Road, Barrow Gurney, Bristol BS48 3SJ
Tel: 01275 475252
www.chefclubdirect.co.uk
Restaurant-quality fresh sea trout.

Fishworks Direct, 17 Belmont, Bath BA1 5DZ
Tel: 0800 052 3717
www.fishworks.co.uk
Fishworks has a strong sustainability policy and buys fish from small, short-trip boats and trawlers. It has shops in Bath, Bristol and Christchurch (Dorset), plus four in London.

Matthew Stevens & Sons Ltd, Back Road West, St Ives, Cornwall TR26 3AR
Tel: 01736 799392
www.mstevensandson.co.uk
Matthew Stevens buys fish from small, local boats and nearby Newlyn Market.

TUNA

Like cod, tuna has become one of the most hunted fish in the world. Chefs sparked the trend for fresh tuna, showing that grilling a slab of blue or yellow fin is as easy as cooking a steak. Then there is the massive trend towards replacing the lunchtime sandwich with a box of sushi. The supermarkets responded to the demand – quite irresponsibly – by happily plucking tuna from the luxury-food pigeonhole where it belongs and throwing it on to every wet-fish counter in the country. And what of canned tuna – can we carry on stirring it into the mayo with a clear conscience? If not, is there any alternative to this wonderful fish?

Are there enough tuna in the sea?

It depends on the type. Most affected by the rush to eat tuna in the last ten years are those that are eaten fresh. Blue fin tuna, from both the northern and southern hemisphere, is classed as 'critically endangered'. We should perhaps not blame ourselves. The Japanese adore tuna, especially the blue fin's *toro*, the valuable fatty belly of the fish. Much of the $50 million daily turnover in Tokyo's Tsukiji fish markets is traded in the tuna auction halls, where you will see tuna from all over the world. We eat blue fin in Japanese restaurants but otherwise mainly yellow fin, whose number is said by the Marine Conservation Society (MCS) to be at safe levels (depending on catch method – see below). Bigeye tuna is rare and classed as overfished, but rarely seen in the UK; albacore, the white tuna beloved of the Spanish and usually sold cooked and preserved in oil, is also classed as overfished. The number of skipjack tuna (the type usually canned) is at safe levels. Tuna numbers are also affected by climate change.

Does it matter how tuna is caught?

Yes – choose your tuna according to the catch method. The use of drift nets, high-tech fish-attracting devices (FADS) and purse seine nets, which encircle and catch whole shoals, is not sustainable.

Dolphins also fall victim to net catch methods. Sustainable methods include:

* **Pole and line** – a traditional method used in the Indian Ocean and parts of the Pacific, mainly for skipjack tuna.
* **Rod and line** – blue fin and the other types can be caught this way but little of it features on the mainstream European market.
* **Troll caught** – a line with a hook dragged behind a boat, used to catch albacore and skipjack.
* **Long line** – this method, which accounts for most of the 'line-caught' tuna in shops, is problematic. A long line of baited hooks is trailed behind boats. It would be sustainable but many other rare marine and bird species can get caught up in the gear. If the fisheries attach coloured 'scare' tapes to the hooks, it prevents this happening, so 'long-line caught' is okay to buy if marked as 'bird friendly'.
* **The Mattanza** – a traditional fishery off the coast of Sicily that corrals and kills huge numbers of blue fin tuna as they make their annual migration to their spawning grounds; it once took place annually but is not permitted now when stocks are judged low.

How can I know if tuna is dolphin friendly?

Be wary, not all dolphin-safe or dolphin-friendly labels are stringent. The best monitoring for dolphin safety is carried out by the Earth Island Institute (EII). It has a logo that reads 'dolphin safe'. However, confusingly, many manufacturers and retailers do not display it, preferring to use the term 'dolphin friendly' (see the supermarket information below).

Is it true that tuna can be farmed?

No, but it can be ranched, i.e. young fish are fattened in ocean pens. This has not reduced the problem with tuna stock, however, and it is frowned upon by marine environmentalists.

What's in the can?

Usually skipjack tuna, but sometimes albacore (white tuna), which is popular in Spain, Portugal and France, and yellow fin, too. Canned tuna is cooked before canning, then heated again once sealed to preserve it. This method gives it the softness that makes it a popular sandwich filling. The quality of canned tuna varies. Good tuna should look like the cross-section of a tree trunk, not like wood shavings. The tuna is preserved in oil, often low-grade refined vegetable or olive oil. Cold-pressed 'virgin' olive oil is used only with European tuna, mainly albacore. You can sometimes buy tuna preserved in salted mineral water. The more common tuna in brine is a good choice because you can then dress it with whatever oil you like.

Is it true that there are mercury residues in tuna?

All oily fish contain traces of mercury, which can affect the nervous systems of unborn children. However, the Food Standards Agency says that levels in tuna should not cause concern and that pregnant women or those intending to get pregnant can eat up to four medium cans of tuna per week.

Is raw tuna safe to eat?

Yes, but most fresh tuna sold in shops has been frozen for a minimum of 24 hours to kill worms that can invade the flesh. This is law when the tuna is to be used in sashimi and sushi sold ready made by retailers (see Sushi, page 393).

Which tuna is in my bento box?

The tuna used in supermarket-sold sushi is usually yellow fin (whose number is at safe levels) but look for information on the pack. It is best to choose line-caught, dolphin- and bird-friendly yellow fin tuna.

What should I eat instead of tuna that is just as enjoyable?

Limiting the amount of tuna you eat means enjoying other oily fish, such as mackerel, herring and organically farmed salmon and trout (see Salmon, page 345, and Trout, page 418). Oily fish deteriorate quickly, so buy from a source of very fresh fish. All these alternatives are delicious salt cured or smoked.

What the supermarkets say

According to the MCS, Tesco, Waitrose and Sainsbury's canned tuna is caught 'in a manner which minimises risk to marine mammals'. Marks & Spencer and Somerfield label their canned tuna as dolphin friendly; all say they buy from fisheries monitored by the EII. It's essential to note, however, that while it's a good thing that manufacturers and retailers are conscious of the importance of saving dolphins and other sea mammals, they are nevertheless selling tuna caught by nets, the most unsustainable method, which could bring about a crisis in overfishing for all tuna species.

If you can't see the information you need on the labels, look at the tin, which will be embossed on the top or bottom with the country of origin. If you see 'Maldives', you can be certain the tuna is sustainably caught by pole and line, as this is the only fishing method used for skipjack by the Islands' fisheries.

The fresh tuna sold in supermarkets is yellow fin. Look for details of catch method – 'bird-friendly' line caught is ideal. Always ask or contact the customer services department; your voice will be heard.

Where to buy canned tuna

Connetable, Bespoke Foods Ltd, Unit 7, 129 Coldharbour Lane, London SE5 9NY
Tel: 020 7737 3777
www.bespoke-foods.co.uk
Rod and line-caught Senegalese yellow fin tuna in brine.

Glenryck Foods Ltd, PO Box 22, 17 Market Place,
Henley-on-Thames, Oxfordshire RG9 2AA
Tel: 01491 578123
www.glenryck.co.uk
Maldives Eco Friendly Tuna Steaks in Brine, from the traditional
pole and line caught fisheries of the Maldives. The cans contain good-
quality whole steaks.

Savoria, 229 Linen Hall – CKp, 162–168 Regent Street,
London W1B 5TB
Tel: 0870 242 1823
www.savoria.co.uk
Sustainably caught Ventresca (belly) di Tonno Rosso (Mediterranean
line-caught blue fin), cured and bottled in the fishing village of Erice
near Trapani. The fish are prepared according to artisan methods,
using the magnesium-rich sea salt of Trapani and a good, local cold-
pressed Sicilian olive oil. Also available is the leaner (cheaper) tuna
fillet and *tarantella* (back meat), plus tuna bresaola (air-dried fillet).

Where to buy fresh tuna

Graig Farm Organics, Dolau, Llandrindod Wells, Powys LD1 5TL
Tel: 01597 851655
www.graigfarm.co.uk
Sustainably caught yellow fin and albacore from the unpolluted
waters of St Helena Island in the South Atlantic. All fish is caught by
rod and line. Home delivery available.

Matthew Stevens & Son Ltd, Back Road West, St Ives,
Cornwall TR26 3AR
Tel: 01736 799392
www.mstevensandson.co.uk
A fish merchant with a conscience, Matthew Stevens sells only hand-
line-caught yellow fin tuna from the Indian Ocean. Home delivery
available.

TURKEY (AND GOOSE)

Adore it, dread it, hate to cook it: no other table bird prompts such mixed reactions, yet each year an estimated 30,000 tonnes of roast turkey arrive on tables at Christmas. But, cooks – relax. How much the oversized bird is enjoyed has much more to do with the turkey you choose to buy than the roasting technique. The right turkey is as interestingly delicious as a game bird, with the bonus of juicier meat and crisp skin. Poorly chosen turkey has dry, pappy, flavourless meat, soggy skin and even associated food-poisoning risks.

Will the way the turkey has been reared affect its flavour?

Take an intensively reared and a naturally reared turkey and you have two birds that have little more in common than their name. Traditional poulterers grow turkeys slowly on a cereal diet, with no fish or animal protein or growth promoters. Young turkeys like access to the outdoors but protection from bad weather; they enjoy grubbing about and are especially fond of nettles. Good feed is very evident in the meat, which will have a stronger, gamy flavour.

Fast-grown, intensively reared birds suffer stress from over-crowding and their bones are not strong enough to hold their vast weight. It takes an average of just nine weeks for these birds to reach a desired size, while a traditional, naturally reared turkey takes about five or six months. Intensively reared birds are killed before they are mature. Ideally, turkeys should be killed on the farm. Long journeys to abattoirs increase stress, altering the PH factor in the meat.

Is breed important?

For decades the only turkeys on sale were white and the traditional breeds were classed as rare, reared as a hobby by a few specialists. But with the revival of the brown-feathered Norfolk Bronze by the Kelly family in Essex, and the more recent commercial comeback of the Norfolk Black with its pronounced breast meat, once again there are turkeys resembling the birds that became so popular as Christmas dinner a century ago. The thicker grain of their meat is a satisfying chew, and the good layer of fat under the skin bastes the bird naturally as it cooks. A white turkey that has been reared naturally in a free-range system can be delicious, too, but never quite so gamy-flavoured as the Bronze or Black.

Is it true that turkeys can be hung like red meat?

Turkeys can be hung, non-eviscerated, for two weeks after slaughter. This causes the collagen in the meat to break down, thus tenderising the meat and developing the flavour. This tradition is legal throughout the EU but is alive only in the UK and Ireland.

Which is better, wet or dry plucking?

Dry plucking by hand produces the best-looking turkey but is time consuming, so expect to pay much more for a turkey finished this way. More and more traditional producers are using molten wax to remove the feathers en masse, which is the next best thing. Least preferable is wet plucking, where the birds are dipped after bleeding into a bath of water and permitted detergent at 60°C to loosen the feathers, then plucked by machine. The skin of wet-plucked turkeys is soft and pale; it rarely becomes perfectly crisp when cooked. Wet plucking increases the risk of contamination with bacteria, so these turkeys must be deep chilled immediately – it is not safe to let them mature by hanging. Incidentally, there is a correlation between the introduction of wet plucking and our Health Authority's advice to cook turkeys for longer than they need in order to be 'safe', hence the often-heard complaint about the dryness of turkey meat.

Is an organic turkey 100 per cent organic?

While the welfare standards for organic turkey are hard to beat – good reason alone to buy organic – be aware that farmers are permitted to use some non-organic ingredients in the feed yet still give it an approved organic label.

What is the general quality of turkey in ready meals?

Most of the turkey used in ready meals and packs of sliced turkey 'ham' is reared intensively unless specified as free range or organic.

Do geese share the same issues as turkey?

Yes, but fewer geese are reared for the Christmas market so the scale of the problem is much lower. Although they are sometimes indoor reared they are not farmed so intensively. As with duck (see page 130), one of the welfare problems associated with geese is that their access to water for swimming is severely restricted, and with this their normal behaviour. Naturally reared geese are usually available from Michaelmas (the end of September), when they will have very little fat on them, until Christmas.

How much should I pay for a turkey?

A 6-kilo naturally reared, dry-plucked bronze turkey, feeding ten to twelve people plus plenty of leftovers, will cost around £60 if organic, less if non-organic. Buying a smaller bird and going for a no-leftovers scenario will reduce the cost – but don't forget to make stock with the carcass.

What the supermarkets say

The Co-op's turkeys are British and French, indoor reared with access to water, perches, bedding and dust baths. They are fed a vegetarian, cereal-based diet, including non-GM soya, and no antibiotics or fishmeal are permitted. The birds are slaughtered after 20 weeks (12 for females), away from the farm.

Marks & Spencer sells standard, free-range and organic turkeys produced in the UK. They are fed a non-GM cereal-based diet that contains fishmeal. Growth promoters are prohibited but antibiotics may be used under veterinary advice. Conventional turkeys are slaughtered away from the farm, but some M&S organic producers slaughter on the farm.

Sainsbury sells both indoor- and outdoor-reared turkeys, plus indoor with access to outdoors. All are provided with perch, bedding and dust-bath facilities. The birds are fed a vegetarian, cereal-based diet that contains non-GM soya. Sainsbury's turkeys are no longer fed growth-promoting antibiotics. The birds travel two hours to an abattoir. Sainsbury also stocks organic turkeys and organically reared geese.

Tesco sells standard, free-range and organic turkeys. The birds are reared indoors with access to water and feed (the free-range and organic birds have access outside). The conventional turkeys are packed in closer together and are given a cereal-based feed with non-GM soya meal, free of growth promoters and fishmeal. Tesco also sells geese that are reared slowly indoors in heated barns. They have access to water and bedding and are fed on a conventional diet (but with no fishmeal or GM).

Waitrose sells organic turkeys plus Redgrave free-range Bronze-feathered turkeys. It does not sell indoor-reared birds. The birds have access to barns and paddocks where they can forage for grubs and worms and graze; their non-GM feed is supplemented with grain. Waitrose also sells free-range geese reared in paddocks but who do not have access to water for swimming. Fishmeal is included in their diet.

Where to buy traditionally reared, dry-plucked turkey

Most supermarkets sell organic and free-range turkeys but the best ones can be bought direct from farms. All the producers listed below offer home delivery.

Copas Traditional Turkeys, Kings Coppice Farm, Grubwood Lane, Cookham, Maidenhead, Berkshire SL6 9UB
Tel: 01628 474678
www.copasturkeys.co.uk
Free-range Bronze turkeys that roam in the farm's cherry orchards. The birds are fed cereal supplements – predominantly oats.

Everleigh Farm Shop Ltd, Everleigh, Marlborough, Wiltshire SN8 3EY
Tel: 01264 850344
www.everleighfarmshop.co.uk
Naturally reared turkeys and also delicious three-bird roasts – a boned turkey stuffed with a boned chicken with a boned pheasant in the centre, and with herb-breadcrumb stuffing between each layer.

House of Rhug, Rhug Estate, Corwen, Denbighshire LL21 0EH
Tel: 01490 413000
www.rhugorganic.com
Free-range Bronze turkeys reared in North Wales.

Kelly Turkey Farms, Springate Farm, Bicknacre Road, Danbury, Essex CCM3 4EP
Tel: 01245 223581
www.kellyturkeys.com
Free-range Bronze turkeys reared by the family who revived the breed.

Peele's Turkeys, Rookery Farm, Thuxton, Norwich, Norfolk NR9 4QJ
Tel: 01362 850237 or 01953 860294
Free-range Norfolk Black, American Red Bourbon and Slate turkeys.

Red Poll Meats, Cherry Tree House, Hacheston, Woodbridge, Suffolk IP13 0DR
Tel: 01728 748444
www.redpollmeats.co.uk
Both organic and free-range Norfolk Black and Bronze turkeys.

Sheepdrove Organic Farm, Warren Farm, Lambourn, Berkshire RG17 7UU
Tel: 01488 71659
www.sheepdrove.com
Organic Norfolk Bronze turkeys, reared slowly (six months) on meadow grass.

Woodlands Farm, Kirton House, Kirton, Boston,
Lincolnshire PE20 1JD
Tel: 01205 722491
www.woodlandsfarm.co.uk
As well as producing organic beef from Lincoln Reds, this traditional Lincolnshire farm specialises in organic Norfolk Bronze turkeys reared in small groups.

Where to buy turkey all year round

Turkey is a good economical meat to store for children's meals or for throwing parties at any time of year.

Manor Farm Game, Berkeley Avenue, Chesham,
Buckinghamshire HP5 2RS
Tel: 01494 774975
www.manorfarmgame.co.uk
Richard Waller rears white turkeys naturally and sells them whole or cut into handy joints – boned thigh is exceptional value. Bronze turkeys available at Christmas.

Sheepdrove Organic Farm (see page 432 for contact details)
Frozen birds available out of season.

Where to buy goose

Goodmans Geese, Walsgrove Farm, Great Witley,
Worcestershire WR6 6JJ
Tel: 01299 896272
www.goodmansgeese.co.uk
Judy Goodman's geese roam free range on grass paddocks and are given additional feed with corn and straw but no additives or growth promoters. Home delivery available.

Sheepdrove Organic Farm (see page 432 for contact details)
Geese sourced from a trusted farm.

VEGETABLE OILS

In an era when shoppers increasingly demand clear labelling, bottles marked 'vegetable oil' are something of a paradox. Foggy definitions like these are deliberate. To most of us, 'vegetable' means 'goodness': carrots, cabbage and other things rumoured to give excellent night vision or make hair curl. But the real components of the ubiquitous refined vegetable oils are more obscure, and high consumption of these oils as an alternative to animal fat may do more harm than good.

What is in 'vegetable' oil?

Vegetable oil sold in the UK is commonly a mixture of refined rape-seed (canola), sunflower, soya, maize, coconut or palm kernel oils. Labels do not have to specify the ingredients.

How is oil extracted?

The seeds, nuts or grains are crushed and heated, then pressed. The high temperature can neutralise or destroy the good antioxidants from the plant and create free radicals – molecules containing oxygen that attack cells in the body. To extract the last 10 per cent or so of oils, processors also treat the pulp with solvents, usually hexane, of which small amounts may remain in the oil. The solvents also retain pesticides that adhere to the seeds and grains. The purpose of this is simply to extract more oil than would normally be possible, so the reasons are purely economic. There is a safer way to extract oil, namely cold pressing, or expeller extraction, which 'drills' into seeds and extracts the oil with minimal exposure to light and oxygen. Look for the words 'cold pressed' on labels.

How is oil refined?

First, any water or gum is removed in a process using citric or phosphoric acid. The oil is then neutralised to remove free fatty acids (FFA), which can lower the 'smoking' temperature of oil. Sodium hydroxide converts the FFA to soap and they are literally washed away. The oil is then bleached with the use of Fullers Earth and more heat, to remove pigments (in the case of red palm oil, much of its goodness is taken this way). Finally the oil is deodorised with high-pressure, very high-temperature steam to remove volatile flavour and odours. Basically, you are left with a pale, virtually flavourless fat – the antithesis of olive oil production, where heat is avoided to enhance flavour and lower acidity.

What is hydrogenated vegetable oil?
This is found in a lot of snack foods and solid cooking fats, such as Trex. It is vegetable oil, treated with hydrogen in the presence of a nickel catalyst. Yum. Again, high temperatures are used. The purpose is to raise the smoking point of the fat, and manufacturers say that biscuits, sauces and other prepared foods made with hydrogenated fat keep better. This is not quite true. Pure butter biscuits can have a long shelf life, too. The point is, butter is more expensive to use. Labels must show the presence of hydrogenated or partly hydrogenated fat.

What are transfats and are they only found in hydrogenated fat?
Transfats are formed when oil is hydrogenated but also in certain oils, such as rapeseed (canola), when they are refined. They are toxic molecules that disrupt cell metabolism and are critically linked to serious health problems such as heart disease, cancer and low-nutrient-quality breast milk. Food labels in the US must show levels of transfats. In the UK, providing this information remains voluntary. The Co-op supermarket has just announced it will give information about transfats on labels.

Can fats be hardened by means other than hydrogenation?
Yes, fats can be fractionated, a means of splitting the saturated and unsaturated fat in the individual oil using centrifugal force. The saturated oil will be thicker, almost hardening on refrigeration. Because the saturated fractionated fat has a high smoking point (it burns at a higher temperature than unsaturated oil) it is useful to

the bread industry. Lower fat vegetable oils can be hardened using 'interesterification', a complex process in which the fatty acid molecules are altered and rearranged using enzymes. There is no clear labelling to explain this but there should be. Ask yourself which you prefer – the product of space age technology or a bit of butter now and then, simply churned?

What are the different saturation levels in fat?

There are three levels: saturated, monounsaturated and polyunsaturated. Saturated fats and partly saturated fats (which include animal fats, palm oil and coconut oil) are normally solid at room temperature, while unsaturated fats (which include olive oil and sunflower oil) are normally liquid. Polyunsaturated fats are still regarded as the healthiest but it would appear, given the concern about transfats, that this is only the case when they are produced by cold pressing. Palm and coconut oils are the most saturated. Coconut oil, however highly saturated, contains good antiviral and bacterial properties that are not lost in processing. The goodness in certain cold pressed oils is a very important part of our diet. They should not be cut out in pursuit of a life of low-fat dieting.

How does the production of vegetable oil affect developing countries?

The demands of the West on countries producing plants for oil can be devastating. Millions of hectares of natural forestation have been cleared to produce soya in Brazil and palm in Malaysia and Indonesia. This affects the eco-system, wild animals lose their habitat, in particular orang-utans, and natural oxygen production is diminished. In Southeast Asia hydrological damage related to oil plantations includes flooding, drought and, in coastal regions, diminished resistance to storm and tsunami damage. Oil production may boost the economy of these countries as a whole, but World Wildlife Fund field workers report that indigenous people in Southeast Asia are being pushed off land by smart lawyers acting for the investing foreign oil 'giants'.

What's in the supermarkets?

Supermarkets predominantly sell large quantities of low-grade refined vegetable oil. You can assume this unless you see the words 'cold pressed' on the bottle. Look out also for the words 'expeller extraction' on labels, which signify the other safe way to extract oil. Supermarkets have not yet tapped into the widening range of cold-pressed oils from plants other than olive – although some sell extra virgin sunflower oil. Rapeseed and hempseed are growing in popularity, so it is likely the first supermarket supply of these oils will become available soon.

See Olive Oil on page 266 for information on supermarket own-brand extra virgin olive oils and a list of smaller suppliers.

Where to buy cold-pressed vegetable oils

It is slowly becoming easier to buy healthier culinary oils, such as rapeseed or hempseed, mainly via home delivery. Afro-Caribbean shops sometimes sell raw red palm oil – saturated oil that is actually very healthy and not to be confused with refined palm oil.

**Farrington Oils Ltd, Bottom Farm, Hargrave,
Northamptonshire NN9 6BP
Tel: 01933 622809
www.farrington-oils.co.uk**
Cold-pressed Mellow Yellow rapeseed oil from Northamptonshire.

**Graig Farm Organics, Dolau, Llandrindod Wells, Powys LD1 5TL
Tel: 01597 851655
www.graigfarm.co.uk**
Sells Bio Planète cold-pressed organic safflower, sunflower, soy, sesame, peanut and rapeseed oils from a small oil mill in France. Home delivery available.

Hillfarm Oils, Home Farm, Heveningham, Halesworth,
Suffolk IP19 0EL
Tel: 01986 798660
www.hillfarmoils.com
Farmer Sam Fair sources local, best-quality UK rapeseed and cold
presses it, retaining all the goodness. Home delivery available.

Merchant Gourmet, 2 Rollins Street, London SE15 1EW
Tel: 0800 731 3549
www.merchant-gourmet.com
Sells Austrian pumpkinseed oil and almond oil. The latter is
recommended as a part substitute for butter in baking. Home delivery
available.

Mortimer & Bennett, 33 Turnham Green Terrace,
London W4 1RG
Tel: 020 8995 4145
www.mortimerandbennett.co.uk
This shop stocks Graf Hardegg Austrian rapeseed oil, a light, cold-
pressed oil in a beautiful old-fashioned bottle, made by a family that
has farmed rapeseed since 1640. Also Philippe Vigean stone-pressed
sunflower and colza oil (rapeseed mixed with olive oil) and Son-
nenetor virgin pumpkinseed oil, cold pressed at source in Austria,
which makes an excellent stir-fry and salad oil. Home delivery
available.

Organic Coconut Oil, PO Box 11045, Dickens Heath,
Solihull B90 1ZD
Tel: 0871 666 1355
www.organic-coconut-oil.com
Virgin oil pressed from fresh coconut meat, packed with natural
antiviral, antibacterial and antifungal lauric acid. It can be used as a
substitute for shortening, vegetable oil, butter and margarine and it
will keep fresh for two to three years unrefrigerated. Home delivery
available.

River Cottage
Tel: 01308 420020
www.rivercottage.net
Produces a 'healthy' hempseed oil, suitable for cooking and salads.
Hugh Fearnley-Whittingstall describes the flavour as 'nutty', with 'a
hint of hay'. The hempseed is UK grown without chemical fertilisers
or pesticides.

Vom Fass, 21 High Street, Chalfont St Giles,
Buckinghamshire HP8 4QH
Tel: 0870 750 0962
www.vomfassuk.com
Cold-pressed oils available via home delivery or straight from the
cask at Selfridges and Harrods food halls in London. Especially interesting are their 'wellness' oils, wheatgerm and evening primrose, but
they also stock a good, dark green pumpkinseed oil for cooking.

WATER (BOTTLED)

We've been hooked since 1974, the year when bottles of Evian and Perrier first twinkled so invitingly on our shop shelves. Life without bottled mineral water and spring water is now unthinkable, but a superfluity of spring-water-based drinks brought to us by those canny drinks companies begs the question whether water is as life enhancing as the labels claim.

What does the label mean?

'Natural mineral water' is as pure as it was at source and its 'mineral profile' remains consistently 100 per cent stable. The supplier must be able to prove this in order to use this phrase on the label. The mineral levels in the water must be listed on the bottle.

'Spring water' is not tampered with, but there is no need for the supplier to prove a consistent mineral content. Both the above are pumped, or rise naturally to the surface (artesian water), from an underground supply. Tap water, or mains water, has, of course, been heavily treated in order to purify recycled water.

Is it true some bottled water comes from the tap?

Yep. It's straight out of the mains, purified (which is mentioned on the label), then the minerals are put back in and a weighty price tag stamped on it.

Which is safer – bottled or tap water?

To preserve its natural characteristics, elements in natural mineral water and spring water are permitted – at safe levels – that would not be acceptable in the tap water supply. It is not recommended, by the way, to give natural mineral or spring water to babies, as the mineral content of some is unsuitable for them. Carbonated mineral water has, on occasion, been found to contain the cancer-causing benzene. Recently bottles of Malvern water were recalled – although it was judged that there was no public health risk. In spite of some other well-publicised occasional scares (remember the Perrier scandal of 1990 and Dasani's embarrassment in 2004?), the Food Standards Agency reports all bottled waters sold in the UK to be safe. The Food Standards Agency says local authorities test natural mineral and spring water 12 times a year, although legislation says testing must be 'periodic'.

Should I believe the health claims of some bottled waters?

Aquaceuticals is the H_2O buzzword in the US, where bottled water is 're-mineralised' – a functional food claiming to be extra good for your heart, bones and so on. It is heavily backed by food conglomerates, well tuned to consumer gullibility, and is a threat to the continued popularity of true natural mineral water, which could become a dead duck in its wake. Suppliers cannot make false claims, however. Coca-Cola's Dasani hit the headlines in 2004, when it was revealed to be not the Space Age answer to all ills but just purified tap water, and contaminated with cancer-causing bromates.

Incidentally, beware when booking into a spa: if they have a natural spring they can claim what they like about their water.

Is the 'fizz' in sparkling water natural?

Naturally effervescent waters do exist, and bottles of this stuff should be accurately labelled as 'naturally sparkling'. Artificially fizzy water should be labelled 'carbonated'. Carbonated mineral waters are often aggressively fizzy, although some water companies make a virtue of their waters being 'gently carbonated', or even sparkling 'lite'.

Is there a real benefit to drinking 'fitness water'?

If you go along with the premise that lots of water with added vitamins is good for you, maybe, but look at the additives in Lucozade Hydro Active (made by GlaxoSmithKline). They include glucose syrup, sweeteners (aspartame and acesulfame K) and acidity regulators. All well and good, but will this drink help England win the next World Cup?

What is in flavoured bottled spring water?

They vary but, as with fitness water, do read the labels to check for sugar content and artificial additives, Volvic 'Touch of Fruit' has a virtual fistful of sugar added – 5.5g per 100ml, which is about half that of Coca-Cola (10.7g per 100ml in regular Coke) but nevertheless not what you expect to find in a bottle of something that to all intents and purposes looks like a mineral water product and not a sweetened drink. Volvic promotes its product as being 'free from artificial sweeteners'. Watch for these words on drinks as they can be a euphemism for 'added sugar'.

Does all bottled water taste the same?

In most cases, the taste of water is subjective, with consumers attributing 'delicious' flavours to certain waters that may simply have high snob value. Some waters, such as Badoit, however, have a distinct saltiness. But do we need water 'sommeliers', like those in trendy New York restaurants? Probably not.

Is there such a thing as organic water?

Because it believes spring water is too 'mobile' to monitor, the Soil Association is yet to certify one – but there is water bottled from springs on organic farms (see below), which has accreditation from the UK's other organic certifying bodies.

How far has my water travelled?

There is a food-mile problem, which is not confined to imported water. Vittel and Evian travel at least 400 miles to our shops, but so does Highland Spring when it is sent south. Fiji water, hailed by the beauty press and the manufacturer as a beauty aid, travels 10,000 miles to the UK.

For many of us, buying locally sourced water is obviously a problem if the main supply emanates from the Highlands, Wales or Cumbria. Cotswold Spring (see below) is an ideal water for food-mile-sensitive Londoners.

If I favour small food and drink producers, where should I buy my water?

Most of the old favourites are now in the stables of the food corporations. Danone owns Evian (the biggest seller), Volvic, Badoit, Chiltern Springs and Danone Activ. Nestlé's water list includes Perrier, Vittel, Buxton and Ashbourne. Malvern is now part of Coca-Cola. Highland Spring is the largest UK supplier; it also bottles Gleneagles and Tesco's Mountain Spring. The wittily dubbed Well Well Well bottles Aquapure, Ashe Park and Stretton Hills.

Which are better, glass or plastic bottles?

Glass bottles are the most recyclable, and you will taste only the water. Occasionally water from plastic bottles has a hint of their flavour, too.

Where to buy water

There are over 150 bottled brands but the following small-scale independent water bottlers are recommended:

Belu Spring Water, PO Box 5380, London WIA 7DT
Tel: 0870 240 6121
www.belu.org

Belu invests all its profits in global clean-water projects – in other words giving and organising clean water in specific areas where the water supply is scarce or polluted. Its water is delicious, and packed in eco-friendlier glass bottles.

Cerist Mineral Water, Llawr Cae, Dinas Mawddwy, Machynlleth, Powys SY20 9LX
Tel: 01650 531263

An official natural mineral water bottled at source on a small-scale organic family farm.

**Cotswold Spring Pure English Water, Dodinton Ash,
South Gloucestershire BS37 6RX
Tel: 01539 59452
www.cotswold-spring.co.uk**
Bottled near Bath from an artesian well under an area of outstanding
natural beauty with absolutely no farmland above.

**Frank Water Company, 25B Great George Street,
Bristol BS1 5QT
Tel: 07866 583844
www.frankwater.com**
From each bottle you buy of this artesian spring water from the
Devon Hills, up to 60 pence in every £1 the company makes goes
towards funding the clean water projects around the world. The
company is otherwise non-profit making.

**Lakeland Willow Spring Water, Willow House, Moor Lane,
Flookburgh, Grange-over-Sands, Cumbria LA11 7LS
Tel: 01539 559452**
Containing traces of the super-healthy salicin, an aquifer-supplying
water that has been filtered through ancient willow-based peat.

**Llanllyr Spring Water, Talsarn, Lampeter, Dyfed SA48 8QB
Tel: 01570 470788**
Water from a spring on an organic farm; it has accreditation from
the Organic Farmers and Growers certifying body.

YOGHURT

The thousands of yoghurts sold each day from thousands of miles of supermarket aisles should surely hint that we are a healthy lot. But many of them have departed somewhat from the wholesome origins of the milk whose acidity and texture are changed with the addition of micro-organisms. Finding a yoghurt that does not contain modified maize starch, heaps of sugar or, worst of all, psychedelic sprinkles can be impossible. Especially when you have a five-year-old tugging at your sleeve demanding the least healthy one, which he or she saw advertised on the telly.

What should be in yoghurt?
Milk and live lactic acid cultures, produced as a result of bacterial fermentation, which also thickens the milk. The acid also restricts the growth of bacteria that could spoil the milk or cause food poisoning.

What else is added?
In commercial yoghurt anything goes; a yoghurt is a palette for the most ardent food technologist to get to work on, unfortunately. Sugar is the main problem. Insipid yoghurt is often oversweetened. Gelling agents are added to very low-fat yoghurt to set it, while stabilisers and starches throw in a bit more bulk, turning watery, low-fat yoghurt into a 'thick and creamy' low-fat style. It's all good stuff for the manufacturer, who need hardly even bother to add milk. Some children's yoghurts contain extraordinarily long lists of ingredients. Reading labels is the only way to check for unwanted additives. Watch for certain colourings in yoghurts or yoghurt-based puddings that may be allergens – for example, sunset yellow (E110), tartrazine (E102), ponceau 4R (E124) and carmoisine (E122).

Must a cow suffer to make yoghurt?
As with Milk (see page 247) and Cream (see page 155), intensive farming can mean poor welfare for dairy cows. Buy organic yoghurt

to ensure higher welfare standards and also because greater care will have been taken not to pollute the environment.

Do yoghurts contain GM material?

Not in so far that the animals who provide the milk are GM, but non-organically kept animals may be given GM feed. Up to 0.9 per cent of the yoghurt's ingredients may be GM without it having to appear on the label.

Do yoghurts contain pesticide residues?

In 2004 55 samples were tested for 11 organochlorine pesticide residues but none were found.

Where does the fruit come from?

Much will be imported – as a frozen purée or preserved compote. Some local suppliers add seasonal fruit to their yoghurts.

Are yoghurts made from fresh, whole milk?

Not always, which sadly means that the goodness in the yoghurt will not be the same as the freshly made real thing. Removing all the fat (in fat-free yoghurts) can take out all the vitamins you need to absorb the calcium, so the yoghurt, instead of being a healthy food, is rendered fairly pointless. Full-fat milk contains an average of just 4.5 per cent fat, so is not a 'fattening' food in any case. Greek-style yoghurts sometimes contain added cream. Some yoghurts are made not with fresh milk but with milk powder – check the label for this. Powdered milk is not a bad food at all but the texture of the yoghurt will be less silky and again it will not be a 'whole' or natural food.

What is 'live' yoghurt?

In live yoghurt, the various organisms added to the milk are not neutralised, or killed after doing the job, but allowed to stay alive. It has long been recognised that, when in the gut, these friendly fauna fight infections, including reducing diarrhoea, and are important to general health. Lactobacillus are especially useful, as they survive the digestive juices of the stomach and pass into the intestine, inhibiting less 'friendly' organisms such as *candida*.

More recently however, much greater claims have been made for the 'probiotic' powers of the organisms added to yoghurts and yoghurt drinks. These include cancer-fighting properties and a reduction in blood pressure. A mass of probiotic drinks and foods have been launched and, due to some skilled promotion on TV, the market for them is now worth over £130 million a year.

Are probiotic yoghurts even healthier than live yoghurt?

Not necessarily. The reason probiotics, or so-called 'friendly bacteria', are being sold as novel foods is that the manufacturers do not have to back the claims they are making in quite the stringent way they would were they selling a drug. It is not that probiotics are either harmful or useless; yoghurt has been known as a beneficial food for centuries and there is recent scientific evidence that those who are vulnerable healthwise – for example, children, the elderly, the sick and those whose immune systems may be compromised by surgery – can be helped by an intake of the good fauna found in probiotics. Note, however, that the small print on some probiotic drinks warns pregnant and breastfeeding women and children that they may be 'nutritionally inappropriate' – so who and what to believe? Some scientists say that if you are physically well you just don't need them. Keep in mind also, especially before you give these novel foods to children, that they can contain sugar (including glucose syrup or sweeteners such as aspartame), flavourings and colour.

What's in the supermarkets?

Supermarkets stock a huge range of branded and own-label yoghurts. While most of them sell good natural yoghurt and organic yoghurt, there are also yoghurts in their chiller cabinets that contain additives, including starch, sweeteners, flavourings, preservatives, colours and much more. Always read the labels of flavoured yoghurts. Look for short ingredient lists that show only the yoghurt (or milk) content, fruit purée or pieces and cane sugar.

Where to buy good natural yoghurt

Davas Cornish Ewe's Yoghurt, Bone Farm, Heamoor, Penzance, Cornwall TR20 8UJ
Tel: 01736 368708

Davas is a live yoghurt made with nothing but ewe's milk and yoghurt culture. Ewe's milk is suitable for those who cannot tolerate cow's milk products.

Neal's Yard Dairy, 17 Shorts Gardens, Covent Garden, London WC2H 9UP
Tel: 020 7240 5700
www.nealsyarddairy.co.uk

Beautifully silky yoghurt made with cow's milk at the Neal's Yard Dairy.

Rachel's Organic Dairy, Unit 63, Glanyrafon, Aberystwyth, Ceredigion SY23 3JQ
Tel: 01970 625805
www.rachelsorganic.co.uk

Rachel's organic wholemilk fruit yoghurts are prepared using organic fruit and organic raw cane sugar. Available from most large supermarkets.

River Cottage
Tel: 01308 420020
www.rivercottage.net

Hugh Fearnley-Whittingstall has commissioned Judith and Clive Freane of Perridge Farm, Somerset, to make an exclusive yoghurt using whole milk from their organically accredited Guernsey herd. Sold in large jars, that can be reused or recycled.

St Helen's Farm, Seaton Ross, York YO42 4NP
Tel: 01430 861715
www.sthelensfarm.co.uk
St Helen's yoghurt is made from pure, whole goat's milk, with no artificial colourings, flavourings or stabilisers. It is available plain or in a range of flavours, including honey, strawberry and rhubarb.

Woodlands Park Dairy, Woodlands, Wimborne, Dorset BH21 8LX
Tel: 01202 822687
A new range of organic ewe's milk yoghurt with fruit.

Yeo Valley Organic Dairy, Mendip Centre, Rhodyate, Blagdon, Somerset BS40 7YE
Tel: 01761 462798
www.yeovalleyorganic.co.uk
Natural live yoghurt made from Somerset cow's milk; also fruit yoghurts and a good range for young children.